What We Believe and Why

Christian faith—from its Jewish roots to its future hope—beyond denominational struggles and doctrinal war.

Insightful, accessible, plain-spoken and a little feisty.

The Rev Dr George Byron Koch
(pronounced *coke*)

Published by

Byron Arts
only the best

Northwoods, Illinois

What We Believe and Why:
Christian faith—from its Jewish roots to its future hope—beyond denominational struggles and doctrinal war.

Unless otherwise indicated, Scripture quotations are from the New Living Translation of the Bible, Second Edition, Tyndale House Publishers, Wheaton, Illinois, 2004. Used by permission. Illustrations created by author, licensed or in public domain.

Second printing May, 2012. Includes minor corrections and updates.

WWBAW 1.2
ISBN13: 978-0-9777226-3-1
ISBN: 0-9777226-3-5

Additional resources, author contact:

WhatWeBelieveAndWhy.com

Published by Byron Arts, Northwoods, Illinois USA. Printed in the United States, England and Australia.

Visit **www.ByronArts.com** for quantity discounts of this and other Byron Arts publications.

Copyediting by George August Koch
GeorgeAugustKoch@aol.com
www.GeorgeAugustKoch.com

Acknowledgements

This book began as a teaching series, and developed over the course of years with feedback from participants and a constant infusion and reformation of content. So many engaged with this process it is impossible to name them all, but I thank them each for their insights, serious questions, and blank stares when I wasn't making sense. They each helped it grow in content and clarity.

Special thanks to my family: my wife Victoria, my sons George and Isaiah (and Freddie the dog), for loving me so much. Thanks to my folks George and Pat, for their unflagging support through many years of adventure (not all of which they signed up for!), and to Bob and Nancy, my brother and sister, who put up with me even when it was hard.

Thanks go to Eileen Healy and Terry Brady for early transcription work, to the Reverend Heather Ann Martinez for her work on the Bibliography, and especially to the Reverend Judith A. Davis, for her early work in content editing. It would have been impossible without them.

I also owe a deep debt of gratitude to my friend, Rabbi Jonathan Kohn, for helping me to understand Judaism, and for his careful review of my text for accuracy, content, Hebrew and even grammar. Thanks also to my Orthodox Jewish friends in Israel for their hospitality, rigorousness, and wrestling to understand *Hashem* and *Moshiach*. At a long distance in time, my thanks also to my seminary professor, Dr. Duane L. Christensen, an Old Testament scholar, for revealing God to me in the pages of the Hebrew Scriptures.

George August Koch, a gifted writer and copy editor, did the arduous work of editing for accuracy, content, form, grammar and clarity, often rewriting what was opaque in my prose into something transparently clear for the reader. It is a privilege to call him my son. He didn't get this job just because he's related to me; it is his profession, and he is very good at it, as other authors have discovered and testified long before me. You can reach him at GeorgeAugustKoch@aol.com.

Thanks to my congregation at Resurrection Anglican Church in West Chicago, Illinois, for loving me, supporting me, and praying for me, and to the ministry team there: Rev Rebecca Teguns, for her discernment, prophetic vision, *havering*, sacrifice of self to Jesus, and always pressing deeply into God's Word; to Deacon Judy Davis, who cares for so many with deep grace, unflagging energy and good humor; to Randy & Mary Fisk for their worship, prayer and vision; to

Rev Ray & Cheryl Waterman for their faithfulness and persistence; to Rev Miguel & Olga Ochoa for caring for the immigrant flock with unflagging willingness; to Rev Heather Ann Martinez for her courage; to Deacon Daniel Park for his wisdom; to Rev Mary Lou Kator for "getting it" in ministry; and to Rev Chuck Ellenbaum for his constancy and humor. Maggie Wuts supported all of us in her daily work as Church Administrator, with grace and excellence (and a houseful of bunnies). None of us can carry the load alone—especially me.

Last but not least, thanks to God, for making everything possible.

Table of Contents

1.
What We Believe and Why

There is a God.
It's not you.

This may seem trivially basic to many, overreaching to some, and exactly wrong to others. I begin with it because the Christian faith starts with this belief, and sees the testimony of both the Old and New Testaments as the inspired narrative and revelation of the outworking of this belief and the God who inspired it.

God manifested in history. God manifests now. Our understanding of this, its implications and our response, are the content of both our theology and our life in Christ—even of all human life.

Whether it sounds trivial or not, it is the foundation on which all else rests. It is sufficient for some. For Christians it is the beginning, but much follows from it. Theology is a description of it.

This book is *What We Believe and Why*. The purpose is to lay out the basics of what Christians believe, the origins of those beliefs, and the arguments for (and against) them. The aim is to provide a well-reasoned and foundational explanation of the faith, without being either tediously basic or hyper-academic. It will cover the key ideas and doctrines, but avoid specialized jargon and denominational particulars: It is a "primer" on what we believe and why we believe it.

Each chapter was created and taught during a year-long course, with feedback, suggestions, objections and more—*havering* (a term I'll explain later)—so that we would all be equipped to stand and deliver for what we believe.

Amazing insights arose during this course. One of them is that *theology* for many Christians is as dry as week-old toast, and apparently just about as useful for daily living.

Somehow we needed to get through the "theories about faith" to the *living* of faith, yet just exactly what THAT meant was not at all clear.

We Christians today are so surrounded by theologies, opinions, denominational fights, schisms, Christians behaving badly and the media's caricatures of Christians, that often we are no longer sure what we believe or why we believe it—or if it's worth the bother!

Even on those matters of faith we may feel strongly about, there is often a challenging opposing voice—sometimes quite sarcastic, and too often from other Christians—that attacks what seems precious and vital to us.

It might help to know that this is not new. One of the early theologies of the Church, *Against Celsus*, was written because the ideas of Christianity were attacked as silly and insubstantial by the Greek philosopher Celsus. More on this later.

As Christians, we regularly face withering and condescending opposition, at least some of which we've brought on ourselves. At the same time, we ourselves often defend vigorously those things about which we are least certain, or worse, those things that may not really be important in God's eyes, but that someone else has loudly insisted are essential.

What *really* matters and what doesn't? That question is rarely asked. As a result, Christians spend at least as much time fighting with each other as they do sharing the "good news." We get hugely distracted about being right and someone else being wrong, and end up debating beliefs rather than loving and serving God and neighbor. This doesn't mean doctrines or theologies are irrelevant, but it shows they are often treated as more important than the things that matter most.

I'm going to try to work through all of this, a bit like cleaning up a messy living room—straightening things out, vacuuming up the dust, and throwing away the old magazines and candy wrappers. In the course of this book I will try to answer these two key questions:

- *What do we believe and why?*
- *What matters and what doesn't?*

Both of these questions are huge. They open up issues of the Christian faith that are deeply important and utterly unsettling—and we will dive into both as fearlessly as we can.

In a sense this is Christian theology—but my purpose here is not simply to add religious concepts to our brains. The goal isn't just to know more *about* God, but rather *to know God more*.

THOMAS AQUINAS

One of the challenges of any theological work is knowing how miserably incomplete it will be—and this has some stunning implications for our life with God. We will unpack these as we go.

For the moment, I am chastened by the life of Thomas Aquinas (1225–1274), one of the fathers of the Church. Aquinas predated the Protestant Reformation, and by most any measure was among the most brilliant people who ever lived.

His writings are widely respected by both Protestants and Roman Catholics. Even the Orthodox Church[1] has commended parts of them.

Aquinas wrote the *Summa Theologica* ("Summary of Theology") so people could understand the *essence* of theology. His "summary" is over 3500 pages long and is extraordinary in its depth and detail, the topics covered and the care with which they are explained and defended.

Toward the end of his life, Aquinas had a personal experience of the Holy Spirit. After that experience, he looked back at his own *Summa Theologica* and all he had written and called it "straw."

The work he did was extraordinary to human eyes. But at the end, he understood that a *relationship with the living God* was fundamentally the purpose of our creation, rather than the detailing of theological issues. No matter how true or profound his theological *concepts* were, they paled in comparison to an actual relationship with God, that is, with the *covenant* (relationship) Jesus offered, with *Life in Christ*.

As a foundational principle, then, we will do *theology* (loosely translated: "God-talk") knowing that our purpose is not only to understand God in a reasoned and logical way, or to spot counterfeits of the faith when they try to divert us, but also to put us on a journey that will find, or rediscover, or deepen, *our own relationship, our covenant* with God.

It will begin with some basic theology, but only to give background and language that will help us move beyond where we began, and beyond where the faith has become entangled in itself and made a mess. Take the time with me, if you would, to put this background and language, these basic concepts, in place. Then we will move, together, beyond them. That at least is my dearest hope.

Before we go on: There are any number of common Christian beliefs that I will reject or defend, about which others who are well-regarded in the Church have taken a different view. Oh well. My efforts will always be to be orthodox, simple, plain: to maintain right teaching while being true to Jesus.

I will also likely be a little feisty and wry as we progress, and some of my illustrations and examples will come from far afield—even mathematics and science fiction. I hope these will be curiously illuminating and even fun!

We should enjoy the journey, even when it is challenging!

But know that I won't teach something I don't believe, and in all things we should discern the Spirit. We should be alert, prayerful, ready to go to Scripture, and willing to use the wonderful minds and *hearts* with which our Creator has gifted us. Read closely, and test what I write with Scripture. Test what I write with the leading of the Holy Spirit.

---

[1] For a basic explanation of these three major divisions of the Church, see the Glossary Plus at the back of the book.

Our journey builds in depth and content chapter by chapter, and some insights of later chapters will be hard to comprehend without the foundation laid early on. It is probably best not to skip ahead, but to take the journey step by step.

We'll begin by carefully defining essentials and non-essentials of the faith, look at Life in Christ and the elements it contains: salvation, sanctification and glorification. These together make up our covenant with Him, our relationship.

We'll look at what salvation means according to Jesus, and whether it is possible to "lose" it. We'll actually ask why we might even bother to be good, and the challenges of living with other believers (sometimes they are *such* a pain!), and with unbelievers—people with other religions or no religion.

Then we will begin to go deeper and wider—perhaps beyond your comfort zone—as we look into common issues of the faith: their basis in Scripture and the history of the Church, how they have separated or drawn us together, and how we can understand each other's Christian faith traditions and concepts, even across significant divides.

We'll study prayer in some depth, and probably upset a lot of preconceived ideas about what it is and how it is done properly. Be patient here—there's a lot to learn!

Then we'll begin to study the Law, a hot topic of both the Old and New Testament writers, and a topic of hot debate even today. This will lead to some revelation about obedience and love (some surprises here), and will challenge some "magical thinking" that rears its head in religious moments.

From there we will dive into covenant. This may well be the most important part of our exploration. *Covenant* is a word not much used in Christian churches, and probably even less understood than used, but it is the key theme of all of Scripture, and the key relationship that God initiates with us, beginning all the way back in Genesis. Hang on during this: It will be high adventure!

We'll then consider the nature and meaning of faith. It might not be exactly what we've grown up thinking it is. We'll let Scripture shed light on it for us.

When faith begins, when we enter covenant, in our relationship with God three astonishing gifts are given to us: peace, mercy, and breath of life. They are the center, the power-store, to lift and carry us through this troubled world. We are left not on our own, to our own devices, but guided and energized by the One who made us and called us into relationship, into covenant.

Next we will learn about heresy. "Heresy" is a common accusation thrown by Christians toward Christians with whom they disagree, especially when they think the other has their doctrine wrong! But "wrong doctrine" isn't what "heresy" actually means; so we'll learn what it means, and then how and when it has arisen in the Church. This helps to protect us from being fooled by counterfeits.

Next, Trinity! Why is it that we assert that there is one God, Who consists of Three Persons? Even on the face of it, this is a challenging concept. How can it be? What does it mean? And how certain can we be of its actual substance? This is not a new question in the Church, and many have wrestled with it for many years—actually many centuries! What can we understand from this important concept? We'll find out.

Bible authority follows. What authority does Scripture have in our individual lives, and in the life of the Church? Why? What can and should we assert about it, and on what basis? If the Bible is just another book of advice, among many others, then we have a serious problem; on the other hand, if we assert things about it that it doesn't even assert about itself (or that have their origins from *outside* of the faith), then we have a serious problem. This will require deep thought and prayer.

As we begin heading toward the end of all this hard (and, I hope, gratifying and exciting) work, we must grapple with a significant problem in the Church: *religious concepts*. As plainly as I can say it, this is a REALLY BIG DEAL. It is critical to knowing who we are in Christ, and what is not *necessary* to that. I won't tease this out here, but suffice it to say that *some things we cling to and love about the Church and the faith actually are not essential to it, and have their origins in another culture altogether*. They are not automatically wrong or bad, but they need to be seen for what they are. Knowing this will remove a significant impediment to…

Reconciliation. The Church in our time and over history has struggled at love and unity. We have split and split again so many times it has made us, and the world watching us, dizzy. Whether the issues were important or not, essential or not, needs to be looked at fiercely, plainly, severely. We will do just that.

Finally, we will deeply engage what Jesus and Scripture teach about how to reconcile, how to find unity, and on what that unity can and must be founded.

Whatever you do, if you desire to read this book, don't put it down until you have read the final three chapters. *Please.* They are key to the future, and whether each of us will be an instrument of the unity for which Jesus prayed, or an instrument of continuing division. I honestly hope that you will work your way to those final three chapters by studying the earlier ones first. There is a lot of careful foundation-building done that will help to deeply comprehend those final chapters. My hope is that you will then share this book—*give it away!*—and share what has been gained from it with other believers and non-believers. I pray that it will be a true seed that will produce twenty-, thirty-, or one hundred-fold of new fruit.

At the back you'll find an extensive "Glossary Plus" of Terms used in the book, a large Bibliography and Recommended Reading list, some funny and Relevant Humor, and an exhaustive Index to topics that have been covered.

The Glossary Plus is nearly a book in itself, and goes into significant detail on the key terms, in English, Greek and Hebrew, that are found in the chapters. I commend it for reading even on its own, but especially if something is unclear when you first encounter it (and some topics are expanded there that are only touched upon in the text).

I hope that you will find the adventure a worthy one, and I ask God's blessing upon you and your journey.

Let's begin.

RELIGION AND PERSONAL TRUTH

I don't believe that each person (or religion) has his or her own truth and that we must regard each as equally valuable and equally true. This is a common response to disagreement, but it fails by ignoring the challenge. The challenge is to discover what is true. To say that everyone has his or her own truth is to refuse the challenge. It's to quit before the journey has begun.

I believe there *is* objective truth and that it is *discoverable*. I believe this because for Christians, objective truth isn't a thing, a philosophy, even a solid theology. It is a *Person* named Jesus Christ. This person, and this Name, have far-reaching importance, well beyond what we normally conceive when we use them.

That is what we must seek, and *Who* we must seek, when Christians do theology. So let's begin to build a foundation.

ESSENTIALS AND NON-ESSENTIALS

The 17th-century Lutheran Peter Meiderlin once said, "We would be in the best shape if we kept in essentials, Unity; in non-essentials, Liberty; and in both Charity." This is an extremely valuable and effective touchstone for our journey. Let's define the terms with precision, and use that precision to our benefit as we proceed. This will prove valuable:

An *essential* is something that is *necessary*, utterly *required* for something to be effective, true or real. You may recall this expression from mathematics: *if and only if.* That defines an essential.

A *non-essential* may be profoundly important, valuable or highly regarded, but it is not *necessary*, not *required*. This is a critical distinction.

Liberty means that we do not force others to conform to our practices or beliefs on issues that are non-essential.

Charity means that we treat others with respect and love, even when we disagree or differ on *either* essentials or non-essentials.

The distinctions for our journey can be usefully illustrated by these concentric circles. At the core are the essentials. Keep this picture in mind as we proceed.

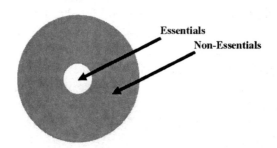

FIGURE: ESSENTIALS AND NON-ESSENTIALS

An example: What is *necessary*, utterly *required* to live a life [as an] independent human being? The *essential* is that you were *born* and are still [alive.] Obviously if you were never born, you don't have a life, and if you've died [you] don't have a life. I'm not saying anything tricky here, just the simple idea that [you] are able to live a life as a human being *if and only if* you have been born and are still alive. That simple. That's the *essential*.

A *non-essential* would be that you are healthy, have shelter, are loved, own a red '58 Corvette, and much more. Be sure to note that because something is non-*essential* doesn't mean it isn't important or valuable.

Some times we use *imprecise* language to emphasize a point. We might exaggerate like this: "Well, you ain't really ALIVE unless you're drivin' a '58 Vette down old Route 66—top off and the pedal to the metal!"

Sounds like a blast, but we all realize the word "alive" is not used with precision. Being alive really doesn't require the '58 Corvette. To some folks, owning one is *valuable and important*, but it is obviously not *essential* to being alive.

Similarly, health, shelter and love are *valuable* and profoundly *important*, but they are *non-essential* in the sense of our definition here: You have life as a human being if and only if you were born and are alive.

If this distinction isn't completely clear, you might pause and imagine some other examples of things that are *essential* and *non-essential* in various spheres of life: travel, games, relationships, location, money, education, and so on. What is the "if and *only* if" and what isn't?

You can go without a healthy diet, without exercise, without having shelter or people who love you—and without a red Corvette—and still have a life. If you are dead, or were never born, then a good diet and exercise mean nothing, and it doesn't matter how great your shelter is, how many people love you, or if your name is on the title to the '58 Vette. You're not alive, so you don't have a life.

Being alive is the only *essential* in this case. The non-essentials may be *important* (or not), but the *essential* of being alive is REQUIRED. The distinction is an important one in doing good theology and living as a follower of Jesus.

This will be applied with care, many times, in our journey together in this book, and I pray that it will become an indispensable tool in your own thinking in doing theology—and in drawing close to God and doing what He commands.

2.
Salvation

Christian evangelists, pastors, teachers, theologians and many others speak about salvation and being "born again" as the beginning of the Christian's life. They speak about it as such because *Jesus* spoke about it as such. How this happens (and how quickly) is described differently in different traditions of the Church, but there is unity in recognizing it as the initiating reality of being a Christian.

It is an *essential* of the faith (many things of the faith are not essential, as we will see).

Salvation is this: Our *trust* in Jesus and His *faithfulness to us* makes us *alive*, now and forever, with God.[2] His righteousness is counted as ours, and we enter an everlasting covenant with Him.

Justification is a closely related term, not identical to salvation, but close: It is that His righteousness is credited to us. In spite of our sin, because of Him we are declared innocent before God.

That's pretty much the central truth of the Christian faith, said simply. Jesus teaches about this, as recorded in the four Gospels—the books of Matthew, Mark, Luke and John—and His followers write about it in the other books of the New Testament. For two millennia Christians have discussed and debated *how* salvation happens, but widely concur that it *must*. So it is a good place to start in our desire *to know God more*.

BIBLICAL LANGUAGES AND CULTURES

Our modern Bibles are in English, and the text is a translation from Hebrew (Old Testament) and Greek (New Testament). The underlying words of the original languages have meanings and nuances of meaning, not all of which come through in our modern language. Sometimes this doesn't matter much at all, but at times the additional meanings in the Hebrew or Greek are important.

There are also ancient cultural assumptions related to many of the underlying words, and modern cultural assumptions about the English words, that simply don't

---

[2] This includes the concepts of accepting Jesus as Savior, of our sinfulness, of His atoning sacrifice, justification, and so on. These will be unpacked as we go along.

correspond, and this can cause misunderstanding. It's one of the reasons we have Bible teachers and pastors who have studied the biblical languages—to help us grasp more fully what is being taught in Scripture. What follows is one of those instances.

BORN AGAIN? CRAWL BACK INTO THE WOMB?

This theologian, or *that* church, might have *this* idea or *that* idea about salvation, and some of those ideas might be worthwhile. Rather than start with those, though, we'll listen in as Jesus explains to Nicodemus what salvation, being "born again," is all about. Jesus is the source of this *essential* truth, so we will intentionally take some time working through the story from the Gospel of John, and looking into some of the original language. The journey will be worth the time spent, but it won't be quick. This is from John 3:1-21, New Living Translation.[3]

> There was a man named Nicodemus, a Jewish religious leader who was a Pharisee. After dark one evening, he came to speak with Jesus. "Rabbi," he said, "we all know that God has sent you to teach us. Your miraculous signs are evidence that God is with you."
> Jesus replied, "I tell you the truth, unless you are born again, you cannot see the Kingdom of God."
> "What do you mean?" exclaimed Nicodemus. "How can an old man go back into his mother's womb and be born again?"
> Jesus replied, "I assure you, no one can enter the Kingdom of God without being born of water and the Spirit. Humans can reproduce only human life, but the Holy Spirit gives birth to spiritual life. So don't be surprised when I say, 'You must be born again.'
> "The wind blows wherever it wants. Just as you can hear the wind but can't tell where it comes from or where it is going, so you can't explain how people are born of the Spirit."
> "How are these things possible?" Nicodemus asked.
> Jesus replied, "You are a respected Jewish teacher, and yet you don't understand these things? I assure you, we tell you what we know and have seen, and yet you won't believe our testimony. But if you don't believe me when I tell you about earthly things, how can you possibly believe if I tell you about heavenly things?
> "No one has ever gone to heaven and returned. But the Son of Man has come down from heaven. And as Moses lifted up the bronze snake on a pole in the wilderness, so the Son of Man must be lifted up, so that everyone who believes in him will have eternal life.
> "For God loved the world so much that he gave his one and only Son, so that everyone who believes in him will not perish but have eternal life. God sent his Son into the world not to judge the world, but to save the world through him.

---

[3] Which translation of the Bible is the "best" is a hotly debated topic in some circles, with thoughtful and sometimes zany arguments about this version or that one. These issues won't be addressed here. Mostly I have used the New Living Translation. When I use a different version, I will indicate it with a notation like *NIV, KJV, NKJV,* etc.

"There is no judgment against anyone who believes in him. But anyone who does not believe in him has already been judged for not believing in God's one and only Son. And the judgment is based on this fact: God's light came into the world, but people loved the darkness more than the light, for their actions were evil. All who do evil hate the light and refuse to go near it for fear their sins will be exposed.

"But those who do what is right come to the light so others can see that they are doing what God wants."

This passage is rich with explicit meanings and implications, but we will focus on just a few key elements for now. It begins with Nicodemus. He is a leader of the Jews and a Pharisee.[4] Not all leaders of the Jews were Pharisees, and not all Pharisees were leaders. But Nicodemus was both.

As a Pharisee, he belonged to a religious sect that rigorously practiced intentional holiness: obedient, observant, even beyond what the biblical text of the Law explicitly required. When Jesus criticizes some of the Pharisees—not uncommon in Scripture—it is typically for pride or hypocrisy, not for attempting to be obedient or to please God. That is another issue, but here the key thing to understand about Nicodemus is his rigorous effort to be holy—part of what it meant to be a Pharisee—and the fact that he is a leader of the Jews, meaning that he is respected and elevated for his knowledge, wisdom, discernment, obedience, character and conduct. Those around him regard him as a wise and holy man.

In fact, proof of his *actual* wisdom and discernment is in the simple fact that he sees the evidence that Jesus has come from God to teach the Jews. The "miraculous signs" of healing, feeding thousands, and more, are a witness to the supernatural power of God, present in Jesus, and Nicodemus understands this. So he comes to see Jesus.

He comes at night. The reason isn't given, but the simple fact that this is mentioned inclines us to infer that he didn't want to be seen. Others—especially those Jesus had accused of hypocrisy or pride—would likely attack anyone who sought out Jesus or believed in Him. (Remember here that Jesus, His disciples, the community, and its leaders are all Jewish. Jesus isn't an "outsider" attacking the Jews as a people, but rather a member of the tribe who has spoken out against corruption in the hearts of those, leaders especially, who pretend to be holy but are not.)

Nicodemus opens the conversation by declaring his belief about Jesus having come from God to teach them. Though he is correct in what he discerns and declares, Jesus responds rather oddly, effectively saying, "Yes, but you missed the more important truth: Unless you are born again, you cannot see the Kingdom of God."

Here is where we need to begin to unpack the Greek meanings. It is obvious this *confused* Nicodemus, who heard it in the original language,[5] right from Jesus' lips. It also is confusing to us, even upsetting, because Jesus leaps in a different direction from where Nicodemus expects the conversation to go. So let's unpack it a bit.

---

[4] See the Glossary Plus for definitions of this and other key terms used in this book.
[5] It may have been Greek, but it also could have been Aramaic or Hebrew.

"The Kingdom of God" isn't a *place* but means *God's power and authority over everything*. If you live in a country without a king, this is a foreign concept and easily misunderstood.

Think about it this way: I was born in Chicago, so I am a citizen of the United States, and I retain that identity regardless of which state I am in. I am under the authority and protection of our Constitution. It gives me rights and responsibilities as a citizen, and no state, mayor, governor, policeman, neighbor or president can deny them to me. Various leaders and institutions have tried over the years to ignore or override the Constitution, but it holds the final authority.

The point is the *source* of authority and protection. In the United States it is the Constitution. In a kingdom it is the *king*. The Constitution is the authority in this country, and the agencies of government are established to enforce that authority. My birth here makes that fully accessible to me.

Were I born into a Roman family in the time of Jesus, I would have been born as a subject of the Caesar (the Roman word for king). The king's rule and authority extend not just to the *lands* that Rome controlled, *but to every person born as a Roman citizen*. Not only am I *subject to* the king's rule and authority always and everywhere, but I am also *protected by* his rule and authority always and everywhere. Which is why, elsewhere in Scripture, the soldiers and others are frightened into treating Paul properly the instant they learn he was born a Roman citizen.[6] Rome ruled the known world. Paul's birth as a Roman citizen meant he was under the *protection* of Caesar.

When Jesus speaks to Nicodemus about the Kingdom of God, He is describing God's *authority over everything*, including Nicodemus, the Pharisees, the Jews, the Romans, the Greeks, the trees, bugs, dirt, stars—everything. But He says you can't enter it—that is, become a citizen of the Kingdom—unless you are born into it. This point would be clear to Nicodemus.

When modern Christians talk about the Kingdom of God, or the Kingdom of Heaven, they often conjure countless adjectives about majesty, glory, honor—as if the main image is heavenly pomp and circumstance, a giant and glorious show, as we all fall to our knees in worship before His Throne.

I love that image, and will be thrilled to fall on my knees at His Throne. But Jesus isn't trying to conjure that vision for Nicodemus. He's making the point that *becoming a citizen* of the Kingdom of Heaven *requires being born* there, and then and only then do all of its *protections* and *obligations* become a birthright.

Jesus is saying, in effect, "In the miracles you have witnessed me perform, you have glimpsed only a tiny flash of God's true power and authority. You have no idea how infinite it really is, and you never will see it fully, nor be a citizen of it, unless you are born again—into the Kingdom of God."

Further, "born again" in the original Greek is *literally* "born from above" (implying born from out of heaven). Both are apt translations, because the point Jesus is making is this: When you are born into this world out of your mother's

---

[6] Acts 22:24-29.

womb (i.e., *of water*[7]), you can then for the first time *see* and participate in this world in which you now live.

Similarly, to see and participate in the Kingdom of God, you must also be born into it, out of the Spirit's womb (i.e., *of Spirit*). Note that the Greek does not say "womb" of the Spirit. I use the term *not* to imply anything about gender of the Holy Spirit, but to help convey *the image Jesus has intentionally chosen* in talking to Nicodemus. It is completely a *birth* metaphor. The terminology *graphically* reflects the act of childbirth.

Nicodemus seems stunned, and Jesus presses the point, basically saying, "You can't see or engage the Kingdom of God because you haven't been born into it yet, so no amount of my describing it to you will give you an understanding of it."

He also asserts that no one else knows about the things of heaven (or the Kingdom of God) except someone who has been there, and no one has gone there and returned. But Jesus says He *came from there.*[8] So He knows whereof He speaks.

Jesus is also making a point here about *all of us*, not just Nicodemus. In both verse 7 ("So don't be surprised when I say, 'You must be born again'") and verse 12 ("But if you don't believe me when I tell you about earthly things, how can you possibly believe if I tell you about heavenly things?"), His use of the word "you" is plural in the Greek.

Which means, of course, that what is necessary for Nicodemus to enter the Kingdom of Heaven, is just what is necessary for us as well. Jesus doesn't explain yet exactly what this *means*, or *how* it happens, or what life will be like *after* it happens, but He does say it *must* happen.

We will continue to unpack this more fully as we move on. But this is where Jesus says it all begins, so we'll take Him at His word.

THE DEATH OF JESUS AND HOW IT IS RELATED TO THE KINGDOM

Jesus then gives a hint of what His death will be like, and what it will accomplish. He makes reference to an event from the Exodus from Egypt, recorded in Numbers 21, when the Israelites grouse against God and Moses, and how much they hate the food God is freely supplying to them.

God sends venomous snakes among them to rebuke them; the people repent to Moses, and at the Lord's command Moses creates a bronze snake on a pole and has it lifted high above them. God promises that whenever a snake bites anyone, all they have to do is look up at the bronze snake on the pole, trusting the promise, and they will live.

---

[7] There are many explanations given by theologians about these references to water and Spirit. I'm not taking sides in any of those debates—I'm simply using a straightforward reading to help understand Jesus' underlying point.

[8] See Daniel 7:13-14. "Son of man" is how Jesus referred to Himself.

(Yes, it is a very odd story, and we might like it better if the narratives in Scripture were a bit more simple like children's stories—but take the cue of the strangeness and sparks in the Bible as an invitation to dig deep. Under them you will find an inexhaustible order and beauty that radiates from the face of God.)

Jesus says the same will be true with Him as with the bronze snake: He will be lifted up (both on the cross and to the right hand of God; see Philippians 2), and just as those who would die from the bite of a venomous snake are saved by looking to the bronze snake on the pole, so those who are poisoned by this world, by sin, by Satan (the serpent in Genesis 3), and who would otherwise *die*, are *saved* for eternity by looking to Jesus.

Jesus then re-emphasizes this in the most famous verse of the New Testament, John 3:16…

> For God loved the world so much that he gave his one and only Son, so that everyone who believes in him will not perish but have eternal life.

It is important in understanding this verse that we also understand what just preceded it. This verse is a part of Jesus encountering Nicodemus and revealing to him what is required to truly see and participate in the Kingdom of God—you have to be born into it—and what is required for that birth: trusting in the One who God sent, who has the power of God to save.[9]

He did just that by the giving of His own life for us at His Crucifixion, when He was lifted up on the pole of the cross.

Jesus continues with Nicodemus, and expands for him about the nature of His coming to live among us:

> "God sent his Son into the world not to judge the world, but to save the world through him.
> "There is no judgment against anyone who believes in him. But anyone who does not believe in him has already been judged for not believing in God's one and only Son. And the judgment is based on this fact: God's light came into the world, but people loved the darkness more than the light, for their actions were evil. All who do evil hate the light and refuse to go near it for fear their sins will be exposed.
> "But *those who do what is right* come to the light so others can see that they are doing what God wants."[10]

Normally this is explained something like this: "If you believe in Jesus you get saved. If you don't believe, you don't get saved." It sounds like your failure to believe buys you a death sentence.

---

[9] As a side note, critics of the faith sometimes claim that God would not give the power of salvation to a "mere man" like Jesus. Yet against this logic is the testimony of Numbers 21, where just such power was given through a bronze snake. If God can do it through a bronze snake, He can do it through anything or anyone He chooses, and most certainly through Jesus.
[10] John 3:17-21.

But that actually isn't what Jesus is saying. He begins with saying God *sent* His Son *in order to save the world through Him.* Not to judge or condemn it, but to *save* it. That's God's intention in sending His Son.[11] So the premise is that this is a rescue effort to save those who are in trouble and want to be saved. When the light appears, they move toward it, seeing that it is for their benefit. No matter how sinful, beat-up, wounded or worn-out they are, when they see the light, they know that hope is here, that their rescue is nigh, and they naturally *move toward the light!* The distance isn't essential—just the direction.

But there are some, dedicated to taking advantage of others, who have used the darkness to their advantage to steal and wound and kill, and the last thing they want is light exposing their malicious acts. *They flee from the same light that draws those who desire to be rescued.*

So it isn't a test to see if you believe the right things *about* Jesus, as you might of a doctrinal or philosophical proposition, and it isn't just that you believe in Jesus in the sense that you merely *assert* your faith in Him, but rather it is that you trust Him *enough* to turn toward Him for His help—and then to live as He tells you to live, to do what He says to do.

And if this doesn't sound orthodox enough, listen to Jesus Himself:

> One day an expert in religious law stood up to test Jesus by asking him this question: "Teacher, what should I do to inherit eternal life?"
>
> Jesus replied, "What does the law of Moses say? How do you read it?"
>
> The man answered, "'You must love the Lord your God with all your heart, all your soul, all your strength, and all your mind.' And, 'Love your neighbor as yourself.'"
>
> "Right!" Jesus told him. "Do this and you will live!"[12]

I recently heard a preacher read these verses, and then quickly add, "Of course when Jesus says, 'Do this and you will live!' it isn't eternal life He is talking about, but a richer, fuller human life."

Such an easy dismissal is stunning. If we want to understand how to get eternal life, who better to ask than Jesus? And when the expert in religious law asks just exactly this question, why would anyone dismiss Jesus' plain and direct answer, and then substitute another interpretation as good Christian theology? Yikes!

So the *essential* of the Christian life, of being born again, the *essential* of being a believer is this: *salvation*, getting *saved*. It is where and how we are *born into* eternal life.

Salvation begins when you trust Jesus to do what He says He will do.

---

[11] See Luke 10. The word here for "sent" has the same root as "apostle," and is the same word used when Jesus sent His disciples to share the good news that the Kingdom of God had come near. God sends Jesus, Jesus sends others: same word, same purpose.

[12] Luke 10:25-28.

And He does! God accepts us because of the righteousness of Jesus (not ours) makes us right before God—justified—and we enter an everlasting covenant. We are reborn as citizens in the Kingdom of God.

This invitation is open to everyone, everywhere, regardless of their religious upbringing or lack of it, and regardless of their sins—whatever they are. No exceptions. No disclaimers. Salvation begins when you trust Jesus to do what He says He will do: take your sin, and love you forever.

To be plain, if you've not yet set your heart on him, not yet trusted him, not yet said, "Yes," you can do it anytime, anywhere. You will be heard and accepted immediately. Even now.

There is more, and this "more" is going to be a huge and lifelong adventure. Salvation isn't only about you being forgiven, getting "born from above" and receiving eternal life. It isn't just a personal, individual transaction with God. Rather, it is all about God's love for the *whole* world, and the freeing of souls that have been trapped in a world of darkness. Not only does Jesus enter this world to accomplish this end—and demonstrate His love by the sacrifice of Himself—He also offers to you, and to each of us, the honor of *being a part* of this invasion into the darkness and the liberation of souls. In truth, He does more than *offer* us the opportunity; He *wants* it of us.

We will look more deeply into what this "more" means in the chapters ahead—the challenges, transformations, and joys—but the important realization here and now is that salvation is not the end of the journey, but the beginning of a new one.

Salvation is birth into a new life, coming *alive* in God's Kingdom.

The "more" has a name as well: *Sanctification*, or learning to love. We will turn next to it.

3.
Sanctification

ESSENTIALS AND NON-ESSENTIALS

One day another pastor and I were standing on a street corner outside of a coffee shop, drinking coffee and talking about our hopes and concerns in serving the people of God.

Some street evangelists came up to us and asked, "Do you know Jesus as your Lord and Savior?"

We grinned and said, "Yes we do!"

They said, "That's wonderful! Have you been baptized?" and we said, "Yes, we have."

Then they said, "You weren't baptized at *our* church!"

"That's true," we agreed, "but we *were* baptized in a Christian church."

They pressed on, "The church outside *our* congregation is so unfaithful that baptism anywhere else has no effect and *you are still lost in your sins.* Come with us to our church right now and if you really truly confess Christ, you will let us baptize you and *only then* will you be saved."

We declined. They were wrong for many reasons, which I'll leave to you to consider. This is an example of a serious problem that abounds in theology and the Church: Many denominations and individuals have become so fond of a particular doctrine, practice, history, culture or tradition, they've mixed it inseparably with salvation. Unless you have absolute conformity to every item of doctrine they believe, they declare you *not saved.* They will argue that many things about our behavior and our opinions—our acts and our theology—the belief in the inerrancy of Scripture through sexual purity, the gender of pastors and the nature of Communion, baptism by immersion and the unbroken apostolic succession, and *countless* others—are also in the center dot, are a part of *salvation.*

They are not!

They may be *profoundly important* to living our life in Christ (or not). But they are not *essential* to *salvation.*

They *follow* salvation, but are a not *requirement for* it. This is where precision and the distinction between *essentials* and *non-essentials* will begin to bear fruit for us:

If we imagine these other things to be *required* for salvation, then the ring of the "non-essentials" shrinks down to a narrow line, containing only such innocuous items as the color or cut of our clothing, or the language we speak—and even *these* would be argued by some as inseparable from salvation!

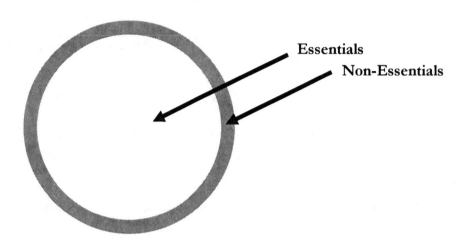

FIGURE: THE COMMON ERROR

Remember Meiderlin's words: "We would be in the best shape if we kept in essentials, Unity; in non-essentials, Liberty; and in both Charity."

When we face issues in the Church about which we disagree, we must first ask, quite rigorously, "Is it a salvation issue?" We must shun the temptation to *make* it a salvation issue in order to falsely elevate its importance. It can be *really important* and still not be a salvation issue. We shouldn't claim that it is just to raise its profile in our debates. And more, if it is *non-essential*, we should grant *liberty*. We should be able to differ—even if we deeply disagree—and do so with respect and love.

Lastly, in *both* the *essentials* and the *non-essentials*, we must show *charity*—which is godly love for each other. This is, sadly, the one thing most often absent in religious discussion and debate.

NOT ESSENTIAL TO SALVATION? WHY DO THEY MATTER?

We have looked at *salvation*, the *if and only if*, the necessary, the required, the essential—being born again from above into the Kingdom of Heaven, accepting the love of Christ, and trusting Him to do what He says. This is the *initiation of a covenant*, a pact, a vibrant *relationship* with our Creator, that will take on great importance in our lives. It begins with a "yes," but it becomes so much more.

Now we can consider the *important* content of a *Life in Christ*, the "more." The theological term for this is *sanctification*. Salvation is spiritual *birth* to a new life; sanctification is *living life*, a Life in Christ, *after* this new birth.

Though sanctification is non-essential *for salvation*, it is essential *for Life in Christ*. We'll unpack this a bit so it becomes clear.

Sanctification is about living a rich, full, abundant, godly life, being harmonized with the will of God, being "conformed to the image of Christ."[1] Sanctification is *learning to live and love like Jesus*. It is at least a life-long process. It matters because Jesus says it does. It isn't essential to being saved, but it is *vital*—essential—to living faithfully *after* being saved. It is where we grow toward wholeness, authenticity and whole-hearted love by the presence of the Spirit of God with us and within us.

In this life, while we have breath, if we have been saved, then what our life *ought* be about is trying to find conformity with God's will for us. We will mess up. Not a day goes by, not an hour goes by, that I don't mess up. But it doesn't affect my salvation—because my salvation comes from God's grace, from what Jesus did for me, *not from what I do.* Hold on to this—it is a key to understanding all that follows.

Think about it: If Jesus saved me just for all the sins I committed up until the moment that He saved me, and I'm responsible for all the sins that come after that, then Jesus was just a *momentary* savior and *I have to be my own savior from then on.*

Well, guess what? I couldn't do it *before* He saved me, and I can't do it *now*. That's what Paul talks about in Romans 7, where he bewails his own sinfulness. And he begins Romans 8 with one of the most important and hope-filled verses in all of Scripture: "But there is now no condemnation for those who are in Christ Jesus."

Cling to that one, because it is truly good news.

THE DISTINCTION BETWEEN SALVATION AND SANCTIFICATION

Let's review again: **Salvation** is the *essential*, the *if and only if*, to begin life in Christ eternally. It isn't *everything*—and by that I mean it *doesn't include all of our growth in Christ*. If our salvation is falsely redefined to include our personal efforts at growth in Christ, then it becomes a salvation accomplished *by us* instead of by the One who did it. Then these other things become a kind of "works righteousness," the things we must do to *earn* our salvation or prove we are worthy. If any of them can do that for us, we don't need a savior. We are our own saviors.

Sanctification is different from salvation, but what has happened in the Church endlessly over the centuries is that some have tried to blend sanctification into salvation. It is extremely important to distinguish between salvation and sanctification—and not confuse one with the other. To begin a *life* in Christ requires salvation. Salvation is the center circle.

The second circle is *growth* in Christ—how this new life becomes rich, abundant, character-building, filled with love, in the shelter of His arms,

---

[1] See Romans 8:29.

nourished by Scripture and the caring of other believers, empowered by the Holy Spirit, working to heal the world and to lead others to life in Him. It is full of high adventure and dismal failure. It is where we try and trip and try again. It is where we desire not to sin and sin anyway. It is where we get confused and then see clearly. It is where we stumble and fall, and are lifted up. It is where we doubt and wail and fight, and are loved anyway.[2]

It is where we make huge mistakes and little ones, grow and seek harmony with God's will for us, where we live as His body and trip over our own feet, where we are being conformed to His image and getting a little too proud of ourselves, and yet are still loved by Him and encouraged. It is where we are helped and help others. This is sanctification. Most of this book is devoted to it.

It is hugely, profoundly, deeply important—but it is not salvation, and *salvation is not dependent upon it.* Sanctification is *not* a necessary condition, and *not* a sufficient condition, for salvation. *If it was, then we repeatedly have to be our own saviors, and Christ's sacrifice for us was insufficient and pointless.*

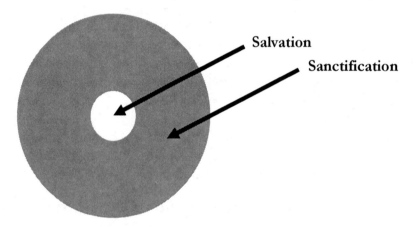

FIGURE: **CLEANING UP THE ERROR**

Moreover, sanctification normatively *follows* salvation, rather than preceding it—so it can't be a required condition that *causes* or precedes salvation.[3]

So salvation does not *depend on* sanctification, on our good works or behavior or the perfection of our beliefs. Cleaning up this error in understanding within the Church (and theologies) is a healthy endeavor—*may it take hold!*

> For by grace you have been saved through faith, and that not of yourselves; it is the gift of God, not of works, lest anyone should boast.[4]

---

[2] Romans 7 and 8 make this process really, really clear.

[3] Note that the Holy Spirit will be active in a person's life, even in the work of sanctification, before that person comes to see Jesus as Savior. This work of the Holy Spirit is *preparing* the person, but not depending on him or her to *earn* salvation.

[4] Ephesians 2:8-9, NKJV.

This point is extraordinarily important to understanding who we are in Christ and, in a more academic way, to having our theology straight. Salvation is something Jesus does. It is not something we do.

LIFE IN CHRIST—COVENANT

I'm including illustrations here and throughout the book to help us visualize the concepts we are attempting to understand. The illustrations are not proofs. They are intended simply as helpful pictures.

Our *complete* Life in Christ is also called by the title of Covenant,[5] which denotes a committed relationship, like marriage or adoption. It includes three key parts: Salvation, Sanctification and Glorification. We'll study this third concept, Glorification, a little later on; for now just hold it open as a category yet to be defined. Our active Life in Christ[6] *begins with Salvation*, is *lived out* as we mature through *Sanctification*, and is *made full* with *Glorification*.

It might be diagrammed something like this:

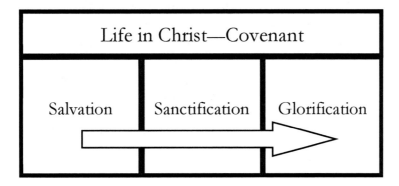

FIGURE: LIFE IN CHRIST—COVENANT

This diagram is pretty straightforward and can be a useful concept to us in comprehending what it means to be a Christian, and how such a life is lived. It is a *concept* about Life in Christ, and of course isn't the actual *living of it*, which happens in daily life in the world, and with other believers in the Church.

Much more on that starting in Chapter 5, "Why Bother to Be Good?"

Unfortunately, some theologians have tried to join salvation and sanctification together by naming the first step—being saved by Jesus—to be "justification." This is not a bad term for it, since it means being made right with God by the righteousness of Jesus. But then they lift the term "salvation" to include all three:

---

[5] Much, much more on covenant later on in the book. Does not refer to "Covenant Theology," but simply to the use of the term *covenant* in Scripture.

[6] We could properly say that Life in Christ begins when we are created, certainly long before we are saved, but doesn't become active or conscious until then. This is a significant subject but one that won't be explored here.

justification, *sanctification* and *glorification*. This wrongly lets them make *any* issue seem like a *salvation* issue! It could be diagrammed like this:

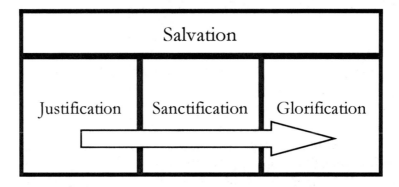

FIGURE: **SALVATION? NO.**

This illustration also displays a *concept* about Life in Christ, and while Justification isn't such a bad term for the first step in this sequence, promoting Salvation to the top category has the unfortunate consequence of making *everything* a "salvation issue." There is a broad, very abstract way in which this is true, but using the term in such a way renders its true meaning unclear, and falsely promotes *non-essentials* as *essentials*. Even if that isn't the motive, it is still confusing. We should avoid that temptation, even if it helps us defend or promote vital concepts, doctrines, practices or theologies that are very dear to us.

It is a *category error*. Vital issues can still be treated as important without being given exaggerated rank.

Issues of belief and behavior, important as they may be—*and they are important!*—are issues of *sanctification*, of being conformed to the image of Christ, of living in harmony with God. They are not issues of *salvation*.

This brings us to, and also sheds light on, a common and important question:

CAN YOU LOSE YOUR SALVATION?

You have become a believer in Jesus Christ. You have accepted His free offer of salvation. You are saved. You are learning to do as He commanded, loving God, neighbor and even enemy; treating others as you wish to be treated.

Can you get yourself unsaved?

This is not a trivial question. Great minds in the Church have asked and debated it. There are highly regarded theologians who would say that once you are saved, you are always saved. There are others who say salvation can be lost relatively easily. *That* assertion, however, is not supported by Scripture. It is also tough to fully support the first position. But the assertion that it is *easy* to lose your salvation is simply not in the Bible.

So let's consider the issue with a few examples:

Theft and the Truck

Sunday morning, you accepted Jesus Christ as Lord and Savior. You received complete forgiveness from God. You are righteous in His eyes because you have the righteousness of Christ. Monday afternoon at work, you steal a notepad and take it home. Does that make you unsaved?

Then, on your way home, a truck hits you and you die. Do you die unsaved and go to hell[7] for stealing? Yes or no?

No.

You are still saved. You have *sinned*, but you are still *saved*. You will have regret when you face your Savior, but He will welcome you regardless.

The Sun and Correct Doctrine

What about Galileo (1564–1642), the astronomer? The Church in his time read Scripture, and made doctrine from it, but much of this doctrine was formed by concepts the Church inherited and embraced from the Greek worldview in which it lived. Simply put, the Church read Scripture through the lens of Greek philosophy. This may sound funny, but it is true. We'll look at this more in depth in later chapters.

In this instance, the Church believed the Earth was the center of the universe. The idea actually comes from Pythagoras (circa 570–495 B.C.) and his students. He imagined that the Earth was the center, and all the planets moved around it, embedded in concentric invisible crystal spheres. The outermost sphere had stars embedded in it. Perhaps you recall this famous hymn, which begins:

This is my Father's world,
and to my listening ears
All nature sings, and round me rings
the music of the spheres.

The Pythagoreans studied music, and musical intervals, and believed that the "spheres" in which the planets were embedded must produce a sound, because they were of different sizes, and arranged together at specific harmonic intervals from Earth. This is the origin of "the music of the spheres"[8] in this famous hymn, although when it was written in 1901 everyone knew the Sun was the center of the solar system. In Galileo's time everyone "knew" that the Earth was the center of a set of concentric crystal spheres.

---

[7] The question of the destiny of the unsaved—whether non-existence, or punishment in a fiery lake, or conscious eternal separation from God, or some other state—may be important to consider at some point, but this isn't it. For now, the common idea that "if you aren't saved, you go to hell" will simply be used in illustrating how and if a person can revert from saved to unsaved.

[8] The Pythagoreans used the term "harmony of the spheres" but the concept was the same.

Well, not everyone. Nicolaus Copernicus (1473–1543), early in the 16th century, formulated the "*helio*centric" model with the *Sun* as the center. A century later, Galileo spoke out publicly in favor of this view.

The Roman Catholic Church condemned this view and said it was contrary to Scripture—or more accurately, contrary to doctrine arrived at because of a Greek philosopher's ideas. The Church told Galileo to stop advocating his view, and he promised that he would.

But he later published *Dialogue Concerning the Two Chief World Systems*, which strongly affirmed heliocentrism. Galileo was arrested, declared "vehemently suspect of heresy," was forced to deny what he had affirmed, and was kept under house arrest for the rest of his life.

Galileo *disagreed* with Church doctrine and disobeyed the order to keep quiet.

Is he therefore going to hell? No.

The Church said Galileo was wrong about doctrine. In fact, *the Church's doctrine was wrong* because the Pythagoreans were wrong. The Roman Catholic Church in 1992 issued a formal apology to Galileo for how they had mistreated him.

This example is about getting doctrine wrong. The Bible doesn't say the Earth is the center of the universe, but the Church developed that *concept*, believing it to be *implied* in Scripture, because the Greeks believed it, and the Greeks were the foundation upon which all philosophy (and theology) was built. The Church *required its members to believe the concept they had embraced.*

So … if Christians don't agree with the Church's concept, do they get unsaved and go to hell?

No.

Getting doctrine wrong doesn't unsave you. It may take you out of harmony with the Church. In fact, if the Church is right about an issue of doctrine, it will take you out of harmony with God; but it doesn't get you unsaved. You don't end your salvation that easily.

The Creeds

How about disagreeing with the Nicene Creed[9]—either in full or in part? If you do that, do you go to hell?

No.

I think the Nicene Creed is valuable. The doctrine is clear. I find it an excellent, short exposition of what Christians believe. Understanding the Creed and coming to the point of accepting what it says can be a valuable part of *sanctification*. But it is not about *salvation*. It is enormously important to make that distinction.

---

[9] Or any other accepted creed of the Church, including the Athanasian Creed, Apostles Creed, and other formal statements of faith.

Bad Teaching

How about a leader in the Church who teaches something that is contradictory to what Scripture says?

Consider: I knew a pastor who was teaching Modalism, which insists there aren't really three Persons: Father, Son and Holy Spirit. Rather, there is just one, and sometimes He wears different masks. Sometimes He acts in the mode of Father, sometimes in the mode of Son, and sometimes in the mode of Holy Spirit. It is called Modalism because He behaves in those different *modes*, but is really (in their concept) just one Person *acting* like three.

This idea has been rejected by the Church for some 1700 years. It is rejected because of the obvious implication that God is a fraud. He *pretends.*

So the questions is, if I am a teacher in the Church, and I have been saved, but then I teach Modalism, do I go to hell? If I am a *false* teacher, do I get *un*saved? That is a really important question.

Scripture is very clear about false teachers in the Church. It says that teachers will be held to a higher standard. But what happens to a teacher who teaches wrong doctrine? We will look at the Scripture.

But before we go there, I want to make again the key point about salvation. If any of these things that I do that are sinful can get me unsaved, then that means I am responsible day by day for my salvation, because if I sin I am not saved any more. *That* would mean I had substituted myself for Jesus, and had asserted that His act on the cross, His death, His willing sacrifice of Himself for me, wasn't sufficient. It didn't do the *whole* job. It was only a partial job and I have to do the rest of it. The fact of the matter is that we can't be (and, thankfully, don't have to be) our own savior, because *His act was complete.*

Scripture says, "But God demonstrates His own love toward us, in that while we were still sinners, Christ died for us."[10] "For by grace you have been saved through faith, and that not of yourselves; it is the gift of God, not of works, lest anyone should boast."[11]

My response to this is profound thanksgiving, because I know myself to be a sinful man. It is certain that with the greatest integrity I can muster, with the greatest care I can take in my study of Scripture and the Church in history, I will teach something that is wrong. And I will believe it when I teach it. Do I get *unsaved* when I do that?

Even as I write these words, I believe God is holding me to a very high standard, so I'm really serious when I study and when I teach, but there *have* to be areas where I am wrong.

There are other teachers in the Church who I believe are in grave error. If people are being intentionally misled by a false teacher, then as far as many

---

[10] Romans 5:8, NKJV.
[11] Ephesians 2:8-9, NKJV.

people are concerned, such a teacher *should* go to hell. But we are not the judge. We don't make those decisions. *God* decides.

Paul writes about teachers in 1 Corinthians 3. He is talking about the teachers in the Church—Apollos and himself, among others—and about how God regards the work they do. He says this:

> For no other foundation can anyone lay than that which is laid, which is Jesus Christ. Now if anyone builds on this foundation with gold, silver, precious stones, wood, hay, straw, each one's work will become clear; for the Day will declare it, because it will be revealed by fire; and the fire will test each one's work, of what sort it is. If anyone's work which he has built on it endures, he will receive a reward. If anyone's work is burned, he will suffer loss; but he himself will be saved, yet so as through fire.[12]

Paul is talking about teachers, though what he goes on to say also applies more broadly to every believer. But here he is addressing teachers, good and bad, in the Church. Everyone's work will be put through the fire to see whether or not it keeps its value.

His allusion is about refining gold. When you take gold that has impurities, and heat it to liquid state, the impurities float to the top. You then scrape them off and throw them away, and the gold is preserved.

If you have gold mixed with hay and straw and you put this mix in the fire, the hay and straw will be burned up. Their ash will be scraped off and discarded. The gold will survive.

Everyone's work, especially those who are leaders and teachers in the Church, will be put through the fire to see whether it keeps its value. If the work survives the fire, that builder will receive a reward. But if the work is burned up, the builder will suffer great loss.

But will he go to hell?

No!

The builder will suffer great loss, but *the builder himself will be saved,* like someone escaping through a wall of flames.

There are teachers in the Church who I would just as soon not have to spend eternity with. I believe they are desperately wrong in what they teach. In the Church worldwide, there are all sorts of people teaching all sorts of wrong things, including fomenting division and violence. *This* will be burned up. The *teachers* will be saved.

But where any of us in teaching have been faithful—*that gold* will survive the fire, and the teachers will be rewarded.

---

[12] 1 Corinthians 3:11-15, NKJV.

CAN YOU LOSE YOUR SALVATION BY SINNING?

So, can you lose your salvation by sinning, whether you are a believer or leader in the Church? The short answer is no.

God doesn't say that now you've been saved, go ahead and sin all you want. Read Romans 6. It makes it clear we are not supposed to sin. But in Romans 7, Paul bewails how, as much as he desires to be free of sin, he still is not. Then in Romans 8:1 he says:

> **But there is now no condemnation**
> **for those who are in Christ Jesus.**

Jesus is really good at saving us. He doesn't need our help to do it.

He doesn't need our righteousness or our works. We can't boast about earning our salvation.

Scripture is clear that though we desire not to sin, we will continue to; but *we stay saved.*

If it is possible to *abandon* salvation, it is not by simple sin. Jesus' sacrifice was complete and sufficient.

LEARNING TO LIVE AND LOVE AS JESUS DID

Our struggle against sin, our maturing as believers, our growth in character, our deepening understanding of Scripture and belief, our worship, our learning to love God, neighbor and even enemy, our learning to live and love like Jesus did—these are all *sanctification.*

They are core to *living and growing* as a Christian, and *fulfilling the covenant God has made with us.* They are vital, inescapable, profoundly important, and we should enter in to them with utmost gravity.

These things begin at our salvation (our spiritual *birth*), but they themselves are sanctification (our *Life* in Christ).

4.
Glorification

In Chapter 1 we considered the wheel illustration and its two concentric circles, Essentials and Non-Essentials. We saw that the center circle is the *if and only if* and the other not so. Non-essentials can be *really important*, but they are still *non-essentials* and shouldn't be falsely proclaimed as essentials just to enhance their visibility.

A good diet is important, but only if you are alive. Being alive is essential to living your life. A good diet is valuable, sustains life and gives health and energy, but it is not essential to living *in the same way* that being alive is.

To say, "Well, you're not really living if you merely subsist on a poor diet, so a good diet really is *essential* to life" is to wrongly tag something as essential just to make it seem especially important. This is a semantic misdirection that hides a category error, and we should avoid it.

In Chapters 2 and 3 this insight was applied to distinguish *Salvation* and *Sanctification*. Life in Christ (see following illustration) begins with salvation—being reborn by the Spirit into the Kingdom of Heaven. Though we sin and fall far short of the sinlessness required to be with God, we are made right with God by Jesus' willing gift to us of Himself—by His self-sacrificing love. We are made just, or "justified," by Christ. *Salvation*, this *birth* into a *new life*, is the *essential* of the faith; without it, there is no Life in Christ. Salvation is "being alive" for believers.

This new birth *begins the process* of our growing up in our faith, in our deepening relationship with God, in our maturing as *disciples*, and in our learning to love more fully. In fact, at its root "disciple" means "to learn by use and practice." Disciples learn to love as Jesus did, by the use and practice of love. In theology this is called *Sanctification*. It is a *hugely* important subject, an adventure, and our *life work*, and we will begin to look at it more fully and unpack its content in the next chapter.

For now, we'll skip over Sanctification to the final stage of Life in Christ, which is called *Glorification*. That is the theological term for *heavenly reward*, for what happens *after our human bodies die.*

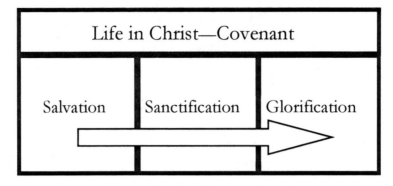

FIGURE: **LIFE IN CHRIST—COVENANT**

This chapter presents a whirlwind tour of what glorification is.[1]

I'll tell you in advance that you may not like this chapter. It is a topic hardly ever discussed in churches, though it is one of the foundational concepts of theology:

The content of our sanctification directly determines the content of our glorification. That is, to be plain, what we do in this life determines our reward in heaven.

That last sentence will raise some howls of protest, but it is what Jesus and the Scripture teach. Hang in there while we look.

This will likely unsettle you and raise all sorts of questions about life, faith, behavior, and what some would call "works righteousness." Even worse, the questions it may raise for you will largely not be answered or even addressed in this chapter. You'll have to wait until we circle back to these issues. But we need to open up the topic because our understanding of it will affect many other parts of our life as Christians—even though we may not even have known the term *glorification* before.

In Philippians 3:20-21, Paul tells us,

> We are citizens of heaven, where the Lord Jesus Christ lives. And we are eagerly waiting for Him to return as our Savior. He will take these weak mortal bodies of ours and change them into glorious bodies like his own, using the same mighty power that He will use to conquer everything, everywhere.

We actually get *changed*. Something happens by the mighty power of God, and we receive what are called *glorified bodies*, and it is *in these* that we live throughout eternity. Whether these are young or old, look anything like we do now, or are very different, we don't know. This is one of those passing references in Scripture that hint at something extraordinary that is coming, but then leaves it an open mystery as to what exactly it means. But somehow, some way, in some form, we get new bodies, and then live in them forever!

---

[1] If you would like to study it at a more leisurely pace, there is a book called *A Life God Rewards* by Bruce Wilkinson. He does a very thorough job of covering the same material.

What will we be doing in these "glorified" bodies? Scripture says we will be judges of angels, rulers of nations, priests of God.[2] This is a stunning revelation and should cause us to tremble at the possibility!

But in this heavenly glorification, who gets to do *what?* And will the opportunities *differ* from person to person? This is not a common topic in most of our churches (or seminaries, for that matter). What do you think?

One common belief is that as long as you believed in Jesus and lived a decent life, when you die you go to heaven, and your reward is pretty much the same as everyone else.

That idea is based on Matthew 20, where Jesus tells us that Kingdom of Heaven is like the owner of an estate who goes out early one morning to hire workers for his vineyard. He agrees to pay the normal daily wage and sends them to work. At 9 o'clock in the morning, he hires more. All the way up to 5 o'clock at night, he hires more people and sends them out. At the close of the day they all stand together to get paid.

> When those who were hired at five o'clock were paid, each received a full day's wage. When those who were hired earlier came to get their pay, they assumed they would receive more. But they, too, were paid a day's wage. When they received their pay, they protested to the owner, "Those people only worked one hour, and yet you've paid them just as much as you've paid us who worked all day in the scorching heat."
> He answered one of them,
> "Friend, I haven't been unfair! Didn't you agree to work all day for the usual wage? Take it and go. I wanted to pay this last worker the same as you. Is it against the law for me to do what I want with my money? Should you be angry because I am kind? And so it is, that many who are first now will be last then; and those who are last now will be first then."[3]

They all got the same wage—a full day's pay—regardless of how much work they did. We assume this may well be true of heaven. Maybe that's why Jesus tells this story…

Well, it is true that it doesn't matter whether you became a Christian at age five and served the Lord until age 95, or became a Christian at age 95, thirty seconds before you died. Everybody gets this same heavenly reward: *eternity with God.* But in a real sense, that reward has already been received: When you were born again, born from above, reborn into the Kingdom of Heaven. That is, eternity with God *begins at your salvation*, not at your death.

A question that we *ought* to ask is, "Is there any difference in the way *people are rewarded* when they spend eternity with God?" The answer is *yes*. There *is* a difference, and it is made by the way you lived your life as a follower of Christ,

---

[2] 1 Corinthians 6:3, Revelation 2:26, Revelation 1:6.
[3] Matthew 20:9-16, NLT First Edition (1996).

that is, by *how you loved*—how you took *willing action for the benefit of others* and to serve God. Some examples from Scripture:

OLD TESTAMENT EXAMPLE

Consider this from Jeremiah 17:10. "I, the LORD, search all hearts and examine secret motives. I give all people their due *rewards*, according to what their *actions* deserve."

NEW TESTAMENT EXAMPLES

You've probably heard quotes like that one from the Old Testament, and then someone objects, "But what we know now is because of Jesus, because everything is forgiven, we are no longer subject to the law, and therefore not subject to this kind of assessment. It doesn't matter if this one did a better job or this one did worse; they are not rewarded according to what their actions deserve. We are all really equal now. We are all one in Christ Jesus."

This *sounds* Christian, religious and theological, but listen to this—this is from *Jesus:*

> "When you fast, comb your hair and wash your face. Then no one will suspect you are fasting, except your Father, who knows what you do in secret. And your Father, who knows all secrets, will *reward you.* Don't store up treasures here on earth, where they can be eaten by moths and get rusty, and where thieves break in and steal. *Store your treasures in heaven,* where they will never become moth-eaten or rusty and where they will be safe from thieves."[4]

So there is *some kind of treasure*, whatever it is, that we can "store up" in heaven. The old saying about heaven is "you can't take it with you," but the implication here is that there *is something* you can put up there, in advance, like an investment account, and get it later when you go there. I know that sounds odd, but that is what Jesus says!

Or what about this? *Jesus again:*

> "Take care! Don't do your good deeds publicly, to be admired, because then you will *lose your reward* from your Father in heaven. When you give a gift to someone in need, don't shout about it as the hypocrites do—blowing trumpets in the synagogues and streets to call attention to their acts of charity! I assure you, they have received all the reward they will ever get."[5]

In other words, the praise they got from the people is their only reward. That's that. There isn't any more reward for what they have given. So if we don't

---

[4] Matthew 6:17-20, NLT First Edition.
[5] Matthew 6:1-2, NLT First Edition.

brag about what we've done—any gift or kindness or act of love—then we will get a reward for it from our Father in heaven.

But wait! You might argue that because the first verse says, "Don't do your good deeds publicly, to be admired, because then you will lose your reward *from* your Father in heaven," that Jesus was describing some kind of reward here on Earth, *now*, in this life, rather than *later*, in heaven.

But actually, the Greek doesn't say that. The Greek says this:

"…because then you will lose the reward *with* your Father in Heaven."

Isn't that interesting? It doesn't say "*from* your Father in heaven." It *is* from Him, of course, because everything is from Him. But it isn't just *from* Him. It comes when you are *with* Him!

Here's another one. Jesus again:

> "If you refuse to take up your own cross[6] and follow me, you are not worthy of being mine. If you cling to your life, you will lose it; but if you give it up for me, you will find it. Anyone who welcomes you is welcoming me; and anyone who is welcoming me is welcoming the Father who sent me. … And if you welcome good and godly people because of their godliness, *you will be given a reward* like theirs."[7]

That is, when good and godly people come, if you welcome them, you will receive a *reward* like theirs. Even more, in the very next sentence Jesus says, "And even if you give a cup of cold water to one of the least of my followers, you will surely be rewarded."

You will surely be *rewarded*, Jesus says.

Another time, Jesus talks about a dinner that is taking place—a wedding feast. The host invites many people. I won't go over the entire story, but Jesus basically says, "Sit at the foot of the table rather than insisting on sitting at the head."

> "For those who exalt themselves will be humbled, and those who humble themselves will be exalted." Then he turned to his host. "When you put on a luncheon or a banquet," he said, "don't invite your friends, brothers, relatives, and rich neighbors. For they will invite you back, and that will be your only reward. Instead, invite the poor, the crippled, the lame, and the blind. Then *at the resurrection* of the righteous, *God will reward you* for inviting those who could not repay you."[8]

In other words, Jesus is saying if we give to those who cannot repay us, knowing that there is no prospect of our giving being returned, then at our

---

[6] By the way, the sense of this is that each of us has a cross, a burden to bear, and it is different for each person. It isn't Jesus' cross that I am taking up. It is my cross. In a sense, it is the cross that is *assigned to me*. The one that Jesus took was one I couldn't carry, but there is a cross, a burden, assigned to me, that I am given in this life. It could be to teach, to care for the needy, to give sacrificially, to feed the hungry, perhaps even to give your life…

[7] Matthew 10:38-40, 41b, NLT First Edition.

[8] Luke 14:11-14.

resurrection, there will be a repayment for us. *God will reward you* for inviting those who could not repay you.

"Hearing this, a man sitting at the table with Jesus exclaimed, 'What a blessing it will be to attend a banquet in the Kingdom of God!'"[9]

He understood what Jesus meant. There will be heavenly reward, and it will differ, based on our actions here on Earth.

Finally this, Jesus again:

> "I tell you, use your worldly resources to benefit others and make friends. In this way, your generosity *stores up a reward for you in heaven.*"[10]

Obviously, a reward is *not stored up* for those who use their worldly resources *for themselves* alone.

In case we had any idea that all rewards were the same when people got to heaven, Jesus is clear that rewards differ based on our actions here on Earth.

MAKING IT PERSONAL

I know folks who are not well-to-do at all. They barely get by week to week. They have to manage their money with extraordinary care. They never go out. They don't have a fancy TV. The car is probably 12 years old. There isn't much in the way of worldly wealth. Yet those people are faithful in their giving to the Church, and to God's work, and to missionaries going overseas, and to beggars on the street. They scrimp and save, and then take a significant percentage (far beyond a tithe) of the small amount that they have, and *they give it freely and with joy.*

There are other people I know who have a medium amount of money, and some with a great deal of wealth, who give hardly anything at all to anything, and when they do give, it is a tiny percentage of what they have. A tithe would be incomprehensible to them. I have heard some of these folks say, "If I win the lottery, I am going to give a whole bunch of money to the Church."

Probably not—more likely this is a self-justifying prediction that would never be lived out.

Jesus says if you are not responsible about small amounts, you are not going to be responsible with big amounts. And if you are not responsible about even small amounts, *God is not going to reward you.* Jesus said that!

Sadly, this can be used very manipulatively by leaders in the church, and I think it is sick and ungodly when it is, but *nevertheless* Jesus is clear that we should bless others with what we have, whether we have little or much, and that those loving actions *will be rewarded in heaven.*

---

[9] Luke 14:15. The Greek actually says, "to eat bread" rather than "attend a banquet." The basic idea is the same.
[10] Luke 16:9, NLT First Edition.

PAUL ON HEAVENLY REWARD

Paul, the most prolific author in the New Testament, says this:

> Spend your time and energy in training yourself for spiritual fitness. Physical exercise has some value, but spiritual exercise is much more important, for it promises a *reward* both in this life and the next.[11]

Finally, this also from Paul:

> After all, what gives us hope and joy, and what is our proud reward and crown? It is you![12]

That is, the people that he has been pastor to, the people that he has taught and led to Christ, will be Paul's proud reward and crown. *He has a reward* that those who have not led others into the Kingdom *will not* have.

SO, YOU *CAN* TAKE IT WITH YOU

There *is* something that you can take with you. When we die and enter heaven—a life much longer than this blink of an eye that we are in right now—there are two things that we can take with us from this life.

The first are *those things that the Lord has stored up for us* in honoring our faithful service. They are there waiting for us. And yes, they differ depending upon how we acted in this life on Earth, on whether we showed love and compassion for others, or simply indulged ourselves.

The other thing that we can take into heaven is *people*—people we have shared the Good News with and invited into the Kingdom, people we have shared our sanctification with, people we have worked shoulder-to-shoulder with, people we have struggled with, argued with, gotten mad at, and reconciled with.

Those folks—we can take them with us. We go together.

No, we can't take gold. (What would you buy with it anyway, in heaven?) But we can take people that we have been given to love, that we have learned to love, and with whom we have shared news of God and Christ. What a privilege that is!

So that is *glorification*. That is that third important theological term.

I expect some of this Scripture made you uncomfortable and raised deep questions in your mind. If so, good! It surely did for me. Theology is supposed to engage us, both to help know God better, and especially to draw us closer to Him.

We will circle back to the likely questions that were raised as we move forward.

In the next chapter, "Why Bother to Be Good?", we'll return to sanctification, the *content* of Life in Christ, and begin to explore the many ways in which this is lived out.

---

[11] 1 Timothy 4:7b-8, NLT First Edition.
[12] 1 Thessalonians 2:19b, NLT First Edition.

5.
Why Bother to Be Good?

We've identified salvation, sanctification and glorification as the three key elements of Life in Christ, of *covenant*, as well as foundational concepts of Christian theology. Looking at *Sanctification* in depth begins here. Recall:

Salvation means being rescued or saved from a life poisoned by sin, thus being born into eternity in God's presence. This comes simply by recognizing that we sin, that we hurt others, ourselves, and the world around us; and accepting the forgiveness that God offers through Jesus. That is salvation.

Sanctification means allowing ourselves to be changed in our thought-life, in our behavior, in our hearts, in the way we live in the world—in essence, to become more and more conformed to the image of Christ. Said differently, to learn to live and love like Jesus did—that is sanctification.

Glorification refers to the life after this earthly one. It is eternity in God's presence, gained in our salvation, and its content is determined in part by the life we live here after we are saved. I believe these are extraordinarily important foundations.

We have identified these three, and looked at *Salvation* and *Glorification*. But we haven't yet really focused on *Sanctification*, the second key element of Life in Christ: learning to live and love like Jesus did.

It sounds noble and all, but why bother? Why bother with sanctification; why bother to be good? If we've gained forgiveness and eternal life with God through our salvation, why bother with the trials and tribulations of being like Jesus? It got *Him* killed.

Who needs the trouble?

Well, for one reason, we know that glorification is better if we are better. That is, our *heavenly reward is greater* if we live godly lives. Scripture says as much. Jesus says as much. But let's be frank. Many people don't find that particularly motivating. I don't. "Be really good in this life, and it will make it all that much better when you get to heaven."

Forget it! There's enough to do with work, kids, neighbors and more; I don't have the time or the desire to be Mother Teresa. So why should I bother to be good?

Even more, much of what the Church focuses on when it talks about sanctification—whether or not it uses that word—is simply *behaving* better: a change in outward appearance but with little attention paid to the content of the heart. And it's usually enforced in a way that I personally find both oppressive and tiresome. So, why bother with sanctification? I hope to begin to answer that here.

SANCTIFICATION

A simple definition of sanctification is "learning to live and love as Jesus did."

Sanctification does not assure us life eternal with God. Only salvation can do that. But the character and the content of eternity in God's presence *is* determined in part by the depth and the nature of our sanctification. But should that be our motivation? Not only does such motivation seem self-centered, it is not likely to have any longevity—a bit like the irresponsible friend who borrowed money and keeps promising to repay. You get tired of promises that don't get fulfilled anytime soon.

But there is a reason to bother with trying to live and love like Jesus. Let's look: Paul's expression "work out your own salvation with fear and trembling"[1] is about sanctification. It helps us begin to understand why we bother. The New Living Translation (First Edition) reads this way:

> Now that I am away, you must be even more careful to put into action God's saving work in your lives, obeying God with deep reverence and fear. For God is working in you, giving you the desire to obey him, and the power to do what pleases him.[2]

In other words, the very desire for sanctification and the power to work through it *comes from God*, not from our hope of reward in heaven.

It is not self-will. This is what distinguishes sanctification from other kinds of human striving, *even from trying to be or do good.* It is powered by the Holy Spirit, who lives in us from the moment we are saved.

Nor is it self-improvement. It is not enlightenment as sought by the Yogis. It is not the Human Potential Movement. It is not self-affirmation, self-aggrandizement or self-realization. It is willing cooperation with the Holy Spirit—sovereign God living in us to help accomplish His loving purposes in us and through us here on Earth. Jesus promised it this way:

> "And I will ask the Father, and He will give you another Counselor, who will never leave you. He is the Holy Spirit, who leads into all truth.
> "The world at large cannot receive him, because it isn't looking for him and doesn't recognize him. But you do, because he lives with you now and later will be in you."[3]

---

[1] Philippians 2:12, KJV.
[2] Philippians 2:12b-13.
[3] John 14:16-17, NLT First Edition.

He was speaking to the disciples just before Pentecost. And here is how what He promised was fulfilled:

> When the Day of Pentecost had fully come, they were all with one accord in one place. And suddenly there came a sound from heaven, as of a rushing mighty wind, and it filled the whole house where they were sitting.
> Then there appeared to them divided tongues, as of fire, and one sat upon each of them. And they were all filled with the Holy Spirit and began to speak with other tongues, as the Spirit gave them utterance.[4]

This is the power of God given to followers of Jesus. The Holy Spirit took up residence in every one of the disciples—150 or more in the upper room on that day—and thousands more shortly thereafter.

Scripture tells us that, likewise, when we accept Jesus as Lord and Savior, the Holy Spirit moves into us.

Paul says:

> He who is joined to the Lord *is one spirit with Him*.[5]

And:

> Do you not know that your body is the temple of the Holy Spirit *who is in you*, whom you have from God, and you are not your own? For you were bought at a price; therefore glorify God in your body and in your spirit, *which are God's*.[6]

Throughout the New Testament, those who become followers of Jesus are described as His friends, disciples, priests, His body and His bride. These terms are used in order to point to an intimacy greater than any of them can express—greater than can be expressed in human language.

Consider now all that has been said about what happens to us when we accept His offer of salvation:

We get filled with God, are made intimate with Him, and are then sent into the world to love others and lead them into the same salvation, filling and intimacy. This is sanctification.

It is a great adventure of cosmic proportions. It is more imaginative than the wildest science fiction.

It is hardly just a personal effort to behave better and live neat, scrubbed-clean lives.

It has more in common with being a medic in a war zone than it has with being polite and soft-spoken. It has more in common with clinging for dear life to a wild lion's mane than it does with staring in a mirror and chanting, "Every day, in every way, I am getting better and better."

---

[4] Acts 2:1-4, NKJV.

[5] 1 Corinthians 6:17, NKJV.

[6] 1 Corinthians 6:19-20, NKJV.

It isn't narcissistic self-improvement. It's not spiritual grooming or holy one-upmanship. It's more like parachuting into the Amazon Jungle in the midst of the Black Caiman crocodiles than it is like trying to be on our best behavior so the gossips won't talk about us.

Let's think about this. There's danger everywhere on this planet, much of it made by humans to hurt other humans—to take advantage of them, rob them, wound them—for pleasure or power or twisted entertainment.

God looks at this and thinks... *What?*

> Then the LORD saw that the wickedness of man was great in the earth, and that every intent of the thoughts of his heart was only evil continually. And the LORD was sorry that He had made man on the earth, and He was grieved in His heart.[7]

And Jesus said:

> "What comes out of a man, that defiles a man. For from within, out of the heart of men, proceed evil thoughts, adulteries, fornications, murders, thefts, covetousness, wickedness, deceit, lewdness, an evil eye, blasphemy, pride, foolishness. All these evil things come from within and defile a man."[8]

Into the midst of this inescapable self-made mess comes the Son of God, the One through whom all things were made,[9] the one whose creation we have been destroying. He comes here, not with storm and fire and lightning to destroy us, but with life and forgiveness—to rescue us from ourselves and the mess we have made. And He invites us to join in the rescue effort, and He gives us power.

John 3:17 reveals His purpose:

> God did not send His Son into the world to condemn it, but to save it.

The Message renders the verse this way:

> God didn't go to all of the trouble of sending his Son merely to point an accusing finger, telling the world how bad it was. He came to help, to put the world right again.

So, *we* have been rescued, *saved!* The Creator, God, came here in person to rescue us, and if we accept His gift, we are saved, forgiven, set free! And then what? Does He simply ask us to live tidy lives and be polite? Hardly! *He invites us to join Him in the effort.* He even offers us inner power and guidance in the Person of the Holy Spirit.

Talk about playing in the big leagues! This is as big-league as it gets. There is training. There is struggle. There is exhaustion, and there is rest. And there is more

---

[7] Genesis 6:5-6, NKJV.
[8] Mark 7:20-23, NKJV.
[9] John 1:3.

struggle and work and even danger. *But lives are at stake,* and we have the enormous privilege of joining Jesus in the rescue—at His request and under His direction.

He doesn't leave us unequipped; in fact, much of sanctification is learning to use the tools and weapons of spiritual warfare, drawing on the power of the Holy Spirit—*supernatural* power.

Here's how Paul puts it:

> A final word: Be strong in the Lord and in his mighty power.
>
> Put on all of God's armor so that you will be able to stand firm against all strategies of the devil. For we are not fighting against flesh-and-blood enemies, but against evil rulers and authorities of the unseen world, against mighty powers in this dark world, and against evil spirits in the heavenly places.
>
> Therefore, put on every piece of God's armor so you will be able to resist the enemy in the time of evil. Then after the battle you will still be standing firm.
>
> Stand your ground, putting on the belt of truth and the body armor of God's righteousness. For shoes, put on the peace that comes from the Good News so that you will be fully prepared.
>
> In addition to all of these, hold up the shield of faith to stop the fiery arrows of the devil. Put on salvation as your helmet, and take the sword of the Spirit, which is the word of God.
>
> Pray in the Spirit at all times and on every occasion. Stay alert and be persistent in your prayers for all believers everywhere.[10]

So this isn't about trying to be good or nice or even behaving well. It is *far* beyond that. It is life and death and high adventure. *This* is sanctification: It is part boot-camp, part revolution, part suffering, part secret-plan, part firefight, part battle-zone medicine, part exhilaration. It is the truest kind of love: willing action to bless others, even in the face of danger.

And it takes work to be in spiritual, fighting trim.

Paul says:

> All athletes are disciplined in their training. They do it to win a prize that will fade away, but we do it for an eternal prize. So I run with purpose in every step. I am not just shadowboxing. I discipline my body like an athlete, training it to do what it should.[11]

Look, there's nothing wrong with being polite, or being nice to neighbors, or being kind to old people—in fact, these are all good things. But at best, these are subsets of subsets of subsets of sanctification: quiet elements of what is essentially high drama, high adventure, on patrol in the war zone against the enemy of all souls, where we are serving the King of kings who has come to rescue His own.

Why bother with sanctification? Because Jesus tells us to, and because every other effort in life is tame beyond words.

---

[10] Ephesians 6:10-18.
[11] 1 Corinthians 9:25-27b.

6.
Living With Believers

This chapter is primarily about living with other believers—Christians—both in a local congregation and in the Church worldwide. In the next chapter we'll look at living with nonbelievers, and living with non-Christian and marginally Christian folk in the everyday world.

This will prove a very short chapter. It will tell you what Jesus told us to do (love each other), look at how well we've done it (we failed) and tell us what to do now (love each other). We keep finding other things to do that *look* busy, important, or holy, but ultimately are a misdirection for our lives and intentions. We avoid the often-thankless work of loving each other as Jesus loved us.

After all...

- Romantic love is more fun, and is easily aided by intoxicants we consume, and endorphins our brains produce when we fall in love.
- Fighting is more exciting—even when frightening and awful and bloody—and is aided by intoxicants we consume and adrenaline and other brain and muscle chemicals our bodies produce.
- Worship is more fulfilling. When we praise God, He dwells in our praises. Our attention is drawn constantly to His beauty and power. We are met, and blessed.
- Music fills us and drives away the cares of the day. Even if the music is bad or the song unsingable, we at least can amuse ourselves in an inner critique of how bad it is.
- Prayer focuses us on God and on the expressed needs of those we love and care about, and our words are directed to God, and He is the perfect listener.
- Bible study reveals to us God's heart and counsel for our lives. We read, mark and inwardly digest His Word.

- Theology captures our imagination—or bores us. If it bores us, at least we can think about what to make for dinner. If it captures our imagination, we can strive to understand God, and build our understanding into a coherent structure of concepts, doctrines and subdoctrines.
- Even fighting heresy can be fun. It's invigorating, sometimes maddening, and it fires off neurons and adrenaline and much more. It excites us.

Unfortunately, *these are not the things that make me a Christian.* Some of them are important elements in a normal Christian life, but only if the key commandments He gives us are actually lived out in our lives.

Here's the point: Being a Christian would be much simpler without having to deal with you. And also without Jesus. *He* complicates my life even more than *you* do:

> So now I am giving you a new commandment: Love each other. Just as I have loved you, you should love each other. Your love for one another will prove to the world that you are my disciples.[1]

But *I* want to prove I'm His disciple by how well I do *theology*, or *sing*, or *pray* or *fight the heretics.* Those things are fun and exciting.

Loving you is hard work. Loving *me* is hard work. It's not just mustering up warm *feelings*; the love of which Jesus speaks is my *intentional action* for your benefit, and *your actions* for my benefit.

Christ's command to us is about loving God and neighbor.

When Jesus speaks above, commanding us to love, the Greek word used for "love" is *agape.* It does not designate warm feelings. It *includes* that, but specifically it's about *taking action* for someone else's success, their benefit, their well-being.

And Jesus doesn't say "love each other when you feel like it." Nor does He say "love each other when you're feeling good about each other" or "…when you're not mad at each other." He says *love*, and He means *take action for that other person's benefit.* Do it even if you *don't* feel like it, even if you *don't want to.* This is not a suggestion from Jesus; it is a *command*: *Love one another.*

Love is action for the other's benefit, for their success, healing, renewal, redemption. And hence because God *is* love, God is *action for our benefit*—in our creation, in His sacrifice, in counsel and empowerment.

Here's how the Apostle John describes it:

> Dear friends, let us continue to love one another, for love comes from God. Anyone who loves is born of God and knows God.[2] But anyone who does not love does not know God—for God *is* love.

---

[1] John 13:34-35.
[2] Recall Jesus' words to Nicodemus (see Chapter 1).

God showed how much he loved us by sending his only Son into the world so that we might have eternal life through him. This is real love. It is not that we loved God, but that he loved us and sent his Son as a sacrifice to take away our sins.

Dear friends, since God loved us that much, we surely ought to love each other. No one has ever seen God. But if we love each other, God lives in us, and his love has been brought to full expression through us. And God has given us his Spirit as proof that we live in him and he in us.

Furthermore, we have seen with our own eyes and now testify that the Father sent his Son to be the Savior of the world. All who proclaim that Jesus is the Son of God have God living in them, and they live in God. We know how much God loves us, and we have put our trust in him.

God is love, and *all who live in love live in God, and God lives in them.* And as we live in God, *our love grows more perfect.*[3] So we will not be afraid on the day of judgment, but we can face him with confidence because *we are like Christ here in this world.* Such love has no fear because perfect *love expels all fear.* If we are afraid, it is for fear of judgment, and this shows that his love has not been perfected in us.

We love each other as a result of his loving us first. If someone says, "I love God," *but hates a Christian brother or sister,* that person is a *liar*; for if *we don't love people we can see, how can we love God, whom we have not seen?* And God himself has *commanded* that we must love not only him but our Christian brothers and sisters, too.[4]

The truth is, we have 20 centuries of failure at this. When we disagree about a concept, a doctrine, a matter of theology, the structure of a worship service, a denomination, or a sacrament, we often do it with *venom*. We get offended with each other over matters large and tiny, and the dishonor with which we treat each other dishonors God.

We are such rank failures at this that Christians have tortured and murdered Christians for hundreds of reasons, from translating the Bible into a language besides Latin to insisting baptism be done only to adults, for poor (or excellent) theology, or for belonging to the wrong church.

I could cite *hundreds* of examples of Christians demonstrating in word and action their hatred of other Christians. Even when we are not killing each other, the sarcasm and disrespect we display is appalling—and *unholy.*

I don't care if some are modern or ancient leaders of the church, and wise or renowned in other ways. *Hating believers is inexcusable. It is wicked.* The Apostle John is spot-on when he says, "If someone says, 'I love God,' *but hates a Christian brother or sister,* that person is a liar."[5]

Further, Jesus told us to love even our *enemies*, and pray for them!

Loving my friends is hard enough. *Loving my enemies is nearly incomprehensible.* Why would anyone do *that?* It seems stupid, foolish.

---

[3] The Greek word translated as "perfect" actually means *complete* or *whole.*
[4] 1 John 4:7-21, NLT First Edition.
[5] 1 John 4:20a.

But though I am to defend the faith, Jesus does not give me the "option" of *hating my opponents*. Whether they are brothers and sisters in Christ, or enemies, it is not permitted. If I claim Christ as Savior, *I don't have that choice.*

And consider this: *We* were *His* enemies, and *He loved us*.[6] Had He hated us, *we would all be dead.* Listen to Jesus:

> "You have heard that the law of Moses says, 'Love your neighbor' and hate your enemy. But I say, love your enemies! Pray for those who persecute you! In that way, you will be acting as true children of your Father in heaven. For he gives his sunlight to both the evil and the good, and he sends rain on the just and on the unjust, too.
>
> "If you love only those who love you, what good is that? Even corrupt tax collectors do that much. If you are kind only to your friends, how are you different from anyone else? Even pagans do that.
>
> "But you are to be perfect, even as your Father in heaven is perfect."[7]

I don't know about you, but I don't particularly like what Jesus has to say there. It makes my life far more difficult than it could be otherwise. But if I claim Him as Lord and He says this to me—and He does—*there is no choice*. I must love my brothers and sisters in Christ. I must also love my enemies. I know that the word Jesus uses for "love" does not mean to try to conjure up warm and fuzzy feelings. It means to take action for their well-being, take action for their benefit, take action *for them*.

Take action for the benefit of your enemies? Yeow!

So what should we do? Frankly, it's easier to fall in love, fight, worship, pray, sing, invent religious concepts, theologize, fight heresy and study the Bible. But this people stuff is very hard work.

The Apostle Paul gives us extraordinary insight into what this "loving each other" means, and the truth is, it is not easy. We have to go out of our way, especially with people who *offend* or *irritate* us. Yet Paul says this:

> But now is the time to get rid of anger, rage, malicious behavior, slander, and dirty language. Don't lie to each other, for you have stripped off your old evil nature and all its wicked deeds. In its place you have clothed yourselves with a brand-new nature that is continually being renewed as you learn more and more about Christ, who created this new nature within you.
>
> In this new life, it doesn't matter if you are a Jew or a Gentile, circumcised or uncircumcised, barbaric, uncivilized, slave, or free. Christ is all that matters, and he lives in all of us. Since God chose you to be the holy people whom he loves, you must clothe yourselves with tenderhearted mercy, kindness, humility, gentleness, and patience.
>
> You must *make allowance for each other's faults* and *forgive the person who offends you.* Remember, the Lord forgave you, so you must forgive others.

---

[6] See Romans 7:5-9.
[7] Matthew 5:43-48, NLT First Edition.

And the most important piece of clothing you must wear is love. Love is what binds us all together in perfect harmony. And let the peace that comes from Christ rule in your hearts. For as members of one body you are all called to live in peace.

And always be thankful. Let the words of Christ, in all their richness, live in your hearts and make you wise. *Use his words to teach and counsel each other.*

Sing psalms and hymns and spiritual songs to God with thankful hearts. And whatever you do or say, let it be as a representative of the Lord Jesus, all the while giving thanks through him to God the Father.[8]

Could Paul be more clear and straightforward? Yet does our behavior or attitude look anything like this at all?

Here's a serious challenge: *Make a list* of Jesus' commands about love, and Paul's and John's examples of what we must do and refrain from doing, if we are to truly love each other. Jesus said:

"So now I am giving you a new commandment: Love each other. Just as I have loved you, you should love each other. Your love for one another will prove to the world that you are my disciples."[9]

If your heart is anything like mine, it struggles and fails to do this. But the simple fact that I struggle and fail to love as Jesus has told me to love does not exempt me from His command.

Learn to love each other.

---

[8] Colossians 3:8-17, NLT First Edition.
[9] John 13:34-35.

7.
Living With Unbelievers

In the previous chapter we looked mainly at living with believers, and I concluded that it would be a lot easier to be a Christian if it weren't for other Christians like you. Having a relationship with each other is hard. But Jesus doesn't give us a choice in this matter. He commands us to love each other. The fact that it is hard doesn't exempt us from His command.

Let's now consider "unbelievers." In the context of this book this means people who, for whatever reason, do not consider Jesus as Savior or Lord.

There are a lot of Christians in the world. And there are a lot of people who aren't Christians. Some belong to other faiths; some have no obvious faith. Some have never considered becoming a Christian, some live in places where doing so would be fatal, and some have considered it and chosen not to. Some regard it as unimportant or irrelevant. Some regard Christians as agents of Satan, and others see them as backwards, superstitious, anti-science, anti-intellectual, and a danger to humanity. Simply put, we seldom enter a relationship with non-Christians where we are given the benefit of the doubt, or where we are looked upon as a gift or blessing.

So how are we to live with non-Christians, and what do we have that is of value to say or show to them?

THE CRUCIFIXION

First of all let us consider the Crucifixion of Jesus. This is really the hinge point of history for Christians. For us it is the time and place where our eternal destiny changed, if we accept what Jesus did for us there.

The Crucifixion of Jesus is looked at by Christians in a variety of ways. Here are two prominent views.

Forensic View

The forensic view of the Crucifixion, held to by Evangelicals, Roman Catholics, Eastern Orthodox, and one way or another by virtually all Christians, is that it was a sacrifice to God to appease His justifiable anger toward us. It was payment of a just sentence and fine on our behalf by someone else. Christ took the sentence, and paid the fine.

Metaphorical View

Another view is that the crucifixion of Jesus on the cross is *a picture, a metaphor,* of what we do to everything God has made: *We crucify it.* This view also says that Christ's Resurrection is similarly a real-life metaphor *of the love God has for us in spite of what we have done.*

If the Crucifixion is a metaphor for the way we treat all of creation, including each other, the Resurrection is God's response to what we've done. This view is often espoused by "universalists" who believe everyone is saved by Jesus, regardless of their awareness of it or their faith in Him.

I think the "metaphorical view" is a valid and extraordinary understanding of the Crucifixion, regardless of whether universalists also concur with it. It is not in opposition to the forensic view, but rather amplifies our understanding of how extraordinary the event of the Crucifixion truly was.[1]

Both of these (forensic and metaphorical) are ways of describing the Crucifixion and attempting to unveil its meaning. Both fall short. Both point to the fact that something extraordinary happened on that cross, on that day, with that man, Jesus—something that transcended mere human action and history, something that invaded our reality and opened a way into an eternal reality. And every description we use of that extraordinary invasion of our reality falls short.

The fundamental and historic understandings and explanations of what happened on the cross are helpful, though they are necessarily limited and finite forms for explaining something unlimited and infinite, and therefore they do not contain the whole truth, because humans cannot comprehend the fullness of God's love.

In any case, we don't even need to get into the minutiae of Crucifixion theology to acknowledge the importance and the meaning of the event. We should be able to step back and simply gaze in wonder, and do so in a way that makes the event accessible to people of other faiths or no faith. Here is why that is important:

Over the years, other interpretations of the Crucifixion have blamed it on the Jews, or the Romans, or the Jewish religious hierarchy of the time. These simple-minded interpretations are both profoundly wrong and misleading. They miss the point. Whoever the incidental agents of His death were, who was actually *responsible* for His death?

You were. I was. All of us. Every one of us. No exceptions. Not just them, whoever "them" might be, but...

Us!

---

[1] To complicate this even more, some of those who consider the Crucifixion and Resurrection a metaphor do believe that both actually happened, some believe the first happened, but not the second, some believe neither actually happened in history but are a valuable fiction, and some believe that whether they happened in history or not is immaterial. We won't unpack these here.

He paid the price for *our* sin. If Christians want revenge against the culprits who killed Jesus, they should look no further. They live inside the skin of the culprit.

The profound truth of the Crucifixion is this: We have all contributed to the harming of others and of our world. We are such miracles of creation, and we live in such a miracle of creation, and yet we not only take it all for granted, but we try to hoard more and more of it for ourselves, and we wound or kill others in the process. We've made a mess of a beautiful garden of life.

If I were God, I'd be really angry about this, and would just crush all these ungrateful, mean-spirited, selfish humans into dust.

Instead, the message of the cross is that God Himself so loved us—even while we were ungrateful, mean-spirited, selfish humans—that He took onto Himself all of that horror that we've done, and offered us complete forgiveness without any cost to us, but at great cost to Him.

For the moment, forget the religion of Christianity that has grown up around this event. Step aside from our religion's competition with other religions and beliefs and faith traditions. Just consider the action of God toward us: *In spite of what we deserve, He loved and forgave us.* He sacrificed Himself for us. That's the fundamental reality of who Jesus is and what He did for us.

This is our most foundational truth: God loved and sacrificed Himself for people still caught in sin.

This is a truth and a bridge into God's love, and to an eternity that stands outside of religion and religious traditions.

It is the direct and intentional invasion of a desperate and needy world by the creator God.

How can I do anything but be stunned and grateful? And if I grasp the wonder of this, how can I do anything but share it with those who haven't heard, or haven't understood?

LIVING WITH UNBELIEVERS

This brings us to *living with* unbelievers, and also why it is so important to understand the difference between salvation and sanctification—which is where we started this whole book.

Unbelievers (meaning those who do not consider Jesus as Savior) come in all kinds: Jews, Buddhists, Hindus, Muslims, Jains and more, plus agnostics, atheists, and some who just never had any religious exposure while they were growing up.

With few exceptions, what they *don't want* from you or me is unsolicited advice on how to behave in a Christian manner (however we might disguise it—morality, patriotism, restraint, etc).

Unbelievers don't desire that from us, hard as that may be for us to believe. That's not what they are seeking. Not only will they not solicit it, they will positively reject it when we try to offer it or force it upon them.

How to live a Christian lifestyle, how to be better conformed to the image of Christ, how to be sanctified: These are things that follow salvation. The very desire to be sanctified comes along with salvation. The presence of the Holy Spirit in us to effect our sanctification, with us and through us, is a gift at salvation: That's when sanctification truly begins.

What has often happened is that we Christians have trotted out the elements of sanctification and tried to give them to, or force them upon, unbelievers. *That is not what they need.*

Ultimately, God desires each human being to be conformed to the image of Christ. But what unbelievers need first is that *miracle*, that *extraordinary invasion* by the Creator into a corrupt and broken world—the sacrifice of Himself for all, with the free gift of forgiveness and eternal life. That is, they need *salvation.*

All that humans have to do is say yes. It is His power to forgive, and His right to forgive. The reason some were offended at Jesus when He forgave a crippled man was this: They believed that there were only two who could forgive a sin, the one who was sinned against, and God.[2]

Because Jesus had not been sinned against by the man He forgave, they read His forgiveness as an assertion of His divinity. To them it was blasphemy because they believed a mere man had made himself out to be God.

Scripture tells us *God is love*. It is an extraordinary gift of this love, beyond my comprehension, that the one who made me would Himself pay the price for my sin, to restore my relationship with God.

UNBELIEVERS

I want to tell you two stories about how Christians treat unbelievers—a "how not to" and a "how to."

HOW *NOT* TO TREAT UNBELIEVERS

We do a bad-enough job with fellow believers, but we are often worse with unbelievers, or with those we suspect might be. We often stink at sharing the Good News.

The Prostitute

I remember many years ago reading the story of a prostitute encountered by a street evangelist. I no longer recall who told the story, or all of the detail, but an overview of it here will serve to make the point:

One night while he was on the street, sharing the Gospel, person to person, an evangelist encountered a young woman who was a prostitute, working the street. He stopped and shared with her the extraordinary gift of God's forgiveness. No matter how great the sin was, God desired to forgive. She listened. She marveled at such love, and right there and right then gave her life to Christ.

She then asked, "Now what do I do with my life, how do I live? What's next?"

---

[2] See Matthew 9:1-8.

He said she needed to find a church and become a part of the family of God in that church. So she left the street, wandered through the neighborhood and found a church that was open where a worship service was underway. The folks inside were singing hymns of praise to God.

She came in the back of the church quietly, came up a couple of pews and moved over and stood there, wondering what would happen next. The congregation heard her come in and turned around. They saw what she was: a prostitute. They looked with extraordinary disdain and judgment, and turned back to the singing of their hymns.

The point is obvious, I know, but there is some further learning we can draw out of this story.

What are the errors made? Let's examine what happened here.

1. First and foremost, Jesus would not have treated her in this way.

2. The congregation condemned her. There is no polite way to put it: Their actions were ugly and profoundly *not* Christian. They may have had many justifications—"light does not consort with darkness; we've separated ourselves from all that is unholy; the evildoers will be left outside the Kingdom; we don't countenance such provocative dress in our sanctuary; we didn't know she had accepted Jesus; and she probably hadn't really or she would have looked more like us. She should have changed her style of dress before she came into our church."

3. Whether she had "accepted Jesus" and just not caught up with the local dress code, or if she was still lost in sin and stumbled into the church by accident, is irrelevant. Jesus did not require holiness *before* He ministered to people trapped in sin—in fact, the opposite is true. Romans 5:8b says that "while we were still sinners, Christ died for us." She should have been accepted and loved as she would have been by Jesus. She should have been treated with kindness and humility, not self-righteousness.

4. The street evangelist failed her as well. He got her to "accept Jesus," and then abandoned her with a few suggestions about finding a church. At a minimum he should have invited her to his own church, or connected her with women who would love and mentor her in her newfound faith, and help solve the problems that had led her to prostitution. Evangelism is far more than closing the sale. It's not *selling* at all. It is bringing others into the Kingdom, and then beginning an eternal relationship with them.

The truth is that as hard as we might think it is even to share the Gospel, that sharing is only one tiny part of living it out. People who do not yet know Jesus or the good news are not prospects we are hoping to turn into customers and then leave behind as we chase after new prospects. People who do not yet know the good news are beloved human beings whom Jesus was willing to die for. If they are that valuable to Him, we had better regard them as just that valuable—not as "wins" in some cosmic sales-contest. We are called to love them and *accompany them* into the Kingdom.

How to Treat Unbelievers

The Boy in Ratty Jeans

A more-hopeful story[3] comes out of a Baptist church. The congregation had largely come in and sat down and were getting ready for the service to start.

An unknown young man walked in from the back of the church—long hair, wearing ratty blue jeans with holes in them. As he reached each pew where there might be a little space, the people would crowd over so he wouldn't sit in their pew. So he just kept moving forward, looking for a spot. He got all the way up to the front pew, and there still wasn't anywhere to sit.

He'd been frozen out of every pew, so he plopped down on the floor, right in the front. Well, you can imagine the unhappiness of the folks in the pews to this tattered young man, who had not only disrupted their holy peace, but was now blocking part of the center aisle.

Then Deacon Brown came in. He was a tall, strong, determined and very well-dressed man. He strode forward to the front of the church, straight for the interloper. The people in the pews began rejoicing as he moved past, *Oh, good! Deacon Brown will take care of this troublemaker!*

Deacon Brown walked up to the young man, bent down and shook his hand, welcomed him, and plopped down on the floor next to him to wait, together, for the service to begin.

That's it! That's it! *That's* how we live with unbelievers.

We share God's love.

We don't share our religion. We don't compete with other religions. We share this extraordinary gift from God, that while we were yet sinners, God loved us. Jesus Christ died for us, so that the forgiveness of sin is free to us, though of great cost to the one who made us. This love, this sacrifice for us, this forgiveness, is available to anyone, anywhere on the planet right now! All you have to do is say *yes*.

That's the miracle of our faith in Jesus. The rest is detail.

How do we live with unbelievers? The same way we live with believers. *We love them as Christ loved us.*

BEING SANCTIFIED IS NOT FORCING CORRECT BEHAVIOR ON OTHERS

Believers should strive to be better conformed to the image of Christ, which is to be *sanctified*. Having such a goal and lifestyle is a good thing. But pushing it on an unbeliever in some vain hope that they'll thank you and begin acting like a believer is not only ineffective, but it drives people away. It is unholy.

---

[3] From the *50-Day Spiritual Adventure* series by Dr. David Mains. Used with permission.

Forcing new "correct" behavior is not *starting* with forgiveness, which is how any unbeliever should first learn about Jesus:

> Then one of the Pharisees asked Him to eat with him. And He went to the Pharisee's house, and sat down to eat. And behold, a woman in the city who was a sinner, when she knew that Jesus sat at the table in the Pharisee's house, brought an alabaster flask of fragrant oil, and stood at His feet behind Him weeping; and she began to wash His feet with her tears, and wiped them with the hair of her head; and she kissed His feet and anointed them with the fragrant oil.
>
> Now when the Pharisee who had invited Him saw this, he spoke to himself, saying, "This Man, if He were a prophet, would know who and what manner of woman this is who is touching Him, for she is a sinner."
>
> And Jesus answered and said to him, "Simon, I have something to say to you."
>
> So he said, "Teacher, say it."
>
> "There was a certain creditor who had two debtors. One owed five hundred denarii, and the other fifty. And when they had nothing with which to repay, he freely forgave them both. Tell Me, therefore, which of them will love him more?"
>
> Simon answered and said, "I suppose the one whom he forgave more."
>
> And He said to him, "You have rightly judged." Then He turned to the woman and said to Simon, "Do you see this woman? I entered your house; you gave Me no water for My feet, but she has washed My feet with her tears and wiped them with the hair of her head. You gave Me no kiss, but this woman has not ceased to kiss My feet since the time I came in. You did not anoint My head with oil, but this woman has anointed My feet with fragrant oil. Therefore I say to you, her sins, which are many, are forgiven, for she loved much. But to whom little is forgiven, the same loves little."
>
> Then He said to her, "Your sins are forgiven."
>
> And those who sat at the table with Him began to say to themselves, "Who is this who even forgives sins?"
>
> Then He said to the woman, "Your faith has saved you. Go in peace."[4]

It is easier to be self-righteous and condemning than it is to love people into the Kingdom. But the truth is, Jesus loved *us* into the Kingdom, and that is what He wants to do *through us* for those who don't yet know of God's love and forgiveness.

It may well be that in the life of someone who could become a Christian there are some things that should change. But let's be honest: There isn't one of us who doesn't have some things that should change.

So let's step into the other person's shoes for a moment. Which will you be able to hear? A condemning, scandalized and self-righteous voice that points out your failings, as the Pharisee did about the tax collector?[5] Or a sinner saved by grace, who knows he or she is saved by grace, who loves you—who takes action for your benefit and blessing—and who tells you that God loves you so much that He offers forgiveness without cost to those who ask?

---

[4] Luke 7:36-50, NKJV.
[5] Luke 18:10-11.

Will you listen to the one who shares the Good News, or the one with sarcasm toward those who don't believe just as he does? Will you trust one who loves you right where you are, or the one who stiffly reminds you of the local rules of conduct?

Once a truly loving relationship has been established, a believer might suggest to an unbeliever that there is something that needs to be faced, resisted or even renounced, for their soul's health. This loves people into the Kingdom, and then helps them grow in it, and it helps deepen their relationship with the Lord. But it begins with *love*, not condemnation; with *invitation*, not regulation. By this I do not mean disingenuous manipulation, but rather *caring* and *walking with* someone in their struggles, rather than simply telling them how wrong or bad they are and expecting them to self-correct. There are times when tough talk is necessary—tough love—but it is profoundly more effective when coming from a trusted friend, than from someone who just wants to let you know you are wrong.

I have seen people brought to tears by the forgiveness of God, who came to the altar in surrender, and who shared there the struggles that had brought them to the church and to the altar. Instead of being welcomed, they were told how terrible their sin was. The accuser had his theology straight but lacked love.

The point of the Gospel is forgiveness, not condemnation.

It is out of the soil of forgiveness that holiness grows, not out of the venom of condemnation. I have heard Christians denouncing both unbelievers and each other, sometimes by murmuring, sometimes face-to-face, using sarcasm and innuendo and clever shaming, to point up a real or perceived sin. What Paul calls, in Galatians 5:15, "biting and devouring one another."

We need to be vigilant, lest we be sucked in by this when it arises. We can speak *very plainly* with others, but only if we do so in love, and lovingly.

Jesus said people should know we are His followers because of the way we love each other. Paul said,

> I, therefore, the prisoner of the Lord, beseech you to walk worthy of the calling with which you were called, with all lowliness and gentleness, with longsuffering, bearing with one another in love, endeavoring to keep the unity of the Spirit in the bond of peace.[6]

The way we often fail with unbelievers—or not-yet-believers—is that we get the "grow in holiness" before the "God forgives." Worse, the "grow in holiness" isn't even really that. It is instead a religious spirit that demands certain behavior, or dress, or speech, to even allow someone to be among us, often long before anyone has even shared the good news with them.

And when someone *has* accepted Jesus as Savior, we often begin on *our* version of what it means to be sanctified, and *our* list of what that person should change, rather than the Holy Spirit's list, which probably will be quite different.

---

[6] Ephesians 4:1-3, NKJV.

This is not to suggest that there are no rules, that everything should be ignored, or that any conduct is acceptable because we all want to be *nice*. Rather, it is to say that even when facing serious concerns, we need to approach people the way Jesus did.

That's what He wants us to learn how to do, after all, in order to be His *disciples*. We learn—*by use and practice*—how to love God, love neighbors, love even enemies, and surely, to love into His Kingdom those who do not yet know Him.

How do we live with unbelievers? By loving them, loving them, loving them, and sharing the astonishing news that God extends His forgiveness to *all of us*, freely.

What we did not deserve and could not earn is given without cost. Jesus did so. Jesus said so.

Say so. This surely is loving those who do not yet believe.

8.
Prayer—Images and Icons

When I first came to Resurrection Anglican Church[1] to be interviewed for the position of Pastor, the search committee met with me down in the basement, and had set aside a certain amount of time for the interview. It didn't take as long as anticipated.

When we finished, the committee members looked at the clock and said, "Oh! We have a little extra time. Let's go upstairs and pray!"

I was amazed that the first thing they would do when they had extra time was go and *pray*. I don't know about you, but in my experience, that's a pretty odd thing in a church. Oh, we pray at formal times, and during meetings set aside for prayer, maybe even spontaneously if someone is in need, but simply to pray because we have a little extra time? *Very* unusual.

We do *other* things together when we have extra time: talk, eat, watch TV, read a book, take a walk.

But pray? Downright odd.

Yet the Apostle Paul exhorted us to "pray without ceasing,"[2] and Scripture is full of examples of prayer and the call to pray. I suspect we don't entirely *get* prayer. I think there are aspects of prayer, even fundamental ones, which we don't usually incorporate into our lives—and that there are also other words and actions that we confuse with prayer, or substitute for prayer. So let's take a serious look at prayer: what it is and isn't. It's a big topic and it is *really important*. It is a key part of the love relationship we have with God, of Life in Christ, of Covenant. It is central to how we are *intimate* with Him. It is our love language. We'll spend three chapters on it and still be just at the beginning.

Of all the subjects covered in theology, prayer is one of the most written about. If you go through Scripture and tally at all the verses devoted to prayer— its nature, character and purpose—it's nearly unending. There is so much in Scripture on prayer, and so much written about it in theology, one hardly knows where to start. But we'll try to tackle the most common issues.

---

[1] Called *Church of the Resurrection* prior to Easter, 2007.
[2] 1 Thessalonians 5:17.

Let me warn in advance that some of this may be off-putting. Parts of it may make you squirm or even get angry or worried – "Where is he *going* with this?" The reason is that I will attempt to unveil how the Church has prayed, across history and denominations, and some of this will be foreign, unfamiliar and perhaps even repugnant to you. My effort here is not to promote everything I describe or explain, but rather to give each of us an understanding of why other Christians pray in certain ways. It's likely that when *they* read here about how *you* pray, they will have similar reactions.

Though this is an imperfect analogy, it is similar to watching courting and marriage customs across cultures: what seems perfectly normal to us looks really odd and icky to people from vastly different cultures, and vice-versa. We may prefer our own, but that doesn't necessarily make the others wrong. On the other hand, there may well be things in the way *they* do courting and marriage that need to be seriously critiqued or corrected (I won't detail these here; you probably can guess at many of them). Equally, there may be common elements of the way *our* culture does courting and marriage that need to be seriously critiqued or corrected.

Just so with prayer.

So I want to take you on a journey through the ways Christians pray. This may seem a bit "granular" at this point, but we will return to a more comprehensive view at the end. Stick with me.

Some of what follows may well be unfamiliar or even seem wrong to you— and it *may* be wrong. But for now just travel with me as I explain how prayer is done, and why people do it the way they do, across Church traditions and history.

Note too, that we may have some ideas or prejudices about the way others pray which misunderstand (or caricature) *what* they do and *why* they do it; we'll try to uncover these and see things clearly.

At the least, this should be an interesting journey of discovery.

Here's a good place to start: Broadly speaking, Christians in the Roman Catholic and Eastern Orthodox traditions use "common prayer." That is, they pray liturgically and simultaneously. They recite prayers together aloud, that were written by someone else, often from a prayer book or worship booklet. To them this seems normal, communal, holy and God-honoring. Many such folks look at modern spontaneous Protestant prayer and feel that it is casual, lacks awe, and is out of order.

Many modern Protestants, on the other hand, look at this liturgical prayer and see it as stiff, impersonal, rote, disengaged and probably not honored by God: Mere ritual. To such Protestants, Jesus is "best friend and savior," the Father is "Abba," and the Holy Spirit is the power present to act and meet needs—why would they want to pray to such an intimate God with anything other than a spontaneous outpouring of their hearts?

I've described these differences a bit in the extreme, but I know you can see my point. We are raised up in, or adopt, a stream of Church tradition that we find familiar or fitting, and it tends to make us look askance (or dismissively) at other streams.

For the next three chapters don't approach this to discover who is right and who is wrong, but rather to grasp how each of many groups within the Church has learned (and loves) to pray. At the end of this journey we'll reflect on what we've learned and how to apply it in our own Life with Christ.

For now, let's explore, and ask some pointed questions, starting with:

CAN WE PRAY TO STATUES, OR THE VIRGIN MARY, OR TO THE SAINTS?

This is a good question, because it reveals many denominational, Protestant, Roman Catholic and Eastern Orthodox theological *distinctions* and *prejudices*. As I noted above, those of us who have been raised primarily in one tradition, and don't have experience in the others, often have really strong (and usually negative) opinions about how *other people* pray. This is true even "among friends" within the Protestant denominations, within the various historical streams in Eastern Orthodoxy, and among the various expressions of Roman Catholicism.

Let's take an example: Is it permissible for a Christian to pray to saints, or to the Virgin Mary, rather than directly to God?

For Roman Catholics and Eastern Orthodox Christians, the answer is a resounding "Yes!" They do this as a normal part of their Christian life. A very few modern Protestants do also, but most would consider it a kind of *idolatry*.

So let me unpack and explain it a bit. My goal—again—is not to promote or attack the practice, but to understand what it is really about. It may not be quite what we thought it was. There are two issues to the question above. To be blunt:

- Is it okay to pray to dead people, saints or otherwise?
- Is it okay to pray to (or at) statues or icons[3] of dead people?

We'll start with statues and icons, and return to "praying to dead people" in the next chapter.

STATUES AND ICONS

Christians have been arguing about statues and icons in the church since the early Church began. Those who are opposed to statues and icons are called *iconoclasts*. They usually base their objections on the Commandment that begins:

> You shall not make for yourself a carved image—any likeness of anything that is in heaven above, or that is in the earth beneath, or that is in the water under the earth; you shall not bow down to them nor serve them. For I, the LORD your God, am a jealous God...[4]

---

[3] An icon is a religious image, usually a saint, typically painted on a small wooden panel.
[4] Exodus 20:4-5a, NKJV.

A strict application of this would prohibit icons, statues, most stained glass, oil and watercolor paintings, pencil and crayon drawings, lawn statuary (now there's a thought!) and even photography of "anything that is in heaven above, or that is in the earth beneath, or that is in the water under the earth." That's a pretty comprehensive ban, and as a side note, one enforced by much of Islam worldwide.

A less-stringent reading would suggest that images are acceptable in and of themselves, but we must not "bow down to them nor serve them." This interpretation is the most common one across nearly all of Christianity today, although there have been periods and countries where the strict view was enforced, and ardent iconoclasts destroyed nearly all icons and statuary in churches. You can read that history on your own.

Note, however, that the most common Christian view today includes *both* those who *permit* and those who *oppose* statues and icons in their churches. How can this be?

While there are exceptions and nuances in this debate, the primary reason statues and icons are *opposed* is due to a misunderstanding of their purpose. This opposition is almost exclusively from modern Protestant Christians, who often assume (or were taught):

- People pray to the statue or icon
- People worship the statue or icon
- People worship the saint depicted by the statue or icon

These are all simply incorrect. In both the Roman Catholic and Eastern Orthodox churches, the *primary purpose of statues and icons*—in addition to the beauty they bring to a sanctuary—is to *remind* Christians of the lives of faithful followers of Jesus who lived before us, and to *encourage* today's Christians to be similarly *faithful*.

In earlier eras, when few people could read, statues and icons (and larger paintings and stained-glass windows) were the "books" of the day to tell the Gospel stories, and to recall the history of the Church in the lives of the saints. They are the Bible and Church history told through art, rather than in words.

Look at this 19th-century statue of St. Francis of Assisi:[5]

---

[5] La Verna, Tuscany, Italy: statue of saint Francis by Giovanni Collina Graziani (1820–1893). This statue is in the Chapel of the Stigmata inside La Verna sanctuary. Photo by Paolo Gaetano.

FIGURE: *ST FRANCIS* BY **GIOVANNI GRAZIANI (1820–1893)**

He wears a rustic garment. He is barefoot. The wounds in his side and hands are "stigmata," representative of Christ's wounds at the Crucifixion. Francis was said to have been given these miraculously during prayer, and the wound in his side often bled and stained his robe. The skull represents death, which all men must face, but from which Christ redeemed us. Other signs are present: the Bible, a rosary, a bird, a cross, a halo. Looking at the statue reminds us of his character, and perhaps even encourages us to be holy, and to simplify our own lives. That is the key to understanding the use of statues of saints in churches. The statue is a three-dimensional *teaching* and *encouragement* to holiness. *That is its primary purpose.*

But what about worship of the saint? Is that a part of the purpose of the statue?

Simply, no. Both Roman Catholic and Eastern Orthodox traditions encourage the *veneration* of the saints, but not their *worship*. This is a huge distinction. Worship is reserved for God alone. To *venerate* simply means to regard with profound respect. The veneration of the saints is encouraged because they are people whose lives can help us learn and grow in our own faith. They are good examples. To *venerate* means *to look to their example as an encouragement for how to live as a follower of Jesus.*

Are there Christians who actually worship saints, or attribute magical powers to statues in church? Yes. But this error is not what is *officially* or *normatively* taught or encouraged by the Church, and both Roman Catholic and Eastern Orthodox teaching would consider this error to indeed be error.

What about icons? What is their purpose? First, to tell a story or depict a saint, as with other forms of art, as above.

But icons have taken on another, special role in the prayer life of many Christians—said simply, they are a *point of focus*, a "window into heaven," to help the people who are praying to deepen their relationship with God and their comprehension of Scripture. The elements of the icon's image all serve to encourage this deepening.

Look at this icon of the *Trinity* by Andrei Rublev (1360–1430).[6]

---

[6] Rublev, Andrei. *Trinity*. n.d. Tempera. Tretyakov Gallery, Moscow.

FIGURE: TRINITY BY ANDREI RUBLEV

This may well be the most famous of all icons. In the original, the wings of the visitors and the chairs on which they sit are gold. Their garments are rich blue, green, red and gold. The chalice in between them is gold. The icon is based on the story in Genesis 18, where three men visit Abraham and Sarah, and predict the birth of Isaac. Read that story (actually, read all of Genesis 18-22!) and then look at this icon. *Really* look at the icon. You will discover all sorts of intentional features that are not obvious at first glance, and whose meanings may not be apparent, but that when you know the story, and some of the interpretation, makes this iconic representation of the story into a powerful image that can draw the mind and heart to meditate on the grace and majesty of God.

I'll give you one key: The table at which the three sit has an opening in front of it, and a channel on the ground below. This is a depiction of the altar in the Temple in Jerusalem where lambs were sacrificed—an altar created hundreds of years after the events of Genesis 18. Note the chalice, reminding us of what Jesus said about His blood at the Last Supper. The blood from the sacrifices in the Temple ran through a drain in the top of the altar, out the opening and into the channel, where it drained away. The opening and the channel of the altar, in the actual Temple, built by King Solomon around 1000 years before the birth of Christ, point to Bethlehem!

The whole purpose of an icon—or a statue, stained-glass window or painting—is to teach us, point us, lead us, to something else: *God.* Do people sometimes confuse the pointer with what it points toward? Of course. But destroying the pointers—icons, statues, etc—doesn't get us closer to God. This is why iconoclasm failed, and it is why destroying images—and, often, the people who prayed using them—produced self-righteous satisfaction for the iconoclasts, but little in the way of love, compassion, or a sense of the holy. Even if the original motivation of the iconoclasts was simply to clear away anything that looked like an idol (even if that idea was mistaken), the action taken was a tragedy, a telling example of people and their ways of worship being destroyed for the sake of a passionately held *concept.* Sadly, to the iconoclasts, their ideas mattered more than the people they attacked.

It is a caution that we should all keep close to our hearts, not just in relation to icons, but to any of the religious concepts we hold dear. In defending them, and in attacking those we disagree with, we destroy objects, concepts and even people. We need to remember that Jesus said "all the Law and the Prophets" depend upon, are subject to, the love of God and neighbor.[7] If we harm someone in defense of a religious concept, we have violated Jesus' clear commands, and missed something fundamental about the character of our God.

So let's ask Him to guide our hearts as we continue to study and understand the nature of prayer, and its expression in the Church.

---

[7] Matthew 22:37-40.

9.
Prayer—To Whom?

In this chapter we'll look at a host of additional prayer issues, beyond stained glass, paintings, statues and icons. These range from praying to dead people (saints and others), to praying directly to God, to confusion about the direction and object (the "to whom") of our prayers. Odds are, there are ways of praying that we *all* misunderstand and misjudge.

As we saw in the last chapter, there may be some people who go into church, see a statue of Mary and pray to it. But the Church has not taught this—not Orthodox, Roman Catholic or Protestant. Rather, the initial purpose of those statues in the church was to communicate things about God and the people of God to people who couldn't read. Even for those who *could* read, it was a 3-D or picture language, rather than a strictly abstract and notational one (which words are). It is why stained-glass windows, paintings, statues and icons were first created. Additionally, these pieces of art have also provided a point of focus for contemplation and prayer. *They were never intended to be the objects of prayer*, but rather a "reminder" for prayer. Have some people over the centuries *misunderstood* this and imagined a statue itself had power and understanding? Certainly.

But the occasional misunderstanding of purpose isn't a reason to destroy this art any more than the fact that people misunderstand Scripture is a reason to destroy Bibles. Some people misunderstand poetry, or neighbors, or jokes, but that's not a reason to destroy any of those either.

That seems pretty simple and straightforward, but it leads us to a related and deeper issue:

PRAYING TO DEAD PEOPLE

Is it okay to pray to dead people? That's a bit blunt, awkward and maybe even disturbing when asked that way, but it cuts to the core of the issue: Some Christians pray to saints, who are dead people. Other Christians, especially some Protestants, find such an idea incomprehensible, repugnant.

But those who don't have a tradition of praying to saints often don't really understand what those who *do* pray to saints are doing, or why. Actually, there are several reasons why people pray to saints. We need to comprehend carefully rather than condemn too quickly. Let's delay judgment until this can be parsed a bit.

"Saints" are usually Christians who have lived exemplary lives, often with special areas of ministry (poor, sick, lepers, etc.), and who have died (at least in terms of their earthly lives). After death, the Church has acknowledged the extraordinary nature of their Christian lives by designating them as saints (Scripture actually refers to all believers as "saints," but the term is also used more particularly to refer to those who were especially faithful Christians).

Over the centuries, many people in the Orthodox and Roman Catholic Churches have made a practice of praying to such saints. So this raises the obvious question—whether such prayer is done before the statue of a saint, or somewhere with no statues around at all: *Does God hear or respond to prayers said to saints?* Or do the saints respond? The answer isn't as simple as many Protestants used to think. Let's look at three different ways that praying to saints might be understood:

- Praying to Saints for Their Personal Assistance
- Praying to a Saint as an Intermediary to God
- Praying to Ask a Saint to Be an Intercessor

1. Praying to Saints for Their Personal Assistance

Some people believe each saint has specific areas of interest and power,[1] and can respond by acting on our behalf. Before we reject this outright, let's consider some of the testimony of Scripture that seems to *support* this concept.

Angels. Angels are not humans, nor are they humans who have died and been sent to earth by God on special missions (as the movies would have us believe). They are another order of creation altogether, and they carry out God's will, including communicating with people,[2] performing supernatural acts and fighting battles, both against other supernatural beings[3] and on behalf of humans.[4] What they demonstrate in this context is that *God often acts through intermediaries* who carry out His will. While we may think of God always being the One who acts—since He is omnipresent, omniscient and omnipotent—Scripture regularly shows His actions as *flowing through others*, who themselves have free will and choose to act as He has instructed, or not. Angels are a prime example of this.

Prophets, Disciples and Apostles. We see God using *people* in *this* way. Recall Moses and the plagues against the Egyptian Pharaoh,[5] Elijah calling down

---

[1] Examples include St. Luke for doctors, St. George for England, St. Olaf for Norway, Saint Maria Goretti for young women, St. Andrew for fisherman. There are dozens of saints so regarded.
[2] Judges 6.
[3] Daniel 10:13.
[4] Genesis 19.
[5] Exodus 7-11.

fire from heaven,[6] Paul healing a man crippled from birth[7] and Jesus sending out 70 disciples with the authority to heal,[8] or the Twelve to heal the sick, cleanse the lepers, raise the dead and cast out demons.[9]

Believers. That is, people we wouldn't normally think of as saints, but who are followers of Jesus, can and do act on God's behalf. There are many places in Scripture where power of God *flowing through people* is demonstrated, but probably one of the most obvious is in 1 Corinthians 12. Here it lists the gifts of the Spirit, the ways that God works through believers to both build up the Body of Christ (that is, the Church) and to reach out to the world. These gifts include supernatural wisdom and knowledge, prophecy, healing and miracles.[10] That is, supernatural things happen through people.

Animals and Things. God acts and touches people supernaturally even through animals, inanimate objects and, well, other weird stuff. A dove brought an olive branch to Noah to signify the end of the Flood,[11] a bush burned in front of Moses without being consumed and God's voice spoke out of it,[12] a pillar of fire and a cloud of smoke led the Israelites through the wilderness,[13] Balaam's donkey spoke,[14] and fingers appeared out of thin air and wrote on a wall.[15] Peter's shadow healed people,[16] as did pieces of cloth that Paul had touched.[17]

Over the centuries, these last two (Peter's shadow and Paul's cloths) have led to an enormous "industry" in the distribution of relics of saints, cloths that have been touched to such relics, plus water, salt, other objects that have been prayed over or blessed by priests or pastors, etc. Some consider this superstitious nonsense; others call it idolatry; still others see either a "placebo effect," a "focal point," or just harmless personal piety. Many others regard this as evidence of the manifold ways in which God shows mercy.

Certainly we can get caught up in "holy objects," and in hoping that they have supernatural power—to the point that we lose sight of the Gospel and the love of Christ, and behave not unlike a superstitious person who carries a rabbit's foot for "good luck." It seems irrational and uneducated. But against this dismissive analysis stands the inconvenient testimony of Scripture of the many and odd ways God acts supernaturally. I'm not suggesting anything be accepted, just a bit of caution in the attitude of our hearts.

---

[6] 1 Kings 18:38-39.
[7] Acts 14:8-10.
[8] Luke 10:1-20.
[9] Matthew 10:8.
[10] 1 Corinthians 12:7-11.
[11] Genesis 8:11.
[12] Exodus 3:1-21.
[13] Exodus 13:21-22.
[14] Numbers 22:28-30.
[15] Daniel 5:5.
[16] Acts 5:14-15.
[17] Acts 19:12.

Where we may see in others an unhealthy devotion to "holy" objects because it seems to supplant devotion to Jesus Himself, we are better led if we speak to them in love, with humility and kindness. God still acts as He chooses, often in ways that defy our personal piety and doctrinal certainties.

Discussing how God uses animals and things, while intriguing, is just a subset of the key concept we're discerning: God *often* uses others to carry out His will. It is well-established in Scripture, and actually very *characteristic* of how He acts.

We need to keep in mind our initial question: Does God act through people who are no longer living? *Can we pray to someone* (a saint, the Virgin Mary, even sweet Uncle Harry) *who has died?* But before we answer this, we need a *little more* preliminary study: we need to consider two additional key ways in which some Christians pray to saints. Whether it is *legitimate* to do so will wait until after we look at these.

2. Praying to a Saint as an Intermediary to God

This is a slightly different idea than praying to a saint for their assistance (believing they each have areas of special power). Here the idea is that a given saint will more or less be the conduit to God through which our prayers flow, and through which then flows the power of God back to us, to help us in our time of need. The saints are, in effect, agents or messengers of God, much like angels, and act to carry our needs to Him, and then act to carry out His will.

Mary is often seen as a special case of this (see also the next section), because she is the Mother of Jesus. The idea seems to be, that if I don't feel worthy to pray to Jesus myself, or I'm frightened, then I can go to Mary (she is a mother, after all!), tell her my fears and needs, and she'll talk to her son. Sort of like the miracle at Cana.[18] People pray to many different saints for similar reasons.

3. Praying to Ask a Saint to Be an Intercessor

This is probably the *least-known* concept for Western Protestants, and yet perhaps *the most common* understanding of the role of saints for believers in the Orthodox Church: The dead saints of the Church can *pray with* you or *pray for* you. They can *intercede*. Does this make any sense at all?

As a 21st-century Protestant, if I am sick, or out of work, or worried about something, I believe it is perfectly fine to turn to a friend and say, "Joe, would you pray for me? Would you intercede about something?"

Does anyone, Protestant, Orthodox or Roman Catholic, think this is wrong? No, we think it is perfectly legitimate. We *encourage* such prayerful intercession for each other!

Until very recently (right on *through* the Protestant Reformation that began in 1517), the common understanding of the Church was that when people died, they

---

[18] John 2:1-11.

stepped from this world into the next, and the distance they traveled was none at all. They 'stepped through a veil.' Though we couldn't see them, *they could see us*. They were as aware of our lives as any living person, standing right beside you, might be.

They were in heaven, with the Father, Son and Holy Spirit, but no one believed they became ignorant of us just because they had gone more closely into God's presence. Heaven was *close at hand*, as Jesus said. Those who had died knew well what was going on in our lives.

Therefore, if my sweet Uncle Harry had passed over, it would not occur to anyone that there was anything wrong in saying, "Harry, please pray for me," even though he was dead. He was just on the other side of the veil. He would be aware I'd asked him for his intercession, and would of course do it. That, broadly, was the understanding of the Church. It was okay to pray to dead people, saints or otherwise. There isn't much in the way of scriptural support for this idea (or against it), but that was a common view.

Over the last few centuries, many Western Protestant theologians have basically declared (an assertion with similarly scant testimony in Scripture) that when people die, one of two things happen:

(1) They go into "soul-rest" and are unaware of anything until the Second Coming, when they are called forth, or

(2) They step into heaven, but become aware of only what is in heaven, and all knowledge ends about what is currently happening on Earth.

In other words, those who have died are unaware of people who are still alive.

Both ideas—that the dead *are* aware of the living, or they *are not*—have been considered normative in Christian belief at some point in history, and *both* are normative in wide portions of the Church today.

Until recently, the Eastern Church and virtually the whole Western Church believed the dead knew of those who still lived, and cared about them. Thus it was considered completely legitimate to ask the dead to intercede for you—maybe even better than asking someone still alive, because the dead are in the presence of God! And the saints—well, if anything, they're a little closer to the throne and their prayers are heard more readily! I'm being a bit flippant here, but I want to make the point that much of the Church still today (worldwide), and nearly all of it in history, believed you could ask the dead to pray for you, and that the saints were especially worthy to be asked, and Mary, Mother of Jesus, was even more so.

This whole idea is very foreign to most Western Protestants, but to dismiss it either because it is unfamiliar, or to assume that it is heresy, idolatry or foolishness, is to ignore the normative practice and belief of the majority of the Church, both today and in history. If these practices are unfamiliar to you, I'm not asking you to start using them, or even to conclude that they are a good idea. Rather, I'm suggesting that understanding the *concepts* of those who practice these methods of prayer can give us insight into why they are so common throughout the world.

As a side note, we might also just observe how a *small shift* in a *religious concept*, i.e., the dead are aware of the living, or they are not (even where there is little Scripture to support one view over the other) can cause us to dismiss a huge part of the family of God and the way it prays.

Who's right? I don't know. But I don't believe God ignores the prayers of anyone's heart just because they ask circuitously rather than directly. Yet what about…

PRAYING DIRECTLY TO GOD HIMSELF

Well, then, do we *need* to go indirectly, through saints, or Mary, or sweet Uncle Harry? Or can we go *directly* to God Himself? We might think this is simple—we go to God, of course! Why not?!

Well, where is our holy fear? Most Jews today will not even say the name of God out loud, much less suggest just wandering into His presence for a chat. Are we wise to be so fearless?

Remember, Moses saw God face-to-face in some (apparently) limited way,[19] but in a later encounter he only saw God's back, because to see Him directly, in all His glory, would have killed him. God said so to him.[20] Uzzah died just by touching the Ark of the Covenant.[21] The high priest, going into the Holy of Holies once per year, would die in God's presence there if he had not first been purified. Yeow!

Maybe this indirect prayer, through the intercession of someone in heaven, isn't such a bad idea! At the very least, it is understandable.

But is it necessary to be indirect in our prayer to God? Here's what Scripture teaches about this:

> Under the old covenant, the priest stands before the altar day after day, offering sacrifices that can never take away sins. But our High Priest[22] offered himself to God as one sacrifice for sins, good for all time. Then he sat down at the place of highest honor at God's right hand. There he waits until his enemies are humbled as a footstool under his feet. For by that one offering he perfected forever all those whom he is making holy.
>
> And the Holy Spirit also testifies that this is so. First he says, "This is the new covenant I will make with my people on that day, says the Lord: I will put my laws in their hearts so they will understand them, and I will write them on their minds so they will obey them." Then he adds, "I will never again remember their sins and lawless deeds." Now when sins have been forgiven, there is no need to offer any more sacrifices.
>
> And so, dear brothers and sisters, we can boldly enter heaven's Most Holy Place because of the blood of Jesus. This is the new, life-giving way that Christ has opened up for us through the sacred curtain, by means of his death for us. And since we have a great High Priest who rules over God's people, *let us go right into the presence of God, with true hearts fully trusting him.* For our evil consciences have been sprinkled with Christ's blood to make us clean, and our bodies have been

---

[19] Exodus 33:11.
[20] Exodus 33:19.
[21] 2 Samuel 6:6.
[22] That is, Jesus.

washed with pure water. Without wavering, let us hold tightly to the hope we say we have, for God can be trusted to keep His promise.[23]

What Hebrews says here is that *each and every one of us*, because of Jesus' sacrifice of on the cross, has *permission* to go into the Holy of Holies—where previously only the great High Priest could go, and only after he had been purified. The curtain that divided the Holy of Holies from the common people has been split in half, and now *we* have the right to go into the Holy of Holies, *into to the very presence of God*. Jesus gave us direct access.

Now, I realize some folks feel they are really not good enough to talk to Jesus, so they talk to His mother. I understand that. "Mary, would you ask Jesus to heal my baby? I'd talk to Him myself, but I'm scared and I'm not worthy and I haven't been a good enough person, so Mary, would you please talk to Jesus for me?"

Similarly, we might seek out a saint known for healing, or for travel safety, or as an advocate or intercessor. I understand this motivation, and I honestly don't believe God dismisses prayers that come to Him in this way. Our fears or misunderstandings don't make God deaf to our prayers. Yet...

What Scripture tells us is that we don't have to be afraid of talking directly to the Father, directly to the Son, or directly to the Holy Spirit. *Jesus did that for us.* That was a gift He gave us by His sacrifice on the cross.

I think we ought to take gifts God gives us and not presume that we are unworthy. *He has made us worthy;* do we think He didn't do a sufficient job? He has declared us worthy; by His act we have become worthy. Therefore we have permission to go into the Holy of Holies without dying. *We should take the gift.*

Yet we should also regard *with love* those who yet believe that an indirect approach to God is necessary. He hears them too.

CONCLUSION—TO WHOM?

Asking a friend for intercession, or praying to saints, shouldn't be used as a replacement for talking to God directly yourself. The most important person who can pray for you is ... you![24] You can have every person on Earth praying for you, or for someone you care about, but if you're not doing any praying yourself, something's wrong. It's basically asking everyone else to go to bat for you but never bothering to join in.

Isn't this why we have prayer—because it's an opportunity to talk with our Creator? It's the means to build an intimate, two-way personal relationship.

Consider God's view—what would He rather have? You, coming personally to talk, or you, always "sending a messenger" in your place? The choice should be obvious!

Pray to God.

---

[23] Hebrews 10:10-23.

[24] Assuming you're not in a coma or otherwise simply incapable, of course.

10.
Prayer—Object, Posture, Purpose and More

In the last two chapters on prayer, we looked in part at the "to whom?" of prayer: Is it permissible for Christians to pray to statues, icons, Mary, various saints, or directly to God?

There still remain a few key issues of prayer to be considered, places where we easily get off track: object, advice, posture, preaching and content. We'll step through these in relatively quick order—not because they are unimportant, but because the issues can be exposed pretty quickly.

OBJECT

The "to whom" question actually wasn't fully addressed in the last chapter. The issue persists even if we have gotten beyond the issues of statues, saints and intercessors, and even if we are praying directly to God. We *still* get confused about the *object* of our prayer. Here's what I mean: To hear some of us pray, you might think it was necessary to insert "Lord," "Father," "Jesus" and "Holy Spirit" into each prayer to ensure *all* the members of the Godhead are addressed. Our prayers often sound like this:

> "Father, we thank You for our sister, Lord, who we bring before You, and we just ask You, Jesus, to heal her back pain, Lord, that she might be restored. And we pray, Holy Spirit, that You would comfort her and counsel her. Be her foundation, Lord Jesus, that her weakness would become strength. Thank You, Abba, Father, for loving her. In Jesus' name. Amen."

Is this prayer heard? Of course. But it is, in a sense, *overstuffed* with names for God, and even with instructions to each member of the Godhead based on our concepts of their differing roles. Perhaps this technique is intended to avoid directing the prayer to the wrong Person of the Trinity—or to ensure *all of them* hear it. Just to be safe, maybe our prayers should begin, "To Whom it may concern…"

I'm kidding, of course. Yet it would serve us well if we remembered this key doctrine of the Christian faith: We believe there is *one God in three Persons*, in mutual submission, mutually glorifying each other, in an eternal loving relationship. The key is: three Persons, but just *one God*.

So when we pray, it doesn't matter whether we pray to the Father, the Son or the Holy Spirit. *Each one* is sovereign God.

So to Whom do we pray? We pray to God. So pick one if you want—Father, Son or Holy Spirit. Or pick two, or even all three. Just don't try to squeeze in all three *for fear of getting it wrong.* You can't get it wrong. Your prayer will be heard!

ADVICE

Do we pray in order to give each other advice? You'd probably quickly answer "no." After all, when I pray, my prayer is with my Creator. It is communion and relationship with God.

In praying to God for you, I'm talking to God *about* you. I am not talking *to* you.

Or so I suppose. Yet we often use prayer as a guise for counseling or correcting one another. For example, Bob approaches me with a question about faith and giving, and so I suggest we go to the Lord about these concerns, and I pray:

"Father in heaven, please show Bob he must give his full tithe as a sign of his faith in You, knowing You will reward him."

That's not a prayer to God; that's me manipulating Bob by pretending I'm praying.

I can also wrongly give psychological advice when I'm "praying." Somebody says, "I'm really struggling with my husband. Would you please pray for me?"

We ought to pray willingly, of course. What we oughtn't do is counsel, for example:

"Lord, please teach Chris, as Your Word reveals in Ephesians 5, to submit to her husband, as a wife should, so it will go well with her."

Or alternatively:

"Lord, teach Chris to stand on her own two feet and resist the oppressive words and actions of her husband."

That's just not prayer. It's counseling *disguised* as prayer.

Are there times when good counsel is needed in addition to prayer? Certainly. But what often happens is the person praying becomes an instant psychologist, and offers advice instead of going to God with the need.

The free advice is masquerading as prayer, and is not prayer. *Avoid this.*

This tactic of disguising advice as prayer also happens on a large scale. Countless times I've been in a church where the pastor, *under the guise of prayer,* exhorts the congregation to do one thing or another.

It was a lecture to the church, but made to sound like a prayer to God. Often this is even done weekly: The pastor preaches, then prays the "pastoral prayer," which is just the sermon points repeated in the form of a prayer to God.

That's not prayer. Prayer is communication with God.

Prayer isn't some big bucket into which we dump all the advice we want to give so that it all sounds holy and submitted to God. When we go to God in prayer, let's actually pray *to Him*, not each other. Perhaps that sounds harsh, but in truth we have developed some odd practices which we call prayer, but are not.

POSTURE

Scripture records a variety of postures during prayer: standing, kneeling, sitting, prostrate, hands spread, beating the chest—and other instances where we have no idea at all what the posture was.

One posture *not* recorded in Scripture is *folded hands*, either hands pressed together or fingers interlaced.

That doesn't mean it didn't happen; it's just not recorded in Scripture.

It doesn't mean it's not legitimate; it's just not recorded in Scripture.

Theories abound about the origins of the folded-hands posture. Some evidence suggests that when the Crusades were underway to "retake" the Holy Land, the Jews there—who apparently also had the habit of folding their hands in prayer—were told by their rabbis they were to no longer pray that way, since it was how Christians prayed.

Some argue that the Jews had adopted this posture from the Christians, while others believe Jews had long used this form (as a paradigm dating back to Abraham's thigh[1]), but that they mostly stopped during the Crusades.

There are several other theories as well; we don't know which, if any, is true.

So, hands held together is traditional; it's just not recorded in Scripture. It's ironic that this has become the norm in so many churches, and that the scriptural forms are often shunned.

More commonly in Scripture, hands are lifted in what is often called the "Orans" position. *Orans* is Latin for "praying."

> Hear the voice of my supplications, when I cry to You, when I lift up my hands toward Your holy sanctuary.[2]
> I desire therefore that the men pray everywhere, lifting up holy hands, without wrath and doubting.[3]

---

[1] Genesis 24:2, 9.

[2] Psalm 28:2, NKJV.

[3] 1 Timothy 2:8, NKJV.

FIGURE: ORANS PRAYER POSITION: 3RD CENTURY – CATACOMB IN ROME

I find it an interesting insight into our cultural biases that this common form of prayer in Scripture is seen by many modern Christians as affected, or "Pentecostal," or unsophisticated and embarrassing to do. We are an odd bunch, aren't we?

Of course, the efficacy of our prayer doesn't depend on whether our hands are raised or folded, or whether we stand, sit or lie prostrate, face to the ground. Prayer is about the conversation of one's heart with the heart of God, and thus all of these postures are acceptable to God. But it's the posture of the *heart* that really matters.

But I'm not going to let us off quite that easily. Posture really does communicate a lot about *us*. We modern-day Christians are so stuck in our heads that we think anything we do with our bodies is somehow unsophisticated or anti-intellectual, and therefore many of us pray only in our heads, and only with words.

If I want to tell Jane I love her (either romantically or as a friend), one way is to say, "Jane, I wanted to let you know that I *really* love you."

Now those are sweet-enough words, but if I give Jane a warm hug, I don't have to say them. I *can* say them *also*, but the hug communicates my affection even without words. And *I experience my expression of love* to Jane *differently* if I only speak to her, or if I hug her. We need to be as aware of the *language of the body* as we are of the *words* that come out of our mouth.

The same is true with God. He doesn't *require* certain postures of us when we pray, but there are things about prayer and *posture* that are tied to the attitude of our heart and our approach to the throne of grace. Posture affects how *I experience* my relationship with Him, and that *matters*.

> When Solomon finished making these prayers and requests to the LORD, he stood up in front of the altar of the LORD, where he had been *kneeling* with his *hands raised* toward heaven.[4]

When I fold my hands and bow my head, in that posture is a sense of humility and submission. When I raise my hands there is a sense of surrender or thanksgiving. When I kneel, there is submission and honor. When I lie prostrate, there is awe and utter surrender in His presence. The posture itself can signify (and become integral to the experience of) the attitude of the heart toward the Creator. In a sense, posture is heart-talk, avoiding the word-generator of the brain that often interferes with or masks our deepest feelings.[5]

Posture communicates, and can be an integral part of, how we pray. We should neither be afraid of it, nor rob ourselves of the gift of *any* of its forms. We should also not be dismissive of others who pray differently than we do.

PURPOSE

We've looked at a number of ways we can go astray in prayer, and a few of the ways to pray. But *why* do we pray? What is the purpose? If God already knows everything that's going to happen anyway, why *bother* to pray?

I might want the future to happen *my way* and I might pray to ask God to *make it happen my way*, but if I figure that God already knows what's going to happen, what's the purpose of praying?

But assuming that "what will be, will be"—that the future is predetermined anyway and God knows it and wills it, and therefore I can't change it—is both unscientific[6] and unbiblical.[7]

There are several reasons we pray. The number-one purpose of prayer is to deepen our relationship, our communion with God. It is both to know Him more fully, and also to serve Him more willingly.

> Prayer puts us on the potter's wheel, reshaping us to be God's vessels. *As we beg that God's will be done on earth* as it is in heaven, *we present ourselves to God to do it.*[8]

---

[4] 1 Kings 8:54.

[5] More on this topic when we look at praying in tongues.

[6] I won't argue this here, but see Heisenberg's Uncertainty Principle, Gödel's Incompleteness Theorem, and Quantum Theory in physics. Some of this is covered in Chapters 11 and 16.

[7] As one of many examples in Scripture, see Numbers 14:17-23, where Moses argues with God and gets Him to change His mind. See my doctoral work on *Healing Prayer*, Chapter 2, for an extended discussion. On GeorgeKoch.com/Writings.

[8] Sider, Ronald, et al. *Churches That Make a Difference*. Grand Rapids: Baker Books, 2002. p. 142.

That is, when we say, "God, Your will be done on Earth," we're not saying, "I'll just sit here and wait until You're finished." No, it means, "I'm a willing participant. Shape me as You need to, use me as You need to, that Your will might be done on Earth."

We are also *commanded* to pray. Jesus very clearly says to pray for our enemies. He didn't say, "If you don't have anything better to do..." He *commanded* us to pray for our enemies. This kind of prayer is very hard. For one thing, "enemies" doesn't just refer to people with guns who might rob us on the street, or to enemy combatants, or to countries or organizations that aim to hurt or destroy us. It includes these, of course. But in some ways they are a bit abstracted from us, and thus easier to pray for at a distance.

But enemies include those people who just get under your skin—sisters and brothers and neighbors and people in church. When I find myself irritated with somebody else, that person has become my enemy. My first human reaction is to say something sarcastic, belittling or complaining, but that's not what Jesus tells me to do. He says to *pray* for that person. We're *commanded* to do that. It is *hard* to do, but *it is what He commanded.*

Another purpose of prayer is to express our needs, whether for guidance, healing, hope, comfort, counsel, courage or even perseverance. We should tell God plainly what we need. He will hear.

So as to purpose, I've mentioned here only a very few. Scripture is replete with purposes for prayer—prayer for enemies, prayer for nonbelievers, prayer for a favorable old age, prayer for children. It goes on and on and on and on. In the end, in each case, the purpose of prayer is conversation and communion with God. Talk with and abide in Him—and He will live in and through us.

CONTENT

"If man is man, and God is God, to live without prayer is not merely an awful thing: It is an infinitely foolish thing."[9]

Amen to that. But what about the content of our prayer? What's in it when we pray? It's one thing to observe, rightly, how foolish we are to not pray, but if we do pray, what is in our prayer? Is it just petition, a list of our needs? Or are there other elements to prayer that also have a place?

Certainly there are some things that should (or shouldn't) be in our prayer, but here I suggest four key parts: *praise, confession, petition* and *listening.* They don't have to be in that order, and all of them needn't be present in every prayer, but each of these parts is foundational to a fully developed prayer life.

Praise. The first part of prayer ought to be praise and thanksgiving. It should be about submission to a gracious God, and about thanksgiving—for other believers, for what Jesus has done for us on the cross, for God's goodness in

---

[9] Phillips Brooks (1835–1893), American clergyman and author.

creating the world we occupy, and more. It should be praise for the wonder of being alive, for the wonder of salvation, for the wonder of the Gospel and being able to share it, for the freedom to worship.

Even when we are in great need, prayer is best entered with a thankful heart. Somehow it sets the relationship on its proper footing between us and the One who gives to us.

Confession. Numerous Scripture passages say God doesn't respond to us when we are not right with Him. It's not that He's so easily offended that if we've done wrong, He's not going to listen. *He always hears.* Rather, *we* have clogged the lines of communication when our lives aren't right. We can unclog the lines by confessing. Confession is simply saying, "Lord, I've messed up again, and I'm sorry again." God's response is *immediate*: "You are forgiven. Clogs are cleared Let's talk." So *confession* is a key part of prayer.

Petition. This is where we bring our heart to God in petition, or intercession. It is really a cry of the heart for favor, for the Holy Spirit. Petition is coming to God and saying, "I'm in need." Or it's bringing before Him a person I love—or a person I hate, for that matter—and asking for blessing, or healing, or conviction or presence. It is asking for grace.

Listening. Do you recall Scripture's criticisms of false gods? Just how does Scripture portray idols? Here's how: They can't hear, they're made of wood or stone, they're powerless, they're fashioned by the hands of men, and they are *speechless.*[10]

That's the criticism in Scripture of false gods: They are speechless. What's the obvious implication? God is *not* speechless! God speaks! God *speaks* and we are to *listen*!

Here are a few examples of God speaking *through people*, and directly *to people*. There are many such examples throughout Scripture:

> You know that when you were still pagans, you were led astray and swept along in worshiping *speechless* idols. So I want you to know that no one *speaking by the Spirit of God* will curse Jesus, and no one can *say Jesus is Lord, except by the Holy Spirit.*[11]

> And finding disciples, we stayed there seven days. They *told Paul through the Spirit* not to go up to Jerusalem.[12]

> "Now it happened, when I returned to Jerusalem and was praying in the temple, that I was in a trance and saw Him *saying to me*, 'Make haste and get out of Jerusalem quickly, for they will not receive your testimony concerning Me.' So I said, 'Lord, they know that in every synagogue I imprisoned and beat those who believe on You. And when the blood of Your martyr Stephen was shed, I also was standing by consenting to his death, and guarding the clothes of those who were

---

[10] See 1 Corinthians 12:1.
[11] 1 Corinthians 12:2-3.
[12] Acts 21:4, NKJV.

killing him.' *Then He said to me,* 'Depart, for I will send you far from here to the Gentiles.'"[13]

"Ask me and *I will tell you* remarkable secrets you do not know about things to come."[14]

We have *a God who speaks!* He speaks in a variety of ways. He does, sometimes, speak with words, and we should listen. But He also speaks with images, dreams, visions, convictions of the heart, signs, wonders, healings, leadings, even whispers—the "still small voice."[15]

He speaks and speaks and speaks. When He does, we must listen and also discern if we are hearing rightly—usually with the counsel of mature believers. But we must listen. We have a God who speaks to us.

Let me tell one small story, of one way He once spoke to me:

One night as I got into bed I felt something on my hand. I had been in some pretty wild places outdoors. I looked down at my hand and there was a tick, about to burrow into me.

I crushed it with my thumb and put it over on the dresser. I got up to check myself for any other ticks. As I stood up, I looked down at the dresser, and the tick was walking around, paying no attention to the fact I had just crushed it.

I took a water bottle with a cap, turned it upside down and smashed the tick ten or twelve times until he was a little mashed-up ball. I went in the bathroom for a more-thorough inspection.

I came back into the bedroom, and there was the tick, moving around again! I smashed him again until the guts were spattered all over. I wrapped him up in toilet paper and flushed him. If he's still swimming out there somewhere, at least he's nowhere near me.

Ticks are like sin. Sometimes when sin begins to get to us we are barely aware of it, might not even feel that little bit of motion, and then it buries itself in us. Isn't that the way it works? You don't even quite really feel it and then, like Lyme disease, it poisons you inside. Maybe even unto death.

Sin is like that. It sneaks in like ticks do, and then begins to do its work, even injecting poison that will inflame your joints and weaken your walk and sap your energy. You've been undone by what looked like a tiny little invasion.

Maybe it was just a tick and there was no message in it.

But as I prayed about that tick, God said, "Let me tell you about sin," and used the tick to reveal how sin sneaks into our lives and poisons us. This was God *speaking* to me, and I *listened.*

---

[13] Acts 22:17-21, NKJV.
[14] Jeremiah 33:3.
[15] 1 Kings 19:12b, NKJV.

Some Comments About "Speaking in Tongues"

It is unfortunate that "speaking in tongues" has long been the subject of debate and controversy, some of it very bitter, and I'm tempted to skip the topic because so many advocates and opponents feel so strongly about it. But the issue isn't going to go away, and shouldn't be left unaddressed.

Tongues was a normative part of the Christian experience in the early Church.[16] While some cautions were given as to when it was appropriate, Paul said he wished everyone spoke in tongues,[17] but even more that they spoke prophetically (see the previous section on *Listening* for a piece of what this means). Scripture doesn't indicate that tongues were reserved for the early Church, and the idea that they stopped toward the end of the first century is quite recent (late 1800s).

I *pray* in tongues and I have for decades. I experience it as *heart-talk*: the deepest groanings and highest hopes of my heart are expressed in a prayer language that is unedited and uncensored by the copy editor in my mind.

I do not believe that those who lack this experience lack evidence that they are saved (as some would assert), nor do I believe that those who do pray in tongues are superior, nor (oppositely) that they are irrational and unhinged. It is a gift testified to by Scripture, one of many that the Spirit bestows as He sees fit, and one that can be sought and received. But it is not a proof of superiority, legitimacy or lunacy.

Finally, the gift of tongues in Scripture actually refers to four or more distinct but related gifts. See the footnote below for a fuller treatment.[18]

The Gift of Prayer

The purpose of prayer is conversation and communion with God. Talk with and abide in Him—and He will live in and through us.

In prayer, we speak to God, and God hears and speaks to us.

God speaks in a million different ways, with Scripture, with words, with visions, with convictions, with hugs and hearts and care and love and healing. (And sometimes with ticks.) Directly and through others, with and without words, our God *speaks and speaks and speaks.*

So we should *listen and listen and listen!* Then our very lives become continuous prayer. As Paul calls to us across the centuries:

> Always be joyful. *Never stop praying.* Be thankful in all circumstances, for this is God's will for you who belong to Christ Jesus. Do not stifle the Holy Spirit. Do

---

[16] See Acts 19:1-6 and 1 Corinthians 14.

[17] The Greek can also be understood to mean that Paul delights that they do.

[18] For a thorough insight into this subject, two excellent books are *The Beauty of Spiritual Language* by Jack Hayford, and *Nine O'Clock in the Morning* by Dennis Bennett.

not scoff at prophecies, but test everything that is said. Hold on to what is good. Stay away from every kind of evil.[19]

What a gift!

---

[19] 1 Thessalonians 5:16-22. The Greek at the end is a bit more elegantly mirrored from a single root word: "Hold on to the good. Hold off the evil."

11.
Rule-Following and Transcendent Love

I talked to my friend Randy Fisk on the phone one Friday. We talked a little bit about what I was going to be preaching about on Sunday, and then at the end of that conversation he said, "Hey, are you okay?"

I said, "Well, actually, Randy, there is something I've been struggling with, and it has put me in a state of ennui.[1] I have been experiencing ennui for weeks now. That causes me to begin to reflect inwardly and ask what is going on in me that makes me feel that way. What is it I'm struggling with? I finally realized I am not writing, and I know one of the gifts God has given me is the ability to write and to write clearly and well and even successfully."

Some of you know I have had success as an author, but hadn't written much until this book other than Sunday-sermon preparation, pastoral letters and the occasional paragraph for the church newsletter. Even after I realized that the problem was that I wasn't writing, I still didn't have the will or discipline to begin.

Randy replied, "Well, a wise man once said to me, 'If you are going to be a writer, you are going to have to write every single day, whether you feel like it or not.'"

I'm the one who said that to Randy! He knew it, and it was to help him finish his first book, which he did. He was pushing my own advice right back at me!

I knew Randy was right, and I knew what I had to do, but there still wasn't the inner drive that comes when I'm really inspired to write. And a part of it came from a kind of personal deprecation: *Who am I to be the one to tell anybody anything? Everything that could be written about theology has been written. Everything that could be written about Christian living has been written. Everything that could be written about how to live life in this world has been written. Who am I?*

That little refrain had been running around in me, and it was one of the things that held me in stasis.

---

[1] I *like* that word. It's pronounced *"ahn-wee."* It isn't exactly depression. It's kind of not feeling that anything, or anything you do, matters; it's a sense of being stuck and the unhappiness that comes from it—ennui.

Then I came to the church for the weekly prayer service. I heard a wonderful teaching about prayer, listening to God and being obedient. As I sat there, the Lord said to me, "Get up, go home, and write." I took a deep breath, picked up my stuff and went straight home and began writing. I got up early the next morning and started writing again. You are reading what came from that: *What We Believe and Why*. This book.

It has been wonderful—because I have started to respond again to what God wants for me. The Lord also said something else really interesting when He said, "Get up, go home, and write." I began thinking, *Well, who am I to...* But He said, "You are who I made you to be. I gave you some unique gifts. I want you to exercise them. You are special. There is something special about the way I made you. There is something special about the way you see things and about the way you express things, and I want you to do that."

INVERTED PRIDE

In a sense, I was insulting God by claiming I was no different and therefore no more able in any way than anybody else ever was at any time. It was a kind of inverted pride and equally unhealthy. It was the same kind of sin as pride.

So, I obeyed and went home and wrote that night; and then at 4:30 the next morning I woke up and—I don't know why—walked out of the bedroom, to the front door and looked outside.

Remember how earlier, when I wrote about prayer, I said that God talks to us? And that one of Scripture's criticisms of false gods is that they are speechless?

God talks to us in a variety of ways. I think for some people, He actually uses human language words. He has done that occasionally in my life. Other times, He uses a variety of languages and signs to get through to us. That morning He used one of those other ways, which in a sense are broader and more profound than mere words.

It was pitch-black outside. A light from our front porch caught my eye. I looked down, and there was a lone firefly—not flying—on the porch. I couldn't even see the firefly, but I could see the light brighten and then dim again. Then it did something I have never seen a firefly do: It held its light on for a long time.

I watched in utter fascination, and I realized the Lord was saying something about me and about every single one of you and about the Church. He was saying that it doesn't matter how small the light is—the darkness is so great that even the tiniest light will be seen from a great distance. *Attend to the light.* It's not our charge to think about who we affect, how we affect them, how big we are, any of those kinds of things. Our first charge is to be *light* amidst darkness. Even if there are only 100, or 50, or even three of us—if we are attentive to the light of the Gospel, the light of Christ, the light given by God as a gift to shine through us, then it will be seen at great distances, because the darkness is so great.

OBEDIENCE

I want to begin looking at the next vital subject: *obedience*. There is something important about this in every one of our lives—and especially in response to a command such as, "Love your neighbor as yourself," or "love your enemies and pray for them," or "do not covet," or even the more personal, "Get up, go home, and write," and "attend to the light."

We will delve more deeply into what obedience is in the next two chapters. But in order to understand what true obedience to God is, we first have to understand what it *isn't*, and this *might not* be obvious:

Obedience to God is not found in mere conformity to religious rules, behaviors, rituals, practices or morality—either to please God or to control Him.

Our utter inability to control God may be self-evident (since He is God and not a vending machine or personal servant), but religious ritual, in many guises, is often used for exactly this purpose: *controlling God*. This is a "magical"[2] view of God where we imagine we control Him by our ritual actions. These range from dress codes to liturgy, from self-flagellation to abstinence. We think that if we say certain words, worship in a certain form, or even *behave* in a certain way, God will do our bidding. It sounds ridiculous and superstitious when put so bluntly, but it is what Christians often do.

Sometimes even non-ritualistic actions take on this same superstitious character: *I did a certain thing once before* (e.g., wore a certain cross), *and God blessed my day and I got a raise. So in the future, if I want a raise, or most anything else, I'll put on that same cross.* Because it is a cross and this is about God, I think it isn't "really" superstition. But it is no different than a rabbit's foot or good-luck charm.

There are many others. Some Roman Catholics believe burying a statue of St. Joseph upside down in the yard will help you sell your home. Protestants call this silly and superstitious—and then turn around and require all prayers end with the phrase "in Jesus' Name" or else God won't hear the prayer. Or they won't put a 13th floor in a building, or move to a home with an address of 666. Years ago I had a phone number where the exchange was 666, and I was stunned at how many people, Christian and otherwise, said I needed to get it changed immediately or bad things would happen to me. I didn't change it. Nothing bad happened. I wasn't surprised.

With a little reflection you can probably think of any number of similar superstitions that we all accept as matter-of-course in church and in Christian life. These are attempts to control God, or our environment, by magical thinking. They are not a part of the faith.

This addresses the error of trying to control God, but what about the other reason we often obey: *pleasing* God? Unfortunately, this is commonly the obverse of the same coin. We're not doing "ritual" or superstition, but we regulate our

---

[2] *Magical* meaning that we can control something by ritual, incantation, secret powers, spells, fetishes, potions, and so on. This is *not* a positive adjective as I use it here.

behavior and even our freedom in the hope that our actions will meet with divine approval and favor: "We will *please* him. And then He will like us."[3]

This kind of "pleasing God" has more in common with the behavior of an abused child, trying to curry parental favor and avoid injury, than it does with giving a gift for the sheer joy of giving pleasure to God or to another person. *Love* characterizes the latter; *fear*[4] characterizes the former. Anything given or done out of fear is an attempt to control or restrain.

The key reason for *true obedience* isn't to try to *control* God, but to *deepen our loving relationship with Him.* As we become more responsive to Him, more and more we move as He moves. As we move with Him, we know Him better and better. There are exceptions, but obedience to God is less like a soldier carrying out orders from on high, and more like a dance where He leads and we follow.[5]

FOLLOWING RULES

There are benefits to obeying rules. We live in society, and we follow more or less what is known as the "social contract." That is, we have rules of behavior that we enforce through law and peer pressure. It is a useful, if limited, approach to making life safe, meaningful and productive. But because we have individual autonomy, we make decisions on our own. Some will carefully follow the rules, others will readily violate the rules, and still others will "interpret" and use the rules to their own ends. Right? This is a pretty unexceptional observation.

In the secular culture, obedience to the rules is how we receive approval, and punishment is how we control those who will not willingly comply. We are approved based on the measure of our conformance to the rules.

This is equally true in Christian churches and in all religions. We do things a certain way because the leaders and tradition tell us to, and if we don't, we are politely ignored, marginalized, shunned, talked about, berated or put out. When we conform, we receive approval and acceptance; when we don't, it's disapproval and rejection. Countries, cities, tribes, social organizations, religions, cultures, gangs,

---

[3] For an extended treatment of this issue, see *TrueFaced* by Thrall, McNicol and Lynch. It is terrific.

[4] Proverbs 1:7 says, "Fear of the LORD is the foundation of true knowledge, but fools despise wisdom and discipline," but the word "fear" used here a is not the kind of fear experienced from an abusive parent, or from someone who points a gun at you. "Fear of the Lord" means reverent awe, realizing that we are in the presence of unimaginable power and grace.

[5] John 5:19-20, NKJV, "Then Jesus answered and said to them, 'Most assuredly, I say to you, the Son can do nothing of Himself, but *what He sees the Father do; for whatever He does, the Son also does in like manner.* For the Father loves the Son, and shows Him all things that He Himself does; and He will show Him greater works than these, that you may marvel.'"
John 12:26, NKJV, "If anyone serves Me, let him *follow* Me; and where I am, there My servant will be also. If anyone serves Me, him My Father will honor."
John 8:29-32, NKJV, "'And He who sent Me is *with Me.* The Father has not left Me alone, for I always do those things that please Him.' As He spoke these words, many believed in Him. Then Jesus said to those Jews who believed Him, 'If you abide in My word, you are My disciples indeed. And you shall know the truth, and the truth shall make you free.'"

families and institutions of all kinds use this to define who they are, and to enforce that definition on members. Again, this is a pretty unexceptional observation.

But what I'd like us to do is examine rules and the way we humans use them in light of the *biblical wisdom* on the subject of rules. Some of Scripture follows the approval/rejection model, but some of it is of *another order* altogether: transcendence.

Hang in here while we take what I think will prove an interesting journey through science fiction and mathematics, for a scriptural insight on this:

THE THREE LAWS OF ROBOTICS

I am fascinated by the fact that much of what science has learned and understood in recent centuries was long anticipated in Scripture.[6] I'm speaking of the thoughtful and careful efforts to understand how the universe works and our place in it as human beings. This has been the lifework of many bright and dedicated scientists and science authors—something commanded by God, by the way, in Genesis 1:26-29.[7]

So, let me illustrate: The 2004 movie *I, Robot* is based loosely on a collection of stories that Isaac Asimov, a science-fiction writer, wrote between 1940 and 1950. These stories incorporate what Asimov called the "Three Laws of Robotics." These are simple rules that are hardwired into the brains of all robots that serve human beings. Those three rules are:

1. A robot may not injure a human being or, through inaction, allow a human being to come to harm.
2. A robot must obey orders given to it by human beings, except where such orders would conflict with the First Law.
3. A robot must protect its own existence as long as such protection does not conflict with the First or Second Law.

Those are the "Three Laws of Robotics." I think they are quite clever, and generations of sci-fi writers and readers have dwelt on the logical rigor and completeness of these three laws.

---

[6] Let me make clear that I'm not referring to "Creation Science," which ranges from quite-competent critiques of scientific hubris and fanaticism to pretty-awful attempts to turn Genesis into Science 101.

[7] Genesis 1:26-29, NKJV, "Then God said, 'Let Us make man in Our image, according to Our likeness; let them have dominion over the fish of the sea, over the birds of the air, and over the cattle, over all the earth and over every creeping thing that creeps on the earth.' So God created man in His own image; in the image of God He created him; male and female He created them. Then God blessed them, and God said to them, 'Be fruitful and multiply; fill the earth and subdue it; have dominion over the fish of the sea, over the birds of the air, and over every living thing that moves on the earth.' And God said, 'See, I have given you every herb that yields seed which is on the face of all the earth, and every tree whose fruit yields seed; to you it shall be for food.'"

The words *fruitful, multiply, fill, subdue* and *dominion* do not intend an abusive dominance, but a mastery characterized by wisdom and insight, since the ones given this mastery were just made in the image of God.

In the movie *I, Robot*, a supercomputer recognizes how difficult it is for robots to obey the Laws because humans are so disobedient, so problematic, so autonomous. Humans make it impossible for robots to fulfill the Three Laws perfectly, so the supercomputer *reinterprets* the Laws to mean that the only ways humans can be kept from harm is by the robots *ruling them* instead of *serving them*. That is the premise of the film.

This is not a new idea. Countless public servants have become tyrants by this same logic. We could surely name many today all over the planet.

In essence, the attempt to make rules, no matter how simple or clearly stated, will fail in application.

If you're anything like me, when you first heard those three rules you thought, *Wow, this is logical and complete. What a good solution!* But in application, the rules fail. They are not sufficient. They are incomplete for the task.

Rules have utility within certain limitations *but cannot be applied mechanically to everything everywhere*. This is the reason Jesus criticizes the Sadducees and the Pharisees and the teachers of the Law. They thought by rigorous application of the rules, everything could be kept in good order, and these leaders were profoundly wrong.

For one thing, rules lack comprehension of present circumstances, and they lack heart, especially when they are applied without love. Jesus and all the New Testament authors understand this, and they work diligently to show us that truth. Rules aren't good for humans if applied without love.[8]

Even the judicial system understands this in a limited way. It expresses the importance of understanding not just the letter of the law but also the *spirit* of the law. That is, not just the literal meaning of the words, but the intent of those who wrote the law. Those people who we like least are those who insist on applying the letter of the law against us, without any care for the spirit of the law.

It is also the reason why "zero-tolerance" is unbiblical, and a fundamentally and horribly flawed notion of rule enforcement.

ARTIFICIAL INTELLIGENCE

Now we'll go from science fiction to current science research: I have followed the development of artificial intelligence, or AI, for decades. Some years ago, AI took a turn toward the development of "neural nets," meaning computers designed to emulate the human brain's ability to think, assess data, understand relationships, make choices, etc. What an idea: Use the model the Maker gave us if we want to make more intelligent machines!

---

[8] Here someone might speak up and say, "This is just that liberal situation-ethics. What the Bible teaches is true in all times and all places. You don't get to change it to just suit your personal wishes." This assertion is profoundly unbiblical and even anti-Jesus. HE was accused of disobeying the rules when He taught, again and again, that love is more important than rules—all the Law and the Prophets depend upon love of God and neighbor.

What this meant was that computers would be designed based on the way humans make decisions, rather than following simple built-in rules. That is, they are designed to learn to make new decisions for circumstances they haven't encountered before.

Asimov grasped the consequences of this decades before computer scientists began their work in AI or neural nets: If you want robots to be at all useful in our complex world, they have to be able to think for themselves to make decisions.

But the moment they can think for themselves and make choices, they have the option to disobey their creators.

Sound familiar to anybody?

In Genesis 2, Adam is given one rule for living in the Garden of Eden: Don't eat of the tree of knowledge of good and evil. One rule given, one rule violated.

After the Fall (the violation of the first rule), God gave additional rules to human beings. These rules were useful in the growing up of humans in helping us understand right from wrong, as parents or teachers do with children. These rules include the Ten Commandments, and another 603 rules throughout the Old Testament: a total of 613.

The Pharisees also followed what is called the "Oral Law," said to have also been given at Sinai by God along with the Ten Commandments, and intended to help them follow the 613 rules in all manner of circumstances, and with specific methods of application and interpretation,[9] all to deal with the problem of the creatures (us) disobeying the Creator. The oral law was their means to fit God's desires for us to the practical and varying circumstances of everyday life. In that sense, it was not a rigid and unreasonable application of rules, but a nuanced and careful effort to be wisely and humanely obedient.

Jesus deeply understood that there was much more to human life than rigidly trying to apply rules to govern behavior. This is a key to who Jesus is, and *who we are called to be* as His followers.

At the beginning of this section I expressed that I personally am fascinated with the fact that much of what has been discovered and understood by science in the last several centuries was long anticipated in Scripture.

The ready disobedience of the creatures (us) is one of those facts: We're like the robots that rebel, and then rationalize the necessity of their disobedience. How like *us*, and just as we are portrayed in Scripture written thousands of years ago!

It gets even more interesting. Just as computer science has begun to face some of these realities addressed long ago in Scriptures, mathematics has also understood the limits of rules. I alluded to this briefly in a footnote back in Chapter 10.

Mathematician Kurt Gödel in 1931 published a paper titled "*On Formally Undecidable Propositions.*" It demonstrates that in well-defined, logical systems, or in any clearly stated set of rules, there will be some decisions or propositions that are undecidable, and that to decide them one must go *outside* of the set of rules to a larger system or reality. Jesus anticipates this in His life and teachings.

---

[9] See *Talmud* in the Glossary Plus for more detail on this.

Listen first to what Paul says in describing the limits of the law, and the coming of Jesus:

> Well then, why was the law given? It was given to show people how guilty they are. But this system of law was to last only until the coming of the child [Jesus] to whom God's promise was made. ... If the law could have given us new life, we could have been made right with God by obeying it. But the Scriptures have declared that we are all prisoners of sin, so the only way to receive God's promise is to believe in Jesus Christ.[10]

That is, we must rely on a reality outside of, and greater than, the one in which we are living.

Again, while we exist within this set of moral, ethical and religious rules, we cannot act, decide or live in a purely loving way. The Law is insufficient.

Kurt Gödel realized in 1931 that no system of rules could answer every question it raised—some 1900 years after Paul talked about this and Jesus declared our freedom.

Nearly two thousand years later, mathematics catches up with Jesus Christ.

Paul, in explaining what Jesus teaches, is in effect saying that there must be the transcendent that comes from beyond the system and its rules—from the Kingdom of God. It is that transcendence by which Jesus brought freedom of action—freedom finally to fulfill the purpose for which we were made:

> Until faith in Christ was shown to us as the way of becoming right with God, we were guarded by the law. We were kept in protective custody, so to speak, until we could put our faith in the coming Savior. ... But now that faith in Christ has come, we no longer need the law as our guardian. So you are all children of God through faith in Jesus Christ.[11]

In other words, Jesus makes it clear that following the rules is insufficient, and He takes us outside of the rules by the invasion of the Kingdom of God into our physical kingdom. He takes us outside of the rules in order to know what is true and to help us to know how to decide what to do, that is, *how to love.*

> But when the Pharisees heard that he had silenced the Sadducees with his reply, they thought up a fresh question of their own to ask him. One of them, an expert in religious law, tried to trap him with this question: "Teacher, what is the most important commandment in the law of Moses?" Jesus replied, "You must *love* the Lord your God with *all your heart, all your soul, and all your mind.* This is the first and greatest commandment."[12]

---

[10] Galatians 3:19, 21b-22, NLT First Edition.
[11] Galatians 3:23, 25, NLT First Edition.
[12] Matthew 22:34-38, NLT First Edition.

Now that sounds like a rule, albeit a really important one. But in fact this command takes us *out* of the rules. It *transcends* them. It brings Heaven to Earth. It connects us to the Creator of the box in which we live. The rules that we had inside the box, inside the system, are insufficient, *incomplete*. Jesus says it, Scripture says it, Gödel the mathematician says it, and scientists and even artists realize it.[13]

Jesus in the First Commandment takes us outside of the box: *Love God.* Why? *Because God is not confined to the box.* God *made* the box.

Then the second is like unto it, and this is how the transcendent moves into the world we occupy: *Love your neighbor as yourself.*

The *transcendent love* of God pours through us into the world we occupy. Simple obedience to the rules—which by themselves cannot work—is insufficient to the task, even when they rest on moral and ethical behavior.

Moshe Chaim Luzzatto[14] reinforces the point this way: "Whoever sets God always before him and is exclusively concerned with doing God's pleasure and observing God's commandments will be called God's lover. *The love of God is*, therefore, not a separate commandment but *an underlying principle of all of God's commandments*"[15] (emphasis mine).

God's concern is always about love, always about loving relationships, always about building up and not harming. He seeks holiness from us, for He is holy. That holiness is His nature, and it requires love from us. His concern is not about the mere fulfillment of ritual obligations, or the following of law.

> So Christ has truly set us free. Now make sure that you stay free, and don't get tied up again in slavery to the law. ... For if you are trying to make yourselves right with God by keeping the law, you have been cut off from Christ! You have fallen away from God's grace. But we who live *by the Spirit*[16] eagerly wait to receive everything promised to us who are right with God through *faith.*[17] For when we place our faith in Christ Jesus it makes *no difference* to God whether we are circumcised or not circumcised [that is, whether we have followed the ritual rules]. What is important is faith *expressing itself in love.* You were getting along so well. Who has interfered with you to hold you back from following the truth? It certainly isn't God, for he is the one who *called you to freedom.*[18]

I don't know about you, but this is very scary to me. It is much easier for me to try to follow, apply and impose rules all the time. The rules were there for a reason.

---

[13]Again I would refer us to Heisenberg's Uncertainty Principle and Quantum Theory, and artist M.C. Escher, who showed how the rules of interpretation of drawing were insufficient to understand fully within the flat plane of the drawing. Also see the book *Flatland* by Edwin Abbot, which explains these concepts.

[14] Also known as Ramchal, 1707–1746. Italian rabbi.

[15] *Mitzvot*, p. 100.

[16] Again, from *outside* of our world, our system.

[17] *Faith*—of an entirely different order than rules.

[18] Galatians 5:1, 4-8, NLT First Edition

They helped us understand right from wrong. But the true *love* that allows us to live as God desires us to live requires *transcendence*. And it calls us to *freedom*.

That transcendence is given to us in the simple command, "Love God" and in the simple application, "Love your neighbor as yourself." When we do this we have fulfilled the law, we have transcended the law, and we have been set free by transcendent love.

Consider also how this makes sense of Jesus' teaching to Nicodemus back in the chapter on Salvation (Chapter 2), that we have to be *reborn* from above by water and the *Spirit*, and the promise that with our salvation, the *Holy Spirit* takes up residence *in us*. We become temples of God's presence. The transcendent—the God Who made the box—now lives in us.

CIRCLING BACK TO APPROVAL AND REJECTION

Earlier we looked at obedience and saw how we can use this in an attempt to control God. We do this as we follow rules, ritual, behavioral controls, or whatever, in order to curry favor or avoid punishment, to gain approval and avoid rejection.

Clearly by now we should see that this is not the same as loving God or our neighbors. Not only are loving God and neighbors *not* an attempt to control God, but their source is a transcendent one that is outside of the system (the kingdom of earth) in which we live. *Transcendent love is of another order altogether*, beyond even the most laudable of human moral and ethical systems. When we act within the system of rules set for us, we behave. We seek approval as we conform. Even if we agree with the morals and ethics of the system, even if we see the value in them in showing right and wrong (as the Law in Scripture is said to do), it is still approval we seek. And within these systems, approval is given when we conform. But...

Approval is a very weak surrogate for love,
and it is *love* we are created to seek.

Love is *transcendent*, it comes from the Source of our creation, and it approaches people and circumstances with a heavenly view, not just a worldly one. Where the Pharisee saw a prostitute, Jesus saw a woman needing the love of God; where those who would stone an adulteress saw the Law violated, Jesus gave freedom from condemnation. Where others saw a despised tax collector, or a Samaritan, or a blind man, or a demon-possessed man, or sick or dead, Jesus saw His *beloved* children, and *His love* brushed aside the judgments of men, *invaded* this kingdom of earth and its laws (including even the laws of time and space), and revealed the *transcendent love* of the Kingdom of God.

It is to this that we are called.

12.
Obedience and Love

God's concern is always about LOVE, always about loving relationship, always about building up and not harming. It is not about the mere fulfillment of obligations, of following religious rules, behaviors, rituals, practices or morality. In fact, these often are *substituted* for love, out of a desire to please or control God, to impose one's will on others, or because the challenge of love is too great. "Following the rules" replaces love. But true love *transcends* the rules and gives us freedom from them.

For many Christians, the thrust of the above paragraph is uncomfortable, perhaps even frightening. The claims do not fit our concept of Christian morality and behavior. Yet listen to Paul's words from Scripture:

> So Christ has really set us free. Now make sure that you stay free, and *don't get tied up again in slavery to the law.* Listen! I, Paul, tell you this: If you are counting on circumcision to make you right with God, then Christ cannot help you.
> I'll say it again. If you are trying to find favor with God by being circumcised, you must obey all of the regulations in the whole law of Moses. For *if you are trying to make yourselves right with God by keeping the law, you have been cut off from Christ!* You have fallen away from God's grace. But we who live by the Spirit eagerly wait to receive everything promised to us who are right with God through faith. For when we place our faith in Christ Jesus, *it makes no difference to God* whether we are circumcised or not circumcised.
> What is important is faith <u>expressing itself in love</u>.[1]

Circumcision was one of many ritual practices and traditions used to show that people were obedient to the Law. Paul uses it here to illustrate how we mistakenly try to make ourselves right with God by following the Law.

Yet *obedience to religious tradition*—whether the Law of Moses, or any other regulations a church has about worship, tradition or conformity to doctrine and belief—is something we hear taught in church, usually in ways that seem to contradict what Paul says. That is, we believe that doing things a certain way,

---

[1] Galatians 5:1-6, NLT First Edition.

perhaps even "in good order," is necessary to please God, to gain His approval, His response, even His love.

It's confusing, isn't it? So we need to spend some time trying to understand this more deeply.

I am not suggesting we simply toss out all the rules, and neither is Paul. Many of them serve us well as a community, help enforce boundaries and safety, and tell us what to reasonably expect and how to treat each other. These are helpful, even a blessing.

Our own church has rules about "appropriate touch," and these are a good example. These guidelines are available to everyone in our church. We publish them because ours is a "high-touch" church. People who have been here a while hug when they see each other in church or on the street; it's common for us. Yet there are ways that touch can be inappropriate, and can feel like a violation or a threat to safety. So we've set out some guidelines for appropriate touch—*not* because we believe they're necessary in order for God to approve of us, but rather because we care for God's people. We love them and want to treat them in a way that encourages a sense of safety, and this helps all of us to be open to the movement of God in our lives.

The problem Jesus, Paul and *many* of the writers of *both* the Old and New Testament address about rules, the Law and religious tradition is something different. It is about a basic *misapprehension* of the character and nature of God.

God does NOT tell us that if we do things in just a certain way, He will approve of us, and if we do other things—like pray, or cook, or weave, or baptize, or take Communion—in just a certain way, He will act as we want Him to. This is a false view of God and couldn't be less helpful.

Let's look at some examples of things we do when we misunderstand God, when we are "obedient" in an unhealthy or mistaken way.

MORE ON MAGICAL THINKING

In the last chapter, I talked about a "magical" view of God. Here I'll expand on it. It is a key understanding for us that will illuminate much of how we understand God and our faith, and I hope it will help us set aside some issues that have divided Christians for centuries.

Let's start with a legend from Greek mythology—Achilles the warrior. He died in battle when a poisoned arrow, shot by Paris and guided by Apollo, struck his heel, his only weak spot.

When he was born, his mother Thetis dipped him in the river Styx to try to make him immortal. But because she held him by his heel, the heel did not touch the water, and thus remained vulnerable. So when Paris' arrow hit his heel, he died. To this day, the term "Achilles' heel" denotes a fatal flaw or weakness.

This is an example of "magical thinking"—that the water of the Styx made immortal only those parts of the body that it actually touched.

Do we Christians do "magical thinking"? *Yes we do,* in a number of ways. One has to do with water: baptism. Generations of Roman Catholics and other

Christians believed that if a child died without being baptized, he or she did not go to heaven. Many still believe this today.

I can't imagine how many parents' hearts have been broken when a child died before the priest got there to perform baptism. Or for that matter, how many baptisms priests perform to this day, even after a child has died, because parents fear that if it's not done then that child will not go to heaven. If this is true, it doesn't say much about God's goodness. *But it isn't true.*

Protestants have magical thinking too. Personally, I believe full-immersion baptism is the most symbolic and meaningful of all methods of baptism, and was probably the most common in the early Church. Some Protestants argue that if you are not baptized by full immersion, you're not really baptized and therefore not really saved and not really a part of the Body of Christ. They refer to baptism by pouring or sprinkling water as "Satan's counterfeit."

Not to put too fine a point on it, but what constitutes "full immersion"? What if your heel doesn't get wet? Are you still saved? How about if 51% of your body gets wet? Is that enough? 33%? 95%?

Or more bluntly, is Jesus' sacrifice for me rendered impotent if my baptism is not done properly? Is His power great enough to save me if I am fully immersed, but insufficient if the water is only poured on me, or *if I am not baptized at all?*

The issue of getting baptism just right or losing salvation is an example of "magical thinking"—"if the ritual is wrong, the magic doesn't work." The flaw is that *Christians don't do magic, not ever.*

We have a sovereign God who is *present*, and who acts. When we pray, when we lay hands, when we bless, we are not managing spiritual *forces*. We are inviting God's presence. *He* acts, not *our "magic"* or ritual or method. God is present and He moves, touches and changes things, as *He wills*—not as *we* direct.

Here is another example.

I grew up in a church that completely rejected the idea that miracles still happened. It would never have occurred to us to lay hands on someone who was ill and ask God for their healing. This changed when, as an adult, I witnessed a profound physical healing following prayer. Later, as a pastor, I wanted our church to learn how to be open to this, and invite God's healing touch. We sought out others with more experience to teach us.

We went many places to be trained. We learned by standing next to, and praying with, people who had long experience in healing prayer. We were *discipled* by them. *We learned by use and practice.*

One time, we were in another church while some of their more experienced folks showed us how it was done. Most of what they did was biblical and straightforward, but there was one method they used that we copied, and later began to worry us. I suspect the technique was one of those things that arose spontaneously one time, and just got copied over and over. Many traditions begin that way, and then harden over time into inviolable requirements.

In prayer for someone who had been sexually abused by a relative, it became clear there were unholy ties to the victimizer—connections (emotional, mental, spiritual) that still bound the victim to the one who had harmed them. The person praying said something like this: "In the name of Jesus, I cut those ties." And they were miraculously *cut*, and the person experienced *immediate release and freedom!* Power of suggestion? Perhaps, but I don't believe so. I believe God sovereignly acted and cut those ties and gave freedom.

I have witnessed many such healings, and it is a great joy to see God move in this way.

But my concern is with what the prayer person said next: "And I seal the end of these cords with the blood of Jesus, so that they can never rejoin!"

This *sounds* good. I see the image. People who have been Christians for a long time often talk about things being "covered" by the blood of Jesus. These words may even have been appropriate the first time they were spontaneously prayed.

We found ourselves praying that same way after we got home.

I remember being present when the same kind of prayer took place, and when another victim with unholy ties to a victimizer was set free. The cord was cut![2] Again, the person we were praying for experienced immediate freedom and release.

The night went on, the person who had been healed left for home, and one of those who had prayed suddenly said, "Oh no! I forgot to seal the ends of the cords with the blood of Jesus. What if they rejoin?" In other words, what if the person gets reattached in an unholy way to the victimizer because *someone forgot a part of the prayer?*

I have to admit, this story probably sounds weird to most everybody, including me. But as odd as it is, I'm sharing it because there is an important error that was made: We had begun *magical thinking* about healing prayer. We had to do it *just right*, be obedient to the ritual form, or it wouldn't work or could go bad later. The cords could rejoin. That's magical thinking. This is *not* what Christians do in prayer.

Rather, we seek the presence of God and He acts.

It is not our management of spiritual forces that make any of this work, and it's not our proper use of ritual that makes anything work.

Remember, *Christians don't do magic.* We have a sovereign God who is present with us when we pray, and when we pray in His will, He acts in ways both simple and miraculous. Our prayers and prayer techniques are not ritual acts that have to be done just right—a false obedience—in order to be effective. In fact, much of the training we do now on prayer is about unlearning bad habits, and "getting out of the way."

MORE ON "IN JESUS' NAME"

In the previous chapter I mentioned in passing the Protestant superstition about saying the words "in Jesus' name" in order for prayers to be effective. Let's unpack this more thoroughly. Here's one place in Scripture from which this idea is deduced:

---

[2] In the New Testament, the word translated as "to forgive," in its Greek root, means to cut a cord, to "release" a legitimate claim that binds one person to another. There is a huge spiritual truth in this, but that's for another time.

The truth is, anyone who believes in me will do the same works I have done, and even greater works, because I am going to be with the Father. You can ask for anything in my name, and *I will do it*, because the work of the Son brings glory to the Father. Yes, ask anything in my name, and I will do it![3]

I often pray in a pattern that follows what is suggested here. At the end of a prayer I will say "in Jesus' name, amen." Many of us were taught that our prayer went unanswered unless it ended *with the words* "in Jesus' name." But that is *not* what it means to pray "in Jesus' name" any more than you can feed someone with the *word* "food."

If I say, "Here, take this food and feed your neighbor," it means you take food I've given to you and bring it to the neighbor and feed them. You don't go over there, without the food, and say the words, "George says take this food." Those aren't magic words, and they won't feed the neighbor.

When Jesus says, "Yes, ask anything *in my name*, and I will do it!" it means He has given us His *authority* to act, to bring healing, to give blessing. The words "in my name" in Scripture are a legal term equivalent to "power of attorney." It means I have the power to act on someone else's behalf, as if I were that person.

If you give me power of attorney, I can sign contracts that obligate you, I can expend your funds, I can make decisions for you, all with the same authority you have over your affairs. In doing so, I act *in your name*. That is precisely what the words mean when Jesus says "in my name."

We are not using some magical incantation by saying, "in Jesus' name." Rather, we are acting in the authority He has given us. That doesn't mean it's wrong to end a prayer that way, even as a reaffirmation of what we believe that He has given us, but we need to know that it isn't just the repetition of the right words that makes things happen, or makes prayers get heard.

MORE AND MORE MAGICAL THINKING

Louis Weil, the man who taught liturgics[4] when I was in seminary, told us a story about the church he attended as a child, a church that was what is often called "High Church," or "Anglo-Catholic." Though Anglican and Protestant, this form of worship looks a lot like a Roman Catholic service.

During Communion, when the priest is up at the altar, he holds his hands up in the "Orans" position[5] and reads aloud biblical prayers from an Altar Book.

In an Anglo-Catholic church, his hands usually stay up the whole time. But the pages in the book have to be turned. Often the priest does this himself, but in this church there were acolytes who turned the page.

The acolytes would kneel on either side of the altar with their hands folded in front of them as the priest read the service. When it got to the point where there

---

[3] John 14:12-14, NLT First Edition.
[4] Simply put, the teaching of the history of worship, its patterns and how to lead.
[5] We looked at this in Chapter 10.

was a page to be turned, one acolyte would rise up, step up to the table and turn the page so the priest could continue. Then he would go back, kneel where he was before and fold his hands again.

When Dr. Weil was growing up, the prayer book his church used was the 1928 edition of the Book of Common Prayer, and the Altar Book followed this. In 1979, the national Church issued a new prayer book, and along with it a new Altar Book to be used during the service, by the priest.

Dr. Weil visited the church of his youth, and as he sat in the pew, watching, sure enough, when the priest came up to the altar table, the acolytes were kneeling on either side of the altar, just as they had when he was young, but the new Altar Book was in place. It stayed open and the priest read from one page to the other *without the page having to be turned* where it used to be.

Nevertheless, when the service reached the exact point where the previous (1928) Altar Book would have required a page turn, the acolyte stood up, lightly *touched* the Altar Book and knelt back down again. The *form* had been preserved even though it was no longer needed!

Dr. Weil said he was so embarrassed, as a teacher of liturgy, that he wanted to crawl under the pew in front of him. Touching the book had no purpose, but it had *always been done that way* and the reason behind it was lost.

Another habit common in Anglican and other churches is to bow at the cross behind the altar table. We do this often in our church. At the end of the service I will usually come up, before I exit, and bow before the cross. I do that because in my heart I honor what that cross is about and what was done for me and for all of us on that cross. It is my body giving praise and thanks without words.

There are churches where this is the rule, the law: If you walk across the front of the sanctuary, past the altar, *you must bow to the cross every single time.* I'm not suggesting that bowing is wrong, but that we can turn something that is a sign of praise and thanksgiving into a regulation—and when we do that, it can be gutted of its meaning. More, it can become a distraction: We get so focused on "doing it right" that we lose our true sense of purpose, which is a deepening of our relationship with God.

I want to be clear here that in the way we worship—whether it includes page-turning by acolytes, or hands in the air, or a circle of neighbors simply holding hands each week and praying—there is nothing intrinsically wrong with many of those things. It's an order of worship, and when it happens consistently, it gives us stability. It's not a bad thing, and can be helpful.

What I want to caution all of us about is "magical thinking"—the idea that if we are stiffly obedient to rules and to ritual, this will gain us God's favor, that it will assure His love for us, and perhaps even ensure our salvation. Or, that when we fail to follow the same rules, He gets mad and withdraws. This is *not* what the Bible teaches. It's not what Jesus teaches, it's not what Paul teaches, and it is not God's message to us.

It is clear, then, that God's promise to give the whole earth to Abraham and his descendants was not based on obedience to God's law, but on the new *relationship with God* that comes by faith.[6]

The word "faith" here means literally *to trust*. The new relationship with God comes about not because we are obedient to the law and earn our way into His favor, but because we *trust* Him and His love for us.

And that's the point; that's what it's about. God is always about relationship; He is always about trust and love. When Jesus sums up the whole law and the prophets, He does it by saying,

> The first of all the commandments is: "Hear, O Israel, the LORD our God, the LORD is one. And you shall love the LORD your God with all your heart, with all your soul, with all your mind, and with all your strength." This is the first commandment. And the second, like it, is this: "You shall love your neighbor as yourself." There is no other commandment greater than these.[7]

God is always about acting in love.

The command to love is greater than any other law, rule, regulation, concept, doctrine, ritual, behavior, order, process, tradition, canon or guideline.

God does not trade our obedience for His help for our wishes. That is, we can't use "obedience" to manipulate God to do our will. This seems obvious when said plainly like this, but the hard truth is that we act, in countless different superstitious (but "holy"-looking) ways, as if our actions will allow us to control God.

That is not a godly obedience, but rather a false and self-centered one.

---

[6] Romans 4:13, NLT First Edition.
[7] Mark 12:29-31, NKJV.

13.
Covenant—Abraham

For a while we've been focusing on obedience—what it *isn't* and how we do it *wrong*. That is, those acts that have the appearance of godliness but lack the power of God. They demonstrate false piety[1] and stem from wrong motives. Whether in ritual or in daily behavior, it is when we do something hoping that we can manipulate God into giving us what we want. If it did, then we would control God, making us Lord and making Him our subject. That attempt is foolish and wrong. That is not obedience.

Now I want to look at what obedience *is*, and how we do it *right*, and that takes us to *covenant*.[2] Covenant is never about pretense nor perfection, but always about willingness. Simply put, covenant is the foundation, the "if and only if," the *essential* of life with God. You may have heard other declarations about what the foundation of life with God is: perhaps faith, or salvation, or holiness, or humility. Each of these is important, but *covenant* undergirds them all. Let's see why.

In the last two chapters, we came back again and again to the insistence by Jesus, by Paul and by other writers of Scripture—both Old and New Testament—that it is not God's intention that we live in fake holiness. Rather, Scripture repeatedly condemns it. In fact, Jesus says of it:

> Hypocrites! Well did Isaiah prophesy about you, saying: "These people draw near to Me with their mouth, and honor Me with their lips, but their heart is far from Me."[3]

Rather than encouraging "keeping up appearances," or obsequious religious displays, or false humility, God's concern is always about a willing, deepening,

---

[1] Piety is considered one of the seven gifts of the Holy Spirit. It is reverence, love and humility before God. False piety "looks like" true piety, but is typically displayed for praise, profit or control.

[2] For the sake of clarity, note that my use of the word covenant throughout this book is not related to "covenant theology," an entire doctrinal worldview on its own. Rather, my effort is to draw out what Scripture reveals about covenant and how it applies to our lives.

[3] Matthew 15:7-8, NKJV.

loving relationship, always about integrity, authenticity, and "making real" those whom He loves.

Thus, true obedience is not about mere fulfillment of ritual obligations, of following the rules to curry His favor. This extends from every one of the 613 *mitzvot*[4] of the Old Testament, all the way through Jesus' New Testament commands about loving God and each other—both of which are themselves commands from the Law in the Old Testament (Deuteronomy 6:5, Leviticus 19:18).

Further, Christians often exhibit a profound misunderstanding of God's Law in the Old Testament. This derives from a misinterpretation of some of Paul's insights about it, and from a shallow caricature of it, especially in dismissing Jews who follow the Law.

I won't unpack it all here, but suffice it to say that Jews do not attempt to follow the commandments of the Law to earn, curry, induce or coerce God's favor, but rather to live healthy and holy lives, in *thanksgiving* for the covenant favor God has *already* shown them. For Jews, following the Law is to remain yoked with God, to live out the marriage covenant with Him, to be His bride.

Jesus' critique of the Pharisees was aimed at those displaying self-righteousness and false piety. He confronted those who required others to behave in holy ways that they didn't behave themselves—He attacked not the holy ways, but the hypocrisy of requiring one thing and doing another.

If we Christians think we have a superior understanding of the Law—that we are now free of it and the Jews are still its slaves—we missed the point. The point that Jesus and Paul make about the Law and covenant is a *deepening* of the relationship between God and His people and *the extension of that covenant beyond the Jews.*

So take a deep breath.

We have the foundation to lay, and then we will spend time understanding God's gift of grace: covenant.

NEITHER A CONTRACT NOR A WILL

First, covenant is neither simply a contract, nor a "last will and testament." It is not an agreement enforced by law.

Though it involves promises and responsibilities, thinking of it just as a "contract" needlessly trivializes its extent and ignores the reality-altering fact that one of the parties to it is God Almighty.

So, discard the notion of contract or will, and we will look at how it is defined and unveiled in Scripture.

---

[4] *Mitzvot* (plural of *mitzvah*) are God's commandments for the Jewish people in the Old Testament, and include rules for diet, living, ethical conduct, worship and holiness. A *bar mitzvah*, literally "son of commandment" (for a boy), or a *bat mitzvah* (for a girl), is the coming-of-age when a child assumes adult responsibilities for fulfilling the *mitzvot*. This is a huge subject, which will not be tackled here. For a good introduction, see *Mitzvot: A Sourcebook for the 613 Commandments* by Ronald H. Isaacs (Northvale, NJ: Jason Aronson, Inc., 1996).

Second, there are several places in Scripture where covenant is declared and defined, but three key instances are:

- The covenant between God and Abraham.
- The Law: the covenant between God and Israel, beginning with Moses.
- The covenant Jesus declared.

The relation of these three, and their interplay, is the topic of Paul's writings, of Jesus' declarations, and of *the covenant that all of mankind is invited to partake in.* We will focus on this central topic in this chapter and the next two.

THE COVENANT BETWEEN GOD AND ABRAHAM

The first covenant to be established was with Abraham and his descendants, in Genesis 15 and 17. Paul refers to it in chapter three of his letter to the Galatians, although he cites only parts of it. Unfortunately, many subsequent Christian writers build theologies solely upon Paul's partial references, and miss a key element of God's covenant with Abraham—one that actually is continued in the Law of Moses and the teachings of Jesus:

> After these things the word of the LORD came to Abram in a vision, saying, "Do not be afraid, Abram. I am your *shield*, your *exceedingly great reward.*"[5]
> But Abram said, "Lord GOD, what will You give me, seeing I go childless, and the heir of my house is Eliezer of Damascus?" Then Abram said, "Look, You have given me no offspring; indeed one born in my house is my heir!"
> And behold, the word of the LORD came to him, saying, "This one shall not be your heir, but one who will come from your own body shall be your heir."
> Then He brought him outside and said, "Look now toward heaven, and count the stars if you are able to number them." And He said to him, "So shall your descendants be."
> And he believed in the LORD, and He accounted it to him for righteousness.[6]

God comes to Abram, reminds him that He is his protector and supply, and then *God initiates* a covenant with a promise to give Abram innumerable descendants, an *exceedingly great reward.* Abram believes (trusts) God when He makes the promise. This means simply that he has faith that what God promises, God can and will do. The text says God credited him for his belief as if it were righteousness.

This idea, that Abram's *trust* was credited to him as *righteousness*, is the source of much theology, study, debate and assertion. Paul focuses on it in Romans as a key to understanding the role of Jesus in the divine plan of salvation.

---

[5] Hebrew שכר, *sakar*, meaning payment (like wages), but hugely disproportionate to what might have been "deserved." Imagine working a minimum-wage job and being paid millions of dollars.
[6] Genesis 15:1-6, NKJV.

The central realization here is that Abram's response isn't belief, faith or trust *in a set of propositions*, or *doctrines*, or even in the Scriptures (there weren't any yet!), but in the reliability, the faithfulness, *of God.*

Abram believes God will do what God says He will do. It's really that basic.

But God credits it to Abram as *righteousness*? That seems like an odd equivalence. Why righteousness?

WHAT IS RIGHTEOUSNESS?

To understand this "odd equivalence," we first have to pause and ask, "What is righteousness?" In normal usage it means *following moral principals*. In Scripture it means *acting in harmony with God's will*. To trust God *is* to be and act in harmony with His will. Thus this equivalence is not an odd one, but a perfectly natural one.

If righteousness is simply a social, moral value, then trusting God is an odd thing to equate with it. But if righteousness is being in harmony with His will, then *to trust Him* is *righteousness.*

SACRIFICE AND DIVIDING

So, Abram trusts God can and will do what He promises, and God credits this to him as righteousness: Abram is in God's will, and God acknowledges it. So far so good. Then Genesis continues with this meaning-laden moment:

> Then He said to him, "I am the LORD, who brought you out of Ur of the Chaldeans, to give you this land to inherit it." And he said, "Lord GOD, how shall I know that I will inherit it?"
>
> So He said to him, "Bring Me a three-year-old heifer, a three-year-old female goat, a three-year-old ram, a turtledove, and a young pigeon." *Then he brought all these to Him and cut them in two, down the middle, and placed each piece opposite the other*; but he did not cut the birds in two. And when the vultures came down on the carcasses, Abram drove them away.[7]

This doesn't signify much to the modern mind, but this sacrifice and dividing was a symbol of agreement in ancient times, an agreement sealed by death and blood—a kind of profound witness (like a notary-public or granite monument), to affirm the seriousness of the covenant. The story continues with an intense encounter with God and a prophecy:

> "Now when the sun was going down, a deep sleep fell upon Abram; and behold, horror[8] and great darkness fell upon him. Then He said to Abram: "Know certainly that your descendants will be strangers in a land that is not theirs, and will

---

[7] Genesis 15:7-11, NKJV.

[8] The meaning in Hebrew is that it was terrifying, not evil.

serve them, and they will afflict them four hundred years. And also the nation whom they serve I will judge; afterward they shall come out with great possessions."[9]

This was a foretelling of Israel's captivity in Egypt, from which Moses would bring freedom and a *subsequent* and *additional* covenant—the Law. We will consider that covenant shortly, but there is still much of eternal importance to understand about this one.

God continues to open the future to Abram, and then shows His presence with fire:

> Now as for you, you shall go to your fathers in peace; you shall be buried at a good old age. But in the fourth generation they shall return here, for the iniquity of the Amorites is not yet complete."
>
> And it came to pass, when the sun went down and it was dark, that behold, *there appeared a smoking oven and a burning torch that passed between those pieces.*
>
> *On the same day the* LORD *made a covenant with Abram, saying: "To your descendants I have given this land*, from the river of Egypt to the great river, the River Euphrates—the Kenites, the Kenezzites, the Kadmonites, the Hittites, the Perizzites, the Rephaim, the Amorites, the Canaanites, the Girgashites, and the Jebusites."[10]

Here God completes the symbol of the covenant (the dividing of the slain animals) by passing His presence between them as a smoking oven and a burning torch, much as His presence in the smoke and fire that would later guide the Israelites in the wilderness, and God promises that Abram's descendants will one day occupy the land (after they leave captivity in Egypt, led by Moses).

Already the covenant with Abram is plainly set forth, its conditions made clear, its future assured, and its promises sealed by God's presence. Just in Genesis 15 alone, we have:

- *God initiates* a covenant with Abram
- *God promises* Abram innumerable descendants
- *Abram trusts* that God will do what He promises
- *God credits* Abram with righteousness for his trust

In addition:

- *God promises* Abram old age
- *God foretells* captivity followed by freedom
- *God promises* Abram land for his descendants
- *God seals the covenant* with cutting, blood and His fiery presence

---

[9] Genesis 15:12-14, NKJV.
[10] Genesis 15:15-21, NKJV.

As if this isn't enough, it gets even more intriguing. This covenant with Abram is repeated, reinforced, and more fully revealed just a few verses later, when he is very old and has still not had a child by his wife Sarai (even though God had promised him innumerable descendants, and Abram *believed* Him):

When Abram was ninety-nine years old, the LORD appeared to Abram and said to him, "I am Almighty God; walk before Me and be *blameless*.[11] And *I will make* My covenant between Me and you, and will multiply you exceedingly."

Then Abram fell on his face, and God talked with him, saying: "As for Me, behold, *My covenant is with you, and you shall be a father of many nations.*

"No longer shall your name be called Abram, but your name shall be Abraham; for I have made you a father of many nations. I will make you exceedingly fruitful; and I will make *nations* of you, and kings shall come from you.

"And *I will establish My covenant* between Me and you and your descendants after you in their generations, *for an everlasting covenant, to be God to you and your descendants after you.* Also I give to you and your descendants after you the land in which you are a stranger, all the land of Canaan, as an everlasting possession; and I will be their God.

And God said to Abraham: "As for you, you shall keep My covenant, you and your descendants after you throughout their generations.

"*This is My covenant* which *you* shall keep, between Me and you and your descendants after you: *Every male child among you shall be circumcised*; and you shall be circumcised in the flesh of your foreskins, and *it shall be a sign of the covenant* between Me and you."[12]

This passage is tightly packed with remarkable requirements and promises, all of which will be revealed and unfold in history—in Abram's life, in the rest of the Old Testament, and right on through the New Testament.

But look how it begins! Something *new* and deeply important: God tells Abram to "walk before me and be *blameless*."

Here God does *not* say, as He did in Genesis 15, "Trust and I will count it as righteousness." Here God says "walk blameless" and He will make an *everlasting covenant* to be God to Abram (renamed Abraham[13]) and all his descendants. He promises not just innumerable descendants, but *nations* of descendants.

The Hebrew for "walk blameless" actually translates closer to "before My face walk and *be* (or become) complete, flawless, whole-hearted." It is a *call to sanctification* in God's presence. It is similar to the righteousness of Genesis 15, which is to live in harmony with God's will, but here it calls for engagement, participation.

This "complete, flawless, whole-hearted" does not mean being frozen in some stiff legalistic stasis, rigidly controlled, never violating the law. Law isn't even

---

[11] Hebrew תמים—*tamiym*—which means complete, whole, wholesome, whole-hearted, innocent, having integrity, authentic, true, perfect, without blemish.

[12] Genesis 17:1-11, NKJV.

[13] *Abraham* means "father of many nations."

mentioned in any of this (it came much later under Moses). The sense is more like a perfect sunset, or a perfectly loving friend, or a profound integrity, authenticity, or *a quick suppleness of response to the leading of the Master*. The sense is the character of our intimate relationship to one that we love and care about, not the frightened response to one we fear will hurt us for the slightest infraction.[14]

So what Genesis 17 further shows us about the covenant with Abram (here renamed Abraham) is that Abraham is:

- to be complete, flawless, whole-hearted, authentic (because pretense hides flaws)
- in God's presence

This should ring a big bell! Remember the chapters on *salvation* and *sanctification*?

In salvation,

- we trust the faithfulness and promises of Jesus,
- His righteousness is counted as ours, and
- we enter an everlasting covenant.

And then in sanctification,

- we grow toward wholeness, authenticity and whole-hearted love…
- …by the presence of the Spirit of God with us.

The covenant pattern with Abraham is the *same* as God's covenant pattern with Christians: *God initiates the relationship* with *eternal* promises, we trust Him and enter the everlasting covenant *He establishes*, and He works with us to grow us up, to make us whole-hearted and complete.

I don't want to be cute or trivial, but an insightful and useful parallel is the attentiveness of a loyal dog. He doesn't really comprehend the nature of our human lives, our possessions or our family connections. He doesn't speak our language, though he learns some of the words we speak to him. But what he *does* do is watch our faces closely, and the most loyal, obedient, and desiring-to-please dogs strive to read our faces and respond to our needs. They spend the time and attention to us needed to learn to do this really well. That's the sense of being before God's face and becoming complete, flawless, whole-hearted. It is ready obedience and suppleness of response.

---

[14] Note: Solomon's "The fear of the Lord is the beginning of wisdom" (Proverbs 1:7) is about the awe we rightly feel when we realize God's holiness, otherness and infinite creative power. It isn't the kind of fear that comes from a mugger's gun or an abuser's wrath.

CIRCUMCISION

For many in the current age and culture, the last element of the covenant with Abraham seems strange and even primitive. God says the sign of covenant will be that Abraham and all his male descendants must be circumcised.

Interestingly, the Hebrew word for covenant, ברית, *berit*, also means "to cut."[15] The Jewish rite of circumcision is called *berit milah*, or *covenant* of circumcision (in the West this is often pronounced "bris"). Keep this in mind.

Now consider this:

> Christ redeemed us from the curse of the Law, having become a curse for us—for it is written, "CURSED IS EVERYONE WHO HANGS ON A TREE"—in order that in Christ Jesus *the blessing of Abraham* might come *to the Gentiles*, so that we would receive the promise of the Spirit *through faith.*[16]

Isn't it an odd collection of claims? Paul is writing to the Galatians, who are Gentiles. They are not a part of the house of Israel. They weren't a part of the promise made to the Israelites, to the Jews. Paul is saying that a promise was made to Abraham that his seed would spread beyond Israel to all the earth. It now has spread to the Gentiles. They are included as part of the promise made to Abraham.

Paul goes on:

> Brethren, I speak in terms of human relations: even though it is *only* a man's covenant, yet when it has been ratified, no one sets it aside or adds conditions to it. Now the promises were spoken to Abraham and to his seed. He does not say, "And to seeds," as *referring* to many, but *rather* to one, "And to your seed," that is, Christ.[17]

Here's the argument Paul is making: The promise given to Abraham—400 years before the law was given to Moses—was that Abraham would be blessed through his *seed*, singular, a single future descendant, and that is Christ.

The covenant made with Abraham pre-existed the Law. It came before the Law was ever established. Paul is saying, "That promise was never broken or replaced." That is, through Jesus Christ, who is the seed of Abraham, *the promise to Abraham is extended to everyone, not just the children of Israel.*

> What I am saying is this: the Law, which came four hundred and thirty years later, does not invalidate a covenant previously ratified by God, so as to nullify the promise. For if the inheritance is based on law, it is no longer based on a promise; but God has granted it to Abraham by means of a promise.[18]

---

[15] Hebrew readers: See the entry for ברית in Gesenius' Lexicon.

[16] Galatians 3:13-14, NASB, italics mine.

[17] Galatians 3:15-16, NASB, italics in original.

[18] Galatians 3:17-18, NASB.

In other words, when the Law was given to Moses, it did not *replace* the promise given to Abraham.

But then what was the purpose of the Law? Paul continues:

> Therefore the Law has become our tutor *to lead us* to Christ, so that we may be justified by faith.[19] But now that faith has come, we are no longer under a tutor. For you are all sons of God through faith in Christ Jesus.[20]

Paul is writing to Gentiles, not Jews, and showing them that *through trusting a descendant of Abraham*—his seed, Christ—they too are now a part of the covenant with God given to Abraham and his descendants.

They have been adopted into the family with full rights and responsibilities as sons.[21] Paul continues:

> There is neither Jew nor Greek, there is neither slave nor free man, there is neither male nor female; for you are all one in Christ Jesus. And if you belong to Christ, then you are Abraham's descendants, heirs according to promise.[22]

Paul sets aside any issues we might have about men and women. You're all one; there is neither male nor female.

"And if you belong to Christ"—here's where the argument draws to his point—"then you are Abraham's offspring, heirs according to promise."

There it is, the promise God made to Abraham was that the whole world would be blessed through his seed!

Paul says the seed of Abraham is Christ and all who trust in him inherit the promise made to Abraham, thus fulfilling it. *Extraordinary!*

We are not done, though; we are still setting foundation stones in place. There is still *a lot* left to understand about covenant and the Law and Christ.

Remember at the start of this chapter I said we'd look at:

- the covenant between God and Abraham,
- the Law: the covenant between God and Israel, beginning with Moses, and
- the covenant Jesus declared.

---

[19] As was Abram!

[20] Galatians 3:24-26, NASB, italics in original.

[21] The Greek in verse 24 uses the explicitly male term "sons" to emphasize that all who are thus adopted are inheritors—legal heirs—of the promise. In Paul's day generally only male descendants could be heirs. Paul reemphasizes this point again in Galatians 3:28. Gender has nothing to do with this inheritance. We are all sons of God, just as we are all the bride of Christ. I delight in the fact that I am part of the bride of Christ. It doesn't worry my masculinity at all.

[22] Galatians 3:28-29, NASB.

Believe it or not, we're still working on the first point! Here's what we have so far:

From Genesis 15:

- God promises to give Abram innumerable descendants.
- Abram believes God's promise, and his belief is counted as righteousness.
- God says Abram's descendants will multiply, go into captivity for 400 years, and then be freed with great possessions, and go to inhabit the land promised to them in this covenant.
- The promise is witnessed with the shedding of blood and with God's presence.

Then from Genesis 17:

- God tells Abram to walk before Him and be blameless (sanctification), renames him Abraham, expands on His promise of many descendants to mean nations (implying non-Israelites), says the covenant will be with him and his descendants, and will be everlasting.
- He promises to be God to Abraham and those descendants.
- He then tells Abraham that the part of the covenant Abraham must keep, as well as his descendants, is that every male child shall be circumcised. This circumcision will thereby also be the ongoing sign of the covenant.

Some 2000 years later, and long after Moses had led the Israelites out of Egypt (fulfilling that part of God's promise to Abraham):

- Paul writes to some Gentiles (that is, people who are not Jews and are not blood descendants of Abraham), and says that by trusting one of Abraham's descendants, Christ, they too become a part of the same covenant with Abraham—adopted into his family—including the promise of God everlastingly to be their God, and are therefore, "Abraham's descendants, heirs according to promise."[23]
- Paul does not make these Gentiles subject to the Law (which isn't mentioned in Abraham's covenant anyway), but refers to it as a "tutor" until faith came through Christ.[24]

We will return to this question of the role of the Law *deeply* in the next chapter.

---

[23] Galatians 3:29b.

[24] Interestingly, most rabbis would agree with Paul and James that Gentiles are not subject to the Law of Moses, but rather the "Noahide" laws from Genesis 2:16 and 9:4, predating even Abram.

14.
Covenant—The Law of Moses

This is an important chapter about an important subject: Law. Specifically, the Old Testament Law followed by religious Jews from the time of Moses right up to today.

But why should we care? Didn't Christ take us beyond the Law? Didn't Paul say it was just a "tutor" until Christ came? Isn't the Law something from "back then" to which Christians are no longer subject?

The Law of Moses is little-discussed in most churches, other than as a "historical" subject, or to show how and why Christians have left behind a key religious requirement of Judaism. It is also one of those "where angels fear to tread" topics for theologians. But like a fool, I will rush in. It is worth the risk.

Most Christian denominations and theologians have a specific and rigorous concept about the relative importance of the Law to Christians, and what effect the coming of Jesus Christ had on the Law and our relationship to it. Most would affirm that faith in Christ frees us from the Law, although just what that means and how it happens is the source of voluminous debate. There are also a few Christian groups that still follow the Law, including keeping kosher[1] and worshiping on the Jewish Sabbath.[2]

It is also true that most Christians, even if they have not really looked into this deeply, have the general impression that those who follow the Law, like the Pharisees, are attempting to make themselves righteous before God by their careful rule-following. We think this at least because Paul *seems* to say as much in his discourses about the Law and the Jews.

You may be surprised to learn that this isn't really the way Paul or religious Jews think about the Law. Thus, in order for Christians to understand the Law of

---

[1] Meaning "clean." See the Glossary Plus.
[2] Beginning Friday night at sundown and continuing until Saturday evening. See the Glossary Plus for more detail.

Moses, and the *covenant* between God and Israel embodied in that Law, we need to first "unlearn" our misconceptions about it. So a little bit of preface:

THE LAW

The source of the "Law" of the Jews, also called "The Law of Moses," is the *Pentateuch*, or the first five books of the Bible: Genesis, Exodus, Leviticus, Numbers and Deuteronomy. Jews call these books, collectively, the *Torah*. Torah is a Hebrew word meaning "teaching," "instruction" or "law." Jews believe this was given them at Mt. Sinai, and many (perhaps most) Jews today (and in Paul's day) believe Moses and they were simultaneously given an "Oral Law" at Sinai, as a guide to interpreting and applying the Law in the Torah to specific circumstances.

This Oral Law comes down to us today in what is called the *Talmud*,[3] a written compilation of the Oral Law itself, surrounded by extensive commentary by renowned rabbinic scholars over the course of many centuries. We'll return to this shortly.

The Torah is central to all Jewish worship, whether Orthodox, Conservative, Reform or Chassidic.[4] Jewish synagogues have a Torah scroll, which is kept in an *Ark*[5] at the back of the sanctuary. The scroll is removed and read with great reverence. Often the congregation touches or kisses it as the Torah is carried out.

Why does this matter? Because rather than as rigid rules imposed on an unwilling people, the Law (Torah) is seen by Jews as the profound and life-giving guidance of a wise, loving, jealous and all-powerful Father—for His children's well-being. This guidance is given not to juvenile recipients, but to adults who choose to live and work as God's partners in the healing of the world. His Torah, His instruction, is His gift to them in this partnership.

Consider these words from Psalm 119:

> Oh, how I love your law! I meditate on it all day long.
>
> Your commands make me wiser than my enemies, for they are *ever with me*. I have more insight than all my teachers, for I *meditate on your statutes*. I have more understanding than the elders, for I obey your *precepts*.
>
> I have kept my feet from every evil path so that I might obey your word. I have not departed from your laws, for you yourself have taught me.
>
> How sweet are your words to my taste, sweeter than honey to my mouth!
>
> I gain understanding from your precepts; therefore I hate every wrong path.
>
> Your word is a lamp to my feet and a light for my path.[6]

This psalm is the longest in the Bible, and it goes on and on with *praise* for the Law, not grudging acceptance or legalistic adherence (nor petulant rebellion). It proclaims that the Law is a blessing and a sure guide for those who obey it, and

---

[3] See the Glossary Plus for a fuller description.
[4] There are other Jewish denominations. These are the largest.
[5] Reminiscent of the Ark of the Covenant, which contained the tablets of the Ten Commandments.
[6] Psalm 119:97-105, NIV.

declares deep love for the Law and thanksgiving for the Lawgiver. God is seen as demonstrating His *grace* by *teaching His ways* to His children through the Law.

The psalmist says, "I have hidden your word in my heart, that I might not sin against you."[7] And, "I take joy in doing your will, my God, for your instructions are *written on my heart*."[8]

The author of Hebrews (in the New Testament) also echoes the psalmist when quoting Jeremiah from the Old Testament:

> For this is the covenant that I will make with the house of Israel after those days, says the LORD: I will put My laws *in their mind* and *write them on their hearts*; and I will be their God, and they shall be My people.[9]

The idea that Christians have a spiritually superior understanding of the Law, and that Jews follow it in attempting to prove themselves righteous, should be a bit suspect by now.

Even the author of Hebrews, who really makes the case about "freedom from the Law," quotes Jeremiah as evidence—that is, the author of Hebrews didn't *invent* his insights about the Law, but rather *restated* what was already present and understood in the "Old" Testament.

Paul's statements about the Law (as tutor) and about circumcision (against the "Judaizers" who insisted Gentiles had to be circumcised before they could become Christians) need to be understood not as rejection of the Law or its blessings, but rather as insights into ways it was misapplied by *some* other Jews of his time.

Rightly understood, the Law of Moses was given by God as a means to guide His people and help them live with each other, and grow into deeper and more intimate and life-giving relationship with Him.

Now, with this in mind, let's begin to look at the nature and content of the covenant between God and Israel, expressed in this *Law of Moses*.

Recall that *Genesis* contains the covenant with Abraham. We move forward to the covenant with Israel in the Law of Moses through these steps:

- Abraham and Sarah beget Isaac.
- Isaac and Rebekah beget Jacob.
- Jacob wrestles with God and is renamed Israel.
- Jacob (Israel) and Rachel beget Joseph.
- Joseph's half-brothers sell him into slavery in Egypt.
- Joseph rises to become ruler under the Pharaoh.
- Joseph's brothers, father and families move to Egypt.

---

[7] Psalm 119:11.
[8] Psalm 40:8.
[9] Hebrews 8:10, NKJV, quoting Jeremiah 31:33.

- They prosper and multiply.
- Later generations of Pharaohs forget Joseph and fear the growing population of Israelites, and so put them into slavery.
- 400 years pass in this process.
- Moses is born to an Israelite family but becomes an Egyptian prince by adoption.
- God calls Moses to lead the Israelites out of Egypt.
- Pharaoh refuses to let them go, and is beset by plagues.
- The Israelites place the blood of lambs on their doorframes, and the Spirit of God "passes over" them but takes the lives of the firstborn of the Egyptians.
- Pharaoh relents, briefly.
- Moses leads the Israelites out of Egypt through the Red Sea.
- *God makes a covenant with the Israelites, the Law of Moses*, the foundation of which is the Ten Commandments, plus many other instructions on how to live and worship. These are contained in *Exodus, Leviticus, Numbers* and *Deuteronomy*.[10]

All of the provisions of the Law are from these four books, though parts of it are anticipated in Genesis and unpacked by the Writings and Prophets (the biblical books of Joshua through Malachi)[11] and also in the Talmud.

Since this is the Law that Jesus, Paul and the author of Hebrews comment on, and that Christians often speak of disparagingly or in caricature, let's carefully consider its nature and key provisions. Rabbi Ronald Isaacs says this about it:

> Judaism has always been more a religion of action and deed than belief and creed. Learning was intended to lead to doing. To that end, Jewish conduct has been governed by a series of commandments, known in Hebrew as *mitzvot* (singular *mitzvah*). The scope of meaning of the word *mitzvah* is a wide one. It denotes commandment, law, obligation and deed, while connoting goodness, value, piety, and even holiness.[12]

James, brother of Jesus, says this very pointedly:

---

[10] *Deuteronomy* means "second law" and is basically a second statement of the Law first enumerated in Exodus, Leviticus and Numbers. In Hebrew this book is called *Devarim*, Hebrew for "words," from the opening sentence. The Jewish sages referred to it as *Mishneh Torah*, meaning "repetition of the Torah."

[11] The Christian "Old Testament" contains the same books as the Jewish Bible, but their sequence is different; also, some books are combined in the Jewish Bible, so that their count is 24, versus 39 in the Christian version.

[12] See Isaacs' *Mitzvot: A Sourcebook*, p. xi. I'm thankful to Isaacs for some of the background in the Jewish understanding of the Law, and also to Jewish rabbis, scholars and friends in the U.S. and Israel. I should note that I don't agree fully with Isaac's comment about creeds within Judaism (I believe they are found in Judaism also), but I won't deal with that now.

What good is it, my brothers and sisters, if someone claims to have faith but does not have works? Can this kind of faith save him?

If a brother or sister is poorly clothed and lacks daily food, and one of you says to them, "Go in peace, keep warm and eat well," but you do not give them what the body needs, what good is it?

So also faith, if it does not have works, is dead being by itself. But someone will say, "You have faith and I have works." Show me your faith without works and I will show you faith by my works.

You believe that God is one; well and good. Even the demons believe that—and tremble with fear. But would you like evidence, you empty fellow, that faith without works is useless? Was not Abraham our father justified by works when he offered Isaac his son on the altar? You see that his faith was working together with his works and his faith was perfected[13] by works. And the scripture was fulfilled that says, *"Now Abraham believed God and it was counted to him for righteousness,"* and *he was called God's friend.*[14]

You see that a person is justified by works and not by faith alone.

And similarly, was not Rahab the prostitute also justified by works when she welcomed the messengers and sent them out by another way? For just as the body without the spirit is dead, so also faith without works is dead.[15]

James is drilling home a key point about faith, works, covenant and relationship with God. Yet some Christians still insist that, since Abraham was justified by his faith, it is our faith in Jesus, alone, that makes us right with God and is therefore sufficient.

It's as if getting "saved" is enough, and sanctification (which includes "works") is an option. But if we believe this half-truth, we have missed this key purpose of the Law, which is the living out of faith in our daily *actions*. As James said above, "You see that his faith was working together with his works and his faith was perfected by works."

In Chapters 2 and 3, I argued that the elements of sanctification shouldn't be stuffed into the requirements of salvation (faith), and I maintain that still. But here is James' point: *Works* are *really important*; they complete what began with faith. They are the outworking, the product and process of our *sanctification*.

Faith is *birth*; works are the living out of a sanctified life *after* birth.

An odd notion has arisen time and again over the centuries, and recently here and there among modern Christians, that somehow the single key to being a Christian is *faith in Jesus*, that having this faith gets us saved, and then our calling is primarily to get others to believe this as well. Often the world and its needs are ignored, or fall far below the priority of leading others to faith.

Social action is often seen suspiciously as the province of the "liberals" and is somehow at odds with the "true gospel," which is wrongly believed to be almost entirely about faith in Jesus as Lord and Savior.

---

[13] That is, completed, made whole.
[14] See 2 Chronicles 20:7; Isaiah 41:8; 51:2.
[15] James 2:14-26.

Paul is sometimes used to defend this view, as against James, who is used to defend the "social gospel" view. Yet the testimony of all Scripture says that these two, faith and action, are inseparable. James says faith is *perfected* (the Greek word here means "completed, made whole") by works. This is profoundly the view of the Hebrew Scriptures (the "Old" Testament), as we will continue to discover.

The New and Old Testaments do not disagree on this point, nor on the purpose of the Law, nor on the requirement to do good works, nor do they disagree on the sequence of faith and works, salvation and sanctification. Only by yanking these out of context can we make the two Testaments seem at odds.

Let's expand on this by looking more deeply at the actual substance of the Law. Rather than assert that it is no longer necessary, let's consider what it actually says:

THE TEN COMMANDMENTS

There are 613 laws in the Torah, but ranking at the top are the Ten Commandments, written on tablets of stone when Moses went up on Mt. Sinai to meet God. Thirteen sentences in Hebrew make up the Ten Commandments. Various Jewish and Christian groups arrange these various ways to get the ten, and the commandments differ slightly in their versions in Exodus 20 and Deuteronomy 5. We won't go into why, how or who. We'll just look at content.

From Exodus 20 (in the most common delineation among Jewish sources):

- I am the LORD your God, who brought you out of the land of Egypt, out of the house of bondage.
- You shall have no other gods before Me. You shall not make for yourself a carved image—any likeness of anything that is in heaven above, or that is in the earth beneath, or that is in the water under the earth; you shall not bow down to them nor serve them. For I, the LORD your God, am a jealous God, visiting the iniquity of the fathers upon the children to the third and fourth generations of those who hate Me, but showing mercy to thousands, to those who love Me and keep My commandments.
- You shall not take the name of the LORD your God in vain, for the LORD will not hold him guiltless who takes His name in vain.
- Remember the Sabbath day, to keep it holy. Six days you shall labor and do all your work, but the seventh day is the Sabbath of the LORD your God. In it you shall do no work: you, nor your son, nor your daughter, nor your male servant, nor your female servant, nor your cattle, nor your stranger who is within your gates. For in six days the LORD made the heavens and the earth, the sea, and all that is in them, and rested the seventh day. Therefore the LORD blessed the Sabbath day and hallowed it.

- Honor your father and your mother, that your days may be long upon the land which the LORD your God is giving you.
- You shall not murder.
- You shall not commit adultery.
- You shall not steal.
- You shall not bear false witness against your neighbor.
- You shall not covet your neighbor's house; you shall not covet your neighbor's wife, nor his male servant, nor his female servant, nor his ox, nor his donkey, nor anything that is your neighbor's.[16]

First Commandment

Note that commandment number one isn't a commandment, but an assertion of authority and power, which is why those that follow it are *commandments* to be obeyed and acted upon, rather than *suggestions* to be entertained. Some sources, both Jewish and Christian, combine the second with the first into a single first commandment, which is then actually a commandment with a preface, but let's consider just the first commandment as enumerated above: "I am the LORD your God, who brought you out of the land of Egypt, out of the house of bondage."

Jews believe that this declaration implicitly requires every Jew to believe that God exists, and that this has practical consequences in how we conduct ourselves in everyday life, as well as in the world to come. Jews believe that lack of belief in the existence of God excludes a Jew from the world to come, and makes understanding and fulfilling the Law impossible.

Recall my comments in the last chapter about righteousness and the Lawgiver. If *righteousness* is what God declares it to be, rather than a creation of humans, then belief in the existence of God is a prerequisite to its understanding and fulfillment. It is defined by God, not by our ideas or agreements.

Because *God exists*, Jews are to respond to this reality by living with this belief all the time, every day, and must not say anything that could lead anyone to believe that God doesn't exist, or that other gods do exist (also reinforced by the Second Commandment).

Nachmanides[17] likened the commandments to the decrees of a king, who requires (and deserves) first his subjects' total faith and trust in his wisdom and power, and then gives them the laws they are to follow. His authority over all things gives them confidence to act as they are commanded, even when they may not fully understand the reasons for the statutes or their consequences. They may well *seek* to understand these things, but their willingness to obey is not based on their first being

---

[16] Exodus 20:2-17, NKJV.
[17] Rabbi Moshe ben Nachman, circa 1194–1270, born in Girona, Spain. Also known as Ramban. As should be obvious about any person I quote, referencing him doesn't mean I agree with everything he believed. But his insights here are valuable and normative.

persuaded of the rightness of the laws. The king who commanded is *trustworthy*, so they obey. Hence, when Moses reads the covenant scroll to the people:

> Then he took the Book of the Covenant and read it aloud to the people. Again they all responded, "We will do everything the LORD has commanded. We will obey."[18]

The Hebrew behind this verse is quite interesting. It actually says literally, "Yahweh we shall do and we shall listen." The Jewish tradition here is profound, and is the bell of faith still rung in synagogues today. The rabbis interpret this word sequence to mean, "God, we are willing to be obedient *even before* we hear what is required of us."

Ponder this. It is deeply *responsive* to God.

Nachmanides also noted that the Ten Commandments are addressed to individuals in the second-person singular—hence to each and every person, not to a generalized plural "you." They are thus incumbent on each and every one of us, personally and individually.

Ibn Ezra[19] points out the First Commandment doesn't have God describe Himself as the Creator of the universe, because no one was there to witness it other than God. Instead He describes Himself as "...your God, who brought you out of the land of Egypt, out of the house of bondage," because this was witnessed by generations (perhaps more than a million Jews who left Egypt in the Exodus), and thus shows that their LORD is a personal God (not a distant concept or force) who is with His people in their lives and times of need.

In other words, Moses didn't free the Israelites. Pharaoh didn't free them. They didn't free themselves. It didn't happen by chance. God was *there* and freed them. Just so, He is *here* and frees us when we call on Him.

In doing so, we are not agreeing to propositions, but are *living in God's presence*.

Second Commandment

God not only declares that *He is LORD and God*, He also makes it clear that *nothing else is*:

> You shall have no other gods before Me. You shall not make for yourself a carved image—any likeness of anything that is in heaven above, or that is in the earth beneath, or that is in the water under the earth; you shall not bow down to them nor serve them. For I, the LORD your God, am a jealous God, visiting the iniquity[20]

---

[18] Exodus 24:7.

[19] Rabbi Abraham ben Meïr ibn Ezra, circa 1089–1167. Also known as Abenezra. Spanish rabbi and brilliant expositor of Scripture.

[20] If you're interested, I've written about the actual meaning of "visiting the iniquity" separately—in Ch. 2 of my doctoral manuscript "Teaching Healing Prayer for the Victims of Sin." This is on my personal Web site, www.GeorgeKoch.com/Writings, and is being developed as a subsequent book titled *Heal!*

of the fathers upon the children to the third and fourth generations of those who hate Me, but showing mercy to thousands, to those who love Me and keep My commandments.

This second commandment is of enormous importance in understanding the centerpiece of both the Old and New Testament teachings, righteousness and Law. Fundamentally, it calls for our full attention and devotion to the one and only God, and explicitly tells us not to give honor or attention to anything else.

This is true in obvious ways—we shouldn't make "gods" out of wood or stone and worship them[21]—but it is also true in the wayward ways of our minds and hearts. We should not worship idols, nor should we worship God by participating in pagan rites, claiming they all point to the same God anyway. Doing so could confuse anyone watching, and could lead others to think other gods *do* exist. Rabbinic law was so strong on this point that bending down to pull a thorn from your foot was prohibited if you were near an idol, lest it look like you were bowing to or worshiping it.

Maimonides[22] makes the point that making an image of God (such as a statue) violates the doctrine that God is One and that God is all spirit—He has no physical body.

Perhaps one of the most interesting Jewish commentators on this topic is the Rebbe of Kotzk (also called the "Kotzker Rebbe"),[23] who says the prohibition against idolatry extends to making an idol out of the commandments—worshiping the map instead of using it for direction!

The purpose of the commandments is not just in the doing (i.e., actions—recall what *James* said), but in the attitude of the heart—the faith, devotion and spirit with which the commandment is fulfilled. Which, of course, sounds just like *Paul*.

The Talmud says the fulfillment of the Second Commandment is so foundational that it is the equivalent of fulfilling the whole Torah. (Jesus makes a similar kind of foundational statement when He says all the Law and the Prophets rest on two commands: to love God, and to love one's neighbor as oneself.) This form of expression ("all things depend on one thing") is an ancient way of highlighting something's importance—the typographical equivalent of **boldface** or yellow highlighting.[24]

Love God

Following the giving of the Ten Commandments, there is this exhortation:

Hear, O Israel: The LORD our God, the LORD is one! You shall love the LORD your God with all your heart, with all your soul, and with all your strength. And these words which I command you today shall be in your heart. You shall teach them diligently to your children, and shall talk of them when you sit in your house,

---

[21] See Isaiah 37:19.

[22] Rabbi Moses ben-Maimon, also known as Rambam (not Ramba*n*), great Torah scholar. Born in Spain in A.D. 1135 and died in Egypt in 1204.

[23] Rabbi Menachem Mendel Morgensztern, 1787–1859, Chassidic rabbi in Kotzk, Austria.

[24] As are ancient techniques of hyperbole and chiasmus. See the Glossary Plus for chiasmus.

when you walk by the way, when you lie down, and when you rise up. You shall bind them as a sign on your hand, and they shall be as frontlets between your eyes. You shall write them on the doorposts of your house and on your gates.[25]

The this passage is the first part of what in Judaism is called the *Shema* ("sheh-mah"), from the Hebrew imperative "Hear!" Jesus quotes the first two sentences of this and says it is the most important commandment.[26] Isaacs observes that "the love for God is one of the first instances in human history that such a commandment was demanded in any religion."[27] He makes three other key observations:

- "The best expression of love for God occurs when people conduct themselves in such a manner as to make God beloved by others."
- "Hosea, Jeremiah, and Isaiah saw God and the Israelites in a love relationship, where God metaphorically was portrayed as the groom and the people of Israel as God's bride."
- "Love of God ... can be done everywhere and anywhere, whenever the opportunity for performing commandments exists."[28]

Remember this quote from Chapter 11 from Ramchal,[29] which reinforces this point: "Whoever sets God always before him and is exclusively concerned with doing God's pleasure and observing God's commandments will be called God's lover. *The love of God is*, therefore, not a separate commandment but *an underlying principle of all of God's commandments*"[30] (emphasis mine).

Deuteronomy 10 concludes this way:

And now, Israel, what does the LORD your God require of you? He requires only that you fear the LORD your God, and live in a way that pleases him, and love him and serve him with all your heart and soul. And you must always obey the LORD's commands and decrees that I am giving you today for your own good.

Look, the highest heavens and the earth and everything in it all belong to the LORD your God. Yet the LORD chose your ancestors as the objects of his love. And he chose you, their descendants, above all other nations, as is evident today. Therefore, change your hearts and stop being stubborn.

For the LORD your God is the God of gods and Lord of lords. He is the great God, the mighty and awesome God, who shows no partiality and cannot be bribed. He ensures that orphans and widows receive justice. He shows love to the foreigners living among you and gives them food and clothing.

So you, too, must show love to foreigners, for you yourselves were once foreigners in the land of Egypt.

---

[25] Deuteronomy 6:4-9 and 11:13-21 and Numbers 15:37-41.

[26] Mark 12:29.

[27] *Mitzvot*, p. 98.

[28] Ibid.

[29] Moshe Chaim Luzzatto, 1707–1746. Italian rabbi.

[30] *Mitzvot*, p. 100.

You must fear the LORD your God and worship him and cling to him. Your oaths must be in his name alone.

He alone is your God, the only one who is worthy of your praise, the one who has done these mighty miracles that you have seen with your own eyes. When your ancestors went down into Egypt, there were only seventy of them. But now the LORD your God has made you as numerous as the stars in the sky![31]

These themes are the core of the covenant between God and Israel in the Law of Moses. Although there are numerous other commandments in this covenant—613 altogether—and some of them have to do with issues we might today consider minor, or non-rational (such as not mixing meat and milk), fundamentally they all center on God's love for His people, and their dedication to loving Him, and to acting in love *as He would.*

Do these sound familiar? They should, because they are taught by Jesus, Paul, John and all the authors of the "New" Testament. *They were not replaced or superseded by Jesus or the Church.* They were *repeated,* quoted from the Old Testament. Jesus said:

"Do not think that I came to destroy the Law or the Prophets. I did not come to destroy but to fulfill. For assuredly, I say to you, *till heaven and earth pass away,* one jot or one tittle[32] will by no means pass from the law till all is fulfilled.

"Whoever therefore breaks one of the least of these commandments, and teaches men so, shall be called least in the kingdom of heaven; but whoever does and teaches them, he shall be called great in the kingdom of heaven.

"For I say to you, that unless your righteousness exceeds the righteousness of the scribes and Pharisees, you will by no means enter the kingdom of heaven."[33]

The Law Jesus refers to is the Covenant between God and Israel, the Law of Moses. Israel declared its willingness to abide by this Covenant in the words I quoted just previously: "Yahweh we shall do and we shall listen." But look also at the sentences that surround this declaration:

Then he sent some of the young Israelite men to present burnt offerings and to sacrifice bulls as peace offerings to the LORD. Moses drained half the blood from these animals into basins. The other half he splattered against the altar.

Then he took the Book of the Covenant and read it aloud to the people. Again they all responded, "We will do everything the LORD has commanded. We will obey."

Then Moses took the blood from the basins and splattered it over the people, declaring, "Look, this blood confirms the covenant the LORD has made with you in giving you these instructions."[34]

---

[31] Deuteronomy 10:12-22.

[32] That is, not even the tiniest part.

[33] Matthew 5:17-20, NKJV.

[34] Exodus 24:5-8.

This Covenant is sealed, like Abraham's, with cutting and with blood.

THE TALMUD

If I had my druthers, I would devote many, many pages to the topic of Talmud. It deserves a full exposition just for Christians, because we miss a lot by not knowing and learning from it, and from those who devote themselves to its study.

Failing that, let me spend just a little time here with it, and give you some references for further study.

Knowing what the Talmud is, and how it is used by religious Jews, will shed light on what Jesus, Paul, and other New Testament authors were actually addressing in their comments on the Law of Moses (hint: see Deut. 10:16).

Jews refer to the books of the Old Testament as the *Tanakh* (an acronym from the initial Hebrew letters of *Torah* ("Instruction or Law"), *Nevi'im* ("Prophets") and *Ketuvim* ("Writings")—hence *TaNaKh.*

The Law (or Law of Moses) comes from the Torah, also called the Five Books of Moses, or the Pentateuch. This Law was given to Moses at Mount Sinai, and contains the Ten Commandments and an additional 603 other rules. This is the Written Law, because it is written down in the Torah. Additionally, most Jews believe God also gave Moses the Oral Law at Sinai, basically the logic and methodology to interpret and apply the written Law to specific situations.

The Constitution

A parallel might be the United States Constitution. Anyone can read it, and most of its provisions are straightforward and not difficult to understand. But it happens that different people will interpret one Article or Amendment one way, and others another way. Also, two Articles might seem to conflict in dealing with a particular issue (the rights of states versus the rights of the federal government, for example).

The Supreme Court is empowered with the responsibility to make the final determination of which (if either) interpretation will prevail when there is a conflict in a given instance. Each judge writes their opinion, and the majority ruling and opinion of the whole Court is also written and becomes the deciding interpretation. This must then be followed and applied by lower courts, other branches of government, and law-enforcement agencies. These opinions, including the dissenting ones, are studied for generations, and also by subsequent incarnations of the Supreme Court, in the forming of future rulings. Certain Supreme Court justices are particularly renown for their deep insights and opinions, and these are studied diligently in law schools across the country.

If the Torah is the "Constitution," then the Oral Law, now written down in the Talmud, is just such a collection of opinions on the Torah, especially the 613 *mitzvot*, or laws, and contains varying opinions from highly regarded sages and scholars of the Law. Sometimes there will be a ruling opinion; other times varying interpretations stand side-by-side with equal respect—without rancor. A *Talmud* page, in Hebrew, follows.

FIGURE: TALMUD PAGE, IN HEBREW

The opinions in the Talmud are not casual or ill-founded; rather, each is rigorously arrived at and defended. To be clear, I do not mean that they are simply passionately defended. Rather, the logic and exegesis used to determine how and why to apply a law from the Torah are thorough, careful, logical and precise.

Although the editors of the Talmud did not begin to write down the Oral Law until about A.D. 200, this rigorous tradition of interpretation and application dates back easily two or three hundred years before Jesus. Tradition would say, of course, that it dates all the way to Moses (about 1350 B.C.), if he indeed received the Oral Law at Mount Sinai.

More relevant for us is that this is just exactly the tradition in which Jesus, Paul and the Jewish authors of the New Testament were trained.[35] Paul especially was a disciple of Rabban Gamaliel the Elder and his school, and any argument he would make—whether for the Messiahship of Jesus or about the Law of Moses—would be naturally formed in the manner of Talmudic debate. This is important, because the book of Romans, written by Paul, explicitly follows such a structure, and disregarding this form of presentation and argument can lead to fatal misunderstanding of what Paul is trying to say.

Even Paul's remark that the Law was a tutor until Messiah came would be regarded as a simple truism, not a revolutionary insight. Note that in Hebrew, a student is a "*talmid*," and the "Talmud" (same Hebrew root) means "instruction." The root in Hebrew, תלם, or *TLM*, means "teach" or "study." *Of course* the Law is our tutor, and the Law is fulfilled when Messiah comes.

In some circles, Christian authors have depicted Paul as the "liberated Jew" who is now crossing swords with the "trapped Jews" still foolishly bound by the Law. While Paul did debate and contest the opinions of other Jews, he did so as a Jew, with Jews, within a Jewish Oral Law tradition. Even when arguing about Gentiles coming under God's grace, he was making his case to Jews in Jewish language, forms, Scripture, hermeneutics, exegesis and logic. Further, even the opinions he expressed were not new interpretations—they were already *well* within the relatively diverse scope of Second Temple Jewish thought. It is during the Second Temple period[36] that Jesus and Paul lived, and in which the New Testament was written and the Church was born.

The claims Paul made about Messiah and the fulfillment of the Law were not new, but were already known and believed by many Second Temple Jews. Paul was just saying, in effect, "Remember what Tanakh says about Messiah? Now it has come true. He's here!"

Paul never quoted the New Testament in making his case, because it didn't exist yet; it was in the process of being written. Paul quoted Scripture only from the Old Testament in making his argument that Jesus was the fulfillment of the Law, and he made his case in the classic "principles through which Torah is

---

[35] Except probably Luke, who was a Gentile.

[36] The Second Temple (Solomon's was the First, destroyed in 586 B.C.) began to be built around 520 B.C. It was destroyed by the Romans in A.D. 70.

expounded" used in the Talmud by the rabbis of his day, and today as well. Key phrases in Romans come right from this pattern: "What shall we then say?" and "May it never be!" or "God forbid!"[37] and the structure of his overall presentation and logic follow as well.

If you go into a modern *yeshiva* (Jewish seminary), you will see men carefully studying Torah and Talmud, sometimes alone, but often in pairs. The pairs are called *haverim*, or friends. They read together and debate, deep, long, rigorously. They ask and challenge each other, point by point. They agree and disagree. "What does it say? How do you read it?"

Does this quote sound familiar? It should!

> One day an expert in religious law stood up to test Jesus by asking him this question: "Teacher, what should I do to inherit eternal life?"
>
> Jesus replied, "What does the law of Moses say? How do you read it?"
>
> The man answered, "'You must love the LORD your God with all your heart, all your soul, all your strength, and all your mind.' And, 'Love your neighbor as yourself.'"
>
> "Right!" Jesus told him. "Do this and you will live!"[38]

Any yeshiva student would instantly recognize the form of this exchange, and especially the question, "What does the law of Moses say? How do you read it?" The question jumps out as a classic form of rabbinic questioning, and of the contesting questions to which the rabbis put their students, and the students put each other. Following is a photograph of a modern yeshiva, where just this kind of arguing is taking place, mostly in pairs, throughout the room.

---

[37] Shulam, Joseph, and Hilary Le Cornu. *A Commentary on the Jewish Roots of Romans.* Baltimore, MD: Lederer Books, 1997, p. 6.
[38] Luke 10:25-28.

FIGURE: A YESHIVA IN SESSION

The foundational assumption is that debate, contest, logic, rigor, open up a space for the Spirit of God to enter in, and reveal His truth. Further, it is not expected that one must win and the other lose the argument. At the end, two or more opinions can stand "side-by-side," with both respected, and those who wrestled with Talmud and each other still remain friends. God's will for a given issue is understood to be discoverable but also sometimes beyond just one result.

Christian theology largely deems a "side-by-side" resolution impossible. One must be right and the other wrong. Somehow God could not possibly allow both. For example: baptism must be *only* for adults, OR it is acceptable for children; the bread and wine *are* Jesus, OR they are merely a "remembrance" of Him, and so on. Denominations have arisen primarily because disagreement led to division and disfellowship.

Frankly, the *rabbinic way* of the yeshiva is healthier. This doesn't mean there are no issues of Christian doctrine that are, in effect, non-negotiable. The Talmud too has opinions where just one is the final ruling. But Christians have a terrible record of insisting on winners and losers, that one is right and the other wrong, of dismissing and then shunning or even harming each other, over opinions that should simply have been left standing, side-by-side, *adjacent*, with equal respect—and that, with continued debate and *no rancor or personal attack*, might even have made space for the Spirit of God to enter in.

Whereas the yeshiva fosters ongoing debate and growth of understanding, we Christians find it tiresome and would rather just separate from those who don't agree with us. That, at least, has largely been our history so far.

I pray for a reformation that brings us together—respecting each other even when we might not agree—rather than dividing yet again because I am right and you, if you disagree, are wrong.

NEW TESTAMENT VERSUS OLD TESTAMENT

The New Testament is not a replacement for the Old. If anything it is more rightly seen as *midrash*, commentary, using the passages of the Old Testament to show how the Law is fulfilled in the Messiah, Jesus, and how God reaches out to the Gentiles through Him. As Shulam and Le Cornu put it:

> The New Testament is indissolubly bound to what Christianity has traditionally erred in calling the "Old Testament." The New Testament as a written text is both a continuation of and a commentary on or explication of the Tanakh, the Hebrew Bible. It cannot be understood without reference to the Tanakh, which provides it with its primary interpretive context. ... *The New Testament is a Jewish text.*[39] [emphasis in the original]

Since the early centuries after the life of Jesus, much of Christian theology has been focused on showing how different it is from Judaism. But the methods used to construct this argument are largely within the confines of Greek philosophical structure, not Jewish thought. Thus, distinctions claimed of "Christianity" from Jewish thought are illusory, manufactured, the product of Greek-style thinking by Gentiles, rather than true distinctions discovered in the text of the New Testament.

Paul's (and other) claims about Law and Grace, about Covenant and Messiah, were not innovations and did not depart from existing streams of Jewish thought, debate and belief. The distinction wasn't what was believed about the coming Messiah—many already believed such things—the distinction was the proclamation that the Messiah had arrived, and His name was Jesus.[40]

So we will turn next to Jesus, and the Covenant He proclaimed.

See next page for a list of resources for further study.

---

[39] A Commentary, p. 6

[40] The issue of Jesus' divinity, and of whether God is One or Triune, is an important one, but will be addressed separately in the chapter on Trinity. It is not, in fact, inconsistent with Jewish thought of that time, but the details of the issue are too extensive for us right here.

RESOURCES FOR FURTHER STUDY

Here are a handful of books on this topic, to help you get started. There is a wealth of research available today that shows how closely related first-century Judaism and first-century Christianity truly are. The **Bibliography & Recommended Reading** appendix has a much more extensive list.

A Commentary on the Jewish Roots of Galatians. Joseph Shulam and Hilary Le Cornu. Academon Ltd: Jerusalem, 2005.

A Commentary on the Jewish Roots of Romans. Joseph Shulam and Hilary Le Cornu. Lederer Books: Baltimore, 1998.

Hebrews Through a Hebrew's Eyes. Dr. Stuart Sacks. Lederer Books, Baltimore, 1995.

Judaism in the New Testament: Practices and Beliefs. Bruce Chilton and Jacob Neusner. Routledge: New York, 1995.

Lost in Translation: Rediscovering the Hebrew Roots of Our Faith. John Klein and Adam Spears, with Michael Christopher. Covenant Research Institute, Bend, Oregon, 2007.

The Real Kosher Jesus. Michael L. Brown. Front Line, Lake Mary, Florida, 2012.

The Talmud, The Steinsaltz Edition (in English). Rabbi Adin Steinsaltz. Random House: New York, 1995 and other years.

15.
Covenant—Jesus

L et's start with what Jesus says on the night before He was crucified, while He and His disciples share the Passover meal:

> And as they were eating, Jesus took bread, blessed and *broke it*, and gave it to the disciples and said, "Take, eat; this is My body." Then He took the cup, and gave thanks, and gave it to them, saying, "Drink from it, all of you. For this is *My blood* of the new *covenant*,[1] which is shed for many for the remission of sins."[2]

When the disciples heard this, they would connect the words and actions with what they already knew and revered about *covenant*, and about *Passover*.[3] Jesus split the bread, saying it was His body,[4] and then declared the wine His blood.

The disciples would hear in Jesus' words a similar image to when Abraham cut in two the animals that were sacrificed in his covenant with God in Genesis 15; and when, in Deuteronomy 24, Moses had the oxen sacrificed (they were cut) and the blood sprinkled on the altar and on the people, as they promised obedience to God's instructions.

A common English expression is "to cut a deal," and some Bible commentators press the point by writing of "*cutting* a covenant" rather than "signing" or "sealing." Note that even these other ways of referring to the act of covenanting have images of physical acts: You *sign* a document, or you *place a*

---

[1] The word for "covenant" in here is a Greek word, since virtually the entire New Testament, as we have it, is in Greek. It is, however, exactly the word used by the Jews in the Septuagint, the translation of the Old Testament into Greek more than 130 years before the birth of Jesus (and parts of it *much* before that). Jesus' use of "covenant" here is precisely what it meant in the Old Testament.

[2] Matthew 26:26-28, NKJV.

[3] Exodus 12.

[4] There has been a debate throughout the Church and throughout the centuries, starting about A.D. 1100—more than *a thousand years* after the Last Supper!—as to whether we are to regard the bread and wine of Communion as a *symbol* of Jesus' body and blood, or as *actually being* the body and blood of Jesus. We will not rehearse this debate here, except to say the early Church took Jesus' words to mean that He would be present in the bread and wine of Communion. They did not debate if or how.

seal on it, in wax, or by embossing the paper. It is not just a "verbal" agreement, or a thought in your head. There is an incarnational *physicality* to covenanting. This was true in Abraham's day, and it is true in ours.

As stated before, the Hebrew word for "covenant," ברית, *berit*, also means "to cut." The Jewish rite of circumcision is called *"berit milah,"* or "covenant of circumcision."[5] The evidence of the covenant (the *cutting of circumcision*) remains on the man—obviously—for his entire life. When Jews look at naked foreigners they usually see no sign on them—no cutting—of the covenant with God.[6] Read 1 Samuel 18 for some further context for this.

Covenant—to God and to Jews—is not a philosophical appreciation of religious principles: It is a *serious, profound union, a yoking together*, physically marked by cutting and blood. Rashi[7] even says that the circumcision is itself the fulfillment of God's command in Genesis 17 to walk "blameless."

I realize I'm going on and on about this, and for some of you it is embarrassing or maybe makes you squeamish, but this is *really* important, and Christians, for the most part, are ignorant of its centrality to the Jewish faith, its centrality to Jesus, its centrality to His disciples, *and its centrality to the covenant that Jesus declared.*

Even more, remember why the disciples are gathered with Jesus for this last supper—it is the *Passover* meal. God promised to free the Israelites from Egypt and leave them unharmed when He moved through Egypt, striking down all of the first-born—except those houses whose doors were marked with the *blood of a lamb*—a lamb "without blemish,"[8] the same Hebrew word used with Abraham when he was told to walk "blameless."

These homes God promised to *pass over*. At this first Passover, they were saved by the blood of the lamb.[9] God commanded the Israelites to memorialize this event every year by celebrating a Passover meal together and retelling the story of their Exodus to freedom.[10]

When, at that Passover meal, Jesus says of the cup of wine, "Drink from it, all of you. For this is *My blood* of the new *covenant*,[11] which is shed for many for the remission of sins," His words are echoes of cutting and blood in covenant, of the lamb without blemish whose blood spared the Israelites, and of deliverance from

---

[5] There are times when this physical event is referred to allegorically, to make an important point, as in Deuteronomy 10:15-16, "The LORD delighted only in your fathers, to love them; and He chose their descendants after them, you above all peoples, as it is this day. *Therefore circumcise the foreskin of your heart*, and be stiff-necked no longer."

[6] Western medicine for many years routinely practiced circumcision on newborn boys, believing it helped prevent certain diseases in adulthood—a topic of debate in the current medical community. But aside from that medical practice, circumcision is generally uncommon except among Jews.

[7] Rabbi Shlomo Yitzhaki, A.D. 1040–1105, French rabbi and the most famed biblical and Talmudic commentator. Typically he is referred to just by the name "Rashi."

[8] Exodus 12:5, NKJV.

[9] Exodus 24.

[10] Exodus 12.

[11] As mentioned, the usage here of "covenant" is just what it meant in the Old Testament. It is not the Greek idea of a will, or of a contract.

the oppression under Egypt. In fact, the word Jesus used, translated "remission," means "deliverance" from the oppression and domination of sin, just as the Israelites were delivered from the oppression and domination of the Egyptians.

Why should someone's blood produce deliverance from sin?

Shed blood atoning (paying) for sin is a common concept to the Jews. Speaking of the altar of incense, God says:

> "Aaron shall make atonement upon its horns *once a year* with the *blood of the sin offering* of atonement; once a year he shall make atonement upon it *throughout your generations*. It is most holy to the LORD."[12]

This is the first reference in Scripture to Yom Kippur, the Day of Atonement, still celebrated by Jews to this day.

So the blood of an animal, offered by Aaron (and the generations of priests that followed him), can produce deliverance from the domination of sin for the people of Israel. The cost of such sin is death—the sacrifice of a *valuable* living being by a high priest of God—and then the people are free from the judgment that sin has caused.

It was not *their righteousness* that brought them atonement; it was the *blood of another*, spilled *on their behalf*, and they *trusted* that it was so, because God told them it would be so.

Remembering this, now listen to Hebrews:

> Jesus has become a surety of a better covenant. Also there were many priests, because they were prevented by death from continuing. But He, because He continues forever, has an unchangeable priesthood.
>
> Therefore He is also able to save to the uttermost those who come to God through Him, since He always lives to make intercession for them.
>
> For such a High Priest was fitting for us, who is holy, harmless, undefiled, separate from sinners, and has become higher than the heavens; who does not need daily, as those high priests, to offer up sacrifices, first for His own sins and then for the people's, for this He did once for all when He offered up Himself.
>
> For the law appoints as high priests men who have weakness, but the word of the oath, which came after the law, appoints the Son who has been perfected forever.[13]

Later Hebrews speaks of the covenant Jesus declared:

> For if that first covenant[14] had been faultless, then no place would have been sought for a second. Because finding fault with them, He says: "Behold, the days are coming, says the LORD, when *I will make a new covenant with the house of Israel and with the house of Judah*—not according to the covenant that I made with their

---

[12] Exodus 30:10, NASB.
[13] Hebrews 7:22-28, NKJV.
[14] This refers in context to the Covenant with Israel through Moses, not with Abraham.

fathers in the day when I took them by the hand to lead them out of the land of Egypt; *because they did not continue in My covenant*, and I disregarded them, says the LORD.

"For this is the covenant that I will make *with the house of Israel* after those days, says the LORD: I will put My laws in their mind and write them on their hearts; and I will be their God, and they shall be My people. None of them shall teach his neighbor, and none his brother, saying, 'Know the LORD,' for all shall know Me, from the least of them to the greatest of them.

"For I will be merciful to their unrighteousness, and their sins and their lawless deeds I will remember no more."[15]

Beginning with the words, "Behold, the days are coming…" this entire text is from Jeremiah 31:31-34. Jeremiah is a prophet in the Old Testament, the Tanakh! So it is not Jesus, nor the author of Hebrews, nor any other follower of Jesus, who *invents* a new covenant to replace the old one.

That is, it is not Jesus nor His followers who suddenly flee the covenants of Judaism and start a new religion, but rather Jesus and His followers claim and live out the new covenant *already promised by the God of the Old Testament*, through the words *of a prophet in the Old Testament, Jeremiah*.

This new covenant declared by Jesus had been promised long before; it was to be one where sin is wiped away, forgotten, by the profound sacrifice of an obedient and sinless man—a sacrifice greater than that of lambs or oxen—and therefore permanent, not temporary.

Further, the covenant Jesus declares is one where those who are redeemed will "know the LORD," and His laws (teachings and instructions) will be internalized and lived out, rather than performed because of external behavior control, whether by peer pressure or because of scrutiny from religious leaders.

That is, people would not harm each other, and would care for each other, not because there were rules, enforced by others, to make them behave, but because God's counsel was incorporated directly in their own hearts and minds!

Note that God says that it will be "with the house of Israel," and Jesus Himself said, "I was not sent except to the lost sheep of the house of Israel."[16]

So this is not a new religion for Gentiles, divorced from its Jewish roots, with a blond, blue-eyed Jesus saving non-Jews who simply declare their faith in Him, and casting off the legalistic Jews who didn't "get it" that He was the Messiah.

Rather, it is the fulfillment of God's promises to the house of Israel that He will be their God and they will be His people, and *they will be so close to Him as to know His heart*, and will *act in ways that make others fall in love with Him*.

Jesus clearly taught in these ways:

He quoted the *Tanakh*[17] and recited the *Shema*:[18] "The first of all the commandments is: 'Hear, O Israel, the LORD our God, the LORD is one. And you shall

---

[15] Hebrews 8:7-12, NKJV.

[16] Matthew 15:24, NKJV.

[17] The Scriptures that Christians usually call the "Old Testament."

love the LORD your God with all your heart, with all your soul, with all your mind, and with all your strength.'"[19]

He quoted the Old Testament: "You shall love your neighbor as yourself."[20]

He told them how to demonstrate that they were His followers, not by proper defense and assertion of theology, not by agreeing to certain propositions or concepts, not by affirming carefully reasoned doctrines, but by how they treated each other: "A new commandment I give to you, that you love one another; as I have loved you, that you also love one another. *By this* all will know that you are My disciples, *if you have love for one another.*"[21]

And on and on He taught, in these instructions and others like them, about loving enemies, and sinners, and those sick, poor, in jail, despised and marginalized by others, giving more than was asked, going further than requested. He Himself made the ultimate sacrifice, the giving of his own life for us, *because He loved us.* The love of God *poured through Him* because the love of God was *in Him*, and He desired that it be also *in us*:

> "I do not pray for these alone, *but also for those who will believe in Me through their word*; that they all may be one, as You, Father, are in Me, and I in You; that they also may be one in Us, that the world may believe that You sent Me.
>
> "And the glory which You gave Me I have given them, that they may be one just as We are one: I in them, and You in Me; that they may *be made perfect in one*, and that the world may know that You have sent Me, and have loved them as You have loved Me.
>
> "Father, I desire that they also whom You gave Me may be with Me where I am, that they may behold My glory which You have given Me; for *You loved Me before the foundation of the world.*
>
> "O righteous Father! The world has not known You, but I have known You; and these have known that You sent Me. And I have declared to them Your name, and will declare it, *that the love with which You loved Me may be in them, and I in them.*"[22]

Though sent *to* the people of Israel, it was *through* the people of Israel, *promised in the covenant with Abraham*, that God promised all people would be blessed—and so the love of God was given to the Gentile as well as the Jew, and all who accepted it were grafted into the vine. And so even Gentiles became followers of the Messiah of Israel, and carry the love of God, placed in their hearts.

---

[18] In Judaism, considered the key statement of the faith; the full Shema consists of Deuteronomy 6:4-9 and 11:13-21 and Numbers 15:37-41, though often just the first two verses are used.

[19] Mark 12:29-30 (NKJV), quoting Deuteronomy 6:4-5.

[20] Leviticus 19:18b, NKJV.

[21] John 13:34-35, NKJV.

[22] John 17:20-26, NKJV.

Christians believe that Jesus[23] Christ[24] is actually God—one Person of a Trinity, the Father, Son and Holy Spirit, who together are one God.

They believe that the Son *is* God, and has *existed since before creation*—that creation happened *through* Him.[25]

Consider the implications of this: What was *created through Him, returns through Him* to come unto the Father. Thus "I am *the way*, the truth, and the life. *No one* can *come to the Father* except *through me*"[26] is an obvious consequence of His creation role in the Godhead.

It is practically a tautology.

But if that is true, then *it has always been true!* Jesus didn't say, "It *used to be* that Abraham and his descendants came unto God by His covenant with Abraham, but *now* they and others can come only through Me." If He is God, then His statement *"except through me"* was *always* true; it's His eternal role as Creator and Redeemer.

If Jesus Christ is indeed God, then He was *present at the covenant with Abraham*, when God promised that the covenant would be *everlasting!*

If He isn't God and wasn't God, then He has no power to overturn an *everlasting* covenant made by God.

In either case, the covenant with Abraham remains just what Genesis says it is: *everlasting*, forever, eternal, unending. And through Israel, and through Jesus Christ, even those outside of Israel are brought into the *everlasting covenant* along with Abraham and his descendants.

SALVATION, SANCTIFICATION, AND...

The order of salvation in covenant is as it always has been: *God initiates* a saving relationship, like a marriage, and promises to be with us eternally. We believe in Him; that is, *we trust* that He can and will do what He promises.

We rely on the promise.

In Jesus, as He fulfills the covenant, we witness the depth of God's love for us: *sacrifice* even unto death, and the power of love so great that it brings resurrection to new life. He lives with us, in us and through us, *to teach us His ways*, so that we too might love those around us—neighbors and even enemies.

That is our sanctification, our being con*formed* to Him, learning to be like Him, *learning to love like Him*.

In these, *salvation* and *sanctification* (and ultimately *glorification*) is *Life in Christ*. It is the *covenant* Jesus taught, and fulfills *within* us, and *through* us.

We are called to covenant. We obey and we hear.

---

[23] "Jesus" is from the Hebrew word *Yeshua*, or Joshua, and deep at its root means "a wide, open, safe place with God." More on this in the chapter on Trinity.
[24] "Christ" is the Greek word for the Hebrew word "messiah," meaning "anointed one."
[25] See John 1.
[26] John 14:6.

16.
Faith

I'd like to encourage you to read Hebrews 11. Much as Psalm 119 is a tribute to God's teaching and counsel (the Law), this chapter of Hebrews is a sweeping, exuberant, compelling paean to faith. It begins:

> Now faith is the substance of things hoped for, the evidence of things not seen.

It is followed, verse by verse, like this:

> By faith we understand...
> By faith Abel offered to God...
> By faith Enoch was taken away...
> But without faith it is impossible to please Him...
> By faith Noah...
> By faith Abraham...
> By faith he dwelt...
> By faith Sarah...
> These all died in faith...
> By faith Isaac...
> By faith Jacob...
> By faith Joseph...
> By faith Moses...
> By faith he forsook Egypt...
> By faith he kept the Passover...
> By faith they passed through the Red Sea...
> By faith the walls of Jericho fell down...
> By faith the harlot Rahab did not perish...

And then concludes:

> And what more shall I say? For the time would fail me to tell of Gideon and Barak and Samson and Jephthah, also of David and Samuel and the prophets: who through faith subdued kingdoms, worked righteousness, obtained promises, stopped the mouths of lions, quenched the violence of fire, escaped the edge of the sword, out of weakness were made strong, became valiant in battle, turned to flight the armies of the aliens.
> Women received their dead raised to life again.

Others were tortured, not accepting deliverance, that they might obtain a better resurrection.

Still others had trial of mockings and scourgings, yes, and of chains and imprisonment. They were stoned, they were sawn in two, were tempted, were slain with the sword.

They wandered about in sheepskins and goatskins, being destitute, afflicted, tormented—of whom the world was not worthy.

They wandered in deserts and mountains, in dens and caves of the earth.

And all these, having obtained a good testimony through faith, did not receive the promise, God having provided something better for us, that they should not be made perfect apart from us.

Hebrews 11 is an intense and sweeping depiction of faith, and the testimony to faith's centrality to life in God. It speaks both of the immediate results of faith, and also of delayed results—where God's higher purposes subsumed faith until a greater result would be revealed.

Faith is *key* to life in God. But rather than dive immediately into faith, we're going to begin by first looking at skepticism.

SKEPTICISM

Beginning in college and continuing for many years, I had a serious interest in other religions and what today would be called "new age" topics: reincarnation, enlightenment, yoga, meditation, and things "spiritual."[1]

After I came to faith in Jesus, something surprising and weird happened. I found that if I went into a bookstore and got close to the "new age" bookrack, it would give me the willies. I couldn't stay near these books. They made me feel creepy and itchy.

Also, *prior* to coming to faith, I had read and appreciated the writings of people who considered themselves "skeptics," meaning broadly that they were rationalists, usually atheists, and relished exposing fraud, trickery and bad behavior among people who believed "spiritual" things, whether astrology, magic or—especially—Christianity.

There is actually a magazine called *Skeptic*, which I used to enjoy reading. Why? At least in part because I found fraud by Christian leaders to be especially repugnant. I still do, by the way!

I remember a radio preacher saying God had told him there was a person listening, right that moment, who had saved up $6000 to buy a car, that it had taken a long time and hard work to get to that point, but now God wanted them to send that money—all of it—to the radio ministry. He said God would multiply and reward that act of faithful giving far beyond the six thousand dollars.

---

[1] To be fair, there are elements of some of these that have enduring value, and that do not compromise one's faith in God—although the discernment to tell the wheat from the chaff is not easily gained.

You just know that this shotgun "prophetic word" would find several targets, people who had saved just that amount of money (or close to it) and were naïve enough to believe that this word was from God and intended for them personally. And they sent in their six thousand dollars, confident that God had orchestrated this radio communication just for their benefit.

I bet you find this as disgusting as I do, and I'm hoping God has a special place in hell set aside for that preacher. I don't mean that literally, but it does express my revulsion to this kind of theft.

Skeptic regularly debunked this kind of fraud. I liked that.

But after I became a believer, I found that if I picked up the magazine, I no longer liked it. Now, as I read it, I felt an emotionally bitter, angry edge in it.

Skeptics usually describe themselves like this: "We just want to look rationally and carefully and make good judgments about spiritual things that people believe, and see whether there is any factual basis to them." This sounds pure, sensible and objective.

But it seldom played out that way. Rather, I found they went into their investigations with an edge of condescension, even anger, toward people who believed things different from what they believed, and this colored their study and reporting.

Even more broadly, though they claim objectivity, we inhabit a universe where complete objectivity is impossible. The observer changes the observed in the process of observation. This happens in a couple of ways:

First, there is a scientific principle called "uncertainty" developed by Werner Heisenberg. He was a German physicist (mentioned in footnotes back in Chapters 10 and 11) who observed that if you try to measure the *momentum* (think *speed*[2]) and the *position* of a subatomic particle, like an electron, you can measure only one or the other with accuracy. The more accurate you get with one, the less accurate you get with the other. You can know exactly where it is at the instant you measured it, but have no idea how fast it is moving. Or you can determine exactly how fast it is moving, but once you have measured it, you have no idea where it is. The reason is that in order to observe an electron flying through space, you have to bounce a photon (a particle of light) off of it.

We see each other because of the photons that come from a light source—like a light bulb or the Sun—as they bounce off of us, and then land on the retinas of each other's eyes. We are so large that billions and billions of photons can bounce off of us without our noticing any effect—we don't seem to get pushed around by them—but at the size of an electron, getting hit by a photon is a big deal. It changes the direction and speed of the electron.

It didn't take long for philosophers to point out that this applied pretty broadly—not just on the subatomic level, but on the macroscopic level too. We affect what we observe by our observation of it.[3]

---

[2] Technically *velocity* times *mass*, but "speed" will do for our illustration in this context.
[3] Actually philosophers realized this long ago. Heisenberg gave support to their insights.

Stamp text:

300

$$\Delta p \cdot \Delta q \sim h$$

Heisenbergsche
Unschärferelation

Deutschland

1,53 €

Werner Heisenberg

2001　　　**Physiker**　　　1901 – 1976

Figure: German Stamp: "Heisenberg's Uncertainty Principle"

Second, there is a related psychological "observer/observed" phenomenon, probably even more familiar. We've all had an experience like this:

You're sitting, thinking about pancakes, or the clouds, or Heisenberg. Your facial expression reflects virtually nothing—or at least it doesn't reflect pancakes or clouds or Heisenberg. But if somebody who thinks you are angry with them looks at you, they think that what is on your face is anger toward them.

You might not be angry at them at all, but they come into it with that assumption; and so they interpret what they see by the bias with which they observe you.

But they can also change *you* when they ask, hotly, "What are you so angry about?" Maybe you weren't angry before they said that, but your adrenaline gets stirred up when they do. The observer has affected the observed.

We color what we observe by what we believe ahead of time, but we also interact with what we observe and change it.

So much for pure objectivity.

This isn't rocket science, and most of us have discovered these simple realities on our own.

Well, guess what? This applies to skeptics. It is impossible to observe without bias the world we occupy. You cannot observe something without affecting the observation and the thing observed. You can try to minimize this effect; that's what good science does. But the idea that you can somehow lift yourself above what it is that we are a part of is not true. In fact, it is often true that what we believe affects what it is that we see.

When a skeptic expects fraud, or incompetent thinking, or scientific naïveté, or gullibility, or religious nonsense, it is what he thinks he finds, even if it is not actually present. In fact, the common skeptical assertion that there is no such thing as the supernatural leads to the inevitable conclusion that anything that looks miraculous is either fraud or misunderstanding. The miraculous is *excluded* as a possibility. The atheist's version of this is, "Because there is no God, there can be no supernatural events caused by God." So the possibility of experiencing God is dismissed, and anything that looks like it might be from God is attributed to foolishness or chicanery.

Skepticism commonly fails because it is not as objective as it imagines itself to be.

That said, a healthy skepticism (minus condescension, self-righteousness and anger) can prove of enormous value. Questioning is a path to the truth, and can free us of a similar failing—*blind* faith.

Yes, it is a challenge!

FAITH

Randy Fisk has written a wonderful book on living with the supernatural: *The Presence, Power and Heart of God.*[4] Randy is a former physicist and now teaches and pastors Christians in learning how to pray. In the book he tells this story:

> A few years ago, the teens in our church befriended a young man named Danny. Danny spent most of his time on the streets. A severe head injury as an infant had affected him mentally. One of his endearing qualities was the way that he would quote clichés usually a little mixed up. For instance, 'I'll believe it when I see it' would always come out as 'I'll see it when I believe it.' We loved that because we realized that with the things of God Danny's words were much closer to the truth than ours.[5]

"I'll see it when I believe it." That actually is what Scripture says about faith. For example:

> Jesus responded, "Didn't I tell you that you would see God's glory if you believe?"[6]

---

[4] Fisk, Randy. *The Presence, Power and Heart of God.* Second Ref Press, 2011.
[5] *Presence*, p. 81.
[6] John 11:40.

Or this, about the blindness of those who don't believe:

> Satan, who is the god of this world, has blinded the minds of those who don't believe. They are unable to see the glorious light of the Good News. They don't understand this message about the glory of Christ, who is the exact likeness of God.[7]

There are numerous other examples. While it is true that believing can bias what we observe (as with the skeptic or a person with blind faith), it is also true that, *somehow*, the willingness to believe—faith—opens our eyes to see what we could not see before.

It is also true that the faith *of Jesus*—that is, His faithfulness to us—will often open our eyes when we ourselves would not see.

When I was a kid, I was taught in church that God produced miracles in the time of Jesus and the Apostles, but stopped doing so around A.D. 100. Instead, He inspired the authors of the New Testament to write down what Jesus and the Apostles did, including the evidences of miraculous power and presence. Our task, in our day and age, was not to see miracles, but to study what was written in the Bible, and use that to govern our daily activities.

Our faith was in *Scripture*, not miracles or the supernatural. In fact, because God stopped performing miracles long ago, anything supernatural that might happen had to be from the devil. *It could not be from God*, even if the effect appeared to be entirely good (a conclusion not unlike the atheist's).

This was a highly intellectualized, even rationalistic, deductive Christianity, and I personally found it disappointing—both because it seemed unfair of God to not perform miracles today, and because the deductive faith seemed so dry and lifeless. And there was no real power in it to sustain you through trying times. Just logic, based on a really odd and unprovable premise:

We believe that a guy who lived some 2000 years ago was actually God and was perfect and never did anything wrong, and came here from heaven, taught for just three years, gathered a few people around Him and taught them—mostly fisherman, tax collectors, prostitutes and rebels. We believe that He was killed on a cross, died, came back to life again on the third day, then went to heaven, and by doing all of that *gave eternal life to each of us who trust Him to give us eternal life.*

Isn't this a weird thing to believe? I mean, think about it. Isn't this a *really* weird thing to believe? It is certainly not logical. I'm not even sure it makes any sense at all, and it costs something. For one thing, it costs us reputation when we are hanging around smart skeptical people. They think us silly or incompetent.

And so, to have a merely intellectual faith, one that is deduced from embarrassingly weird premises, leaves one without solid foundation, other than perhaps trenchant fundamentalism.

---

[7] 2 Corinthians 4:4.

Wouldn't it help if the Lord *showed up?* If His presence and power were here? Wouldn't it help people to believe He is real? I can tell you *that* was how I finally became a believer.

I am often stuck in my head, thinking important and deep thoughts (of course), following rational pathways and creative imaginings, and it takes a big boot to get me loose.

That is exactly what the Lord did for me. That is exactly how I came to faith; it was the presence of the Holy Spirit in power—really hard to debate, or to raise skeptical arguments against! It is why it says in Mark, "And they went out and preached everywhere, the Lord working with them and *confirming the word through the accompanying signs.*"[8]

So, it costs for believers to believe these weird things that we believe, but it's like Danny said: "I'll see it when I believe it." There is a kind of door into the eternal that is not opened by a rational progression of thought. It comes from two directions:

- from our believing, we *see*, and
- from the *power* being seen, we believe.

Also, look at how freely the experience of God appears in Scripture. It is depicted as normative, and normative of belief:

> Rid yourselves of all malice and all deceit, hypocrisy, envy, and slander of every kind. Like newborn babies, crave pure spiritual milk, so that by it you may grow up in your salvation, now that you have *tasted* that the Lord is good.[9]

If someone makes a purely rational decision to believe in Jesus and accept His offer of salvation, of course He will say, "Amen, welcome into the Kingdom."

But few people are ever argued logically into the Kingdom, and even at the end of a compelling, logical argument, they must still take that step of faith.

Pascal said, "The heart has its reasons that reason does not know."[10]

Thus, instead of being convinced by argument, most recognize their own frailty, their own sinfulness, and their hearts respond to the offer Jesus makes to forgive and accept them. All this requires is that we accept the gift.

In this world we Christians are looked upon as aliens. We are viewed as people with an odd belief system, a strange religion to which we cling. We are often scorned as not really fitting the culture in which we live—and the truth is, we don't.

Scripture says that we will continue to struggle. We will even continue to sin. We will continue to have calamities. There will continue to be suffering. But in spite of all of that, we are and remain children of the living God, brothers and sisters of Jesus Christ, royal priests in a royal kingdom—a kingdom of Heaven.

So we should act like it!

---

[8] Mark 16:20, NKJV.
[9] 1 Peter 2:1-3, NIV.
[10] From *Pensées*.

The spirit of God, who raised Jesus from the dead, lives in you.[11] ... For all who are led by the Spirit of God are children of God. So you should not be like cowering, fearful slaves.[12]

Don't apologize for your faith. Don't be ashamed of the Gospel. Be willing to take the ridicule. Be willing to be considered an intellectual lightweight, because your faith does not conform to the logic that a skeptic requires of you. Never mind the fact that the skeptic's faith is built on less.

You should behave instead like God's very own children, adopted into his family—calling him "Father, dear Father." For his Holy Spirit speaks to us deep in our hearts and tells us that we are God's children. And since we are his children, we will share his treasures—for everything God gives to his Son, Christ, is ours, too.[13]

Faith and belief are very odd things in this day, but the truth is that there isn't anyone, skeptic or believer, who doesn't live on faith, who doesn't live by belief. I can choose, if I want, to believe that the universe began without purpose and without a creator. I can choose to believe, if I wish, that the aggregations of atoms and molecules came together and made life happen purely by accident.

I can't prove that, however. It is a statement of faith. And as a statement of faith, it does nothing to change how I live or how I behave, how I treat other people, or how I treat my enemies.

And so, in that sense, as much as I might want rationally and skeptically to cling to the accidental-creation theory, I find it of little value. As Kurt Gödel would point out, there are questions, problems, challenges in this system that cannot be solved within this system.[14]

But when I look at Jesus, and I hear what Jesus said about loving God, loving our neighbors as we love ourselves, and loving even our enemies, I find there a truth, a wisdom, a presence and a power that *transcends* all the rest—that goes beyond it.

God breaks open the physical world in which we are confined, and drives into it an entirely new dimension of life and reality. If we taste it, we find that it is good.

C.S. Lewis said:

I believe in Christianity as I believe that the sun has risen: not only because I see it, but because by it I see everything else.[15]

If I have to choose one or the other, skepticism or faith, accident or intentional creation, deduction or presence, then though I will fail again and again in so many ways, nevertheless:

I choose to believe so that I might see.

---

[11] Romans 8:11a, NLT. First Edition.
[12] Romans 8:14-15a, NLT. First Edition.
[13] Romans 8:15b-17a, NLT. First Edition.
[14] See Chapter 11.
[15] From "Is Theology Poetry?" (1945)

17.
Peace, Mercy, Breath of Life

Three deeply related gifts come to us when we enter the Kingdom of God and begin to live in covenant, in relationship with God: Peace, Mercy, and the Breath of Life. We will look at these and their intimate relationship.

PEACE

In normal conversation, the word "peace" typically refers to a state of calm when there are no wars underway, whether between nations or neighbors. But peace in Scripture isn't that. It isn't the absence of conflict. It is a state of the soul.

It is extraordinarily important for each of us to find that peace that comes from God—even in the face of grief, of conflict, of great trial.

We will consider several aspects of this peace, from different places in Scripture, and then see how they all relate to this state of the soul, to peace.

Let's start in the book of Isaiah. It was written some 600 years before the birth of Jesus, and has many passages that are prophecies of the coming of the Messiah, "the suffering servant." One of them is in chapter 42. Here Isaiah, speaking for God, says:

> "Look at my servant, whom I strengthen.
> He is my chosen one, who pleases me.
> I have put my Spirit upon him."[1]

The word "spirit" in Hebrew is *ruach*, and it means "breath" as well as "spirit." This same word is used both to describe what God breathes into Adam's lungs to give him life, and the Holy Spirit (*ruach HaKodesh*, literally *spirit the holy,* or *breath the holy*) in the Old Testament.

God is speaking through Isaiah about the coming Messiah. He continues:

> "I have put My Spirit upon Him;
> He will bring forth justice to the Gentiles.
> He will not cry out, nor raise His voice,

---

[1] Isaiah 42:1a.

Nor cause His voice to be heard in the street.
A bruised reed He will not break,
And smoking flax He will not quench;
He will bring forth justice for truth.
He will not fail nor be discouraged,
Till He has established justice in the earth;
And the coastlands shall wait for His law."
Thus says God the LORD,
Who created the heavens and stretched them out,
Who spread forth the earth and that which comes from it,
Who gives breath to the people on it,
And spirit to those who walk on it:
"I, the LORD, have called You in righteousness,
And will hold Your hand;
I will keep You and give You as a covenant to the people,
As a light to the Gentiles,
To open blind eyes,
To bring out prisoners from the prison,
Those who sit in darkness from the prison house."[2]

The Messiah literally is to be given as a *covenant to the people*. Here is Jesus, at the Last Supper:

Then he took a cup, and when he had given thanks, he gave it to them, saying, "Drink from it, all of you. This is my blood of the covenant, which is poured out for many for the forgiveness of sins.[3]

And Jesus also gave sight to the blind, and His followers were literally freed from prisons, thus fulfilling this prophecy.

But even more broadly than this, in Jesus people are freed from *internal* prisons, places they have been trapped and bound by sin—by abuse, false belief, tradition, culture, self-righteousness, self-condemnation, pride and more.

Freedom in Christ

But what is this freedom Jesus gives? Is it *just* being cut loose from sin?

Remember the scene, in a hundred different movies, of the thief and long-time prisoner being released from jail? He gets a new suit, maybe $20 in his pocket, and he walks out of the prison—to what?

In some films he is picked up at the door by his old partners in crime, and immediately re-enters his old lifestyle—robbing others to gain wealth for himself.

---

[2] Isaiah 42:1b-7, NKJV.
[3] Matthew 26:27-28, NIV.

In other films he walks out alone—no one to meet him or lend a hand—and he begins walking, facing an empty and bleak future, not knowing how he will succeed in a changed and hostile world.

But in a few movies ... even though he has been a thief, and was convicted of a crime, he is met by family and friends, who had continued to love him anyway, and visited him while in prison. As he is set free from jail, he is warmly greeted and taken back into the bosom of the family—who care for him and commit themselves to work with him through the challenging and rocky adjustment to his new life of freedom.

Which of these three futures, once we are set free, do you suppose God intends for us? Which future has God *always* intended for us? Do any of us imagine that God's intention was simply to make us free to do anything we wanted, unrelated to the One who made us and loves us? Is the purpose of freedom in Christ to live unguided and vain lives, pursuing wealth, or addiction, or entertainment, or laziness, or self-indulgence—to go back to the life of sin?

Do we imagine He intends to leave us on our own to make our way in the world, forgiven but abandoned in our freedom?

Rather, *what comes with freedom* after forgiveness is just exactly what God has always desired from us—*us*.

Jesus said this:

> "A rich man had a fertile farm that produced fine crops. He said to himself, 'What should I do? I don't have room for all my crops.'
>
> "Then he said, 'I know! I'll tear down my barns and build bigger ones. Then I'll have room enough to store all my wheat and other goods.
>
> "'And I'll sit back and say to myself, "My friend, you have enough stored away for years to come. Now take it easy! Eat, drink, and be merry!"'
>
> "But God said to him, 'You fool! You will die this very night. Then who will get everything you worked for?'
>
> "Yes, a person is a fool to store up earthly wealth but not have a rich relationship with God."[4]

What is important is not just the point Jesus is making about wealth and its inability to give eternal life or even complete satisfaction, but what He says about a *rich relationship with God*. THAT is what He has always desired.

Isn't it true for many of us, and for much of the Church around the world, that our focus is *not* on a rich relationship with God? It's about something else that appears religious or spiritual or even holy, but is just us, *acting* in what we imagine is a religious, spiritual or holy way. God is not in it. We may think it is better than wealth, but it is the same action of the heart. It is idolatry.

Sometimes this "religious spirit" is a certain kind of behavior or a certain kind of dress. Sometimes it is adherence to certain doctrines, which may even be

---

[4] Luke 12:16-21. Some translations say "rich toward God," but the implication is about relationship, not possessions or tithing.

true and important. But the focus is on the *behavior, dress or doctrine* rather than a *rich relationship with God.*

It is making an idol and missing God.

So Jesus focuses us on relationship with God. Each one of us needs to take this *personally* because this is what Jesus wants *for* us and *from* us. It is what the Holy Spirit wants for us and from us. It is what God the Father wants for us and from us—rich relationship with our Maker.

We were not created to be abandoned, but to love and to be loved.

In the face of this, we chased other gods like wealth, status, fame, success—and we abandoned our Source. We imprisoned ourselves in our lusts (far more than just sexual desires), and couldn't escape.

Yet though *we* abandoned *Him*, He came to find us, sacrificed Himself to *free us* from our prison, and called us back to His bosom. He wants us to live with Him, with the family, and He will work with us through the rocky and challenging adjustment to this new life of freedom. It is what He has always desired for us.

Jesus makes the promise this way:

> Jesus replied, "Anyone who loves me will obey my teaching. My Father will love them, and we will come to them and make our home with them."[5]

That is pretty clear. Jesus says "we"—plural—will come to them and will live with them. The family (the Godhead, if you will) comes to those who had been lost, to live with them. In this passage, Jesus goes on to promise peace and the Holy Spirit:

> "Peace I leave with you; *my* peace I give you. I do not give to you as the world gives. Do not let your hearts be troubled and do not be afraid."[6]

The peace Jesus speaks of is not the absence of war, or absence of conflict with another, but an inner gift from Him of His own peace, in order that our hearts would be calm and fearless.

Consider what His peace looked like: At His most troubled moment, knowing His painful death was near, did He stew silently and alone? Did He drink away His fears (alcohol and drugs were used then as now to numb the pain of living and the fear of dying)? No, He went to the Garden of Gethsemane to talk to His heavenly Father. When He stood before Pilate, did He quake in fear? No. He was calm, fearless, resolute. When He was whipped and scourged and a crown of thorns pierced His head, He endured it unafraid. When He was mocked and spat upon, He was at peace. When He was crucified, He calmly spoke to a condemned criminal and promised him paradise that day, gave the disciple John to His mother, and forgave the soldiers and others who were killing Him.

Such was His peace!

---

[5] John 14:23, NIV.
[6] John 14:27, NIV.

It is this peace, His peace, that He gives freely to us, that our hearts might not be troubled or afraid. It is a peace that is not the absence of strife, conflict or pain, but of calm poise in the midst of it. Such is the peace of Christ. We obtain it by allowing Him into our lives and hearts.

MERCY

Mercy is described in Paul's letter to Titus:

> Once we, too, were foolish and disobedient. We were misled and became slaves to many lusts and pleasures. Our lives were full of evil and envy, and we hated each other.
> But—"When God our Savior revealed his kindness and love, he saved us, not because of the righteous things we had done, but because of *his mercy*.
> "He washed away our sins, giving us a new birth and new life through the Holy Spirit. He generously poured out the Spirit upon us through Jesus Christ our Savior.
> "Because of his grace he declared us righteous and gave us confidence that we will inherit eternal life." This is a trustworthy saying, and I want you to insist on these teachings so that all who trust in God will devote themselves to doing good. These teachings are good and beneficial for everyone.[7]

Let's remember that He saved us, not because of the righteous things we had done, but because of *His mercy*. And that mercy isn't just forgiveness, as great a gift as that is in itself. Rather, when He washed away our sins, His mercy also gave us *new birth* and *new life* through the Holy Spirit.

What is the nature of this new life? It is the very breath of life itself, the Holy Spirit in us. Here's what Scripture tells us:

BREATH OF LIFE

Pause and recall Jesus' encounter with Nicodemus (see Ch. 2). The teaching that Jesus gave to Nicodemus is just what is reflected in Paul's words above, and just as in the Old Testament Holy Spirit (*ruach HaKodesh*) means "breath holy," so in the New Testament, Holy Spirit (*pneumatos hagiou*) also means "breath holy." In both languages the word for *spirit* also means *breath*. From Genesis:

> And the LORD God formed a man's body from the dust of the ground and breathed into it the breath [*ruach*] of life. And the man became a living person.[8]

Think of the image of a child when it is born. It hasn't breathed when it is in its mother's womb. When it is born, it takes breath, and then it can live on its own. So long as it has breath, it has life. Jesus told Nicodemus that to enter the

---

[7] Titus 3:3-8.
[8] Genesis 2:7, NLT First Edition.

Kingdom of God, to be saved, he had to be reborn of water and the Spirit. The *new life* Paul speaks of here is just that!

Now recall Psalm 104:

> O LORD, what a variety of things you have made! In wisdom you have made them all. The earth is full of your creatures.
>
> Here is the ocean, vast and wide, teeming with life of every kind, both great and small. See the ships sailing along, and Leviathan, which you made to play in the sea.
>
> Every one of these depends on you to give them their food as they need it. When you supply it, they gather it. You open your hand to feed them, and they are satisfied.
>
> But if you turn away from them, they panic. When you take away their breath, they die and turn again to dust.[9]

I want you to try something just for a few seconds. Without taking a breath in, *stop breathing*. Just hold your breath right now. As you do that, pay attention to what you feel. It is scary, isn't it?

The psalmist speaks of the life of creatures on Earth, how they are all fed by God, and how when He turns away from them they panic. When He withdraws their breath, they die.

As a young baby coming out of the womb cannot live on its own unless it breathes, so we cannot live in relationship to God without the Holy Spirit given to us—without the Holy Breath that we breathe.

And without the Holy Spirit, the Holy Breath, we have no peace. Without the Spirit, it is like what happens when we stop breathing. We get anxious. We become frightened because that which gives us life has stopped.

The peace that we do not have in this world is because we do not have peace inside. And we do not have peace inside if we do not breathe, if we do not have the holy breath—the Holy Spirit living in us, breathing in us, giving us life.

Without it, we become anxious. Then our outer life begins to reflect that.

That isn't what God wants for us.

For reasons beyond our comprehension, God loves us and desires relationship with us, covenant with us. For reasons beyond our comprehension, God loves us and desires to give us mercy. For reasons beyond our comprehension, God loves us and desires to save every last one of us, and give us breath, the Holy Spirit.

We will never fully comprehend why, but...

All we need to do is say "yes."

Yes, I would like to breathe.

Yes, I would like Your presence living in me.

Yes, I would like *rich relationship* with You.

What God desires of us is ... *us*.

---

[9] Psalm 104:24-29, NLT First Edition.

And so let *each of us* make this *very personal*. Pray something like this, but in your own words:

"Lord, I seek rich relationship with You as close as my very breath—not simply a set of instructions, doctrines, or ways to behave, but You living with me and in me. I ask Your forgiveness for all the things I've done that have kept me from You. Come to live with me, in me, through me. Make this covenant with You full."

That close—as close as the breath that goes to every cell of your body.

Pray for that kind of covenant, that relationship, that close, *that close* and *that rich*—now, and everyday. It is peace, mercy, breath of life.

18.
Heresy Explained

Most of us don't have occasion to use the word *heresy* in our daily conversations. It's one of those highly charged words that is seldom employed except perhaps by theologians or people hotly engaged in church debate, and occasionally in the press when someone expresses an unpopular position on any topic. It is most commonly used to put down someone—on either side—who disagrees.

This is not to imply that one opinion in a disagreement is just as valid as the other. Rather, it is to observe that "heresy" is often misused to smear an opponent and frighten his or her supporters, especially in church disagreements. More, it is commonly used as a synonym for "wrong doctrine." Even though wrong doctrine may be an issue, that isn't what makes for heresy, nor does holding wrong doctrine make you a heretic. It is *not what you think*, but what you *do* with what you think.

As with Law, we have some unlearning ahead of us:

The Greek root of our word "heresy" is *hairesis*. Let's begin with a couple of key places where this word is used in Scripture, and then I'll give its actual definition.

In Acts 24, some Jewish opponents of Paul (also a Jew, of course) accused him before the local governor of causing strife. Paul defends himself this way:

> And they neither found me in the temple disputing with anyone nor inciting the crowd, either in the synagogues or in the city. Nor can they prove the things of which they now accuse me. But this I confess to you, that according to the Way which they call a sect, so I worship the God of my fathers, believing all things which are written in the Law and in the Prophets.[1]

This is the important verse: "But this I confess to you, that according to the Way which they call a *sect*, so I worship the God of my fathers." The word translated as "*sect*" is the Greek *hairesis*, or heresy. Remember Paul is a Jew, so this isn't a Jewish-Christian dispute. It is a different group of Jews than those who believe what Paul believes, and they are accusing Paul of *promoting a sect*.

---

[1] Acts 24:12-14, NKJV.

Elsewhere, Peter uses that same word, which the New King James Version renders "heresies." Other translations use "heretical doctrines," "sects," "lies," "things that are wrong" or "teachings."

> But there were also false prophets among the people, even as there will be false teachers among you, who will secretly bring in *destructive heresies*, even denying the Lord who bought them, and bring on themselves swift destruction.[2]

Haeresis, the Greek word for "heresy," actually doesn't mean something negative or wrong. It means an opinion, or a way, or a choice. In fact, there is an early Christian writer who talks about the "heresy of the Gospel." As he uses it, the expression refers to the *way* of the Gospel. It is not a criticism of the Gospel, but simply the use of that word to mean a way or a path. So one of the confusions of this word "heresy" is that in Greek it can refer to something neutral or even positive.

When Peter uses the word in the passage above, he modifies it with a strong negative adjective, *apoleia* ("destructive, ruinous, pernicious"), to make his point. And in fact, when it is used in the sense of a destructive opinion, what that connotes primarily is "to break into factions"; in other words, to take the unity that exists and break it by promoting an idea that will divide believers. That is the negative sense in which this word—with an adjective or by the context—is used. Eugene Peterson's *The Message* captures the key idea of heresy in this verse effectively:

> They'll smuggle in destructive divisions, pitting you against each other...

One more example from Scripture. In Galatians 5, starting in v. 19, Paul says this:

> When you follow the desires of your sinful nature, the results are very clear: sexual immorality, impurity, lustful pleasures, idolatry, sorcery, hostility, quarreling, jealousy, outbursts of anger, selfish ambition, dissension, division...[3]

Division—that English word here is from the word *hairesis*. It is still the same word that means choice or sect, but it is translated *division* because in context (a long string of negative words) it implies an opinion, a concept, a sect, that is driving a wedge between believers. The point Paul is making here is that people are destroying the Body of Christ, including through contrary opinion used to divide.

Simply put, heresy refers, in a neutral way, to a choice, a way or an opinion. When it is used negatively in Scripture, with an adjective such as "destructive," or when it is clearly negative by context, it means to *break into factions*, to *cause* division or schism (another word for division).[4]

---

[2] 2 Peter 2:1, NKJV.
[3] Galatians 5:19-20.
[4] The Greek word *skhísma* means a tear, separation or division. It is distinguished from heresy in that it is the *result*, whereas heresy is the *cause*.

"Heresy" doesn't mean "wrong doctrine." In the negative sense it means using something—doctrine or practice or gossip or subversive leadership—to break up the loving community of the church.

Wrong doctrine can be used for such heresy—to divide—*but so can right doctrine!* In fact, many of us have experienced individuals and groups within churches that have used correct doctrine in such a legalistic, self-righteous way that they have caused division and harm to others in the church. This is heresy at its finest.

One of the reasons the church constructed the creeds (Nicene, Athanasian, Apostles) was to combat wrong doctrine—that is, a misunderstanding of the basics of the faith. That is a sufficient reason in and of itself, like a good dictionary or map. But the creeds also helped to combat heresy that came from misunderstandings of the faith. A more-proper term for those misunderstandings is *heterodoxy*—deviating from the norm.

Heresy happened when these heterodoxies were being used by certain people to cause factions. They promoted heterodoxies to produce an isolating, self-righteous sect. The First Edition of the New Living Translation pointedly puts it this way:

...the feeling that everyone is wrong except those in your own little group.[5]

Many people use the word *heresy* to mean "bad doctrine." Bad doctrine is a real problem, but it is not in itself heresy.

Heresy is creating faction or division, rather than being simply bad doctrine. *Even correct doctrine can be heresy.* Even *accusations* of heresy can themselves be heresy, if delivered in a way that sows division or hurtfully attacks the accused.

Let's listen again to more from this chapter of Galatians, as Paul contrasts the attitude and behavior of a sinful versus a loving life. He is writing to Christians. The italicized words specifically address the issue of doctrine, conflict and heresy in the Church:

For the whole law can be summed up in this one command: "Love your neighbor as yourself." But if you are always *biting and devouring one another*, watch out! Beware of destroying one another.[6] ... When you follow the desires of your sinful nature, the results are very clear: sexual immorality, impurity, lustful pleasures, idolatry, sorcery, *hostility, quarreling, jealousy, outbursts of anger, selfish ambition, dissension, division, envy*, drunkenness, wild parties, and other sins like these. Let me tell you again, as I have before, that anyone living that sort of life will not inherit the Kingdom of God. But the Holy Spirit produces this kind of fruit in our lives: *love, joy, peace, patience, kindness, goodness, faithfulness, gentleness, and self-control.*[7]

---

[5] Galatians 5:20, NLT First Edition. The Second Edition (2004) simply says "divisions." See footnote 3 and Galatians 5:19-20 quote on previous page.

[6] Galatians 5:14-15.

[7] Galatians 5:19-23a.

We seem to have little difficulty seeing the sinfulness of sexual immorality, idolatry or lust, but we quickly indulge in hostility, dissension and division to "defend the Gospel." It's the same as claiming that we commit adultery or worship idols to "defend the Gospel"! They are *all* sin, and *none of them* can be excused as a defense of the Good News.

With this understanding of heresy ("to cause division") in the life of the Body of Christ, let's look at some of the classic challenges to the faith—heterodoxies—over the centuries.

MODALISM

One heterodoxy that produced heresy is modalism (also called *Sabellianism*). Modalism is this idea: In the Godhead, there are not really three separate Persons (Father, Son, Holy Spirit). There's just one God, and He acts in different "modes." Sometimes He acts in the mode of the Father, sometimes in the mode of the Son, and sometimes in the mode of the Holy Spirit, depending upon the need. Said differently, He wears different masks depending upon His intention and purpose at the moment.

The problem with this idea is it says God fundamentally is a fraud: He pretends. That is why it was rejected by the Church. It also makes a hash of events such as the baptism of Jesus, where the Holy Spirit descends on Jesus and the voice of the Father is heard to say, "This is My beloved Son, in whom I am well pleased."[8] *Is the Father also standing there as Jesus, and descending on Him, and calling Himself His own beloved Son?* Modalism does not hold up under scrutiny.

What the Church very early said is that there are three Persons but one God. Many writings, including famously those of St. Augustine, address this doctrine, and it is set forth clearly in the Athanasian Creed.[9] Here's a key sentence from it:

> For there is one Person of the Father, another of the Son, and another of the Holy Spirit. But the godhead of the Father, of the Son, and of the Holy Spirit, is all one, the glory equal, the majesty co-eternal.

ARIANISM

A related early heterodoxy that also caused heresy was Arianism, promoted by a fellow named Arius who lived in the 4th century. He said God *created* before all things a son, but he was neither equal to nor co-eternal with the Father. According to Arius, Jesus was a *supernatural creature* not quite human, not quite divine. Another way this was presented was to say that God the Father, God the Son and God the Holy Spirit are of different *substances*, that is, different natures or orders of being.

---

[8] Matthew 3:17, NKJV.

[9] A good, concise review is found in Robert Krueger's "The Origin and Terminology of the Athanasian Creed" at www.wlsessays.net/files/KruegerOrigin.pdf.

And so the Church, in the face of this heresy (which was producing division), asserted *homoousios* (pronounced *homo-u'-see-os*). That means *of the same substance*. The Nicene Creed includes a sentence to combat this specific heterodoxy:

> We believe in one God the Father Almighty, Maker of heaven and earth, and of all things visible and invisible, and in one Lord Jesus Christ, the only-begotten Son of God, begotten of the Father before all worlds, God of God, Light of Light, Very God of Very God, *begotten, not made,* being of *one substance* with the Father by whom all things were made.

"Begotten, not made" makes the point that Jesus was not *created* by the Father but was with Him before anything was created, and "one substance" means that Jesus is God in His very nature.

As you can see, both Modalism and Arianism are controversies over the fundamental nature of God, and of the person and role of Jesus Christ. Other heterodoxies disputed on this same issue, and one purpose of the creeds was to clear up misunderstandings, and reduce the disputes and subsequent divisions they caused.

DOCETISM

Notable among these other heterodoxies is something called Docetism, which is an element of another heresy called Gnosticism (we'll get back to that). The idea of the Docetists—and this is similar to Arianism—was Jesus was not really fully human. He may have been God, but He never became fully human. They might say He was fully divine, but He only *pretended*, or *seemed*, to be human. Again, the root of the problem here is the implication of fraud in the Godhead.

There is one old Docetist text that describes the Crucifixion. It pictures the body as Jesus hanging on the cross suffering, and the *real, divine* Christ standing on a distant hill watching and laughing—because as God He cannot suffer.

That is the Docetist heresy. It shows us a God who is a fraud, who never actually had His own physical body nor died on the cross, who fundamentally lies to us in His relationship with us.

DONATISM

The last heresy I want to talk about in this chapter is called Donatism. And this one is especially important to us today because it is raging worldwide in the Church, across denominations, and in many forms. The idea of the early Donatists was this: Only those living a blameless life belonged in the Church.

Their idea was the Sacraments, of which there were two key ones—Baptism and Communion—were *ineffective* if the person celebrating them was not sinless. Also, any ordination performed by a bishop who was not sinless had no effect and no ordination truly happened.

Donatism was considered a holiness movement in the early Church—where those who were in it strove to be holy, and they excluded from their company those who they did not believe to be blameless and sinless. *This still goes on today!* It ranges from not allowing people to sing in the choir if they are having troubles at home, to refusing to receive Communion at the hands of a bishop, priest or pastor whose theology differs from your own—especially on hot, controversial issues.

Don't mistake my point here: I'm not saying that differences in theology are irrelevant. They can be extremely important—can even be salvation issues—but to suggest that the minister's own sinlessness is essential to God's being able to be present—in Communion, Baptism, ordination or anything else—is to assert God's powerlessness in the presence of His sinful creatures.

Can our sin get in the way of our relationship with God? Of course it can. But does God depend upon the sinlessness of His followers and pastors to be able to be present in Communion, baptism, ordination, prayer, care, teaching or anything else? No.

The fundamental idea of the Church is we are all sinners gathered together. Our responsibility to each other is as we should teach what we know to be true, hold each other accountable, love and edify each other, and speak with humility, love and directness when we believe that there is sin in someone's life.

What the Donatists did while the Christian Church was still basically one church, with local bishops leading geographical regions called dioceses, was to set up competing bishops in every diocese of Northern Africa, where they held most of their influence. They created competing Churches, separate from those of the original and undivided Church, because they believed that any bishop in the original Church was a sinner, and therefore nothing he did had any effect. His actions were deemed to be unholy in their roots and unholy in their effects.

St. Augustine (A.D. 354–430) is the one who wrote convincingly about the Donatist heresy (and note that it was *heresy*—it intentionally divided the Church by claiming sinlessness and establishing competing Churches!). Augustine drew the heart of the Church to understand that though filled with sinners, it was the *unity of the Body* that mattered, and that the division into another separate parallel Church was heresy. It was *heresy* because it was breaking into factions. It cut off part of the Body of Christ. That is the division that the Church contested.

Augustine's arguments were important, because just as the Donatists claimed that actions by the original church bishops were ineffective because they were sinners, so original church bishops claimed actions by the Donatist bishops were ineffective because they were heretics! It cut both ways, and still does today!

Here's what Augustine said in *Epistle 185*,[10] paragraph 43, in refusing to rebaptize someone who had strayed from the faith and was being restored, and *who had been baptized by Donatists*:

> "Because I do not … [refuse to recognize] the stamp of the monarch, when I correct the ill-doing of a deserter."

Augustine was familiar with the Roman military's tradition of tattooing the hand of soldiers to mark them as the emperor's. His quote means that if you are tattooed (or cut as in circumcision) as a soldier or servant of the monarch, then even

---

[10] http://www.newadvent.org/fathers/1102185.htm

if you have deserted, you still bear the emperor's mark.[11] Said differently, the evidence of marking *remains* even if you have fled or misbehaved. When you return you may need correction, but you are still his and don't need to be marked again.

What he means is it that it doesn't matter who baptized you or when—once baptized, you are marked as Christ's own forever! You do not need to be baptized again. The mark is already there and is permanent.

What's interesting about this is the Roman Catholic Church today does not follow what Augustine said. If you have been baptized in a Protestant Church and you want to join the Roman Church, they will re-baptize you.

If you have been baptized in an Anglican Church and you want to join a Baptist Church, they will re-baptize you. If you are baptized as an infant, anywhere, the Baptists will re-baptize you.

One of the primary arguments Augustine made in settling the Donatists' heresy is we do not re-baptize in the church. We believe that when you are baptized, you are baptized. That is what Augustine said.

The Donatist *heresy* was the breaking off of a group who considered themselves holier, basically without sin, compared to the rest of the Church. The reason the Church declared that to be heterodoxy is because we are *not* blameless. We all sin and fall short of the glory of God, and we are all in the same boat together. That is the reality of it, and the Church said it very early on—that any pretensions to being pure, blameless and holy are wrong. They are contrary to the Gospel. They are contrary to Scripture. They are contrary to the unity of the Body. They divide it into factions.

As a side comment on all of this is the sheer size of Augustine's argument. It is called *Epistle 185* (to Boniface from Augustine), and it goes on to about 60 pages. What is remarkable about Augustine's argument is his profound concern for the unity of the Church, that we all be one undivided body.

Augustine followed Jesus, who said,

> "I am praying not only for these disciples but also for all who will ever believe in me through their message. I pray that they will all be one, just as you and I are one—as you are in me, Father, and I am in you. And may they be in us so that the world will believe you sent me. I have given them the glory you gave me, so they may be one as we are one. I am in them and you are in me. May they experience such perfect unity that the world will know that you sent me and that you love them as much as you love me."[12]

If we are honest with ourselves, we have failed to listen to the prayer of Jesus for us, and have failed to be convinced by Augustine when he reminded us of it.

---

[11] "The recruit should not be tattooed with the pin-pricks of the official mark as soon as he has been selected, but first be thoroughly tested in exercises so that it may be established whether he is truly fitted for so much effort." P. 8, from the 4th-century book *Epitome of Military Science*, by Flavius Vegetius Renatus, translated by N. P. Milner, Liverpool University Press, 1996.
[12] John 17:20-23.

19.
Heresy Continued

WRESTLING ABOUT DOCTRINE

The very challenge of discussing heresies, ancient and modern, makes my head hurt. The debates that rage are often so rancorous and bitter that I don't even want to read the stuff—even from people I agree with.

Hence I want to warn you in advance that while we continue to review heresy, heresies and heretics, there will be, at the end, a quite-severe critique of all of this—not self-important, I hope, but what I believe is a necessary and overdue upbraiding of the Church's doctrines, and the cost of those doctrines, regardless of whether they are right or wrong. More later.

HOW TO DISAGREE

I believe we *do* need to be serious in understanding what the Lord wants us to know about Him, and what isn't true about Him. Right doctrine *is* important. But it never trumps love.

There will be points at which we will disagree. So long as we abide by the two commandments that Jesus has declared supreme, and on which our doctrine should hang, we can keep on talking to each other and loving each other. Jesus said,

> "'You shall love the LORD your God with all your heart, with all your soul, and with all your mind.' This is the first and great commandment. And the second is like it: 'You shall love your neighbor as yourself.' On these two commandments hang all the Law and the Prophets."[1]

Even if we have got our doctrine "right," if we apply it in a way that violates those two commandments, we've got it *wrong*.

This is a very hard thing for us to remember, because in the Church, people disagree—just as with politics, sports, families and life in general. Then they get

---

[1] Matthew 22:37-40, NKJV.

angry and bitter, and quickly dash to the violation of those two foundational commandments Jesus gave.

And when someone complains that the debate has become rancorous and mean, the charge is laid that the peacemakers value being "nice" over being in accord with God's will, that they stick their heads in the sand or are afraid to name aloud what is seriously wrong. Those who do not approve of vicious attack are themselves attacked—accused of being wimps, or quislings, or traitors—apparently in the hope of silencing them, or justifying the hateful attacker's words and methods.

My desire is that as we face serious issues in the Church, we approach them consistently with Jesus' two commands. Otherwise, it doesn't matter if we are *right about where we stand*, because we are *unholy at the roots*.

BLASPHEMY AGAINST THE HOLY SPIRIT

One of the worst manifestations of mean-spirited attack is the accusation that another person's belief is "blasphemy against the Holy Spirit."[2] "Blasphemy" means slander, contemptuous speech, verbal attack. This expression is an intentional weapon used—like the accusation of heresy—to condemn a point of view and frighten others away from it.

Again, I am *not* suggesting all points of view are equally valid. In fact, I believe some are profoundly mistaken, even dangerous. My objection here is to loveless, sarcastic, personal attack, and the hyperbole often used against opponents, raising emotions to a fever pitch. *This behavior is not of Christ.*

The reason *this* accusation is particularly egregious is that "blasphemy against the Holy Spirit" is the one sin Jesus calls unforgivable, which is why accusers use it. To accuse an opponent of an opinion or belief that is *unforgivable* and a *blasphemy against God*, however thrilling it might be to make such a charge, is to ignore Jesus' clear direction on how we are to treat each other.

More, biblical scholars are not agreed on what the expression "blasphemy against the Holy Spirit" actually means, so wielding such an accusation freely against one's opponents is the height of presumption.

I have heard this claim made so many times about so many points of dispute in the Christian faith that I think it is scandalous and reprehensible. We should avoid it with extraordinary care.

In *Epistle 185* (mentioned in Ch. 18), Augustine addresses the question of what blasphemy against the Holy Spirit really is. Here's what he says in paragraph 49:

> But this is the *hardness of heart even to the end of this life*, which leads a man *to refuse to accept remission of his sins* in the unity of the body of Christ, to which life is given by the Holy Ghost.

I think he is probably more right than any of the people I have heard claim that those who disagree with them have committed this unforgivable sin.

---

[2] Matthew 12:31.

I revisit this again here as a reminder that the fundamental issue of heresy is not wrong doctrine, but *causing division in the Body of Christ*. This can be done with wrong doctrine, but it can also be done with *right doctrine and wrong attitude*.

That said, let's look at a few more heresies that have arisen in the Church throughout history, and that we often still face today. Then we will consider a serious critique of all of this.

Mormonism

My best friend when I was growing up was a Mormon. If you know anything about the Mormons—"The Church of Jesus Christ of Latter-Day Saints"—then you know this is a church with an extraordinary focus on family. They set aside each Thursday as "Family Night," just to have the family together. They don't do anything else. They don't go out skating or playing hockey or to the movies. They spend the time with the family.

This is hugely reminiscent of Shabbat, the setting aside by Jews of one day a week to rest and do no work (from the 4th Commandment). Shabbat begins on Friday evening at dusk, with the family gathered for a meal, prayers and blessings, and time together.

(In theory Sunday is the "Christian Sabbath," but in practice we no longer set aside the entire day for rest and time with God and family. We may attend church, but then for most Christians it's back to the daily routine of our lives. I find it telling that we vocally affirm the Ten Commandments, even fight for the right to post them in public places, and yet so easily ignore this inconvenient one: "Six days you shall labor and do all your work, but the seventh day is a sabbath to the LORD your God. On it you shall not do any work…"[3])

But back to the Mormon Family Night. This is a wonderful idea. We adopted the concept in my family as soon as we heard about it. The focus on family is surely one of the things that attracts people to Mormonism.

Then what is it about Mormonism that is heterodoxy, or wrong doctrine? It clearly self-identifies as Christian, and Mormons actively promote Christian values in the public square. So what's the problem?

Simply this: Mormon doctrine says that God—the God of this earth, the One we worship—was once a man on a previous earth—not this planet, but another one elsewhere in space. Because He lived an obedient life, the reward for His obedience was that He earned a planet to populate and be God. We are literally His offspring.

You too, if you are male, can become God of your own planet. To do so you must have many children, be successful in business, and obey all of the commandments—633 from the Old and New Testaments (if you're keeping track, rabbinic Jews count 613).

There is much more to basic Mormonism, from the source of the Book of Mormon to baptizing one's ancestors, that is seriously problematic, both in

---

[3] Exodus 20: 9-10a, NIV.

doctrine and in *the separation from other Christians caused by those doctrines*, but these two issues should be sufficient to understand why Mormonism is considered both heterodoxy and heresy.

JEHOVAH'S WITNESSES

The Mormons and the Jehovah's Witnesses are the only two current organizations I will mention, primarily because they are the two you're most likely to encounter at your front door, and it helps to know what they believe—especially those things they won't share with you at the door.

The Jehovah's Witnesses usually really know their scripture, and they share a beautiful vision of a redeemed earth with all people and creatures living in peace.

Like the Mormons, there are many issues of concern with doctrine and separation that are foundational to what Jehovah's Witnesses believe. First is that they do not believe in the divinity of Jesus Christ, nor in the purpose and value of His death on the cross.

To sustain their views, they have created their own translation of the Bible, called the "New World Translation." Compare the first sentence of the Gospel of John, as read in the New King James Version, and in the New World Translation:

> In the beginning was the Word, and the Word was with God, and the Word was God. (NKJV)

> In [the] beginning the Word was, and the Word was with God, and the Word was a god. (NWT)

Notice that final word *god* is lowercase. If you ask them what that means, they will say there is only one God and Jesus isn't a part of it. There are many smaller gods, and Jesus was one of those. (Also, the "a" in "a god" isn't in the Greek and isn't implied in the Greek, even though Greek grammar allows it.[4])

Elsewhere they substitute "stake" for "cross," insert words and punctuation not in the original Greek or Hebrew, and make the English text conform to their theologies, rather than let their theologies be formed by the text.[5]

They also believe that just 144,000 people will reach heaven. The challenge is to be one of those 144,000 out of the 10-100 billion people who have ever lived on Earth. That's a tough challenge, even if you are one of the seven million Jehovah's Witnesses. *(Half-humorous, half-serious aside: If there are seven million Witnesses, and only 144,000 will reach heaven, why do they bother trying to convert anyone? Isn't that just making more competition?)*

---

[4] That is, nouns can have a definite article, *the*, but the indefinite article, *a*, isn't a feature of Greek. When no word appears before a noun, the context might determine whether it should be understood in English to be "a" or not.

[5] To a degree this is true of all translations, but it is particularly overt in the NWT.

Jehovah's Witnesses separate from the rest of the Body of Christ based on these beliefs. Thus it is heterodoxy and heresy.

ANCIENT HERESIES – WHY DO WE CARE?

Below are a handful of ancient heresies, condemned by the Church many centuries ago. Why do we care? Well, in part because understanding how someone got it wrong can help us avoid similar errors, but also because most of these are like perennial weeds—they keep reappearing, though in new guises.

GNOSTICISM

The Gnostics believed that they lived by special revelation, and that this was because they were superior beings to the great unwashed masses—basically, you and me. *Gnosis* means "knowledge" in Greek, and is the root of the word "Gnostic." The Gnostics believed in *salvation through secret knowledge*.

Gnosticism was a problem in Ephesus, so one of the purposes of Paul's letters to the Ephesians and to Timothy (who was sent to be pastor to the Ephesians) is to refute some of the Gnostic ideas. This is more obvious in the Greek text than in English, because Paul intentionally uses Gnostic terms in his writing in order to refute or redefine them. This was similarly true with the Colossians.

The Gnostics taught that there was a vast array of principalities and powers, godly beings and thoughts, and it emanated wisdom to the initiates (the "superior people" who were Gnostics). This vast array in Greek is called, by the Gnostics, the *pleroma*—a word that means, basically, fullness.

Paul makes the point that all of the Godhead and all "principalities and powers" are contained in Christ:

> Beware lest anyone cheat you through philosophy and empty deceit, according to the tradition of men, according to the basic principles of the world, and not according to Christ. For in Him dwells all the *fullness* of the Godhead bodily; and you are complete in Him, who is the head of all principality and power.[6]

The word translated as "fullness" in English is *pleroma*, and not by accident. Paul was making a point. It was and is all about Christ, not an imagined heaven populated with beings who whisper secrets to the initiated superior humans.

Lest this seem like ancient and irrelevant heresy, Gnosticism has enjoyed a heady revival in recent decades, especially with the discovery in 1945 of the Gospel of Thomas. It was found near Nag Hammadi, Egypt, along with a collection of Gnostic manuscripts, and begins by declaring, "These are the secret sayings that the living Jesus spoke…" It purports to be the hidden way to enlightenment, obtained only by those initiated into the mysteries that Jesus secretly taught.

---

[6] Colossians 2:8-10, NKJV.

The Gospel of Thomas was widely known and rejected by the early Church as a false gospel, falsely attributed to the Apostle Thomas. It is not surprising that it would appeal to a culture now so committed to private, individualistic spirituality and "spiritual enlightenment," but it is far from the mark of orthodox Christian belief.

MONTANISM

Montanism was a movement within the Christian Church that arose in the second century. It said, in effect, "The Second Coming of Jesus is almost here—any minute, any day. He will be here."[7] Montanus, Prisca and Maximilla were the leaders of this sect, and purported to prophesy under the power of the Holy Spirit. When they spoke, the words they used were in the first person, as if God Himself were speaking through them, and they were passive conduits of His voice. Their prophecies were considered normative and had to be followed, even if they contradicted Scripture—because theirs was a further revelation, a new thing that the Spirit of God was doing.

Their public declarations were spectacular and ecstatic worship events, big productions, along with rigorous personal holiness, fasting, and regulations for sexual purity. Their version of Christianity spread like wildfire.

This same problem exists today. There are sects and "prophetic" parachurch ministries that do exactly the same thing.

Does this mean anything that smacks of the supernatural and the presence of the Holy Spirit is untrustworthy or heretical? No. But it should put us on guard not to be swept away by showmanship, drama and the purported voice of God speaking through charismatic leaders in the Church. Paul teaches balance and discernment on prophecy:

> Do not stifle the Holy Spirit. Do not scoff at prophecies, but test everything that is said. Hold on to what is good.[8]

Yet there are sects all over the world that regularly claim to prophesy from the Holy Spirit in ways that are flat-out contradictory to what Scripture says. If you ask them how they can do that, they will say this is a new Word for a new time. This is the Montanist heresy, and it brings us to Humanism.

HUMANISM AND THEISM

Do you recall Jean-Jacques Rousseau, Voltaire and the French Enlightenment? They are key elements in the growth of Humanism (sometimes also called *Modernism*). Without getting mired in specifics, let me suggest that beyond the "heresies" listed above (and aware that each has reappeared in new guises), there is a wider battle underway in the Church and culture. This battle shapes the language,

---

[7] Numerous cults say the same thing, and claim their leader is the Second Coming of Christ.
[8] 1 Thessalonians 5:19-21.

nature and understanding of many of our debates. It is between *Humanism* and *Theism*. There are two layers to this contest, and we'll address the most recent first. The older, lingering layer will be addressed shortly, in the *Severe Critique*.

To oversimplify a bit, the *Humanists* tend to be atheists, agnostics and Deists,[9] and believe "man is the measure of all things,"[10] meaning that *there is no external standard by which we live* (such as from God), but that all standards, including our moral values, come from humans, arise from our circumstances, and may differ depending upon needs and choices.

The *Theists* tend to believe that God is the measure of all things, and He communicates His will and Law through revelation, and holds humans accountable to it. In effect, *He is the external standard by which we live.*

Both the Humanists and Theists have able proponents of their worldview, some quite winsome, others quite mean or condescending. Not a surprise.

I want us to be conscious of how much we are the descendants of debates that have been underway not just for years but for centuries.

Humanism

I consider myself a child of the Enlightenment. My first degree is in physics. I love science and the scientific method. I love that whole approach to understanding the world. It is not the only approach that I love, but I love that approach.

So, I honor the Enlightenment and even the democratic ideals from the French Revolution, such as the overthrow of the hereditary class-system and a parasitic aristocracy. But I'm also aware of how amazingly intolerant this movement is to those who do not support it. One of the worst examples was Voltaire himself, always a good source for condescension and sarcasm, who said he looked forward to the day when the last aristocrat was strangled with the intestines of the last priest.[11] Or my own, much-milder experience in a liberal seminary, where the few of us who were more conservative were regarded as "fundies" and dim bulbs (not too bright) by others. If there is a most-common sin in this movement, it is a sense of intellectual superiority. In fact, one subgroup of this movement has even named itself "the Brights."

This is understandable, since Humanism elevates human reason above all else, and in fact sees it as the source of all values and progress.

Simply put, the liberal, modernist movement in Christianity is heir to the values of Humanism, and is itself sometimes labeled "Christian Humanism." There are debates within the camp, of course, which I will avoid for now. My

---

[9] A fast definition: An atheist believes God does not exist, that there is no deity at all. An agnostic is unconvinced whether God exists or not, or believes that such existence is unknowable. A Deist believes there is a God but that He is uninvolved in the universe or human life other than as original creator.

[10] Protagoras, Greek philosopher, ca. 485–410 B.C.

[11] Note, of course, that both the aristocracy and the Church in France were riddled with corruption and privilege. It wasn't hard for anyone to hate both.

point is that if we realize the origins and foundational truths of Humanism within liberal Christianity, we will understand why it sees the world as it does, why it defends and supports various causes, and why it reacts as it does to more conservative or orthodox Christians.

Theism

Theism has its own strengths and sins. As against Humanism, it tends to have a robust sense of the existence and actions of God. For theists, God is not a superstition or abstract principle, nor an irrelevant Creator who made the world and left it on its own. He is present, involved, concerned, directive and holds humans accountable to the standards that He set. He reveals Himself through Scripture and encounters the world, nations, cultures and individuals, directly, consciously, immanently, omnisciently and omnipotently. (I acknowledge that there are "liberal" Christians who would affirm every word of this basic description of theism. My point is not to deny such robust faith, but to draw broad outlines of the two camps and how they generally differ.)

I consider myself a child of Christianity. I love Jesus and all that He taught and did, for the world and for me, to reconcile us to God. I find in Him wisdom that stands the test of time, is a solid foundation for moral decisions, and yet also breaks open prisons of thinking and selfishness. He teaches me to love far beyond what I am naturally inclined to do. I love Paul and all the authors of the New Testament. They challenge my values and my actions, and they help lift me to new heights of servanthood and care for others.

I love the Old Testament, though I find nothing "old" about it at all. I find a robust, living God there, and a people like me, who declare their willingness to be faithful and then fail again and again. God encounters them again and again, and not as some distant abstract Being, but as a jealous, emotion-charged Creator and lover of souls, who again and again calls them, loves them, forgives them, sticks close to them and never gives up on them. Israel is His bride, and He loves her like crazy.

I'm fully aware of the huge range of depictions of God in these pages, from angry to joyful, from gentle to brutal, from loud to silent. But I am not dissuaded from belief in Him or His love by these depictions—rather, I am made more aware of how Other He is than I am, and how much I must stretch and be stretched to come to any understanding or harmony with His will and love for the world.

Further, I see the life and teachings of Jesus as naturally consistent with the God I meet in the Old Testament. It was the *only* Scripture Jesus read, taught or explained, and *never* did His teachings depart from or disagree with what was written there—though He often challenged the interpretations of others, most especially when they exempted themselves from its teachings, or held themselves up as holy and superior.

So I also consider myself as a child of the faith, an orthodox Christian and a *theist*. There are also many debates within this camp (some noted in these last two chapters), which I will avoid for now. But I'm also aware of how amazingly intolerant this movement is to those who do not support it.

This intolerance is excused ("Souls are at stake!") because the end—salvation, or orthodoxy, or right doctrine, or right worship, or right discipline, or holiness—is *so* important. But the end contains the means, and either enriches or poisons it.

At its worst, it has killed those who would not agree (as have the Humanists), but even more mildly it can be self-satisfied, arrogant and sarcastic.

It claims tradition and honest scholarship as its guide, and holds Scripture to be a pure transmission of God's revelation, as over against the "revisionists" who it believes rewrite or reinterpret the past and Scripture to suit their own desires and theories.

My point is that if we realize the origins and foundational truths of *Theism* within conservative, orthodox Christianity,[12] we will understand why it sees the world as it does, why it defends and supports various causes, and why it reacts as it does to more-liberal Christians.

We can comprehend why and how these two camps, *Humanism* and *Theism*, see the world and each other. I joke sometimes that it is the fight between John Wesley and Voltaire, being replayed in our age. We are the inheritors, the descendants, of a disagreement that has persisted in open conflict since the Enlightenment, though its origins extend back into the mists of time. There is plenty of intolerance to go around, and it shows up regularly on both sides.

Each side caricatures the other in order to show itself more worthy, yet the best of each still suffers from failure, as human weaknesses and selfishness rise up in each. Each side needs to listen to the best critiques from the other: They make us aware of our flaws and help keep us from lying about or hiding them.

For my part, I find great value in both Humanism and Theism, and great human weakness in both, but I come out on the side of Theism.

I take God seriously and believe Him to be active in the world, though profoundly unconfined by my theologies about Him. Which brings us to…

A SEVERE CRITIQUE

You may remember back in Chapter 14, "Covenant—The Law of Moses," I quoted Rabbi Ronald Isaacs, who said, "Judaism has always been more a religion of action and deed than belief and creed."

This is a deep and historically profound insight, and if understood is likely to remake how Christians understand who they are, and how to live life more fully in relationship to our Creator.

Philosophers love to draw parallels and make connections across centuries and cultures. The abstractions and categories created in doing so can provide insights

---

[12] In this I include Eastern Orthodoxy, Roman Catholicism, Anglicanism and Evangelical Protestantism, among others.

into how humans live, believe and behave—and there are surely deep commonalities among human communities, even when widely separated by distance or time.

But such abstraction and categorization is not universal. That is, not all cultures *think* this way. Oh, they do to a degree, but the real flowering of this approach to analyzing and describing human life and the world is essentially Greek in its origins,[13] especially in the West, and especially in Christianity.

Think of it like this: The entire Old Testament is essentially a narrative story about a people, *the Jews*, and their robust, constant, joyful, rocky, rebellious, dedicated, awestruck and argumentative love affair with God. They are so familiar with Him that they will yell and wrestle with Him, even turn on their heels in fits of pique, and yet they are so profoundly in awe they will not even say His name aloud. In the entire Old Testament there is virtually not a word of doctrine, nor a foundational philosophical proposition.

A philosophically minded person could look at it, and *impute* doctrine or philosophy, just as could be done with any narrative, but neither of these are in the worldview or methods of Hebrew thought.

The Greeks, on the other hand, developed a philosophical approach to human life and the world. "The unexamined life is not worth living," Socrates said, and this conviction characterizes their passion to examine and explain. They abstracted, categorized and organized what they observed, and drew parallels and distinctions. From these they were able to establish foundational propositions, and from these came doctrines: definitions of what fit or didn't fit the foundational propositions.[14] Whether it was the Platonists, the Aristotelians, the Stoics, the Rhetoricians, the Epicureans, the Cynics or the Skeptics (to name a few), the approach of abstraction, categorization, organization, proposition and doctrine was essentially the same: The various schools differed primarily on what values were key, and which were not. They had many gods, some of which were icons of these points of view, others of which were a means to self-satisfaction, or defense, or spiritual mystery. The Greeks were complex and deep thinkers, as well as being sensual and pleasure-seeking.

Greek philosophy intersected Hebrew thought at several key points throughout history:

- When Alexander the Great (356–323 B.C.) conquered the known world and Hellenized it. Greek became the common language of all the nations he defeated. (It's because of this that the New Testament was written in Greek.)

---

[13] Which has its own roots, of course, and elements of which also arose elsewhere and elsewhen across the globe.

[14] I know that something roughly parallel to this can be found in the Talmud, but the dating and place of its development actually supports the point I will be making shortly.

- When Rome, whose leaders were all trained by Greek teachers, conquered all the lands of Alexander, and more. Greek continued to be the common language, and Greek philosophy the way of thinking about the world. Pilate, the Roman governor, said to Jesus, "What is truth?"[15] This was a profoundly Greek question.

- When Paul, the Apostle to the Gentiles, explained the God of Israel (and Jesus) to people who didn't know how Jews thought, and didn't know the Old Testament, but who were accustomed to thinking in Greek philosophical categories (including their beliefs about Greek and Roman gods) and listening to rhetorically sound argument. Read Acts 17:16-34 for a quick insight into this. Paul was trained in rhetoric and continues this approach throughout most of his letters to the Gentile believers.

- When the expanding Church defined and defended itself in debate over many centuries, most of which took place between Gentile authors and leaders (starting in the second and third centuries), hence imbued with and expressed through Greek philosophical and rhetorical methods.

- When Thomas Aquinas discovered the writings of Aristotle, which had been lost to the West for centuries, and began to explain Christian theology in Greek philosophical terms (even transubstantiation, substance and accident are concepts from Aristotle).

- When Humanism arose, heavily dependent on Greek ideas, and began to claim values arising from human reason (in which the Greeks delighted). Remember that "man is the measure of all things" is from a contemporary of Socrates, the Greek philosopher Protagoras, who predated even Alexander the Great.

- When science arose, contesting religion for primacy in the lives and faith of people, and showing its superior and growing ability to cure disease, tap power from the atom, and travel even into space. It remains dominant to this day. Its roots, like the Enlightenment and Humanism, are largely Greek.[16]

Each of these intersections of Greek philosophy and Hebrew thought have affected how we understand and respond to the God of Israel, Who we Christians (along with Jews and Muslims[17]) believe to be the One True God.

Now, you may not have thought about it this way before, but the fact is that much of the theology that we do today, and that has been done in the Church

---

[15] John 18:38a.

[16] In the last few centuries the West has also been influenced by other great civilizations from the East and South, including in the areas of philosophy, mathematics, medicine and agriculture.

[17] I won't open up this topic further here. Muslims believe the God of the Old Testament is the one they call Allah (from the Hebrew *Elohim*). That's my only point.

since the second or third century, has, in *structure* and even in *content*, been fundamentally a *Greek philosophical debate*.

It is a Herculean effort to *explain* God, to abstract, categorize and organize what the Jews and followers of Jesus *experienced*, and then to draw parallels and make distinctions. From these were established foundational propositions, and from these came *doctrines*: definitions of what fit or didn't fit those propositions.

In this process we have Greekified the God of Israel. We have been misdirected into a philosophical structure and debate. Even the Theists, who proclaim a living and involved God, still promote and defend Him in philosophical terminology.

Instead of a robust, constant, joyful, rocky, rebellious, dedicated, awestruck and argumentative love affair with *God*, we have given our hearts to *propositions*. We have fallen in love with *our own thoughts* about God, and *missed* Him. I realize this is a difficult thing to hear or countenance. I myself want to jump up and defend good doctrine: Bad doctrine can lead to disaster. *I know!* And Paul warns us:

> For the time will come when they will not endure sound doctrine, but according to their own desires, because they have itching ears, they will heap up for themselves teachers; and they will turn their ears away from the truth, and be turned aside to fables.[18]

"Doctrine" here in Paul's quote is the Greek word *didaskalia*, and means "teaching, precept, proposition." And we do want to get that right, and not be led astray by fables instead of the truth.

But the truth isn't a concept to Jews or Christians: *God* is truth. So the issue fundamentally isn't about getting the doctrine right, so much as it is about getting the *relationship* right. If bad doctrine can lead us away from relationship, let's point it out and move on, seeking Him. *But right doctrine can and does also lead us away from Him*—when we focus on it *instead* of Him, and when we try to *grasp and explain Him* by doctrine.

We've now endured centuries of this approach to God, and we've missed the point, which is—well, *God*. It isn't our intellectual assent to propositions about Him that He seeks. It is our trust. It is intimacy. It is wrestling. He offers *love* and *covenant*, marriage, not highly ordered thoughts and explanations about Him. There is no explaining Him.

This problem began early, with the Hellenization of the Mediterranean and Middle East under Alexander the Great. It affected Judaism and Pharisaic methods in the Talmud, and it continued under Paul, both in his training as a Pharisee, and later as he sought to reveal the God of Israel in terms and concepts his Hellenized Gentile audience would grasp.

I understand this and don't even really object to it, as it is. It was a door for the Gentiles, an opening, to a new way of life and to salvation and the love of God. Paul taught them in their language, in their own modes of thought. But his

---

[18] 2 Timothy 4:3-4, NKJV.

goal was not to have his philosophy beat the other philosophies—it was to introduce them to their Creator and Savior.

In our day and age we have virtually abandoned the prospect of life with God, and have settled instead for debates about His nature and intentions.

Even the struggle between Humanism and Theism is almost entirely within the Greek philosophical arena. The Humanists adopt basic Greek philosophical ideals about the nature of man, from Socrates, Aristotle, Plato, from the Skeptics and others, and posit a world of human relations in which God is absent at best, and we are left to determine what we will value and what standards we will maintain.

But the Theists, though they proclaim a God in intimate relation with humanity, act largely like Deists, and posit their own worldview in carefully structured, detailed and defended doctrines, deduced from Scripture and Tradition, and re-formed into a philosophical system of considerable breadth and compass. Their thought is dialectical: One way is right and the other wrong. The smallest deviation is cause for attack. But even if it was consistent to the *nth* degree, and "right" in some elemental and universal system of "truth," it is still *Greek* and not *Hebrew* in its approach to God and to life.

Well, *so what?* Is God a Jew? Do we need to think like Hebrews in order to love God or be saved? Doesn't Scripture tell us that God is the God of all nations, and that in Him we are neither Greek nor Jew?

Yes, of course. But I contend that by putting all of our effort into explaining God, arguing about God, understanding God and defending God in philosophical terms, in debates about doctrine, we have fled the door labeled "God" and packed the hall for "lectures about God," delivered by contesting theologians.

We claim that we Christians are a wild olive branch, grafted into the root of Judaism. It would be more accurate to say we have cut ourselves off from the root, confident that we don't need the sustenance it supplies. We left Israel, moved to Greece, and were assimilated. Our memories of our Hebrew ancestry are just that, only memories—faded pictures in dusty boxes of a life lived by others long gone.

Christian liberals and Christian conservatives alike are essentially Greek in their approach to God and life. We differ on philosophy, we align with sparring schools, we accuse each other of ineptitude and bad motives, and we fight about how we each define and explain God.

We instead need to be married to God, and let Him have His way with us. We need to be ravished, not lectured.

20.
Trinity

In this chapter we are going to look at the Trinity. This is a concept that is easily discarded—and only with great foolishness, I believe. Note however that I said "concept." This will prove important as we seek to understand what Christians believe about that nature and character of God, and how that is applied in their conduct in the church and in the world.

By the way, this is one of the key issues that separates Christians and Jews, Christian and Muslims, Christians and Hindus, Christians and Buddhists, and Christians and _____ (fill in the blank). It even separates some Christians and other Christians, though either side of *that* divide would claim the other wasn't actually "Christian."

So, after I set forth the normative and confessional concept of the Trinity within orthodox Christian theology, then we'll go a step further, and engage the issue of *concept* and *ontology*.[1] Stay tuned. There is much to be revealed here, in history and in how we think.

Christians believe Scripture teaches that there is one God in three Persons.

Not three gods in competition with each other.

Not one God operating in three modes.[2]

But rather, Christians believe that there are three Persons who coexist eternally in unending, loving relationship with one another—glorifying each other, edifying each other, working with and through each other.

Yet we need to recognize that what we know about God and what we assert about this "Trinity of Persons in one God" is *deduced* from what is *revealed* to us in Scripture. That is, nowhere in either the Old or New Testament do we find an explicit statement that the nature of God is "three Persons in one God," nor that

---

[1] A study of the ultimate, intrinsic nature of something. More later.
[2] Modalism, discussed previously in the chapter on heresy (Chapter 18).

the Father, Son and Holy Spirit are of one substance (Greek *homoousios*[3])—also a part of the normative definition of Trinity in Christian theology.

So let's look at what is revealed in Scripture.

Remember the story of Jesus on the road to Emmaus with a couple of His followers, shortly after the Crucifixion and Resurrection? He said to them:

> "You foolish people! You find it so hard to believe all that the prophets wrote in the Scriptures. Wasn't it clearly predicted that the Messiah would have to suffer all these things before entering his glory?" Then Jesus took them through the writings of Moses and all the prophets, explaining from all the Scriptures the things concerning himself.[4]

The Greek actually begins something more like, "You who *don't perceive* and whose hearts are *slow to believe*…"

The "Scriptures" referred to here are the Old Testament, because those were the only Scriptures of Jesus and His followers. "The writings of Moses" refers to Genesis, Exodus, Numbers, Leviticus and Deuteronomy (*Torah* in Hebrew). The "prophets" (*Nevi'im* in Hebrew) refers to Joshua, Judges, Samuel, Kings, Isaiah, Jeremiah and Ezekiel, plus the 12 "Minor Prophets."[5]

Jesus used passages from these Scriptures to explain to these followers who and what the Messiah was foretold to be. That is, the Redeemer of Israel (and the world) was spoken about in 1500 years of biblical writings, and the events, signs and sufferings of this coming Messiah were foretold. Jesus showed them how He fulfilled these prophesies, and their eyes were opened: They now *perceived* what they had previously failed to perceive, and *believed* what they had been slow of heart to believe.

All well and good. Israel was yearning for a Messiah to free her—especially from the yoke of the Romans, and Messiah had been predicted. Jesus helped these two (on the road to Emmaus) understand that He fulfilled what had been foretold about Messiah.

There have been many others who claimed to be Messiah, even in Jesus' time, and the claim has been made repeatedly among the Jews, and a number of Christian sects, right down to our own day.

---

[3] In the early Church's debates over the Trinity, some argued the three Persons were of one substance—*homoousios*. Others contended the three Persons were of "similar" substance—*homoiousios*. These two words differ by one letter—*I*—called *iota* in the Greek alphabet. The wags of that day thus said there was only "one iota" of difference between them. And that's as much as we'll go into the issue here.

[4] Luke 24:25-27.

[5] Hosea, Joel, Amos, Obadiah, Jonah, Micah, Nahum, Habakkuk, Zephaniah, Haggai, Zechariah and Malachi.

Such a claim is not rejected out of hand by Jews, of Jesus' time or ours, and messianic fever was and is common. The question is whether *Jesus* was and is the Messiah, or if it is someone else.[6]

Does Jesus qualify, according to the prophecies of the Old Testament? Without expanding on the point here, the simple answer is *yes*, and certainly as fully as any other who has been claimed to be the Messiah.[7]

But whether Jesus is Messiah is *not* the key point of dispute over the issue of Trinity; rather, it is: Is Jesus *God*? And, does God consist of three Persons?

Many Jews would accept the *possibility* that Jesus is the Messiah, but recoil from the claim that He is God. This seems like blasphemy to them—*a man can't be God*—and God *cannot be divided!* So let's look at the issues.

THE SINGULARITY OF GOD

Consider this from Deuteronomy:

> Hear, O Israel: The LORD our God, the LORD is one![8]

This is the first sentence of what is called the *Shema*[9] (sheh-<u>mah</u>), and religious Jews recite this every day. It is a declaration that God is *indivisible*, and there is nothing like Him. He *alone* is God. This assertion immediately set ancient Jews apart from all of their neighbors, who believed in numerous gods with various powers and areas of authority: a god of war, another of fertility, weather, harvest, sunlight, darkness, etc. But the Jews had one. Just one.

Christianity arose as a Jewish sect, followers of a rabbi, Yeshua ("Jesus" is the Germanized or Anglicized version of this name), whose followers believed Him to be the Jewish Messiah.

It is in this context that Jesus and his followers arose—that is, as *monotheists*, deeply dedicated to the concept that God is one, alone, singular, unique, and there is nothing like Him or with Him (that is, no other gods). God Himself said,

> You shall have no other gods beside me.[10]

---

[6] John's two disciples found Jesus and said to Him, "John the Baptist sent us to ask, 'Are you the Messiah we've been expecting, or should we keep looking for someone else?'" (Luke 7:20, NLT)

[7] Including Theudas, Judas the Galilean (see Acts 5:33-39), Bar Kochba and the Lubavitcher Rebbe, among *many* others. See *50 Jewish Messiahs: The Untold Life Stories of 50 Jewish Messiahs Since Jesus and How They Changed the Jewish, Christian and Muslim Worlds*, in the Bibliography.

[8] Deuteronomy 6:4, NKJV. The entire *Shema* includes Deuteronomy 6:4-10, 11:13-21 and Numbers 15:37-41.

[9] שמע – *shema*, Hebrew for "Hear!"

[10] Exodus 20:3, NIV.

His followers were not to worship other "gods," as did those of neighboring cultures. *Neither Jesus nor His followers would abandon this foundational claim and identity.* To do so would have been repugnant to them.

Jesus Himself quotes the *Shema* when asked what the greatest commandment is.

> Then one of the scribes came, and having heard them reasoning together, perceiving that He had answered them well, asked Him, "Which is the first commandment of all?"
>
> Jesus answered him, "The first of all the commandments is: 'Hear, O Israel, the LORD our God, the LORD is one. And you shall love the LORD your God with all your heart, with all your soul, with all your mind, and with all your strength.' This is the first commandment. And the second, like it, is this: 'You shall love your neighbor as yourself.' There is no other commandment greater than these."[11]

So this *singularity* of God seems firmly established, and the Jews (including Jesus and His followers) seem committed to it. But some words and passages in the Old Testament should lead us to question just what it is that is being so strongly affirmed: Is this about *number*, or *nature*, or *uniqueness*, or *otherness*—or what?

Let's look: The word translated as "one" from Hebrew is *echad*.[12] But the word *echad*, though it is singular, can also be used in describing a *composite unity*, and it *is* used that way in the Old Testament. Here is one example:

> Therefore a man shall leave his father and mother and be joined to his wife, and they shall become one flesh.[13]

Two persons, yoked together, joined in marriage, are called *one* flesh—*echad*—the same word used to describe God in the Shema. There are other times when the word "one" is used in the Old Testament to describe a composite unity. Here God directs that two sticks become one:

> The word of the LORD came to me: "Son of man, take a stick of wood and write on it, 'Belonging to Judah and the Israelites associated with him.' Then take another stick of wood, and write on it, 'Ephraim's stick, belonging to Joseph and all the house of Israel associated with him.' Join them together into one stick so that they will become one in your hand."[14]

In fact, the original Hebrew is even more intense about oneness than the English translation reveals. It reads something more like this (admittedly quite awkward in English):

> And you son of Adam, you take for you *one* stick and write on it for Judah, and for sons of Israel, partner of him and partners of him take *one* stick and write on it

---

[11] Mark 12:28-31, NKJV.

[12] אחד, Hebrew for "one."

[13] Genesis 2:24, NKJV.

[14] Ezekiel 37:15-17, NIV.

for Joseph, stick of Ephraim, and all the house of Israel partner of him and partners of him, and join *one* to *one* for you to *one* stick, and they become *ones* in your hand.[15]

Every place you see the word *one*, it is the Hebrew *echad*.[16]

The point here is that the word used in Hebrew for "one" does not preclude a unity of parts, such as trinity. It doesn't *prove* God is a trinity, of course, but it demonstrates that this possibility is not outside of the normative use of the Hebrew word for "one."[17]

A kingdom, a nation, a city, a family, a book, a house, a sentence, a meal, an hour, a person, an atom, a neutron—each of these is one thing, but each is also a gathering of parts that compose that one thing. We might even say that there is nothing in human experience that is not a composite of other parts,[18] and even the *Shema* leaves open the possibility of this result.

Thus, the idea that *God is one* does not contradict the idea that there are three Persons in one God—not even in the Old Testament language about God. It doesn't prove it, but it doesn't preclude it.

There's more. You probably remember the story of Abraham and Sarah in Genesis 18:

> God appeared to Abraham at the Oaks of Mamre while he was sitting at the entrance of his tent. It was the hottest part of the day. He looked up and saw three men standing. He ran from his tent to greet them and bowed before them.[19]

This encounter is also the subject of a very famous icon by Andrei Rublev, discussed back in Chapter 8. It is titled *Trinity*, and is a drawing of those three men as they visit Abraham and Sarah. These three men are referred to in Genesis as God (Yahweh). Does this prove God is a trinity? No. But it is more than suggestive.

Here's another:

> In the beginning, *God* created the heavens and the earth. The earth was formless and void, and darkness was over the surface of the deep, and the *Spirit* of God was moving over the surface of the waters.[20]

What this illustrates is complexity in the nature of God. That is, the *one* that God is, is not an undifferentiated, impenetrable, pure singularity. In fact, such an ideal is more Platonic than biblical. The God of Scripture is robust, emotional and complex.

---

[15] Ezekiel 37:15-17, my translation.

[16] In the above translation, "*ones* in your hand" is not a typo. The word *one* is plural in the Hebrew—אחדים—because it refers to *they*, and grammatically, its ending has to match the plurality of *they*.

[17] See *The Jewish Trinity* by Yoel Natan for an extended study.

[18] Probably including the quark and the Higgs boson, or "God particle."

[19] Genesis 18:1-2, *The Message*.

[20] Genesis 1:1-2, NASB.

Still another: Note the singulars and the plurals are in the original Hebrew.

> Then God said, "Let *Us* make man in *Our* image, according to *Our* likeness; and let them rule over the fish of the sea and the birds of the sky and over the cattle and over all the earth, and over every creeping thing that creeps on the earth." So God created man in *His* own *image*; in the image of God *He* created him; male and female *He* created them.[21]

Let's just unpack that for a moment. God creates man and woman. "Man" is from the Hebrew word *adam*, meaning "mankind"—not a male, but male and female. Male and female, God created mankind in "*Our* image." One *could* even deduce from this that God is a *duality* of persons in one God (male and female). I'm not suggesting this, but rather I cite it to show that Scripture implies that *more than one* is present in the Godhead.

More: In Genesis 11 the people had decided that they were going to build a tower up to heaven so they could climb up and see God—the Tower of Babel. God decides this is arrogant on their part and decides to put an end to their enterprise. Here is what it says. The plural is in the Hebrew:

> "Come, let *Us* go down and confuse their language, so that they will not understand one another's speech." So *the LORD* scattered them abroad from there over the face of the whole earth; and they stopped building the city. Therefore its name was called Babel, because there the LORD confused the language of the whole earth; and from there the LORD scattered them abroad over the face of the whole earth.[22]

God says this to *whom*? One singular being says this to Himself? Let "us" go down? I suppose this could be some sort of majestic, royal circumlocution (some have argued this), but if so, it is quite odd. The plain reading would imply some *one* speaking to *another* one, or to other *ones*.

STILL MORE COMPLEXITY

Consider this parallel between Psalm 33 and John 1:

> By the **word** of the LORD the heavens were made,
> And by the **breath** of His mouth all their host.[23]

> In the beginning was the **Word**, and the Word was with God, and the *Word was God*. He was in the beginning with God. All things were made through Him, and without Him nothing was made that was made.[24]

---

[21] Genesis 1:26-27, NASB.
[22] Genesis 11:7-9, NASB.
[23] Psalm 33:6, NASB.
[24] John 1:1-3, NKJV.

John 1 is a parallel to Psalm 33. Both imply some agency, some part of God, the **Word**, as the means by which everything is made. Note also the "**breath** of His mouth" is the same word as the "**Spirit** of God" that moved over the waters in Genesis 1:1. Psalm 33 could be understood to imply a trinity of Persons in one God.

Another hint is from Proverbs 8. This is rather stunning—it is declared to be the voice of *wisdom*, personified, who was *with God* at the beginning of creation, and *with whom* the world was made, and *in whom* God delighted!

> "When He prepared the heavens, *I was there*, When He drew a circle on the face of the deep, When He established the clouds above, When He strengthened the fountains of the deep, When He assigned to the sea its limit, So that the waters would not transgress His command, When He marked out the foundations of the earth, *Then I was beside Him as a master craftsman*; And *I was daily His delight*, Rejoicing always before Him, Rejoicing in His inhabited world, And my delight was with the sons of men. Now therefore, *listen to me, my children*, For blessed are those who keep *my ways*. Hear instruction and be wise, And do not disdain it. Blessed is the man *who listens to me*, Watching daily at my gates, Waiting at the posts of my doors. *For whoever finds me finds life, And obtains favor from the LORD.*"[25]

Of course, some might assert that this personification of wisdom is mere poetic license, an indirect and elegant way to speak of wisdom, and not any sort of proof of another "Person" in the Godhead. But such an easy dismissal of the self-referential language here seems like hand-waving. It is facile: It simply dismisses what it cannot explain.

While we might assert that "whoever finds me finds life" merely means that wisdom is good and helpful in living, expressions like "I was beside Him as a master craftsman," and "I was daily His delight" do not make much sense as poetic license, for that would imply a God who relates to a mere concept (wisdom) as if it were a person. It would be more true to the words to accept the presence of this *person*, wisdom, even surrendering any claim to understand it (or him or her).

"I don't know" seems more genuine than dismissing the possibility of another person present at creation because it is incompatible with a traditional or Platonic ideal of singleness.

Besides, this is God's *nature* we are discussing, and *we can't penetrate it*, however excellent our propositions might seem to us.

GOD SPEAKS TO GOD

Then there is this difficult bit in Psalm 110:

> The LORD said to my Lord, "Sit at My right hand, Till I make Your enemies Your footstool."[26]

---

[25] Proverbs 8:27-35, NKJV.
[26] Psalm 110:1, NKJV.

The Hebrew reads:

> Yahweh[27] declares to Adonai, sit at My right hand until I make Your enemies Your footstool.

Both Yahweh and Adonai (printed as LORD and Lord in the New King James and many other English versions) are titles for God. So God is speaking to God, and telling Him that He will make His enemies His footstool. One God, two Persons, one promising something to the other.[28]

We find those precise words, from Psalm 110, used by Jesus in Matthew 22:

> While the Pharisees were gathered together, Jesus asked them, saying, "What do you think about the Christ[29] [Messiah]? Whose Son is He?"
>
> They said to Him, "The Son of David."
>
> He said to them, "How then does David in the Spirit call Him 'Lord,' saying: 'The LORD [Yahweh] said to my Lord [Adonai], "Sit at My right hand, till I make Your enemies Your footstool"'? If David then calls Him 'Lord,' how is He his Son?" And no one was able to answer Him a word, nor from that day on did anyone dare question Him anymore.[30]

Jesus raises this messianic Psalm of David before the Pharisees. David has referred to the coming Messiah, the Redeemer, as Lord [Adonai], who is spoken to by the LORD [Yahweh], with a promise of victory. The Pharisees believe the Messiah is to be a descendant (son) of David. How can a descendant of David also be his Lord? The implication is that the Messiah pre-exists David, is God, and yet will be born from David's line of descendants.

Does this prove that the Messiah is God? No. Not in a strict logical deduction, but it is a legitimate inference from the Psalm. You can bet this unsettled the Pharisees there with Jesus.

But perhaps more importantly, the Psalm does imply divine activity between two beings, both God, more than a thousand years before anyone suggested the concept of three Persons in one God.

Psalm 110 is also echoed in Ephesians 1:

> That power is like the working of his mighty strength, which he [the Father] exerted in Christ when he raised him from the dead and *seated him at his right hand*

---

[27] "Jehovah" is the Germanized version of "Yahweh," but note that the actual Hebrew word contains four consonants and no vowels. We do not know how or even *if* it was ever pronounced. Many Jews today will not say this word out loud (except in some prayers), and instead substitute "*Hashem*," which means simply "the name."

[28] Ramban (Nachmanides) in *The Disputation at Barcelona* asserts that the use of Adonai here refers to David as king, and that this Psalm was written by him to be sung by the Levites. There are difficulties with Ramban's assertion, but I won't open up the issue here.

[29] Again, remember that *Christ* is simply the English form of the Greek word for *Messiah*, from the Hebrew word *Moshiach*.

[30] Matthew 22:41-46, NKJV.

in the heavenly realms, far above all rule and authority, power and dominion, and every title that can be given, not only in the present age but also in the one to come. And *God placed all things under his feet* and appointed him to be head over everything for the church, which is his body, the fullness of him who fills everything in every way.[31]

It is also referred to explicitly by Peter in Acts 2:

> God has raised this Jesus to life, and we are all witnesses of the fact. Exalted to the right hand of God, he has received from the Father the promised Holy Spirit and has poured out what you now see and hear. For David did not ascend to heaven, and yet he said,
> "The Lord said to my Lord: 'Sit at my right hand until I make your enemies a footstool for your feet.'"
> "Therefore let all Israel be assured of this: God has made this Jesus, whom you crucified, both Lord and Christ."
> When the people heard this, they were cut to the heart and said to Peter and the other apostles, "Brothers, what shall we do?"[32]

Psalm 110 contains even more that is later found in the New Testament. Verse 4 (NKJV) says this:

> The LORD has sworn and will not relent, "You are a priest forever according to the order of Melchizedek."

And the author of Hebrews makes an extensive scriptural argument about the role of the Jewish priesthood, and the coming of the new covenant, and in Hebrews 7 explicitly quotes Psalm 110:

> "The LORD has sworn and will not relent, 'You are a priest forever according to the order of Melchizedek.'"[33]

This underscores the depiction of Jesus as the fulfillment David's messianic psalm—the very psalm in which Yahweh God spoke to Adonai God—two Persons in conversation, and both God. Thus here in Hebrews we have two plain implications: that Jesus is the Messiah, and is also one of the Persons who is God.

ISAIAH ON THE TRINITY OR DUALITY OR...

The last piece of Scripture I want to share with you is Isaiah 48. When we read the book of the prophet Isaiah, there are certain chapters that Christians usually read more than others—43, 53 and 61—but typically not chapter 48.

---

[31] Ephesians 1:19b-23, NIV 1984 Edition.
[32] Acts 2:32-37, NIV 1984 Edition.
[33] Hebrews 7:21b, NKJV.

There is some very disconcerting language in Isaiah 48, particularly if you are a monotheist who doesn't believe there are three Persons in one God. If you are a Jew, for instance, you might think the Trinitarian concept that Christians hold is made up from whole cloth. But listen to Isaiah. Here I am intentionally using the Jewish Publication Society 1917 translation, so it is clear some Christian translator hasn't fudged the translation from the Hebrew.

Isaiah 48:11 For Mine own sake, for Mine own sake, will I do it; for how should it be profaned? And My glory will I not give to another. 12 Hearken unto Me, O Jacob, and Israel My called: I am He; I am the first, I also am the last. 13 Yea, My hand hath laid the foundation of the earth, and My right hand hath spread out the heavens; when I call unto them, they stand up together. 14 Assemble yourselves, all ye, and hear; which among them hath declared these things? He whom Hashem[34] loveth shall perform His pleasure on Babylon, and show His arm on the Chaldeans. 15 I, even I, have spoken, yea, I have called him; I have brought him, and he shall make his way prosperous. 16 Come ye near unto Me, hear ye this: From the beginning I have not spoken in secret; from the time that it was, there am I; and now the L-rd[35] GOD[36] hath sent me, and His spirit. 17 Thus saith Hashem[37], thy Redeemer, the Holy One of Israel: I am Hashem[38] thy G-d[39], who teacheth thee for thy profit, who leadeth thee by the way that thou shouldest go.

Note that everywhere "Hashem" (the name), "L-rd," "GOD" and "G-d" appear, it represents a Hebrew name for God. See the footnotes for the specifics.

Let's open up this Scripture to see the revelations it contains. Verses 11-13 are God declaring Himself and His authority. He makes very clear that He is the one speaking through the mouth of Isaiah. He is the first and the last. He will not give His glory to another. He laid the foundations of the earth, and He spread out the Heavens. They all obey Him.

In verses 14 and 15, He speaks of how someone that He loves will perform His will against the Babylonians and Chaldeans (the specifics of this are not my focus right now).

Now read verse 16 again:

Come ye near unto Me, hear ye this: From the beginning I have not spoken in secret; from the time that it was, there am I; and now the L-rd GOD hath sent me, and His spirit.

God says, "Come ye near unto Me, hear ye this" and declares:

---

[34] Yahweh.
[35] Adonai.
[36] Yahweh.
[37] Yahweh.
[38] Yahweh.
[39] Elohim.

- He has not spoken in secret, even from the beginning (though His listeners may not have been paying attention; see verse 8).
- He has been there all along, as God.

Then Isaiah says:

> and now the L-rd GOD hath sent me (Isaiah), and His spirit.

Which either means that God and His spirit sent Isaiah, or God sent Isaiah and His (God's) spirit.

Finally, Isaiah concludes in verse 17:

> Thus saith Hashem, thy Redeemer, the Holy One of Israel: I am Hashem thy G-d, who teacheth thee for thy profit, who leadeth thee by the way that thou shouldest go.

No matter how you read this, God and God's spirit are differentiated: They are two. There is even the possible reading of a third presence here: "thy Redeemer."

Capitalization in the quoted verses is from the original JPS text. Hebrew has no upper- or lowercase letters, so the capitalization was added in the JPS English to help understand the references in the Hebrew grammar.

In other words, God said, *What there is to be revealed about Myself has been revealed. It's there. It hasn't been a secret. You may not have seen it. You may not have had the eyes to see it, but it is there.*

Hold all of this in mind for a moment. He has declared, "I am He, I am the first, I am the last. Surely My hand founded the earth, and My right hand spread out the heavens."

That echoes John 1 again: "Through him, all things were created" (v. 3). Through the Second Person of the Godhead, the Redeemer, all things were created. And in Revelation 21, Jesus says, "I am the Alpha and the Omega, the Beginning and the End" (v. 6a).

It is the same speaker with the same message of redemption that came through the lips of Isaiah speaking on behalf of the Lord some 700 years before Jesus was born. In fact, Jesus' very name is a Hebrew compound of "Yahweh" and "saves."

I trust this is eye-opening and heart-warming.

CONCEPT, ONTOLOGY AND FREDDIE

Finally this: Ultimately the Trinity is going to remain a mystery to us. What we know and what we understand about it is only what God has *revealed*. As He opens our eyes to see more, we may see more. Ultimately the deepest, deepest, deepest truth of the Trinity is something that human minds will never, *can* never understand—any more than our little dog Freddie can understand our family. I don't mean to trivialize this. I believe this parallel will help our comprehension of

Trinity, and the little bit that we understand of it, but also why the Godhead must remain fundamentally opaque to us. It should temper our hubris.

As much as Freddie the *dog* loves each of the *people* in our family, he does not *even slightly comprehend* the relationship between my wife and me, or between me and my sons. He knows we love each other, like a pack; and he knows we all treat him with love.

He knows we are different from each other. My wife is the one who really dotes on him and gives him affection, and he just loves to be with her. My oldest son takes care of him at night after everyone else is in bed. My youngest son is his buddy and teases him about squirrels and other dogs.

As for me, I am the Father, the Alpha Dog, the Master: Fred can be a block away, and everybody else can be calling, "Come on, Freddie, come on, Freddie," and they'll get nothing; Fred will be too interested in something or other, and he will ignore their pleas. But I can shout "Fred" just once, and it doesn't matter where he is or what he is doing—when he hears *my voice*, he returns instantly.

(Fred, like all dogs, "gets" this concept of "the master's voice" better than we do—a dog comes running when the master calls, but humans tend to just ignore. Or pretend they don't hear. Part of the whole point of it all is that when *our* Master calls, we ought to do as dogs do—come running.)

Fred could write a theology of the four persons of the family, and it would be accurate as far as Fred could understand it—the Master, the One Who Dotes, the Caregiver at Night, and the Buddy. But he would not understand, ultimately, what the relationship amongst the four of us actually is. It is above his pay grade, beyond his understanding, outside of his ability to comprehend. He gets love, attention, care, food and direction from us, and he guards us when he perceives a threat (or imagines one—theologians take note!), and he lives with us in love. But he cannot know what is beyond his dog mind's ability to know.

So it is with us and the Godhead. Both Testaments are replete with references to God that reflect enormous complexity and diversity and numerous assertions and implications of activities and of living *beings* present in the Godhead, beyond only one—yet affirming *one God*. Christians assert that the correct number within the one God is three: Father, Son and Holy Spirit. Even if we are exactly right about that number, the actual content of the Godhead is still above our pay grade, beyond our understanding, outside of our ability to comprehend. We cannot know what is beyond a human mind's ability to know.

Which bring us at last to *concept* and *ontology*.

Much of what has seemed, over the centuries, like a vital defense of God, or of Jesus, or of the Christian faith, has in fact been a battle of concepts within a philosophical framework that is ultimately foreign to the God who reveals Himself in the Bible. Just because these debates have used biblical terms does not make the debates either holy or meaningful.

Much serious scholarship has gone into defining and defending the Trinity over the course of many centuries, and that scholarship has been valuable in encouraging us to conceive of God as three Persons in unending, *loving relationship* with one another—glorifying each other, edifying each other, working with and through each other. It has helped to remind us that it is *in this image we are made* (and hence we should treat each other this way). But the inescapable reality is that to our human minds, Trinity is a *concept*. That is, Trinity is a philosophical proposition used to help us conceive of God, affirm the authority and divinity of Jesus and the Holy Spirit, and guide us in our worship and behavior.

I am not saying that the concept of Trinity is wrong, nor that it is "just" a concept. As deeply real as the Trinity is within the Godhead, there is still an issue here that needs to be seen and understood.

For all of the theology, hermeneutics and apologetics expended to prove that this concept of Trinity is right and the others wrong, the *concept* is still something erected within Greek philosophical thought forms and the study of *ontology*—the study of being, existence and reality.

However excellent a job is done in constructing this proposition, this *concept of Trinity* is *not God*, and it cannot contain (or even well describe) God's actual nature. In fact, what God reveals about Himself in Scripture, if anything, upends every human attempt to capture or really understand Him. God says, "I am that I am."[40] He confuses those at Babel who want to climb up to see Him. He says quite explicitly, "My thoughts are not your thoughts and my ways are not your ways."[41] He even says that if we were to look at His face we would die.[42]

Whatever it is that He is, He does not play by our rules and will not be confined to our concepts about Him, however bright, competent, accurate and scholarly they might be.

I don't want to seem dismissive of the thoughtful and prayerful work of centuries of Christian and Jewish authors—many of whom I find enormously insightful—but my playful analogy of little Freddie really does parallel our own attempts to know God's nature—except that *we are even worse off* than Freddie in this regard. The distance between his dog mind and our human minds is tiny when compared to the distance between our minds and the mind of God—*that* distance is unbridgeable. God Himself says so again and again.

My counsel is that we all keep our confidence (and hubris) in check when asserting our *concept* of the Godhead against that of others—both those who believe in Trinity, and those who argue against it, including Muslims and Jews.

I see Trinity as an insightful means of seeking to respond to God's character, but also as a necessarily weak and doomed attempt to bound or define His nature. It is a *concept*. It is not God.

So, we have to kneel and recognize that by God's grace He has revealed the image in which we are made—that is, to be in loving submission and loving care for one another, with a Father, a Redeemer-Lord-Messiah-Son, and a Holy Spirit—all revealed in Scripture—in both Testaments, however we describe these to coexist,

---

[40] Exodus 3:14. The Hebrew actually says something more like, "I will be what I will be."
[41] Isaiah 55:8, *God's Word* Translation.
[42] Exodus 33:20.

relate, proceed or be numbered. I'm not trying to be cute or heterodox here, but rather acutely aware of our own human limitations, and therefore humble in our assertions.

Christians deduce and conceive Trinity from the revelation of Scripture, and we should, by God's power, do our best to live out its implications and imperatives. *But we should not confuse a concept, however well-formed, with the reality of God.*

At this point some readers may be getting a bit irritated or worried that I'm trying to toss out a fundamental doctrine of the Church—Trinity. I'm not. That's not my goal nor is it the point of this line of analysis. It's a different issue, but sometimes hard to grasp initially.

So let me press deeper. Permit me a moment to give a parallel example, because what we are trying to understand is *really* important:

Imagine that a man, Phillip, will be coming to our church. For whatever reason, he's decided to find a new church for his family, and ours is a possibility.

I'm told that he is the son and heir of billionaire parents, has been to all of the best schools, received top grades, and is in charge of numerous international companies. He is married to a rich, equally accomplished wife, and they have children, all in private schools.

I'm also told that he is so full of himself that there's barely space in a room to be with him. I'm informed he is rich, smart, powerful, arrogant and obnoxious.

What goes on in my heart and mind as I anticipate his arrival? For one thing, I'm anxious. Not shaking in my boots, but who wants to deal with someone who is rich, smart, powerful, arrogant and obnoxious? Yet I'm also thinking maybe if I'm really nice to him, some of that wealth will come our way. He could help build our new church. I'd even be willing to name the fellowship hall after him.

Some in the church hear that he is coming to visit, and insist that when he gets here it be a "come to Jesus" meeting. That is, someone has to call him to account, name his sin for him, to get him straight with God and face-to-face with his arrogance.

Others counsel overlooking his obnoxiousness, and treating him with deference. After all, people like him are used to giving orders and having them followed immediately. We need to do no less if we want to win him to our church. We can eat humble pie for the good of the whole church.

Now, you're probably thinking I'm going to ask, "What is the right response to such a man?"

But I'm not. We are missing something far more important here: *the man!* We haven't yet had the tiniest relationship with Phillip. ALL we have had is a *concept* about Phillip—whether accurate or not—and all of our thinking, contest and struggle has been with a concept—not the man! We have been stuck inside our heads in an internal debate about a concept, a proposition, an idea.

We must get outside of our own skin and have *an **actual relationship** with another human being*, Phillip. That relationship is real, human, tangible, palpable, incarnate, and *can* embody the love of God. Right now *the concept is in the way!*

Phillip may be arrogant or humble, rich or suddenly broke, smart or recently brain-damaged, and we may find him difficult or sweet, full of himself or seeking genuine friendship. We may find constant joy with him, or we might wrestle and argue till the cows come home—*but those are all realities that unfold in relationship with the actual human being, Phillip,* and it is only *there* that the love of God matters.

Whether our concept about Phillip is accurate or mistaken, it will *always be insufficient,* because it is a *concept.*

It is not Phillip.

We can debate our concepts about Phillip forever and it will be worth exactly nothing, no matter how true the limited description is to which we cling. In the end, all that really matters is if there is a *relationship* with *Phillip.*

Just so with the Trinity.

Many great minds have worked for many centuries to spell out exactly what our precise concept is of the Trinity, what the characteristics are of each of the persons: Father, Son, Spirit. What their relative roles and responsibilities are, how they relate and proceed to and from one another, and on and on and on.

But we cannot have a relationship with a concept—that's all inside our own heads! We can only have a *relationship* with God. We must get out of our own heads and have an actual relationship with our Creator.

Knowing God is not the same as having well-defined and defendable concepts about God.

For Christians, the ultimate example of knowing God is contained in the life and willing sacrifice of Jesus (*Yahweh saves*). Jesus didn't simply have a better set of concepts about God or Trinity. *He had relationship with the Father!* And out of this relationship, Jesus says, "He who has seen Me has seen the Father."[43] Jesus also says that He and the Father are one.[44]

We can spend much ink and heat in deducing and debating philosophical propositions from this assertion—whether the Two are actually a Single One, of the same or similar substance, whether this is just metaphor, or if it describes reality, whether One is lesser than or equal to the Other, whether One is begotten or created and what exactly that means (more ontology), whether Both existed before time, whether the Spirit is separate from the Two, and whether He proceeds[45] from One or Both, and on and on. But when we do so, we have often trapped ourselves in *concept,* and missed *relationship.*

We live like intellectual Deists, asserting there is a God, but often having nothing actually to do with Him.

Some claim that the whole Christian faith is based upon the concept of the Trinity, and insist that good Christians must subscribe to it to truly be counted as Christian. But the danger is that *this* then has become our foundation: not God,

---

[43] John 14:9b, NKJV.

[44] John 17:11, 21.

[45] This debate has gotten so convoluted that one side defends the use of "proceeds" depending on whether the word used is Latin or Greek!

but our well-defined and defended *concept about God*. However accurate the concept is, *it is not God*. Knowing the concept is not the same as knowing God. *Knowing a concept is not a relationship.*

Maybe some solid, thoughtful Trinitarians will say, "Yes, of course. What's important is the Trinity Itself, not our explanations of it. This is obvious. Of course that's what is important. Of course that's what we mean and defend."

But I don't believe that is what we have actually seen through history.

Instead, *we fell in love with concepts* in a Greek philosophical system, worked out structures and appurtenances to the *nth* degree, and gave religious and biblical labels to the parts. We fought over which was the most beautiful, refined and true, yet they often became idols made by our own hands and minds—and we spoke bitterly of, shunned and even killed those who made and embraced other ones.

We have made idols of our concepts, and fought over them.

In so doing we neglected relationship with the One true God.

Trinity is a valuable, useful concept to help us understand the nature of the Godhead, but no matter how true or accurate a concept it is, *it is not God*, and it is not *relationship* with God.

Relationship is in *covenant*, not concepts.

21.
Bible Authority

In this chapter we will be looking at the authority of the Bible. This is not trivial, and parts of it will be a little bit complex, so I ask your indulgence.

Let's be honest: The Bible is not the most user-friendly book you can read. Here are some great reasons NOT to read the Bible:

- It's long and intimidating, and it's not put together like a novel or a "how-to" book or a textbook or most any other kind of book you can buy.

- Different Churches and traditions don't even agree on which books belong in it and which ones don't.

- There are many different translations, and advocates for one or the other often fight bitterly and publicly against translations other than their own favorite.

- Starting at the beginning and reading through to the end is often boring and really difficult.

- Really creepy people have used the Bible to (try to) justify everything from segregation to religious persecution to murder.

You have to wonder why anyone would even bother to begin to read it.

On the other hand, the Bible is obviously an extraordinary and profoundly important book.

This is true even if you don't believe in God at all.

Year after year it is the single best-selling book on the planet—far beyond whatever is in second place.

Why? Well, for a bunch of good reasons.

- It contains some of the deepest insights into human character ever written.

- It has some of the most beautiful poetry and astonishing dramas ever penned.

- It shakes people up. It jolts them out of their self-centeredness and gives them a wider vision of who they are and why they are alive.

- It sweeps across thousands of years of human history.

- It challenges authority and condemns tyranny.

- It attacks hypocrisy, and it honors the downtrodden.

- It offers comfort in ways no human institution has ever been able to do.

- It is used by billions as a source of counsel, comfort and understanding of their place in the world.

- You likely know some of the stories from childhood about Adam, Eve and the serpent in the Garden of Eden, about Moses escaping Egypt with a million Jews only to wander in the wilderness for 40 years, or Jesus feeding 5000 people with a few loaves of bread and a couple of fish.

- Such stories can be told to children on a very basic level, and they will understand the story and the basic moral of it.

But there is much more than meets the child's eye in each of these stories. One of the remarkable things about the parables of Jesus is that rather than saying, "Here are the rules to follow. Rule one, rule two, rule three, rule four...", Jesus told stories that can illustrate a moral or spiritual truth on many different levels.

The first time we hear it, we get level one. Then as we mature, we get level two and level three. We can't exhaust the levels or depth of the parables that Jesus tells, nor exhaust how widely applicable they are in our lives.

The same is true of the entire scope of the two Testaments: They contain narrative that does not simply relate history, but teaches us about ourselves.

The Bible is something we ought to take seriously, but Christians have to ask the question: "What is its *authority* in our lives?" Secular opinions include:

- Who cares?

- It's a bunch of fairy tales and outright lies.

- It's just a book written by people in one ancient cultural context and with primitive superstitions about a god who created them. Nothing more.

- It may be interesting to cultural historians and may even contain some good ethical ideas, but as a book, it's not much different than other religious texts, from other cultures, in other times. Just one of a bunch.

- It's an instrument of oppression used by a patriarchal institution—the Church—to control women and other oppressed minorities. It's all about domination and control.

Many versions of each of these views are common, and range from measured academic assessment to bitter disdain.

At the other end of the spectrum is the view that Scripture is the infallible and inerrant word of God written by men under the direct inspiration and control of the Holy Spirit—and that those who do not accept this view threaten the future of the Church and risk their immortal souls.

If you have not already had your view of the Bible demanded of you by those holding *any* of these points of view, just wait—your time will come.

As for me, I believe we can trust the Bible as God's reliable and intentional revelation of Himself without being drawn into any of the partisan fighting. So, let's unfold the history and the issues and see where it leads us.

THE ORIGINAL MANUSCRIPTS

First, do we really know what the *original* manuscripts said? We don't have any of them, not one. We only have copies. This causes several problems:

Authors can make up conspiracy theories that excite and mislead their readers, and no one can *prove* they are wrong. One group believes the Church was in control of the Scriptures for centuries, so they could make it say *whatever* they wanted it to say—and did, in order to keep the people under their control.

One variation of this has it that Justinian I, when he was the Roman Emperor, intentionally excised from the Bible all references to reincarnation, because the Emperor and his wife Theodora didn't want us to know about it.

Usually these descriptions of the way the Bible has evolved are done semi-conspiratorially with a wink: "We know what the Church did. It took out those parts that wouldn't allow it to control the people. So what we have left is only what the 'powers' in the Church want us to read."

Conspiracy-lovers love *that* one. There are many variations on this theme about Scripture and its unreliability: Since we don't have any of the original manuscripts, *who knows* what the original said? How can we *possibly believe* what we read in the Bible?

It turns out there are actually some pretty solid reasons for believing that what we have is, with few possible exceptions, what the authors originally wrote. We have quite-good evidence of this.

Let's start with the historical textural evidence and the abundance of early manuscripts. One great review of this evidence comes from Bible scholar F. F. Bruce, in *Are the New Testament Documents Reliable?*[1]

Bruce wrote some terrific books, including *Hard Sayings of the Old Testament* and *Hard Sayings of the New Testament*. One of his key points is how historians accurately ascertain the *original text* of a document. Of course, they can use carbon dating to compute the age of the paper or papyrus, and they can use archaeological location and context to figure the age based on other objects or documents found near it. But those tell just the age of the *base material* of a document, not the age or accuracy of the text written upon it.

Further, what we usually find is not the original document but a copy, or a copy of a copy. In fact, we have do not have the original documents of the New or Old Testaments—so how can we be sure the *text* in our copies is what the original documents actually contained?

Well, it turns out there is a method, now greatly aided by computers, called textual criticism. This is a technique intended to recover, as well as possible, the original text based on a multitude of copies. The technique is quite ancient (it was in use thousands of years ago) and consists of looking at how the copies we have *differ* from one another. Here's a simple example to illustrate the principle. A teacher writes a sentence on the board, and three students copy it onto three pieces of paper. The papers read as follows:

1. I went to the corner store and bought ten peanuts.
2. I went to the general store and bought ten pennies.
3. I sent to the corner store and sought ten peanuts.

The teacher erases the board and leaves. We are given only the students' copies of what was once written there. Which one is most likely to be accurate? Don't go on to the next paragraph just yet. Look at these three and see if you can figure it out. Then read on.

What did you conclude? The correct answer is number one, because that sentence is more likely, sensible and logical, but also because in those places where #2 and #3 differ, parts of them are the same as number one. So, "went," "corner," "bought" and "peanuts" were *probably* in the original.

But what if 30 other students were also present, and we found their copies, and all of them, independently written, at the same time as the first three, read:

---

[1] Originally published in 1943, with subsequent editions from Wm. B. Eerdmans Publishing Company, Grand Rapids, MI, 1954, and Martino Publishing, Mansfield Centre, CT, 2011. Nicky Gumbel and his book *Questions of Life* has a great and more extended review of this evidence from F. F. Bruce.

I sent to the corner store and bought ten peanuts.

A textual critic would conclude this last one is statistically more likely to be an accurate rendition of the original. Of course, all 30 additional students may have made the same scribal error, but that's highly unlikely. Rather, the odds are excellent that "I sent to the corner store and bought ten peanuts" is the true original. The more copies you have that agree, the more likely it is that what you have is what was in the original. There's a lot more to this analytical process than simply numbers of copies and the logic of the content and words, but you get the general idea.

When it comes to ancient documents, the *more copies* we have that are consistent with each other, and the *more places they are from*, the *more likely* that what we believe to be *content of the original* is actually so. This is a widely accepted principle in the study of many ancient texts, not just Scripture.

What is compelling about Scripture is how many copies we have that can be dated not far from when the original (now-missing) document was written.

For non-Scripture documents, we have few copies, and they were made long after the original.

> For Caesar's Gallic War (composed between 58 and 50 B.C.) there are several extant MSS [manuscripts], but only nine or ten are good, and the oldest is some 900 years later than Caesar's day. ... Of the fourteen books of the Histories of Tacitus (c. A.D. 100) only four and a half survive. ... The text ... depends entirely on two MSS, one of the ninth century and one of the eleventh.[2]

To be clear: *Caesar's Gallic War* was written about 50 B.C. No one knows where the original is, nor do we have any of the many copies made between 50 B.C. and A.D. 900. They are all lost, destroyed, or yet to be found. *The earliest copy we have* is from A.D. 900, and yet no one doubts the accuracy of the copy. The words we have are what Caesar wrote, though no one has seen the scroll on which they were first written. Similarly with Tacitus, and also with *Livy's Roman History*, and the histories of Thucydides and Herodotus, and many more.

We have few copies of these important and ancient writings, and the copies date typically hundreds of years after the creation of the originals.

The case with the New Testament, however, is profoundly different. It was written beginning between A.D. 30 and 40, and likely completed about A.D. 100. There are *thousands* of copies of the books of the New Testament, many dating to A.D. 200-300, just a couple centuries from their being written. More, these New Testament books are *quoted by other authors* from the first century on, which provides another confirmation of their accuracy.

Sir Frederic Kenyon, an expert in these documents, says this:

---

[2] F. F. Bruce, *Are the New Testament Documents Reliable?*, p. 20.

The interval then between the dates of original composition and the earliest extant evidence becomes so small as to be in fact negligible, and the last foundation for any doubt that the Scriptures have come down to us substantially as they were written has now been removed. Both the *authenticity* and the *general integrity* of the books of the New Testament may be regarded as finally established.[3]

That is an opinion not just of Christian theologians but of secular historians who look at ancient texts. The vast numbers of manuscripts, all virtually identical in content, and all of the very early references to them by writers in the first through fifth centuries, fundamentally make it impossible for "the Church" to have "rewritten the Bible to control people." Like it or not, what we have is what was written, with only tiny differences.

Some might not agree with the content of the New Testament, but it is highly probable that what we read is what the authors wrote. Justinian and Theodora, who ruled in the sixth century A.D., did not go in and take out references to reincarnation, nor did any of the other conspiracies to change the content ever happen. For one thing, too many people already had too many copies of all of the New Testament Scriptures at that point, and they weren't about to let the Emperor and his wife (or anybody else) decide to take part of it out. They couldn't have gotten away with it.

So that deals with the issue of whether what we have is what the authors wrote. We have lots of evidence.[4]

INCONSISTENCIES IN SCRIPTURE

There is another reason we believe that Scripture as it is written is likely to be accurate. This is going to sound funny when I first say it, but follow me on this logic: The evidence that what we have is what they wrote is the Bible's *inconsistency*.

That is, the *same event* is described by *different authors* in *different ways*. In some cases, there seems to be an explanation that helps this make sense. In others, not so.

For instance, Matthew 15:38 says Jesus fed 4000 men plus women and children with seven loaves of bread "and a few small fish." But Mark 6:41 says Jesus fed *5000* men with "*five* loaves of bread and *two* fish." So which is it?

This one is particularly easy to clear up because in Mark 8, the disciples are thinking about food and Jesus asks them, starting in verse 18:

> "'You have eyes—can't you see? You have ears—can't you hear?' Don't you remember anything at all? What about the 5,000 men I fed with five loaves of bread? How many baskets of leftovers did you pick up afterward?" "Twelve," they

---

[3] Sir Frederic Kenyon, *The Bible and Archaeology* (Harper & Row, 1940), cited by F. F. Bruce in *Are the New Testament Documents Reliable?*, pp. 23-24.

[4] An equally compelling argument can be made about Old Testament texts and the scribal tradition, but we won't cover that here.

said. "And when I fed 4,000 with seven loaves, how many large baskets of leftovers did you pick up?" "Seven," they said.[5]

Jesus Himself said He did both. The two reports are of different events. It is not a discrepancy. Thank you, Mark.

But there are some other places that aren't quite as simple. Here is an example. Matthew 28, on Easter Day:

> Early on Sunday morning, as the new day was dawning, Mary Magdalene and the other Mary went out to visit the tomb. Suddenly there was a great earthquake! For an angel of the Lord came down from heaven, rolled aside the stone, and sat on it.[6]

But in Luke 24:1-4, it says this:

> But very early on Sunday morning the women went to the tomb, taking the spices they had prepared. They found that the stone had been rolled away from the entrance. So they went in, but they didn't find the body of the Lord Jesus. As they stood there puzzled, two men suddenly appeared to them, clothed in dazzling robes.

Wait a minute, where is the angel sitting on the stone? In this telling, the stone had *already* been rolled aside. Who was it who went there? Matthew says "Mary Magdalene and the other Mary." Luke says, "The women who went to the tomb were Mary Magdalene, Joanna, Mary the mother of James, and several others."

How about this? Gospel of John, chapter 20:

> Early on Sunday morning, while it was still dark, Mary Magdalene came to the tomb and found that the stone had been rolled away from the entrance. She ran and found Simon Peter and the other disciple, the one whom Jesus loved. She said, "They have taken the Lord's body out of the tomb, and we don't know where they have put him!" Peter and the other disciple started out for the tomb.[7]

Add to this that all of these stories have Jesus encountering different individuals in different places (near the tomb, the road to Emmaus, or Galilee), for different reasons and at different times, all immediately post-Resurrection. Just read through each of the accounts in the Gospels and you'll see how these disagree. Some have tried to argue that each detail did happen exactly as reported, and that they are all consistent parts of a single greater whole.

Well, maybe, though no one has been able to construct such a meta-story that made sense of the smaller stories. Many have tried, but reading through them, one gets the sense they are trying too hard. Better to just leave it unexplained, as the early Church did.

---

[5] Mark 8:18-20.
[6] Matthew 28:1-2.
[7] John 20:1-3.

Countless other conflicts and contradictions exist, and also many instances of believers behaving badly:

Partisan Spirit

> Some of you are saying, "I am a follower of Paul." Others are saying, "I follow Apollos," or "I follow Peter," or "I follow only Christ."[8]

Infighting Among Leaders

> But when Peter came to Antioch, I had to oppose him to his face, for what he did was very wrong. When he first arrived, he ate with the Gentile Christians, who were not circumcised. But afterward, when some friends of James came, Peter wouldn't eat with the Gentiles anymore. He was afraid of criticism from these people who insisted on the necessity of circumcision. As a result, other Jewish Christians followed Peter's hypocrisy, and even Barnabas was led astray by their hypocrisy.[9]

Paul is the writer in both of these cases, and is presenting his own point of view, but in both cases he reveals struggle in the young church. In the first instance, church members are taking sides, and acting as partisans for one top leader or another (Paul, Apollos, Peter). In the second instance, Paul accuses Peter of hypocrisy for acting one way among Gentiles and another way among Jews. This is, of course, the same Paul who said,

> When I was with the Jews, I lived like a Jew to bring the Jews to Christ. When I was with those who follow the Jewish law, I too lived under that law. Even though I am not subject to the law, I did this so I could bring to Christ those who are under the law. When I am with the Gentiles who do not follow the Jewish law, I too live apart from that law so I can bring them to Christ. But I do not ignore the law of God; I obey the law of Christ.[10]

This is also the same Paul who argued so vehemently against circumcision,[11] and also circumcised Timothy.[12] So why does inconsistency or bad behavior give us confidence in the reliability of what we read? Because Scripture doesn't try to "pretty up" things by rendering as consistent all of the accounts that are told, or by hiding the flaws of the people it describes. It's all there in gritty, authentic realism.

If you really wanted to take something and make sure it was exactly the same all the way through so everybody would believe it is a perfect and complete gift

---

[8] 1 Corinthians 1:12.
[9] Galatians 2:11-13.
[10] 1 Corinthians 9:20-21.
[11] See Galatians 5 for example.
[12] See Acts 16.

from the Holy Spirit, without error, consistent and infallible, would you let this stuff through?

The Church from the earliest time has been aware of these inconsistencies. But it has also been honest enough about its regard for Scripture not to disguise or hide these things. It has wrestled with them, yes. But it has been authentic about what was written.

The bottom line on that is, nobody copy-edited these documents to force consistency on them. What we have *today* is probably what was written *then*, by the *original authors*, with some possible minor copying errors that crept in over the years.[13]

I don't know which of the stories of the Resurrection is the most accurate telling. Perhaps in eternity I will discover that the event as it unfolded actually included all of those parts, but in some way that I can't really perceive right now because I am at such a distance from it.

Is it possible that one of the writers of the Scripture remembered it wrong, or heard the story from someone who remembered it wrong? Well, it is a common human experience that several people at the same event will remember it differently, and not all will accurately recall it. That *may* be what's at play here, though some theologians would find this an *impossible* explanation—they believe the Holy Spirit caused the authors of Scripture to write and thus *God kept their original writing infallibly accurate, perfectly controlling each thought, each choice of a word, and each stroke of the pen.* Such theologians *might* accept that copying errors crept in, but would assert that when the words were first written down—such documents are called "original autographs"[14]—no error was present or possible, because the Holy Spirit was completely in control. The author was a mere instrument in the Holy Spirit's hand.

Others will grant that there could be human error or misunderstanding present,[15] even in the original autographs, but in matters of faith and morals, the Scripture is *inerrant* (without error).

Several versions of these claims of inerrancy are made by different groups, almost all of them Protestant. Similar claims are made by the Roman Catholic and Orthodox churches about the *infallibility* of Scripture, but also of the *bishops* of the Church when meeting in official councils.

The point I really want to make here is that those who assembled the Canon[16] of Scripture did not smooth things over and make them all look consistent or

---

[13] These include simple mistakes in copying as well as marginal notes and other scribal marks that may have been incorporated accidentally. But the sum total of such errors is a minuscule fraction of the whole, and generally without consequence for the meaning. I won't go into the specifics here. They are easily learned from a good study Bible.

[14] In theology this word doesn't refer to a signature, like a celebrity's autograph on a photo. It simply means the actual document the author wrote.

[15] An example of this would be mistaken conceptions about the nature of the solar system, or the weather, which are repeated in these writings.

[16] "Canon" refers to the collection of books accepted as Scripture by the Church. A good resource for this is F. F. Bruce, *The Canon of Scripture*.

praiseworthy. There was no "spin." They accepted conflicting stories, and conflicts between individuals, and did not excise reports about important, godly people behaving badly. This says a great deal about their integrity and honesty as they assembled God's Word and passed it down to us.

In other words, they looked at Scripture and said, "This is inspired by God's Spirit; we dare not change it even if we can't explain the differences and difficulties."

The Old Testament was completed long before Jesus was born. The New Testament books began to be written perhaps A.D. 30-40, and were likely complete by the year 100 or so. But they circulated individually and separately, copied and passed hand to hand (along with *many* other early Christian writings—some terrific, some not), long before they began to be collected together into the "New Testament" that we have today.

Assembling the Bible—including deciding which writings to include and exclude—was a complex process of debate, prayer, time and the seeking of the Holy Spirit.

There was plenty of hand-wringing and disagreement along the way, and it took until the year A.D. 397 before it was complete.

Even at that—with all of the prayer, hard work and argument that went into choosing which books to include and which to leave out—there are still advocates for change in the list of "acceptable" books to include.

Martin Luther himself, the vocal proponent of *Sola Scriptura* ("Scripture Alone") as the source of faith for all, called the Book of James "an epistle of straw" and didn't think it measured up to being included in the New Testament.

Recently some have advocated adding the Gospel of Thomas (an old Gnostic text rejected by the early Church) as a fifth gospel book, and there remains ongoing debate about the inclusion of "intertestamental"[17] literature—the Apocrypha—in the Bible.

Most Protestants exclude the Apocrypha entirely, some include it as "non-canonical" but valuable for its spiritual insights, and some (including Roman Catholics) include it as a regular canonical part of their Bibles. I won't open up these debates other than to acknowledge that they exist.

My regard of Scripture is similar to that of the early Church as they assembled the Canon: I believe it is reliable and inspired by the Holy Spirit, but I do not feel the need to explain away areas of contradiction or conflict.

The Apostle Paul says:

---

[17] Books written after the completion of the Old Testament and before the writing of the New Testament.

All Scripture is inspired by God[18] and is useful to teach us what is true and to make us realize what is wrong in our lives. It corrects us when we are wrong and teaches us to do what is right.[19]

This is a valuable and healthy understanding of Scripture. In this quote Paul is referring to the *Old Testament*, because the New Testament didn't exist yet. Paul's letter to Timothy was then, well, a letter to Timothy from Paul.[20] Today we also accept this letter, and the whole New Testament, as also "God-breathed" and "useful to teach us what is true." We affirm the work of the Holy Spirit in the mind and heart of the authors as they wrote the text that we read today.

INERRANCY

"The inerrancy of Scripture" is a common affirmation in statements of faith among some Protestant groups. What does this mean?

The noun *inerrancy* goes back only to 1818, to *An Introduction to the Critical Study and Knowledge of the Holy Scriptures* by Thomas Hartwell Horne. Ironically, he used the word for the opposite purpose of its more-recent advocates, in saying, "Absolute inerrancy is impractical in any printed book."[21]

The adjective form, *inerrant*, is a little older, from the Latin root *errare*, "to err or wander." This was first used in English in 1652 to refer to "wandering" stars—that is, planets. "Inerrant" thus referred to "fixed" stars—actual stars so far away that they didn't appear to move (though in reality, of course, they do).

There are obvious errors in the many *copies* we have of the original texts of Scripture,[22] and thus the claim of inerrancy isn't made about the copies—which are all we have. We know they are not without error.[23] For those who affirm inerrancy the claim is instead made about the "original autographs." They are perfect, it is said, because the Holy Spirit inspired the authors. Holy Spirit inspiration is a good thing!

Nevertheless, we should ask: If God inspired the authors of Scripture, would He not also inspire the readers? If we are given the Holy Spirit when we become believers, does He take up residence in us for no purpose? Didn't Jesus say the Holy Spirit would lead us into all truth? And if Scripture contains truth about God and His purposes and counsel for us, wouldn't the Holy Spirit naturally lead us into it?

---

[18] The Greek word translated as "inspired" is *theopneustos*, "God-breathed."

[19] 2 Timothy 3:16. More literally the Greek reads, "Every writing God-breathed and helpful toward instruction, toward correction, toward straightening up, toward training in what is right, that the person of God toward every good work might be wholly equipped."

[20] Some authors suggest that it was Scripture the instant the pen touched paper to write it. Maybe so. But Paul was not referring to his own writings when he made this statement. He was referring to the Old Testament, period.

[21] He wasn't referring to the "original autographs" but to the process of producing books.

[22] Though not many inconsistencies, and not particularly important ones at that.

[23] There is actually one small sector of inerrantists that insists that one of the copies of Scripture, the *textus receptus*, is without error; another smallish group insists that the King James Bible, in English, is inerrant. These are noted, but will not be addressed here.

God inspired the writers of Scripture, but He didn't leave it simply to ink and paper to carry His Word and His intentions to our hearts. He also inspires us as we read it. Just as God was very serious when He inspired the authors of Scripture to write, so also He is very serious when He inspires the committed readers of Scripture to read, and *we* should be very serious when we invite Him to lead us in our study of the Bible.

We don't meet just words on paper in the Scriptures, however perfectly recorded. We meet *Him.* And though we will often get things wrong, He honors our willingness and guides us patiently to the truth.

How to See the Bible

Here is a simple three-step way for dealing with the authority of the Bible:

First, God was and is intentional and serious about restoring and maintaining a relationship with us. He was intentional and serious in causing all of Scripture to be written. He was intentional and serious in the historical process of many minds and hearts who discerned what was to be a part of the Canon of Scripture and what did not rise to that level.

This doesn't mean that some of the other books written in New Testament times, or even in modern times, aren't true or don't contain valuable insights into God's character. The *Epistles of Clement*, Augustine's *Confessions* and *Mere Christianity* are shining examples … but they don't rise to the level of Canon.

The Bible stands alone in both form and content. There isn't anything else like it even among the most profound scriptural texts.

Second, it does God and us a disservice to pick verses out of context and build belief systems on them. We need the whole counsel of God in Scripture, and we need it in order to understand any verse truly and fully. That means we need to take the whole of Scripture seriously. We should not read it with a razor blade.

Thomas Jefferson is an example of this. He made his own version of the Bible by cutting out every verse he didn't like or agree with and then pasting together the ones that remained. As smart as Jefferson was, I don't think that was his best idea.

God was serious in the creation of Scripture. We need to be serious in its absorption. If a particular verse or part of the Bible offends me, rather than skip it or declare loudly that I disagree, I should consider it instead a red flag indicating that there is something I don't understand yet, that God *wants* me to understand. I should dig deeper rather than run away or cut it out. This may seem counterintuitive to some, but it will yield great rewards: *Press in* rather than flee.

Third, don't be intimidated by either those who reject the Bible or those who insist you aren't a Christian if you do not take it literally.

Rejecting the Bible completely, saying, "It's just a creation of another culture; we don't really need to pay attention to it," is misguided.

Taking it literally makes nonsense out of its poetry, imagery, metaphor and parables. It is equally misguided.

Take it seriously. It is reliable, and it contains all things necessary for salvation.

INFALLIBILITY

Infallible (adj.) means "incapable of error." *Infallibility* is a noun that refers to this (asserted) incapability to commit error. The Roman Catholic and Eastern Orthodox churches maintain that the Holy Spirit will not allow error in the Church's teachings, within ecumenical councils, and (in Roman Catholicism) for certain declarations of the Pope (such as the Immaculate Conception of Mary and the Assumption of Mary), and the teachings of the "ordinary and universal Magisterium."

Without going into detail, it should be noted that this infallibility is asserted for 21 councils (historical meetings over many centuries, mostly of bishops, which made doctrinal statements) by the Roman Catholic Church, for 7 by the Eastern Orthodox Church, and for the "Christological statements" of the first seven by some Protestants. (A reader will search in vain for a Christological statement in the seventh council. It's in a footnote.)

These conflicting claims of infallibility cannot all be true.

How to See the Great Councils of the Church

I believe the teachings of the Church and the councils can be taken with great gravity without imposing upon them either the idol or the onus of infallibility.

THE COVERING AUTHORITY

All of Scripture, and all of the councils and teachings of the Church, stand under the covering authority of two great commandments, and so must we. Those two great commandments come from the lips of Jesus, and He said this:

> "'You shall love the LORD your God with all your heart, with all your soul, and with all your mind.' This is the first and great commandment. And the second is like it: 'You shall love[24] your neighbor as yourself.' On these two commandments hang all the Law and the Prophets."[25]

That is, every word of Scripture, everything about our faith, belief, practice, doctrine, theology, church polity, teaching, authority, and our daily living in the world, stands under the force, command, and the covering authority of those two great commandments. Jesus said *all the Law and the Prophets* hang on these two commandments. They are the standard and touchstone for all that we believe and do.

Yet what is true of many of us as Christians is that while we may believe that all the Law and the Prophets stand under those two commandments, we don't think *we* have to, particularly if we feel threatened by doctrine, practice, theology, people—or other religions. Then it is okay to behave with sarcasm, with bitterness, with anger

---

[24] Go read the whole of Luke 15 for insight into what Jesus means about love.
[25] Matthew 22:37-40, NKJV.

towards our enemies, attacking them, belittling them, caricaturing them, putting them down, treating them as less than worthy of the love Jesus commanded.

But we are *not* exempt. We too, like the Law and the Prophets, must stand under those two great commandments. If we believe the Scriptures and the Church have authority in our lives, there is no other option.

22.
Religious Concepts

The Gospel is arguably God's greatest revelation to us, but if we worship our Concepts about it, rather than live it, we render it worthless—and *we* can become dangerous.

WHAT MATTERS AND WHAT DOESN'T

A couple of chapters back I said:

> Much of what has seemed, over the centuries, like a vital defense of God, or of Jesus, or of the Christian faith, has in fact been a battle of concepts within a philosophical framework that is ultimately foreign to the God who reveals Himself in the Bible. Just because these debates have used biblical terms does not make the debates either holy or meaningful.

That was in the chapter on the Trinity. Now I want to apply this more broadly, and focus even more deeply on essentials and non-essentials, on *what matters* and *what doesn't*.

If I do this well, you will likely find this chapter very unsettling. It may make you angry. At a minimum, it will be an intellectual, emotional and cultural challenge.

We all have methods of *thinking* and *feeling* about things—analyzing, measuring, judging, accepting, rejecting, praising, weeping—to determine whether something is to us: true, valuable, dangerous, trite, profound, unimportant, beautiful, and so on.

These methods are partly rooted in our common humanity, and partly taught to us by our cultures, our experiences and our educational training in the social, scientific, religious, psychological and emotional worlds we all inhabit. These vary considerably across the world and through history.

It is a very difficult thing to try to see and feel something afresh, free of these methods, or even to realize that *these methods are limiting us in how we comprehend and emotionally respond.* And yet even if that assertion is granted, and the desire is present to realize and then step beyond our ingrained methods of thinking and feeling, it is *really* hard to do—near to impossible!

Yet essential.

So try to hang in with me to the end—this chapter and the two that follow it—and then turn it over to God for His judgment.

Two Doors

Two doors stand before us. One is labeled "God," and the other, "Lectures About God."[1] Everyone is lined up to go through the second, because going through the first is too frightening. But if (as Scripture reveals) there is a God who is Creator of us and all that is around us—and who is Other than us and beyond our comprehension, but who desires *relationship* with us and reveals Himself to us (to the degree that we can receive it, which He knows)—and makes *covenant* with us and offers us access to Himself and reconciliation even when we have left Him … then *why would we choose lectures instead?*

The testimony of Scripture, which is the testimony of generations of people He created and led and loved, is just this: He desires and makes available to us a loving, chastening and deepening relationship with Himself, a covenant. He offers counsel on what makes this possible and what hinders it. He chases after us even when we rebel. He desires us to be with Him so much that He willingly suffered death to demonstrate it. He cares for us and tells us to care for each other.

We find other things to do instead.

We ignore Him. Or deny He exists. For agnostics and atheists, at least they can claim no obligation to follow His commands, or His teaching on love. Instead they must construct their own systems of relationships, justice and organization. And these stand or fall based on efficacy, or power, or inattention.

But for those who claim to believe in God, we seem largely to fail often, and often miserably, at living out what He called us to do as *our part* of the covenant. As His creations, you'd think following His lead would be our heart's desire.

We find other things to do instead.

Distractions and Ambitions

These "other things" include the obvious: work, entertainment, hobbies, food, sports and other distractions. These are not ungodly in and of themselves; they are an issue only when they consume us and diminish or replace love of God and each other.

But there is another class of "other things" that *is* innately ungodly, though it has the guise of godliness: when we elevate "things" over love of God or people.

---

[1] A paraphrase of Søren Kierkegaard, who is said to have imagined two doors, one labeled "Heaven" and the other "Lectures About Heaven."

Here I do not just mean the conspicuous "things" of ambition: wealth, fame, success, possessions. These can easily replace God on the throne of our hearts, and our *pursuit* of any of them can run roughshod over people who get in our way.

Wealth, fame, success and possessions *can be* handled with humility and caring, but they carry obvious danger both in their pursuit, and in reliance upon them once obtained.

But this is all well and often proclaimed. It is not my focus here. Rather it is our willing idolatry of religious things, and our vicious defense of them.

RELIGIOUS IDOLATRY

What is most insidious among those who claim belief in God is the idolatry of religious doctrine, worship, polity[2] and culture, and the use of disagreement on these as an excuse to mistreat others. This ranges from disregard to verbal attack to physical assault to murder to genocide. All in an alleged defense of God, who is omnipotent and needs no defenders. It would seem silly were it not so profoundly tragic.

There is a reason Jesus spoke of *two* great commandments rather than just the one to love God. He saw that those who claimed to love God were using it as an excuse for all manner of ungodly behavior toward other people.[3] He said, "All the Law and the Prophets hang on these two commandments."[4] Then He immediately illustrated the command to "love your neighbor as yourself" by describing to His listeners a neighbor who was a Samaritan—a despised outsider whose religious beliefs were flawed.[5]

Jesus eliminated the loophole of claiming "neighbor" to be someone like us who we love anyway (or who has religious beliefs we approve of). And on the outside chance that someone might claim that an "enemy" fell outside even the broadest category of neighbor, He said, "Love your enemies, do good to those who hate you, bless those who curse you, pray for those who mistreat you."[6]

He didn't leave any loopholes.

Let me first spell out explicitly how we have violated Jesus' commandments in seeming to be His followers, and then propose a heart-understanding He has given us that can act as a corrective to this misapprehension and misapplication of His teachings and sacrifice—so that His love for us may no longer be wasted. Or worse, that He does not even recognize us as one of His own.

This will be very plainspoken. If it doesn't make you squirm or shout *hallelujah*, then either I'm not doing my job or you've failed to understand my point. I'm not hopeless about the problem—in fact, I'll suggest a way out—but I won't pull any punches.

---

[2] The organizational structure and rules of a church or denomination.
[3] See Mark 7:6-13 and John 8:1-11 for a couple of examples.
[4] Matthew 22:40, NIV.
[5] See Luke 10:25-37 and John 4:20-22.
[6] See Luke 6:27-36 for the full text.

We Christians have a serious problem, and we need to see it and confess it before we can be redeemed from it. So I will be blunt and thorough in describing it, and I will pray for God's grace in its solution.

Once more: Much of what has seemed, over the centuries, like a vital defense of God, or of Jesus, or of the Christian faith, has in fact been a battle of concepts within a philosophical framework that is ultimately foreign to the God who reveals Himself in the Bible.

Different denominations have different philosophical structures (of doctrines, worship styles, etc). Different theologians and movements within and outside of denominations also have different philosophical structures they defend.

The followers of these many structures constantly and fiercely attack one another, and are praised for doing so by their fellow adherents. The overarching battle of concepts rewards and promotes this ungodly behavior, because this battle of concepts is founded on "defending God" by means of attacking those who do not share their beliefs. In the process of "defending God," they violate Jesus' command to love God, neighbor and enemy.

Please hang in here with me as this problem is laid out more fully. It is a very serious issue for the Body of Christ, and it has gone largely unnoticed or intentionally ignored, with far-reaching consequences.

There have been battles over small parts of it, but the larger issue has been missed. I believe God is afoot in bringing us to a realization of the problem, and intends to redeem us and it to His good purposes, but we have to face this disorder and call it out.

How the Problem Arose

The Old Testament[7] is largely a narrative telling (a story, or "testament") in Hebrew of the adventures of human beings, primarily Jews, and their *life with God*. It contains God's counsel on that relationship, His counsel on living with each other and in the world, and plenty of examples of people behaving badly—toward God and each other—as well as examples of love and self-sacrifice.

The New Testament continues the story in this pattern, but introduces some new elements: It is in Greek[8] (at least the copies we have of it); it explicitly extends the invitation of relationship with God to non-Jews; it declares that in the person of Jesus, the love of the Father God is revealed in and through a human being; and it reminds all, Jew and non-Jew alike, what the basic requirements of living with God and each other are. It also promises the assistance of the Holy Spirit to counsel, comfort and lead us.

Both Testaments are a large body of writing, and are highly diverse in form, content and theme, though all of it, ultimately, returns the reader to the same fundamental message of love of God and each other.

---

[7] In case I haven't said this before, "old" doesn't mean "outdated." It means that it came before the "new" Testament.

[8] Some parts may have originally been in Hebrew, Aramaic or Syriac.

Building Religious Concepts From Scripture

Our modern age and the whole Western world owes its foundation to ancient Greece. In the several hundred years before the birth of Christ, Greece produced some of the greatest minds of all time, and from them whole schools of philosophy, geometry, science, and more.

In most cases those schools of thought encompassed all of these topics as an integrated whole: The universe was seen by many of these gifted thinkers with the beauty of pure geometric forms expressed in the symmetry of nature, in the planets and their motions, in the mathematical means to build great buildings and temples with extraordinary precision, or simply to think through the pure discipline of geometry and the proofs that could be deduced from simple premises.

Just the names of these thinkers conjure awe: Socrates, who taught Plato, who taught Aristotle, who taught Alexander the Great. Euclid, Pythagoras, Archimedes, Diogenes, Zeno. Dozens and dozens more.

What they had in common was an extraordinary ability to examine the world around them, its objects and its people, its ideas and its methods, and extract from these sources a collection of elements: ideas, themes, and similarities; and then carefully abstract and categorize them into highly organized arrays of concepts—very geometric, taut, connected—like rows upon rows, shelves upon shelves, within vast multi-story warehouses of ideas, each warehouse a school of philosophy with a genius in charge. A place for everything and everything in its place.

It wasn't absolutely perfect, and things sometimes got miscategorized, misunderstood or missed, but the basic approach was there: analyze, extract, abstract, fabricate. Organize the objects of thought into categories: build concepts, subconcepts. Use logic and deduction and get it all in mathematical order. It was science, mathematics, philosophy and even physical culture (the origin of the Olympics) and government (the invention of democracy), all evolving together in one of the greatest thinking and living revolutions of in human history.

We are all heirs of this extraordinary flowering of thought and civilization.

This foundation spread to all of the Mediterranean world, and to Israel and Judah and northern Africa before 300 B.C. It continues to this day, and was the fire and foundation of the Renaissance (the *re-awakening* of Greek methods of thinking) and the Enlightenment.

Science owes its foundations to ancient Greece, as do all *modern academic methods in all fields*, including *theology* and all of the *arts and humanities*.

Take literature, for example. A novelist may do a wonderful job of telling a complex, exciting story, full of adventure, characters, secrets, surprises and emotions. The story fulfills its purpose and *affects the reader by the power of the telling of it.*

An expert in literary form can take this novel and examine it—expose it to scientific scrutiny, if you will—extracting specific ideas, themes and methods: How was the character development of the main protagonist accomplished? What were the challenges faced and how were they overcome? How were the scenes and the sense of place constructed? Was the language vernacular or sophisticated?

What was the pacing—fast, slow, erratic? What was the form: romance, adventure, science fiction, fantasy? How extensive was the vocabulary? At what level of education was it aimed? Were there technicalities of profession or time and place that gave the story substance? Was it derivative, like another novelist or school of writing, or unique, or simply ill-formed? What themes did the author intend to convey, and what methods were used to accomplish this? Did the author have a "message" that the reader was expected to absorb and perhaps adopt?

Asking questions like these, and hundreds more, a good literary analyst can disassemble a story into what he or she sees as its structural and thematic elements, and fabricate from them a *concept*, if you would, of what this book is about and how it accomplishes its purposes.

The literary analyst takes a story apart and *analyzes* it. The results of the analysis can exceed by many times the volume of the story itself. And with even the very best analysts, sometimes they get it right, and sometimes they don't. The author might hear the analyst's conclusions and say, "That's pretty accurate. That is what I intended and how I went about it." Or, the author might say, "Not even close! That wasn't what I meant at all."

Sometimes analysts will fight over who did the best job of analysis, and they will often disagree markedly and rabidly with each other. Sometimes they will even tell the author he did not understand his own story correctly!

Literary analysis (which is founded on Greek philosophical methods) is a rich and complex undertaking, and creates complicated and detailed arrays—scaffoldings of thoughts, themes, conclusions, opinions—that take on existences independent of and often beyond the original story they purport to understand. They are not necessarily wrong in this, but they are always obviously something *other than* the story on which they are based.

Why do we care about this in a book about what Christians believe and why? Because that is just how Christian thinking has worked out its ideas, year after year, since the time of Paul. *It is a thoroughly Greek process*, creating vast structures of themes and ideas: analyzed, extracted, abstracted, fabricated, and put up in giant conceptual arrays, like tall warehouses, filled with row after row, shelf after shelf, of analysis after analysis.

The problem is, they aren't the story the Author wrote, and they aren't the Author who seeks relationship with His followers. They are Concepts fabricated by the minds of people, based on a disassembly and analysis of the story.

Various groups and individuals have pulled from the scriptural narrative various *themes* and *ideas, fabricated* them into a philosophical *structure*, a religious *Concept*, have used this to guide the production of Doctrine, Ritual, Polity and more—as well as to interpret other themes and ideas in Scripture and in the world—and have given the Conceptual structure an independent status and reputation of its own.

Saying that various religious groups *fabricated* them is not meant to imply fraud, but rather an extended and complex process of analysis, extraction, abstraction, categorization, comparison, critique, deduction, induction and careful fabrication—piece by piece, category by category, syllogism by syllogism, reference by reference—until whole Concepts emerged from this pulling of *themes* and *ideas* from the scriptural narrative.

As these major religious Concepts evolved, they generated layers of subconcepts, including doctrines and practices, patterns of worship, methods of authority and organization (polity), forms of both promotion and defense, and more. Vast warehouses of Concepts, often each headed by a religious genius.

Were each Concept's vocabulary not so overtly religious and dependent on the Testaments, and the Apocrypha, it might simply be perceived as only another Greek philosophical school, much like the Platonic, Utilitarian, Stoic, Pythagorean and Aristotelian—most of which also contained religious concepts. Each Concept has the same structure as those schools do; it fits within the same basic worldviews. In fact, had Christianity not become so dominant after Constantine, it might *still* be regarded as just another Greek philosophical school, one among many.

The whole fabrication process of Christian religious Concepts is simply Greek in its origins and methods. As noted, all of the Mediterranean world and the Middle East had been under the deep influence of Greek philosophical teaching and culture for *centuries* before the first New Testament book was written. Even the Old Testament itself had been rewritten in Greek[9] because it was a language most Jews spoke—like nearly everyone else in that day and place.

This Concept-building process, at least in its early stages, may not even have been an intrinsically bad thing. In humble hands such Concepts could help to share God's love with others.

One might even say that this is just what Paul did in taking the Gospel to the Gentiles. He "contextualized" the God of Israel into concepts that his hearers would understand, so that they might accept the invitation of forgiveness and salvation, the covenant that Jesus shared and embodied.

However, the key point is that much of early Christian writing and debate— as well as the establishment of the Church after Constantine, the complete integration of the Church into the Roman Empire, the energetic establishment of Doctrine and Creed, Rituals, Practices, forms of Worship, Polity, Hermeneutical methods, the development of Systematic Theology, and then the division of the Church into countless denominations (tens of thousands at this point)—all owe their foundations to Greek philosophical methods and culture.

These produced Concepts about God and man, and these Concepts multiplied and gained independent recognition and authority. They were about God, and about Scripture (the Story of Life with God: both Old and New Testament), and they contained vocabulary from Scripture (as well as Greek philosophy), *but they were neither God nor Scripture.* They were *Concepts.* See the *Concept Creation* illustration that follows to help visualize the issue.

Note also that the Church, as it became embedded in the Roman Empire, followed the organizational model of Rome, whose education was led by Greek teachers over many centuries. Even Rome's military, like all subsequent military

---

[9] The Septuagint, completed about 132 B.C.

forces up to today, studied the methods and principles of Alexander the Great, the pupil of Aristotle. The Church grew large while nurtured and trained in this environment.

More, the Church was steeped in things Greek even from its first moment, because the culture of the Middle East had already been Greek *for more than three centuries*. As the Church matured, this influence of Greek philosophical methods—of thinking, analyzing, categorizing and describing—only deepened. In the centuries after Jesus, it changed the Church from a Greek-influenced Jewish movement in and about Judea, to a largely Greek-culture religious institution throughout the Mediterranean, with a Roman governmental structure and Roman norms of authority and hierarchy.[10]

Alfred North Whitehead once wryly observed that European philosophy "consists of a series of footnotes to Plato."[11] And although some modern philosophers might draw the lines from early Greek philosophy straight to the Renaissance and the Enlightenment, Greece clearly also provided the foundational thought-forms (ways of thinking) for the Church from its inception, and later quite explicitly for Aquinas (who seems to have learned of Aristotle from Islamic scholars), and continuing through all of the systematic theologians who followed him, right up to this day.

But again: Long before Aquinas "rediscovered" the Greeks and their methods of reasoning, their ways of doing philosophy, their ways of fabricating philosophical structures, Greek philosophy was *already* the foundation of the Christian Church's religious Concepts. It was in the DNA of the Church, though the Church seemed unaware of it, or unaware that it had been so thoroughly infiltrated and overtaken.

This is not a new revelation or big secret. It is the analytical and creative *thought process* by which Christian religious Concepts, and their subsequent doctrines, dogma, creeds, rituals, liturgy, worship, practices, polities, canons and even hermeneutics were formulated. (This is not to deny the work of the Holy Spirit in any of this, but as we will see shortly, the products of the process take on a life of their own.)

It is worth noting that early Christian religious Concepts were not readily accepted as equals to the work of ages of Greek philosophical schools. Critics in the Roman and Greek cultures in the first two centuries found the Church's philosophical efforts inept and even dangerous, and ridiculed them—beginning at least as early as Paul, recorded in Acts 17 and elsewhere.[12]

---

[10] The Roman Catholic Church has a hierarchical structure that is a precise copy of the Roman Empire's, because after Constantine, a prelate (church official) was placed in a parallel position to each official at each level of the Roman government. The Pope is the equivalent of Caesar (with similar authority), the Cardinals are Provincial Governors, etc.

[11] Whitehead, Alfred North. *Process and Reality*. New York: Free Press, 1978, p. 39.

[12] See his speech in Acts 17, and his letters to the Corinthians, Ephesians, Galatians and Timothy (among others) for examples.

The Church's development of *detailed* and *extensive* philosophical Concepts arose in part in response to the ongoing and condescending criticism it received from its critics, and in part as various Christian religious Concepts arose and conflicted with each other.[13] The works of Origen (*Against Celsus* and *On First Principles*[14]), Justin Martyr (*First Apology*), Irenaeus[15] (*Against Heresies*) and Tertullian[16] (*Apologeticus*) are examples of just such responses. Attack and defense occurred on both sides of the debate, and over the course of centuries.

---

[13] "The Christianity of the first century had yet to develop an assailable system of belief or a fixed canon of writings from which such beliefs could be educed." From *Celsus, on the True Doctrine: A Discourse Against the Christians*. Trans. R. Joseph Hoffman. New York: Oxford University Press, 1987, p. 24.

[14] Here Origen (A.D. 185–254) is commonly seen to develop his concept of Trinity based in part on the "triadic emanation" ideas of "Middle Platonic" philosophies. It is quite worth reading about his life and philosophical efforts in understanding the point being made in this chapter about religious Concepts.

[15] Also, it should be noted, one who argued that Christian unity comes by humbly accepting one doctrinal authority—that of councils of bishops.

[16] From whom we get the Trinitarian concept of "three Persons, one Substance," although he was later spurned as unorthodox by the Church when he became a Montanist.

Concept Fabrication
Analysis, Extraction, Abstraction, Fabrication

How to read the illustration on the next page: Start at the upper left—humans were created by and experience **Life With God** over the centuries.

The authors of Scripture **wrote about Life With God**, creating the **Old** and **New Testament** (and the Apocrypha, though its inspiration is disputed). Most Christians believe the authors were inspired by the Holy Spirit in their work.

Because Greek culture and philosophical methods were so dominant throughout Judea and the Mediterranean world, when the Scriptures were read in the centuries after Christ, these **Greek Philosophical Methods** were used to **analyze** the texts and **extract** themes, ideas, parallels, grammatical structures and textual forms. These were then **abstracted** into categories, and philosophical **Concepts** were **fabricated**. These complex religious **Concepts** are a distinctively Greek way of thinking about life, and Life With God.

These Concepts then led inevitably to the creation of **Doctrines, Rituals, Canons** (laws), **Worship, Practices, Polities** (ways of organizing)**, Creeds** (conceptual statements of faith) and **Hermeneutics** (ways of reading and interpreting Scripture). Since the New Testament was compiled from numerous sources, and since many sources were rejected in this compiling, these Concepts and Hermeneutics also affected which sources were included in Scripture, and *continue to affect how Scripture is read and interpreted.*

All of this is the description of the process that occurred, and is intended to be observational, not critical. The *critique* of its consequences is a separate issue, and follows in the text.

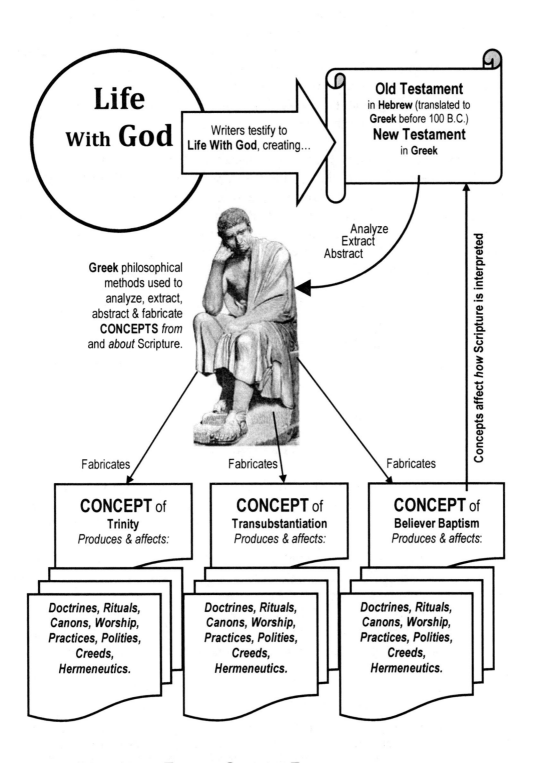

FIGURE: CONCEPT FABRICATION

I'm aware of the debates over the Hellenization of the Church stretching back to Hippolytus, Tertullian, Luther, Schleiermacher, Barth and others, and of the rejection of this by advocates of the modern Roman Church, which view it as a "Protestant problem." If anything this is just another proof of my assertion that this whole process of analysis, extraction, abstraction and fabrication of Concepts produces a framework of beliefs that divides the Church.

Further, these Concepts have more in common with scientific *hypotheses*[17] than they do with settled truth, yet over time they are treated as if they have arrived fully revealed from the pen of the Almighty.

The reason it is sometimes called a Protestant problem is because Scripture is held in high esteem by many Protestants (i.e., *Sola Scriptura*—"Scripture Alone" is the authority), and Church Tradition is held to be nonessential, or at least less essential. Roman Catholics (and some Protestants, including Anglicans and Lutherans) on the other hand, hold Church Tradition very high, along with Reason. But what is so highly esteemed in this theological trinity (Scripture, Tradition and Reason) is also its weakness: The way in which Greek philosophy provided the framework of Tradition and Reason led to Concepts that were fundamentally *analyses*, not laws; they may have been well-thought-through, but they were not proofs and not revelations from God—and though the Holy Spirit is invoked looking back at the process, His presence is not so self-evident as the proponents claim. These Concepts may have seemed important and valuable in the growth of the Church, but they were elevated beyond their function and station, and the Greek origin of the process was largely considered of no great matter. But it was *key* to this entire development.

WORSHIPING DOCTRINE

It gets even more problematic: One important product of Christian religious Concepts is Doctrine, essentially a set of ideas and themes drawn from a Concept, and woven together to assert a specific philosophical tenet that generally was often not explicitly present in the scriptural text, but was imputed from it by linking several verses and ideas found there. Many of these have been examined in the previous chapters. Some are fairly straightforward and provoke little controversy, while others continue to be contested.

Some of these Doctrines are labeled heresies, usually because they tended to divide the Church into factions, or because they contained elements that appeared to misrepresent God, or contradicted the dominant Doctrines of the period.

---

[17] In scientific methodology *concepts* lead to *hypotheses*, which are tested to see if they are true and accurately describe reality, which lead to *theories* (accepted hypotheses), which if proven over the course of many tests, lead to "*laws*," which generalize many observations. Though not all of this is easily applied to religious concepts, it should at least make us wonder why theologians and the Church go so quickly from Concepts to Doctrines.

There is an old saying: "History is written by the victors." This helps in understanding why we believe what we believe today in the Church, at least in terms of Doctrine.[18]

The problem begins to unveil itself here: Once a Doctrine gains sufficient prominence, it tends to draw not just advocates, but *worshipers*. Instead of worshiping God alone, we worship Doctrines about God, and promote and defend them passionately. They are easier to understand and control than a Being Who is Holy, Wholly Other, Omnipotent and Omniscient.

Even if I believe God loves me, and desires loving relationship with me, His power and *otherness* frighten me—as they should.

Doctrine doesn't scare me. As with wealth, fame, success and possessions, I want to hold on to my doctrine and defend it. And like wealth, fame, success and possessions, I can and do make an idol of it.

We die for and kill for idols all the time. Humans always have. We still do. Whether "honor" or position, fame or religion, nationalism or race, gender or beauty, we tend to *idolize* what we want or want to keep, and we fight for it, often regardless of the harm we do to other people or to our world.

We make idols and fight to defend them. We justify such battles with self-righteous explanations, and we labor to get others to bend to our will or submit to our vision. Such idolatry is not unique to Christians, or even to religion, but it is common to our humanity. This is why Scripture is so compelling, and why we must listen again to God's first commandment:

> You must not have any other god but me. You must not make for yourself an idol of any kind, or an image of anything in the heavens or on the earth or in the sea. You must not bow down to them or worship them, for I, the LORD your God, am a jealous God who will not tolerate your affection for any other gods.[19]

In the event that anyone thinks this passage is simply about tribal gods made of stone or wood, and not about idols like *pride* or *fame* or *property* or *wealth*—or idols of Doctrine, Ritual, even Hermeneutics—just read the Bible. It is replete with such idols and exhortations against them. We began all of those kinds of idolatry right at the beginning, and they were well-known to God and to the ancient authors of Scripture. We were warned early!

Our idolatry of Concept—especially the part called Doctrine and supposedly all about God and holy behavior—leads us to attack, disfellowship, injure and hate others who cling to different Doctrines, or to none.

---

[18] Some might ask, "Wasn't the Holy Spirit leading the development of doctrines?" The difficulty in this assertion is that many doctrines held as essential in various divisions of the Church are directly contradictory to those held elsewhere. Which is just exactly the problem under study here! The doctrines are worshipped and the Holy Spirit is claimed by all sides as their author. See **Infallible** in the Glossary Plus for more detail.

[19] Deuteronomy 5:7-9.

Even if their Doctrines *are* wrong, we conduct our debates as if *we are exempt from God's commandments* about loving neighbors and even enemies. We attack and belittle others. We treat them with condescension and sarcasm, full of ourselves and with self-righteousness. At our worst, we murder our opponents *en masse*. The partisanship for and the idolatry of our Doctrine wounds the heart of God. Our actions are *wrong*—even if our Doctrines are *right*.

The problem is rooted in our focus on *Doctrines*, and debate about them, rather than on *loving relationship with God and neighbor*.

This rabid debate over Doctrine stretches from the authors of our day back to Luther, Aquinas, Augustine, Irenaeus and others. As respected as anyone might be for contributions to the faith, to the development of settled Doctrine, or to a rigorous debate on a point of theology, each also is personally culpable when engaged in loveless attack. The former does not justify the latter.

With every debate over Doctrine, division follows. People are kicked out, or leave, and another sect or denomination arises—another group with its own correct way, and defenders of its correct way, angrily contesting against the "false way" of the group they just divorced.

The children of such divorces learn from their parents what to do when they disagree: Attack the *person*, and divorce again. It is ironic that voices who most loudly denounce divorce in the marriage of people often celebrate the divorces of *churches*—their own, or those of their founders.

> "So why do you keep calling me 'Lord, Lord!' when you *don't do what I say?* I will show you what it's like when someone comes to me, listens to my teaching, and then *follows it*. It is like a person building a house who digs deep and lays the foundation on solid rock. When the floodwaters rise and break against that house, it stands firm because it is well built. But anyone who hears and doesn't obey is like a person who builds a house without a foundation. When the floods sweep down against that house, it will collapse into a heap of ruins."[20]

The foundation Jesus speaks of here is not transubstantiation, Trinity, inerrancy, systematic theology, baptism, apostolic succession, textual criticism, epiclesis, Orthodoxy, Roman Catholicism, Protestantism or any such thing. The solid foundation is *following* what Jesus taught: "when someone comes to me, listens to my teaching, and then *follows it*."[21]

If we want evidence that the Church has forgotten what Jesus taught, we need only consider the state of the Church—disputing not over how better to live as Jesus called us to live, or about love of God and each other, *but over Concepts:* doctrine, worship, authority, liturgy, baptism, gender, Communion, translation, hermeneutics, tradition, tongues, evolution, end-times, titles, music, Rapture and the internal structure of God. And a thousand thousand more. We have collapsed

---

[20] Luke 6:46-49.

[21] Of course it has to be in human language and concepts and the like. The point is about doing what He said, rather than condemning each other.

into a heap of warring factions, followers of *this* Concept fighting followers of *that* Concept. We are obsessed.

The problem is that our foundation is not God, not even Scripture. It is instead Philosophy, and its *Concepts*.

We are not doing what Jesus told us to do.

We love Concepts and fight about them in the "Lectures About God" lecture halls. We avoid the door labeled "God."

Even now, seeing this achingly clearly perhaps for the first time, we will likely return to our fights, and we will find other things to do. We will justify our sin as a defense of God.

THE CONCEPTS WE FIGHT ABOUT

I've described the problem in broad terms above, and likely you can readily imagine or recall examples and particulars of where it has impeded or delayed the advance of the good news in your own life, church or denomination.

But let me give a few explicit exemplars of this problem of religious Concepts, specifically in Doctrine and Practice, knowing the actual scope of the issue is monumental and daunting in every way, able merely to be touched upon here. But it is a huge barrier to (and distraction from) doing the work of Christ, and must be exposed and acknowledged. Then I will suggest a way forward.

Some common examples of where and how the problem manifests:

BAPTISM

Baptism with water[22] in Scripture is a physical action with spiritual meaning. It signifies initiation and acceptance by God, was and is used by Jews to signify repentance and purity (both literally and figuratively), and occurs in the New Testament with John baptizing both repentant Jews, and Jesus. Later Jesus instructs His disciples to take the Good News to all nations and baptize them "in the name of the Father, and of the Son and of the Holy Spirit."[23] We later read of the disciples doing just this.

There are no rules given in Scripture regarding who can do baptism or receive it, although many rules have been formulated based upon various verses referring to baptism, as well as upon varying *Concepts* of God and the Church.

Nowhere in Scripture will you find a formula for only an adult making a specific and individual profession of faith in Jesus Christ as Lord and Savior, and then being fully immersed in water, with certain unfailing words, in order to be baptized and become a member of the church. But today you will find certain sects of Christians who will insist that certain specific rituals and practices about this are *necessary*, or *not*, to the true faith.

---

[22] "Baptism" is also used in other contexts to refer to a struggle, and also the coming of the Holy Spirit.
[23] Matthew 28:19.

- Some will baptize infants unfailingly, and adults only if they had not been baptized as infants. These sects will not re-baptize an adult if he or she was baptized as an infant, believing baptism can only happen once, though they normatively require someone baptized as a child to go through "confirmation" when they reach the age of reason, and *then* profess their faith in Jesus.
- Others refuse to baptize infants, insisting that only an adult can make a true profession of faith, and only *after this* can baptism occur. If an adult was baptized as an infant, it is considered no baptism at all, and re-baptizing is *required* (though of course it isn't considered "re-" because the first baptism isn't acknowledged).
- Some sprinkle or pour water for baptism; others call this "Satan's counterfeit" and require full immersion.
- Some denominations recognize baptisms done by some other denominations. Others consider them meaningless, and insist on baptizing anyone joining their church from outside the denomination.
- Some ritually baptize ancestors who died outside of their denomination, and even outside of the faith.
- Some churches will allow followers of Jesus to receive Communion in their church only if they have been baptized. Others will allow anyone professing faith to receive Communion. Still others will allow anyone who desires it to receive Communion. Some will allow only members of their denomination, and who have been baptized in their denomination, to receive Communion in their church.
- And some believe, as in the story I told back in Chapter 3, that unless you have been baptized in their single local church, you are still lost in your sins.

Every one of these positions on baptism is argued voluminously by countless authors over many centuries, and those who disagree with any of these positions have either fled or been forced out of their churches. Although *today* these debates consist, at best, of lengthy analysis and argument, and at worst of *ad hominem* accusations, sarcasm and disfellowship, over the centuries thousands of people were literally *tortured* and *killed* for choosing one side or another in this disagreement.

It was and still is a scandal.

Every one of these rituals and practices (as well as the Doctrines and Canons that accompany them) came from a religious Concept, drawn from pieces of Scripture and tradition, and reasoned out in a thoroughly analytical Greek way, and then used as a plumb line by which to judge the faith and worthiness of individuals and other Concepts.

COMMUNION

The night before Jesus died, He gathered His disciples for a Passover meal.

While they were eating, He took some bread, and after a blessing He broke it, and gave it to them, and said, "Take it; this is My body." And when He had taken a cup and given thanks, He gave it to them, and they all drank from it. And He said to them, "This is My blood of the covenant, which is poured out for many."[24]

Then He told them whenever they gathered for a meal, to do this again to remember Him.

This was a simple moment, clear, foreboding and hopeful.

But the Church, over many centuries, via many sects and their Concepts, has turned it into a complex series of competing Doctrines and Practices, which divide the Church into bitter rivalries, and thereby ignore the One who asked to be remembered.

- One group allows only ordained clergy to preside at the serving of bread and wine at Communion. Some of these allow ordination by the local congregation, to serve in ministry to it, or to be sent by it to serve elsewhere.
- Some of these have no process for ordination at all, and believe only in the "priesthood of all believers."
- Others require ordination by a regional group, with rules set down at the national level. Some of these require ordination by a bishop, who is overseen by a cardinal, primate, or regional bishop. Some of these require that every bishop ordaining every cleric have been ordained by a bishop in the "unbroken apostolic succession" of bishops from the time of the Apostle Peter. Others deny any such succession exists, or that it is unbroken.
- Some believe the wine Jesus used was actually grape juice, because surely He wouldn't have used anything that contained alcohol. Some are offended if grape juice is offered instead of, or in addition to, wine.
- Some use gold or other costly materials for chalices to hold the wine and have everyone drink from the single chalice. Others allow only a priest to drink the wine. Still others use small plastic cups with grape juice.
- Some use only unleavened bread. Some use only leavened bread. Some use either.
- Some have used milk and cookies—literally. Others found this to be blasphemy.
- Some break the Communion wafers into nine pieces, and drop them in the wine, serving the mixture of both with a tiny spoon.
- Some will allow anyone, even a single individual alone by him or herself, to have bread and wine, remembering Jesus as He asked.

---

[24] Mark 14:22-24, NASB.

- Some believe the bread and the wine literally become the body and blood of Jesus. Some explain this as "transubstantiation," a concept fabricated by Aquinas from an idea he got from Aristotle and Plato. Others prefer the idea of "consubstantiation," while still others go for "dynamic presence."
- Some believe it is literally the body and blood of Jesus, but don't explain how that can be true.
- Some believe in the "Real Presence" of Christ in the bread and the wine. Others find this idea superstitious and unnecessary.
- Some believe the bread and wine become His body and blood during the Communion service, and continue to be so. Others believe they revert to just bread and wine right after the service.
- Some don't believe they are His body and blood at all, but bread and wine eaten merely as an act of remembering Him.
- Some sects revere any leftover bread and place it in a special box or frame, and allow people to worship at it (because they believe it *is* Jesus). Others simply throw the leftovers in the garbage.
- Some allow laypeople to gather close at the altar; others fence off the altar area with railings or screens and permit only the ordained clergy and their aides to enter.
- Some permit any ordained person to preside at Communion.
- Some permit only certain classes of ordained people to preside.
- Some permit only ordained men to preside, believing that this person is standing in Christ's place and is the groom, welcoming His bride the Church to the holy meal. Some of these will recognize the ordination of the presider only if it was conducted by men who have never ordained women.
- Some see the meal as fellowship of Christ's followers, with no gender restrictions, and no assumptions about the leader being a groom or others being the bride.
- Some see bride and groom as a metaphor, one among many, of the love of God for His people, and not as a prescription for how Communion is to be conducted. Others treat this metaphor as if it were an inviolable command from God.
- Some call this gathering a Eucharist, or Great Thanksgiving; some call it Communion; others, the Last Supper or the Lord's Supper. Some use all of these terms, while others restrict themselves to just one or two. It is typical that many people who call it "The Lord's Supper" do not even know the term *Eucharist*, while those who always call it Eucharist rarely us the term *The Lord's Supper*.

Each of these many Concepts on the meal Jesus shared with His disciples, and whether and how His followers might recall the event, has fierce advocates and defenders.

Over the centuries, these Concepts about Communion have gained layers of Doctrines, Subdoctrines and Practices, volumes of arguments by theologians, canons (laws) and books of ritual, and each has grown into a mighty fortress alone and apart, a tall idol, whose followers worship there and declare other fortresses, other tall idols, other Concepts, to be anathema, unholy and unworthy (a mighty *fortress* is our god). It is sad irony that *communion*[25] actually means to be *in union*, in fellowship together, and that it has been used to produce *division*.

This process has been repeated not just about baptism and Communion, but for *countless other Concepts in the Church*, from apostolic authority, to ordination, to celibacy, to monogamy, to polygamy, to candles on the altar, to *having* an altar, to the use of instruments in worship, to dressing up for God on Sunday, to plain dressing, to women wearing head coverings, to men without moustaches—issues that seem large or trivial depending on who is judging them.

Religious Concepts of Jesus range from believing He is actually literally also Father God and Holy Spirit (manifesting Himself as each as needed), to three Persons in One God, to belief that He was a liberal political activist (not divine at all) railroaded to death by conservative enemies. All of these, *and thousands of others*, are the excuse for bitter dispute, division, divorce, disfellowship, and with many, even torture and killing.

What in heaven does this have to do with loving God and neighbor?

It is attention to things, not God or people. Even if we are thoroughly convinced that our Concept is superior to the other Concepts, how sad it must make the heart of God to see us viciously attack and separate from each other for the defense of our favorites.

We elevate things above people. Even though our "things" are built with religious words, and are partly derived from Scripture, they are still *Concepts*, not *God* and not *human beings*! Jesus did not set aside the Law and the Prophets, but He *did* insist they hang upon, and are subservient to, *love of God and neighbor*.

We fabricate religious Concepts, worship them, and *we hurt actual people while defending them.* We fail to *preserve* the love of God and neighbor.

Do our Concepts outrank love of God and neighbor? Sadly, the answer is yes. No excuses. It is what we have come to. God forgive us. What shall we do?

---

[25] See 1 Cor. 10:16. The Greek is *konionia*—partnership, fellowship, Communion.

23.
Reconciliation

It is my deep prayer that we all find our hearts broken by the lovelessness we have shown for one another in the Body of Christ. Though we all claim Jesus as Lord and Savior, we defend our religious Concepts, doctrines and practices as if they are our gods, and other people as if they are obstacles to our worship of these gods. We act as though such things matter and people don't.

We would rather be right in our own eyes than loving in God's eyes. Even when we realize we have spoken evil of others, rather than repent, we justify our words or actions with a "yes, but…" and an explanation. Yet Paul said to:

Speak evil of no one … be peaceable, gentle, showing all humility to all men.[1]

He also cautioned us to…

Avoid foolish disputes, genealogies, contentions, and strivings about the law; for they are unprofitable and useless.[2]

Instead of real unity in Christ, we war over our differing Concepts about Him. What a mess we've made of fulfilling "that all of them may be one, Father, just as you are in me and I am in you."[3]

We can change this! Here is what we are called to:

And all of this is a gift from God, who brought us back to himself through Christ. And God has given us this task of reconciling people to him. For God was in Christ, reconciling the world to himself, no longer counting people's sins against them. And he gave us this wonderful message of reconciliation. So we are Christ's ambassadors; God is making his appeal through us. We speak for Christ when we plead, "Come back to God!"[4]

---

[1] Titus 3:2, NKJV.
[2] Titus 3:9, NKJV.
[3] John 17:21a, NIV.
[4] 2 Corinthians 5:18-20.

We are called to bring the Gospel message of reconciliation to the world, *yet we ourselves have failed to be reconciled with one another,* and have too easily discarded the Jesus' clear commands about love of God, neighbor and even enemy!

So what shall we do? First we need to realize what this call to reconciliation *is **not***. Then we must understand what it *is*, and how to live it out. Let me summarize where we have gone wrong, then recall what Scripture calls us to do.

LOVE OF GOD AND NEIGHBOR

The life of a Christian should be one of sanctification, learning to live like Jesus: *Love God, neighbor and even enemy.* It is not about fighting over religious Concepts, and specifically as they form and then produce:

- Doctrines, Creeds, hermeneutics and apologetics
- Forms of worship, music or liturgy
- Structures of authority in the organization of the Church
- Traditions, whether ancient, modern or middle-aged
- Teachers, leaders, preachers or others

…and then harming (or even just marginalizing) those who disagree with or don't care about *our* favorite and well-thought-through Concepts.

Yet we are so entangled in the ways we have thought about all of this, that the most common immediate reaction to the warning above is fear—fear that the faith will be lost if any ground is given to those with different Concepts about … *see the list above!*

Here's where our thinking typically goes:

- we must be true to the faith once delivered to the saints, or
- we must be true to the Holy Catholic Church, or
- we must be true to the great Reformed Tradition, or
- we must be true to the progressive tradition, or
- we must be true to the Orthodox Church, or
- we must be true to the Historic Creeds, or
- we must be true to the Heidelberg Confession, or
- we must be true to the Westminster Confession, or
- we must be true to the Dogmatic Definitions of the undisputed Ecumenical Councils of the undivided Church, or
- we must be true to the Anglican tradition, or
- we must be true to our Evangelical witness, or
- we must be true to the insights of post-modernism, or
- we must be true to the 1769 Standard Text of the 1611 Authorized Version of the Holy Bible, or
- we must be true the insights of the Enlightenment, or

- we must be true to science and Christian Humanism, or
- we must be true to the orthodox faith of the Church, or
- we must be true to the founders of _____, or
- we must be true to the Social Gospel, or
- we must be true to our Baptist distinctives, or
- we must be true to *Sola Scriptura*, or
- we must be true to the insights of textual criticism, or
- we must be true to who we are, or
- we must be true to the tradition of scholarship, or
- we must be true to our academic foundations, or
- we must be true to our experience, or…

I could go on for pages. This is not a "conservative" or "liberal" problem. We are *all* caught in this familiar trap—so familiar that we don't realize we are captive to it, and we are *very* defensive of our own position.

Whatever our own theology is, we can't take a step out of it and consider whether there might be a *wholly different* way to live and move forward: a new heart-understanding. But we fear that even *considering* this puts our faith at risk—as if the only alternative to defending our religious Concepts is to fall into a pit of syncretism[5] or Universalism,[6] or into the jaws of our opponents' worldview, error or sin.

It is not so.

Stay with me on this—it is a key to deep reformation and reconciliation in the faith, but it will likely also make your brain hurt as we work through it. Perhaps your heart as well. It makes both of mine groan.

You may remember that back in Chapter 11, "Rule-Following and Transcendent Love," I talked about Kurt Gödel:

> Mathematician Kurt Gödel in 1931 published a paper titled "On Formally Undecidable Propositions." It demonstrates that in rigid, logical systems, or in any clearly stated set of rules, there will be some decisions or propositions that are undecidable, and that to decide them one must go *outside* of the set of rules to a larger system or reality. Jesus anticipates this in His life and teachings.

I'm going to reprise some of that here. It sets the foundation for escaping the trap that holds us all captive:

Listen first to what Paul says in describing the limits of the Law, and the coming of Jesus:

> Well then, why was the law given? It was given to show people how guilty they are. But this system of law was to last only until the coming of the child [Jesus] to

---

[5] In this context, the mixing of faiths.
[6] Declaring all faiths equally valid or true, or that all get saved, regardless.

whom God's promise was made. ... If the law could have given us new life, we could have been made right with God by obeying it, but the Scriptures have declared that we are all prisoners of sin, so the only way to receive God's promise is to believe in Jesus Christ.[7]

That is, we must rely on a reality outside of, and greater than, the one in which we are living.

Again, while we exist within this set of moral, ethical and religious rules, we cannot act, decide or live in a purely loving way. The Law is insufficient.

Kurt Gödel realized in 1931 that no system of rules could answer every question it raised—some 1900 years after Paul talked about this and Jesus declared our freedom.

Nearly two thousand years later, mathematics catches up with Jesus Christ.

Paul, in explaining what Jesus teaches, is in effect saying that there must be the transcendent that comes from beyond the system and its rules—from the Kingdom of God. It is that transcendence by which Jesus brought freedom of action—freedom finally to fulfill the purpose for which we were made:

> Until faith in Christ was shown to us as the way of becoming right with God, we were guarded by the law. We were kept in protective custody, so to speak, until we could put our faith in the coming Savior. ... But now that faith in Christ has come, we no longer need the law as our guardian. So you are all children of God through faith in Christ Jesus.[8]

In other words, Jesus makes it clear that following the rules is insufficient, and He takes us outside of the rules by the invasion of the Kingdom of God into our physical kingdom. He takes us outside of the rules in order to know what is true and to help us to know how to decide what to do, that is, *how to love*.

> But when the Pharisees heard that he had silenced the Sadducees with his reply, they thought up a fresh question of their own to ask him. One of them, an expert in religious law, tried to trap him with this question: "Teacher, what is the most important commandment in the Law of Moses?" Jesus replied, "'You must *love* the LORD your God with *all your heart, all your soul, and all your mind.*' This is the first and greatest commandment."[9]

Now that sounds like a rule, albeit a really important one. But in fact this command takes us *out* of the rules. It *transcends* them. It brings Heaven to Earth. It connects us to the Creator of the box in which we live. The rules that we had inside the

---

[7] Galatians 3:19, 21, NLT First Edition.
[8] Galatians 3:23, 25-26, NLT First Edition.
[9] Matthew 22:34-38.

box, inside the system, are insufficient, *incomplete*. Jesus says it, Scripture says it, Gödel the mathematician says it, and scientists and even artists realize it.[10]

Jesus, in the First Commandment, takes us outside the box: *Love God.* Why? *Because God is not in the box.* God *made* the box.

Then the second is like unto it, and this is how the transcendent moves into the world we occupy: *Love your neighbor as yourself.*

The *transcendent love* of God pours through us into the world we occupy. Simple obedience to the rules—which by themselves cannot work—is insufficient to the task, even when they rest on moral and ethical behavior.

God's concern is always about love, always about loving relationships, always about building up and not harming. His concern is not about the mere fulfillment of ritual obligations, or the following of law.

> So Christ has truly set us free. Now make sure that you stay free, and don't get tied up again in slavery to the law. ... For if you are trying to make yourselves right with God by keeping the law, you have been cut off from Christ! You have fallen away from God's grace. But we who live *by the Spirit*[11] eagerly wait to receive everything promised to us who are right with God through *faith*.[12] For when we place our faith in Christ Jesus, it makes *no difference* to God whether we are circumcised or not circumcised [that is, whether we have followed the ritual rules]. What is important is faith *expressing itself in love.* You were getting along so well. Who has interfered with you to hold you back from following the truth? It certainly isn't God, for He is the one who *called you to freedom.*[13]

I don't know about you, but this is very scary to me. It is much easier for me to try to follow, apply and impose rules all the time. The rules were there for a reason. They helped us understand right from wrong. But the true *love* that allows us to live as God desires us to live requires *transcendence*. And it calls us to *freedom*.

That transcendence is given to us in the simple command, "Love God," and in the simple application, "Love your neighbor as yourself." When we do this, we have fulfilled the law, we have transcended the law, and we have been set free by transcendent love.

Consider also how this makes sense of Jesus' teaching to Nicodemus back in the chapter on Salvation (Chapter 2), that we have to be *reborn* from above by water and the *Spirit*, and the promise that with our salvation, the *Holy Spirit* takes up residence *in us*. We become temples of God's presence. The transcendent—the God Who made the box—now lives in us.

---

[10]Again I would refer us to Heisenberg's Uncertainty Principle and Quantum Theory, and artist M.C. Escher, who showed how the rules of interpretation of drawing were insufficient to understand fully within the flat plane of the drawing. Also see the book *Flatland* by Edwin Abbot, which explains these concepts.

[11] Again, from *outside* of our world, our system.

[12] *Faith*—of an entirely different order than rules.

[13] Galatians 5:1, 4-8, NLT First Edition.

CIRCLING BACK TO APPROVAL AND REJECTION

Earlier we looked at obedience and saw how we can use this in an attempt to control God. We do this as we follow rules, ritual, behavioral controls, or whatever, in order to curry favor or avoid punishment, to gain approval and avoid rejection.

Clearly by now we should see that this is not the same as loving God or our neighbors. Not only is loving God and neighbor *not* an attempt to control God, but its source is a transcendent one that is outside of the system (the kingdom of earth) in which we live. *Transcendent love is of another order altogether*, beyond even the most laudable of human moral and ethical systems. When we act within the system of rules set for us, we behave. We seek approval as we conform. Even if we agree with the morals and ethics of the system, even if we see the value in them in showing right and wrong (as the Law in Scripture is said to do), it is still approval we seek. And within these systems, approval is given when we conform. But…

Approval is a very weak surrogate for love,
and it is *love* we are created to seek.

Love is *transcendent*, it comes from the Source of our creation, and it approaches people and circumstances with a heavenly view, not just a worldly one. Where the Pharisee saw a prostitute, Jesus saw a woman needing the love of God; where those who would stone an adulteress saw the Law violated, Jesus gave freedom from condemnation. Where others saw a despised tax-collector, or a Samaritan, or a blind man, or a demon-possessed man, or sick or dead, Jesus saw His *beloved* children, and *His love* brushed aside the judgments of men, *invaded* this kingdom of earth and its laws (even the laws of time and space), and revealed the *transcendent love* of the Kingdom of God.

It is to this that we are called.

Do you remember what Paul taught us about the Law? That it was our overseer, our guide, our teacher, until we grew up. The Law was not wrong, not bad, not in error—it was simply *insufficient* for the whole task of actually loving God and neighbor, of transcending the external rules and having God living and reigning in our hearts. And Jesus promised this: God, the Holy Spirit, living IN US and leading us into all truth! He *didn't* promise elegant, well-thought-through Concepts and our skillful application of them to each life circumstance, but instead He promised the discernment of *God in us*, living through us!

This is the fulfillment of the promise of Jeremiah:

But this is the covenant that I will make with the house of Israel after those days, says the LORD: I will put My law in their minds, and write it on their hearts; and I will be their God, and they shall be My people.[14]

Just as Jesus desired to free His followers of rule-following, whether those of the Pharisees or Sadducees, whether written Law or Oral Tradition (or the Talmud), so He also desires to free us.

As we have fabricated extensive Doctrines, Liturgies, Polities and ways of reading and explaining Scripture, to give us rules by which to judge right and wrong, and just as we have created edifices of these Concepts upon Concepts, and have argued them and scorned and harmed each other in the struggle to be right, Jesus once again wants us to transcend our own Rules.

Are some of our Concepts more right than others? Are some just plain wrong? Certainly. Who was right about the resurrection of the dead—the Pharisees (believed in it) or the Sadducees (didn't believe in it)? Jesus sided with the Pharisees. They were right! But Jesus didn't applaud them for this; instead, *He criticized them for their loveless enforcement of rules!*

As long as our focus is on fighting over Concepts, our modern version of the Law (whatever *side* we are on), we are simply replaying the loveless battles of the Pharisees and the Sadducees, and *not doing what Jesus told us to do.*

We can say "Lord, Lord," all we want, but He says *He will know us by our love,* not our Concepts, no matter how perfectly formed and right (or not) they are. We have taken a Greek philosophical methodology, used it to create highly complex and detailed Concepts (philosophies, if you will), sworn allegiances to one or another, worshiped them, and fought with each other over who was right. One had to win, and the other lose.

Again and again, in countless ways, in specific exhortations and in parables, in healings and declarations of forgiveness and love for even the most despised, Jesus teaches and demonstrates to us that *people matter.* Yet we have so elevated Doctrine and our divisions and disagreements—and who's "in" and who's "out" as a result—that *love of neighbor* simply is set aside when our *Concepts* are at risk. Things outweigh people.

How do we escape this error?

MOVING BEYOND WINNING

I've personally been involved in many reconciliations—and attempted reconciliations—between individuals and other individuals, or with their families, churches, and even their histories and identities.

The work of reconciliation stinks. It is enormously difficult and often nearly impossible. The primary cause of failure is self-righteousness. One side, usually

---

[14] Jeremiah 31:33, NKJV.

both, thinks reconciliation consists of the other side confessing and admitting he or she was wrong.

This is not reconciliation. It is *triumph*! Even when I act all friendly and cooperative, saying that I truly want to reconcile with you, to be restored, my true-but-unspoken agenda is for you to admit I was right all along. I want to be vindicated and I want you defeated. If you'll surrender, *then* we can be reconciled.

Generally people who are against each other have a long list of grievances, of "wrongs" done to them, accusations of revisionism (recalling history in a distorted, self-serving way), little willingness to reconsider their own actions and opinions, and even less willingness to actually *love* the other, especially in the sense that Jesus called us to. Oh, I might *claim* to love you, even make a show of reconciling, but afterward I want nothing to do with you again. I may forgive you for your sins—real or perceived—but I won't confess or ask forgiveness for my own.

These flawed notions of reconciliation are even more pronounced when it comes to our favorite religious Concepts, and our denominations and allies—even when all involved call themselves Christians. It becomes all about our side *winning*. And though we seldom admit it, it is equally important to us that your side *loses*.

Our hearts are not right.

Reconciliation is never about winning and losing. It is about loving God and neighbor. This love is an *act of blessing*, not a warm feeling. It is faith lived out by showing love, care, protection, *not* by believing the right things.

Believing the right things is worthless when we are loveless. Faith is empty when it is without love.

> Yes indeed, it is good when you obey the *royal law as found in the Scriptures: "Love your neighbor as yourself."* But if you favor some people over others, you are committing a sin. You are guilty of breaking the law. For the person who keeps all of the laws except one is as guilty as a person who has broken all of God's laws. For the same God who said, "You must not commit adultery," also said, "You must not murder." So if you murder someone but do not commit adultery, you have still broken the law.
>
> So whatever you say or whatever you do, remember that you will be judged by *the law that sets you free.* There will be no mercy for those who have not shown mercy to others. But if you have been merciful, God will be merciful when he judges you.
>
> What good is it, dear brothers and sisters, if you say you have faith but don't show it by your actions? Can that kind of faith save anyone? Suppose you see a brother or sister who has no food or clothing, and you say, "Good-bye and have a good day; stay warm and eat well"—but then you don't give that person any food or clothing. What good does that do?
>
> So you see, faith by itself isn't enough. Unless it produces good deeds, it is dead and useless.
>
> Now someone may argue, "Some people have faith; others have good deeds." But I say, "How can you show me your faith if you don't have good deeds? I will show you my faith by my good deeds."

You say you have faith, for you *believe* that there is *one God*. Good for you! Even the demons believe this, and they tremble in terror.[15] How foolish! Can't you see that faith without good deeds is useless?

Don't you remember that our ancestor Abraham was shown to be right with God by his actions when he offered his son Isaac on the altar? You see, his faith and his actions worked together. His actions made his faith complete. And so it happened just as the Scriptures say: "Abraham believed God, and God counted him as righteous because of his faith." He was even called the friend of God. So you see, *we are shown to be right with God by what we do, not by faith alone.*

Rahab the prostitute is another example. She was shown to be right with God *by her actions* when she hid those messengers and sent them safely away by a different road. Just as the body is dead without breath, so also faith is *dead* without *good works*.[16]

This passage from James bears reading again and again. It is relentless in separating declarations of faith, and even right doctrine, from what really matters: love manifested by *action*. This love—*agape* in Greek—really means to bless or protect someone by action, rather than warm feelings or positive declarations that do nothing.

Acting to serve and bless another is the core of such love. It may produce deep feelings of affection in its wake, but it is the *willing action* to show mercy that is its true character.

More, this *willing action* is not just to help those we like! It means everyone, including pagans, atheists, heretics, legalists, denominationalists, polemic authors, the self-righteous, those who refuse to reconcile, dangerous enemies and cranky neighbors. *No exceptions.* Jesus put it this way:

> "You have heard the law that says, 'Love your neighbor' and hate your enemy. But I say, *love your enemies!* Pray for those who persecute you! In that way, you will be acting as true children of your Father in heaven. For he gives his sunlight to both the evil and the good, and he sends rain on the just and the unjust alike. If you love only those who love you, what reward is there for that? Even corrupt tax collectors do that much. *If you are kind only to your friends, how are you different from anyone else?* Even pagans do that. But you are to be perfect,[17] even as your Father in heaven is perfect."[18]

If we take these words seriously, surely they must bring us to our knees in repentance. Each of us, individually, is such a rank failure at loving in this way that we shun even looking seriously at our own sin here. It is much easier to justify my self-righteous scorn for those with whom I disagree, than it is to consider my own sinfulness in the way I have treated them, spoken of them and

---

[15] The demons have their doctrine right. It doesn't save them.

[16] James 2:8-26.

[17] Greek *teleios*, meaning "mature, grown-up, whole, complete."

[18] Matthew 5:43-48.

thought about them! I can call them "enemies of the Cross" or "the scarlet whore," or any of a thousand other epithets, and justify my violence—verbal or physical—as a defense of Jesus and the Gospel, but I can only do this by ignoring the actual requirements of Jesus and the Gospel.

Step one in reconciliation is to repent for our own lovelessness, and stop it.

We have to actually admit that our attitudes, judgments, words and actions against others are partisan, unloving and scornful. In the worst of times they are even violent. They are sin, plain and simple. *We need to stop.*

More, such sin toward others cannot be excused by accusing them of the same sin, or by pointing out how wrong or hurtful *their* actions and religious Concepts might be. Even if we are absolutely right in our Doctrine, our scorn in its defense is divisive: It is heresy because of its lovelessness.

Jesus' response to wrong Concepts, false charges and hurtful actions gives us the model of what followers of His are to do:

> When false witnesses testified against our Lord and Savior Jesus Christ, He remained silent; and when unfounded charges were brought against Him, He returned no answer, believing that His whole life and conduct among the Jews were a better refutation than any answer to the false testimony, or than any formal defense against the accusations.[19]

Instead of condemnation of others, Jesus counsels loving action for their benefit. He demonstrated His love through His life and conduct, not through self-defense. Instead of judgment, He counsels *not* judging. Above all, even where we have been wronged (or where we believe Jesus and the Gospel have been wronged and we want to raise swords[20] in their defense), Jesus says:

> "Do not judge, and you will not be judged. Do not condemn, and you will not be condemned. Forgive, and you will be forgiven. Give, and it will be given to you. A good measure, pressed down, shaken together and running over, will be poured into your lap. For with the measure you use, it will be measured to you."[21]

So Jesus says don't judge, don't condemn, but *give* (this is love as *willing action*), and *forgive.*

Treat others the way you want to be treated.

---

[19] Origen, *Against Celsus*. The very first sentence.
[20] See John 18.
[21] Luke 6:37-38, NIV.

Step two in reconciliation is for us to forgive.

This is required even when it has not been asked of us, because until we forgive we are still bound to our adversary. The word *forgive*[22] that Jesus uses means to set free. It does not mean to approve of what someone else has done. In fact, the idea really is to give up a *legitimate* claim. For example:

Shortly after college I left a job and moved across the country. I was close to broke and just scraping by when making the move. My employer owed me one final paycheck and promised to send it when payday came. He didn't. In spite of many calls, he never did, knowing—I suspect—there was nothing I could do about it from such a distance. I had a legitimate claim. He owed me the money, and for years I remembered being cheated by him, and my anger and scorn remained regular (if faded) visitors. I wanted my money, and I wanted to get even, or more. He owed me both the paycheck and an apology, but my chances of getting either were nil.

Finally, after becoming a Christian and gaining insight into the meaning of forgiveness, *I released my legitimate claim:* I forgave him. By doing this, the legal, emotional and spiritual cords that had bound me to him were cut. Anger and scorn left. My need to win left. I experienced shalom, heart-ease, peace. I was freed.

The example is a simple one, but illustrative of many in the course of my own life, and in the lives of others who have learned of this stunning freedom that comes when we forgive. Jesus knew what He was giving us.

True forgiveness does not require the other person to concede to me, to confess to me, to repent to me, or to ask for forgiveness from me—only that *I forgive*. And like love, it is not a feeling to be waited upon, but rather an action, a choice. Feeling will follow, but what matters is the action to forgive, to release the legitimate claim.

Confession, repentance and even *punishment* for my enemies *may* be necessary for the well-being of their souls, but are not necessary for the well-being of mine. In fact, if I require them of others before I'll forgive them, then I am still seeking triumph, not love.

Full reconciliation and restoration requires that both I and the other repent and forgive, but I cannot withhold mine until the other completes his or hers. Such a precondition keeps me bound.

My willingness to forgive *without precondition* is how I complete my second step in reconciliation. This willingness frees me from the bondage of desiring vindication, of needing to win, and needing my adversary to lose. This is true about sin done to me, whether about money, love, family, work, culture, oppression, abuse or religious Concepts.

> "You have heard the law that says the punishment must match the injury: 'An eye for an eye, and a tooth for a tooth.' But I say, do not resist an evil person! If

---

[22] Greek *apoluo*, "to free, loose, release."

someone slaps you on the right cheek, offer the other cheek also. If you are sued in court and your shirt is taken from you, give your coat, too."[23]

If we really dwell on what Jesus commands here, it must unsettle us deeply. He's asking for more even than just forgiveness, which is the dropping of a just claim. Normal justice is getting back what has been taken—literally, getting *even*. Forgiveness is *not* seeking recompense, *not* seeking payback, *not* getting even. It is releasing the claim. Yet Jesus calls for more: love. Yes, *love!* No, not warm feelings toward an adversary, but *action* to bless them! That's the point of offering the other cheek to someone angry with you, or giving your coat to someone who is awarded your shirt by a judge. It may not make a lot of sense to our rational mind, or in our litigious culture, or even to our sense of personal justice, but it is how Jesus says we are sons of God.

Let's be honest: This is utterly beyond any of our normal concepts of equity, justice or fair dealing. It is downright outside of the box! Which brings us back to Gödel, of course, and to Jesus transcending the box we live in, going beyond its structures and rules.

Yet it is how we learn to truly love each other, even neighbor and enemy.

We might have a glimmer of understanding about the nature of such transcendent forgiveness in our relational lives, with family, friends, acquaintances, neighbors, perhaps *even* political adversaries—and all the struggle and emotion these relationships contain. But we seem to fiercely resist forgiveness when we are defending our culture or our nation. We resist *even more so* when we defend our religious Concepts. It's as if their religiousness exempts us from the clear instructions of Jesus about forgiveness. *It doesn't!*

Again, the issue here is not whether my Concepts are more "right" than your Concepts, or even if you've treated me badly in attacking my Concepts. It isn't about *getting even*. The issue is whether I'm willing to do what Jesus asked of me, and that is to *repent* of *my* hard heart, and *forgive you* for yours.

> God is not looking for repayment, but repentance. What heals a broken relationship is sincere love and contrition. What's wrong with us isn't a rap sheet of bad deeds, but a damaged heart, a soul-sickness, that plunges us into fearful self-protection, alienation from God and others. Paradoxically, this leads to death: "whoever would save his life will lose it" (Matthew 16:25).[24]

With repentance and forgiveness, I can move beyond winning and discover reconciliation, which is, simply, to truly love God, neighbor and even enemy. But will I? Or will I persist in my self-justification and lovelessness?

It is time to decide.

---

[23] Matthew 5:38-40.
[24] From *Why We Need Hell* by Frederica Mathewes-Green.

RECONCILIATION

I believe we are at the beginning of a major reformation of the Christian faith—a Reconciliation of believers across many boundaries that had once separated us and put us at swords with one another. It would be easier for any of us to remain cocooned, but the Lord is afoot and calling us to common cause: His.

Our denominationalism, our religious wars, our vitriolic doctrinal disputes, and the holy isolation we use to keep ourselves separate and untainted by each other's patterns of worship and belief, belie any claim we make to all be Christ's own. We each act like He is our private possession, formed according to our image of Him, blessing just *our* worship, and approving only *our* doctrine and *our* orders of ministry. We imagine that at best He *tolerates* the worship, doctrine and polity of those who are not like us. What amazing pride we have.

> Then Jesus told this story to some who had great confidence in their own righteousness and scorned everyone else: "Two men went to the Temple to pray. One was a Pharisee, and the other was a despised tax collector. The Pharisee stood by himself and prayed this prayer: 'I thank you, God, that I am not a sinner like everyone else. For I don't cheat, I don't sin, and I don't commit adultery. I'm certainly not like that tax collector! I fast twice a week, and I give you a tenth of my income.'
>
> "But the tax collector stood at a distance and dared not even lift his eyes to heaven as he prayed. Instead, he beat his chest in sorrow, saying, 'O God, be merciful to me, for I am a sinner.' I tell you, this sinner, not the Pharisee, returned home justified before God. For those who exalt themselves will be humbled, and those who humble themselves will be exalted."[25]

The Pharisee is certain that he knows it all, and it seems he has it all correct—doctrine, behavior, tithing, isolation from the sinful—but *none of it counts before God.* Yet the prayer of the sinner, seeking mercy, counts for everything.

Maybe Oswald Chambers had it right when he said, "The certainty that I do not know—that is the secret of going with Jesus."

With this in mind, listen to Revelation:

> After this I looked, and there before me was a great multitude that no one could count, from every nation, tribe, people and language, standing before the throne and before the Lamb. They were wearing white robes and were holding palm branches in their hands. And they cried out in a loud voice: "Salvation belongs to our God, who sits on the throne, and to the Lamb."
>
> All the angels were standing around the throne and around the elders and the four living creatures. They fell down on their faces before the throne and worshiped

---

[25] Luke 18:9-14.

God, saying: "Amen! Praise and glory and wisdom and thanks and honor and power and strength be to our God for ever and ever. Amen!"[26]

The pattern for us is in heaven: All the angels and tribes around the throne aren't arguing about who is most right, nor jostling to see who gets to sit at Jesus' right hand. They are *not identical*, but they are side-by-side, *adjacent*, in awe and ministering together to the Lamb.

The earthly incarnation of this heavenly scene is just how we should work together. It is the heart of Jesus, and it should be our heart as well. It should be *your* heart.

It should reflect this common desire: We respect each other's tribe. We work and minister together, yoked to each other and to Him. We love each other as one.

Jesus makes this blazingly clear in His prayer for His disciples and for us:

> "My prayer is not for them alone. I pray also for those who will believe in me through their message, that all of them may be one, Father, just as you are in me and I am in you. May they also be in us so that the world may believe that you have sent me. I have given them the glory that you gave me, that they may be one as we are one—I in them and you in me—*so that they may be brought to complete unity. Then the world will know that you sent me and have loved them even as you have loved me.*"[27]

We have failed miserably to do this in our past. Perhaps now we can at last begin to do as Jesus commands.

THE KEY TO THE FUTURE

So to restate the point: We have taken the narrative telling of Life With God, written down as Scripture, and (in a process that owes its methods to Greek philosophy) drawn from it multitudes of religious Concepts, and from them multitudes of ideas about doctrine, worship, polity, hermeneutics, behavior, dress, ordination and much more, and then we have separated into religious tribes, each idolizing and worshiping its own Concepts, and fighting the tribes that idolize and worship other Concepts.

The Concepts can have usefulness in drawing and introducing people to God, and in helping them understand what He desires of them. But more often then not, they grow instead into idols, and are worshiped in place of the God that they were developed to help explain.

Some may be more helpful than others, and some may well be quite wrong, but this difference provides no justification of the scorn and often violence we have shown toward each other. Worse, the way we have behaved is radically *contrary* to what Jesus has *told us to do,* and it is Him who we all claim as *Lord!*

---

[26] Revelation 7:9-12, NIV.
[27] John 17:20-23, NIV.

For a true Reconciliation of the faith to occur, there must be a reconciliation of the faithful, and a coming together to embody the unity for which Jesus prayed. *We do not have to surrender* our favorite Concepts, or patterns of worship, polity, ordination or even doctrine, *to be reconciled.* We can even continue to wrestle with each other about these, but we cannot do so without first acknowledging our own idolatry, confessing our lovelessness toward each other, repenting of it, *stopping it*, forgiving each other, and taking action to bless and protect each other—that is, we have to *incarnate the love* Jesus *called us to do* toward others.

Listen to Paul's counsel on just this point:

Accept other believers who are weak in faith, and don't argue with them about what they think is right or wrong. For instance, one person believes it's all right to eat anything. But another believer with a sensitive conscience will eat only vegetables. Those who feel free to eat anything must not look down on those who don't. And those who don't eat certain foods must not condemn those who do, for God has accepted them. Who are you *to condemn someone else's servants? They are responsible to the Lord*, so *let him judge* whether they are right or wrong. And with the Lord's help, they will do what is right and will receive his approval.

In the same way, some *think* one day is more holy than another day, while others *think*[28] every day is alike. You should each be fully convinced that whichever day you choose is acceptable. Those who worship the Lord on a special day do it *to honor him*. Those who eat any kind of food do so *to honor the Lord*, since they give thanks to God before eating. And those who refuse to eat certain foods also want to *please the Lord* and *give thanks to God.* For we don't live for ourselves or die for ourselves. If we live, it's to honor the Lord. And if we die, it's to honor the Lord. So whether we live or die, we belong to the Lord. Christ died and rose again for this very purpose—to be Lord both of the living and of the dead.

So why do you condemn another believer? Why do you look down on another believer? Remember, we will all stand before the judgment seat of God. For the Scriptures say, "'As surely as I live,' says the LORD, 'every knee will bend to me, and every tongue will confess and give praise to God.'"

Yes, each of us will give a personal account to God. So let's stop condemning each other. Decide instead to live in such a way that you will not cause another believer to stumble and fall.

I know and am convinced on the authority of the Lord Jesus that no food, in and of itself, is wrong to eat. But if someone believes it is wrong, then for that person it is wrong. And if another believer is distressed by what you eat, you are not acting in love if you eat it. Don't let your eating ruin someone for whom Christ died. *Then you will not be criticized for doing something you believe is good.*[29] For the Kingdom of God is not a matter of what we eat or drink, but of living a life of goodness and peace and joy in the Holy Spirit. If you serve Christ with this attitude,

---

[28] This is a difference in Concepts, and the Doctrines they produce.

[29] Remember, even correct doctrine can be heresy if it causes division.

you will please God, and others will approve of you, too. *So then, let us aim for harmony in the church and try to build each other up.*[30]

This isn't just about food or special days, of course, but about how we treat others—perhaps of weaker faith (though you or I might be that one!)—who are not just like us, but for whom Christ also died!

Paul is saying that every person, in his or her own way, is honoring God by serving Him the way they do, so who are we to condemn them? *They are servants of Jesus.*

Your tribe is going to be next to my tribe before the throne, and we will not be arguing about who had the right Concepts, doctrine, polity, worship or anything of the sort. We will be in awe before the Lamb, one, in unity, glad to be side-by-side, adjacent, in His service.

He desires that unity from us—honoring, safeguarding and building each other up—not just when we reach heaven, but *now.* But we each have to confess, forgive, and then live with reconciling love for the faithful, refusing any longer to scorn or harm each other in defense of ourselves and our religious Concepts.

> Remind the people to respect the government and be law-abiding, always ready to lend a helping hand. *No insults, no fights.* God's people should be *bighearted and courteous.*
>
> It wasn't so long ago that we ourselves were stupid and stubborn, dupes of sin, ordered every which way by our glands, going around with a chip on our shoulder, *hated and hating back.* But when God, our kind and loving Savior God, stepped in, he saved us from all that. It was all his doing; we had nothing to do with it. He gave us a good bath, and we came out of it new people, washed inside and out by the Holy Spirit. Our Savior Jesus poured out new life so generously. God's gift has restored our relationship with him and given us back our lives. And there's more life to come—an eternity of life! You can count on this.
>
> I want you to put your foot down. Take a firm stand on these matters so that those who have put their trust in God will concentrate on the *essentials* that are good for everyone. Stay away from mindless, pointless quarreling over genealogies and fine print in the law code. That gets you nowhere. Warn a quarrelsome person once or twice, but then be done with him. It's obvious that such a person is out of line, rebellious against God. By persisting in divisiveness[31] he cuts himself off.[32]

We need to stop trashing each other! It doesn't matter how many religious words we use, how many Scriptures we quote, how much we disagree with the religious Concepts, doctrines or practices of other believers—*we do not have the right to treat them with lovelessness.* In truth, we are required to treat them with love—*action* to bless them. And let's be clear: Pretending to "love" someone by "enlightening" them with sarcasm, shame or cruel words is not *love.* It is sin.

---

[30] Romans 14:1-19.
[31] That is, *heresy* in the true sense of *causing division.*
[32] Titus 3:1-11, *The Message.*

If Paul says we are to honor them as servants of God—even if we disagree with their Concepts, doctrines, polity, worship styles, food or other elements of how they serve God—then surely the way to love them is to care for and protect them. That is the love, the action to bless them, which reverses and neutralizes the trashing we and others have done. And there is a covenantal beauty to it: Though we serve differently, we stand up for each other. We do not simply refuse to attack; rather, we positively act to safeguard them. It is just exactly what the Good Samaritan did for the wounded Jew.[33]

"Treat others the way you want to be treated" becomes incarnate in such intentional safeguarding and covering. We make the Church and its wild variety of believers, a wide, open, safe place where God is.

You may have already come to this realization, and already act in a loving, protecting, covenantal way toward other believers, even those quite different from yourself. If so, praise God! Keep it up. Proclaim it fearlessly—the Church needs this reformation of hearts, this reconciling love of God and each other.

If this is new, and the attack upon others has been a part of how you "defended the faith," stop it. Work to bless and safeguard them instead. Go the extra mile or two; repent, forgive, bless.

Reconcile.

FINAL REFLECTION AND INSIGHTS ON TRUE UNITY IN THE CHURCH

Watching denominational wars, doctrinal battles, struggles over worship forms and all other forms of Christians behaving badly, leads me to wonder aloud what it is we should unify around, if anything. Many attempts at this have been made in the last decades, usually built on agreed-upon doctrine, creeds, confessions and/or traditions. As smaller pieces of the whole Church come together to make common cause, these are helpful. But for the whole Church to be in unity, the foundation must be both more encompassing and less contractual. Perhaps what Jesus taught could provide that solid common ground.

WHAT JESUS TAUGHT

With any text as large and content-rich as the New Testament is, one could probably pick any of a hundred themes and construct a Concept out of it and proclaim it to be the central message of Jesus. Even knowing this, and being aware of all that I've just cautioned against, I'll dare to suggest that Jesus' key teaching is just exactly what has been addressed above—*reconciliation*—the reconciliation of people to God, and to each other. This is salvation, and the beginning of the covenant He offered.

---

[33] Luke 10:25-37.

This reconciliation unfolds through love, repentance and forgiveness, but it begins with love. The character of love is embodied in how Jesus lived and opened the way to God for others. Though He made it clear that He had come not to abolish the Law, but to fulfill it,[34] He quickly recast the understanding of God's intentions. God was not a rule-giver who required rule-following in order for anyone to have approval or access; rather, He offered openness to all, even those desperately lost in sin. He did not approve of sin, but He did invite sinners to come close to Him. When they came close, they fell in love, their hearts turned, forgiveness was granted, and they were reconciled with God. This was and is salvation, the initiation of Life in Christ, covenant with God.

Even Jesus' own name[35] embodies this. We've all heard that "Jesus" means "God saves," or something of the sort, and it does, but a little more deeply it means even more. "Jesus" comes from two Hebrew roots, the first of which is *Yehovah* (*Jehovah* is the Germanic version of this), and the second *yaw-shah*, which is usually said to mean "salvation." But *yaw-shah* actually means "to be open, wide or free," and hence implies giving safety, salvation, deliverance to one who lacks these. In effect, in Jesus we have a open, wide, free place where God is present, just like the Promised Land for the Israelites! (The one who took the Israelites into the Promised Land after the death of Moses was *Joshua*—the same name, in Hebrew, as *Jesus*.)

The many stories of Jesus eating with and encountering sinners, which rankled the self-righteous religious people around Him, gives testimony to this open presence of love in Him. But perhaps one of the most compelling testimonies is also the shortest:

> Tax collectors and other notorious sinners often came to listen to Jesus teach. This made the Pharisees and teachers of religious law complain that he was associating with such sinful people—even eating with them![36]

The second sentence shows how the religious people responded to what Jesus did with sinners, but dwell just a moment on the *first* sentence: "Tax collectors and other notorious sinners often came to listen to Jesus teach."

What a revealing insight: The despised agents of the Romans, and notorious sinners, somehow feel *safe* with Jesus. You know it wasn't because He was saying their sins were of no concern. But does anyone suppose for a moment that they flocked to be near and learn from the self-righteous religious people who looked down on them and condemned them? Of course not.

Look at Jesus' stunning encounter with the woman caught in adultery. The self-righteous said she should be stoned for her sin, to which He replied that the

---

[34] Matthew 5:17.

[35] Hebrew: יהושע *Yehoshua,* or ישוע *Yeshua* (a shortened version of the same name).

[36] Luke 15:1-2.

one without sin should cast the first stone. After they all fled, having been convicted by His words,

> He said to her, "Woman, where are those accusers of yours? Has no one condemned you?" She said, "No one, Lord." And Jesus said to her, "Neither do I condemn[37] you; go and sin no more."[38]

Jesus doesn't tell her the sin was not sin, but He implicitly forgives her for it, and then tells her not to do it again. Certainly the love she experienced in this encounter filled her and strengthened her not to fall so easily again.

She is treated as one beloved, who has been lost—not as one despised who must be publicly shamed and harmed.

So it makes perfect sense that Luke follows this story in his text with the quote I shared just above:

> Tax collectors and other notorious sinners often came to listen to Jesus teach. This made the Pharisees and teachers of religious law complain that he was associating with such sinful people—even eating with them![39]

...then he recounts how Jesus then told the self-righteous complainers three parables:

Parable of the Lost Sheep

> So Jesus told them this story: "If a man has a hundred sheep and one of them gets lost, what will he do? Won't he leave the ninety-nine others in the wilderness and go to search for the one that is lost until he finds it? And when he has found it, he will joyfully carry it home on his shoulders. When he arrives, he will call together his friends and neighbors, saying, 'Rejoice with me because I have found my lost sheep.' In the same way, there is more joy in heaven over one lost sinner who repents and returns to God than over ninety-nine others who are righteous and haven't strayed away!"[40]

The shepherd doesn't punish the lost sheep, doesn't humiliate it or condemn it, doesn't shame it into proper behavior. It was lost, and now that it is found, the shepherd celebrates its return, and calls friends and neighbors together to join in! And of course this isn't about sheep; it's about people—and Jesus says there is *joy in heaven* over one lost sinner who repents and returns to God!

Often when we hear the word "repent!" it comes with a booming voice dripping with disapproval and condemnation. And though we may feel

---

[37] The Greek word used here means "judge down."
[38] John 8:10b-11, NKJV.
[39] Luke 15:1-2.
[40] Luke 15:3-7.

brokenhearted when we have sinned, the word "repent"[41] in New Testament Greek means *to turn around mentally, to change your mind*, or *to feel compelled to do so.* In Hebrew it means *to be sorry*[42] or *to draw back, retreat, return.*[43] The core idea is to be restored to relationship with God. Jesus makes the point that this is cause for celebration.

Parable of the Lost Coin

The second parable He tells them (He's driving His point home) is about the woman who loses one silver coin, and searches for it until it's found, then calls friends and neighbors together to rejoice with her. Jesus explains the parable to them by saying, "Likewise, I say to you, there is joy in the presence of the angels of God over one sinner who repents."[44]

Parable of the Prodigal Son

Next is the famous and often-repeated parable of the Prodigal Son—one of Jesus' longest and most pregnant parables. I believe it contains in a single story the most foundational and important elements of Jesus' teachings. What the Pharisees and teachers of religious law heard next was the unadorned Gospel, the good news of God's reconciling love for mankind. I'll put the whole story here, so we miss none of it:

> Then He said: "A certain man had two sons. And the younger of them said to his father, 'Father, give me the portion of goods that falls to me.' So he divided to them his livelihood. And not many days after, the younger son gathered all together, journeyed to a far country, and there wasted his possessions with prodigal living. But when he had spent all, there arose a severe famine in that land, and he began to be in want. Then he went and joined himself to a citizen of that country, and he sent him into his fields to feed swine. And he would gladly have filled his stomach with the pods that the swine ate, and no one gave him anything.
>
> "But when he came to himself, he said, 'How many of my father's hired servants have bread enough and to spare, and I perish with hunger! I will arise and go to my father, and will say to him, "Father, I have sinned against heaven and before you, and I am no longer worthy to be called your son. Make me like one of your hired servants."'
>
> "And he arose and came to his father. But when he was still a great way off, his father saw him and had compassion, and ran and fell on his neck and kissed him. And the son said to him, 'Father, I have sinned against heaven and in your sight, and am no longer worthy to be called your son.'
>
> "But the father said to his servants, 'Bring out the best robe and put it on him, and put a ring on his hand and sandals on his feet. And bring the fatted calf here and

---

[41] μετανοέω *metanoeo.*

[42] See entry in Strong's Hebrew Lexicon for *nacham* H5162 for more detail.

[43] Strong's entry: *shuwb* H7725 for more detail.

[44] Luke 15:10, NKJV.

kill it, and let us eat and be merry; for this my son was dead and is alive again; he was lost and is found.' And they began to be merry.

"Now his older son was in the field. And as he came and drew near to the house, he heard music and dancing. So he called one of the servants and asked what these things meant. And he said to him, 'Your brother has come, and because he has received him safe and sound, your father has killed the fatted calf.'

"But he was angry and would not go in. Therefore his father came out and pleaded with him. So he answered and said to his father, 'Lo, these many years I have been serving you; I never transgressed your commandment at any time; and yet you never gave me a young goat, that I might make merry with my friends. But as soon as this son of yours came, who has devoured your livelihood with harlots, you killed the fatted calf for him.'

"And he said to him, 'Son, you are always with me, and all that I have is yours. It was right that we should make merry and be glad, for your brother was dead and is alive again, and was lost and is found.'"[45]

Jesus shows us ourselves in relation to God in this story. We are given what we demand as our own, even though we are not its creator, and we leave home and the Father to do as we wish with it. In that day as in ours, this means narcissistic self-indulgence. Then as now it consumes our wealth and leaves us destitute. The Prodigal found himself living with pigs, and *there he realized his foolishness, and turned from it.* This was the moment of repentance, literally.

He decides to head back home, not demanding rights, but humbly, realizing the Father treats even the servants better than he is living now—hoping just to become one of them.

Now here comes the fundamental truth Jesus is teaching: *the response of the Father.* He does not stand aloof, looking away. His arms are not folded, his foot tapping impatiently, his brow furrowed in disgust. Rather, he sees the son from a great distance and *runs* to him! He has *compassion.* He pulls him close and tightly *embraces* him (that's what "fell on his neck" means). He *kisses* him!

The son repeats to the Father what he has realized of his failing, his sin. He is speaking his repentance aloud, though it had happened in his heart before he even began his journey. The Father knew simply by the son's return that this had occurred, and he rejoiced.

Shaming doesn't follow, nor does punishment. There is no humiliation or wounding. No earning of forgiveness is required, no proof before forgiveness is extended, no repayment demanded. The Father's unbridled love is pure grace, unmerited favor, and it is neither grudging nor measured: It is joyful and abundant. The prodigal is given a clean robe, sandals, and a ring—signifying sonship. He is restored beyond his wildest imaginings by a Father who loves him more than he can conceive.

That moment of embrace and kiss—the love of the Father and the restoration of the lost son—that wide, boundless, safe, open and complete reconciliation— *that* is the good news. All the rest is commentary.

---

[45] Luke 15:11-32, NKJV.

All the way back in Chapter 2 I talked about salvation. This is it. It is being reconciled to God, and it comes not through our efforts to be good, or *right*, but by the love of God. When we realize our distance from Him, how we have wasted what we have received, and realized—at last—that life with the Father even in its most humble forms is better than life with the pigs, then He willingly restores us—joyfully, with abundance, with sonship! That is *salvation*; that is what the name *Jesus* means, in His very name, and in His teachings, life, love and sacrifice. He is the author and finisher of reconciliation, because our faith in Him brings all of us before Him, *together*. He is the foundation we all can stand upon *together*. He is the One who can bring unity to all believers.

All who know this love can stand adjacent together before the throne, *fully reconciled though they differ* in religious Concepts, doctrine, worship, polity and all the rest.

They honor each other's tribe, and even *honor what is important to that tribe*, even when it is not essential to Salvation, or Sanctification, or Glorification.

They watch out for and protect *each other*, rather than themselves.

They do not fight over the pedigree of the other's fellowship.

They cling to the *essential*, which is the reconciling love of God that Jesus offers, and the Life in Christ that it initiates.

They enter into covenant.

They listen and do simply as Jesus said:

Love God, neighbor and even enemy.
Treat others the way you want to be treated.
People matter. Things don't.

There is no "yes, but..." There is confession, repentance, stopping, forgiveness, love and unity in the One who came to reconcile all of us to God, and to keep us in His covenant.

This truly is good news. Let's choose to live it, beginning now.

24.
Application and Haverim

From Matthew Henry's commentary on Psalm 122:

> If all the disciples of Christ were of one mind, and kept the unity of the Spirit in the bond of peace, their enemies would be deprived of their chief advantages against them. But Satan's maxim always has been, to divide that he may conquer; and few Christians are sufficiently aware of his designs.
>
> Those who can do nothing else for the peace of Jerusalem, may pray for it. *Let us consider all who seek the glory of the Redeemer, as our brethren and fellow-travellers, without regarding differences which do not affect our eternal welfare.* Blessed Spirit of peace and love, who didst dwell in the soul of the holy Jesus, descend into his church, and fill those who compose it with his heavenly tempers; cause bitter contentions to cease, and make us to be of one mind. Love of the brethren and love to God, ought to stir us up to seek to be like the Lord Jesus in fervent prayer and unwearied labour, for the salvation of men, and the Divine glory.[1]

Recall, if you would, all the way back to Chapter 1:

> The 17th-century Lutheran Peter Meiderlin once said, "We would be in the best shape if we kept in essentials, Unity; in non-essentials, Liberty; and in both Charity." This is an extremely valuable and effective touchstone for our journey. Let's define the terms with precision, and use that precision to our benefit as we proceed. This will prove valuable:
>
> An *essential* is something that is *necessary*, utterly *required* for something to be effective, true or real. You may recall this expression from mathematics: *if and only if*. That defines an essential.
>
> A *non-essential* may be profoundly important, valuable or highly regarded, but it is not *necessary*, not *required*. This is a critical distinction.
>
> *Liberty* means that we do not force others to conform to our practices or beliefs on issues that are non-essential.
>
> *Charity* means that we treat others with respect and love, even when we disagree or differ on *either* essentials or non-essentials.

---

[1] *Matthew Henry's Commentary on the Whole Bible: Complete and Unabridged.* Nashville: Thomas Nelson, 2008, p. 561.

I want to consider this again for just a few more paragraphs, and then press in to some examples of how it can be applied. We need to realize that something can be non-essential in one context and essential in another.

- Plain, modest dressing is essential to being Amish, but it is not essential to being a Christian.
- Ordination is essential in many denominations to be a priest or pastor, but it is not essential to teach or care for others.
- Apostolic Succession is essential to the polity of a church in the apostolic tradition (Roman Catholics, Anglicans, others), but it is not essential to salvation or sanctification.
- The Liturgy is essential to the worship of a "liturgical church," but it is not essential for a church to be Christian.

Similarly, though *sanctification* is non-essential to salvation,[2] it is *essential* to Life in Christ, to Covenant. Recall this illustration:

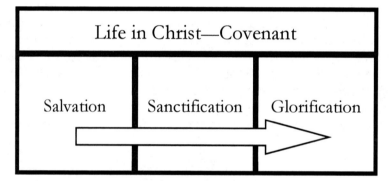

FIGURE: LIFE IN CHRIST—COVENANT

Covenant, Life in Christ, begins with salvation, is lived in sanctification, and finishes in glorification. *Sanctification* is the process of learning to live and love as Jesus did. Sanctification is the very means by which we are each conformed to Christ's image, where we become more like Him, where we learn to love.

So, *what is essential to sanctification?* What is the *if and only if* of sanctification? What *must* it have to proceed? And what can it proceed *without*? Here's the key understanding:

To the degree that any of our church concepts, doctrines, worship styles, polity and so on aid us in our sanctification, they are helpful, perhaps even important, *but if sanctification can proceed without them*, they are not *essential* to sanctification, and not *essential* to life in Christ.

---

[2] It follows salvation, but salvation doesn't require it. Life in Christ, covenant, requires it.

Life in Christ, covenant, is what all Christians have in common. Sanctification is basically the living out in daily life—and in our faith tradition—of this covenant with Him. It is where we are formed in His image, where we are made into His bride without spot or wrinkle, where we mature in learning to love as He did. *It is life with and in Christ during our walk on this earth.* That's *sanctification*, and every Christian *grows up* through it. It is to be discipled and be a disciple—to learn "by use and practice." To learn to love.

Sanctification is essential and unavoidable for a Christian. It is our daily walk and growth. So the big question is: are the elements of your church tradition *required* for sanctification, and therefore for life in Christ? Are they *essential*? I'm not asking if they are valuable or perhaps even important. I'm asking if they are essential, *required* for sanctification. As valuable and honored as they may be, the answer is almost certainly, "No."

Let me offer an example from a non-Protestant tradition: confession to a priest in a confessional booth in a Roman Catholic church.

Going in and admitting all you've done wrong to another human being, and receiving forgiveness, can be a petulant, mechanical and worthless effort—or it can be key to God's helping you to leave sins behind and press forward in service to Him. It *can be* a valuable and hugely important part of your sanctification. Yet millions of Christians, including Protestants and many Roman Catholics, have lived lives in Christ, in covenant with Him, with sanctification underway in profound measure, without once setting foot in a confessional booth. The confessional booth (and all that it entails) can be important and valuable—but it is not *required for sanctification* nor to life in Christ. And *just so* with many, many elements of *every* church tradition.

The issue is not a new one—consider that my Meiderlin quote about essentials and non-essentials is from a 17th-century Lutheran, and he is actually reflecting back to treatises by Luther in the 16th century. Luther used a Concept, *adiaphora*[3] (matters of indifference), which itself traces back to the Greek Stoic philosophers. The Stoics used it to refer to things neither required nor forbidden by moral law.

Luther adapted this Concept to define which actions of Christians, specifically in worship, are required or forbidden by Scripture, and which actions are neutral—that is, where Scripture does not give specific direction. His goal, in part, was to free worship from man-made rituals—to require only what Scripture required, and leave individual churches and groups free to add their own ritual elements—so long as they did not impose them on others or violate Scripture.[4]

Now, all of this sounds a lot like the point I am trying to make here, but Luther's treatises were written when it seemed like the only real distinctions (in

---

[3] Greek ἀδιάφορα, "indifferent things."
[4] From Article VII of the Augsburg Confession "And to the true unity of the Church it is enough to agree concerning the doctrine of the Gospel and the administration of the Sacraments. Nor is it necessary that human traditions, that is, rites or ceremonies, instituted by men, should be everywhere alike."

theology and worship) were to be found between Protestants and the Roman Catholic Church (and, to a degree, within a handful of Protestant sects).[5]

Even at that, bitter division ensued over what constituted "matters of indifference." Some felt, for instance, that the concept of transubstantiation, and the practice of veneration of the saints (both approved within the Roman Catholic Church), should be permitted (though not required) in order to bring peace among the churches.

Others found such a suggestion a direct threat to the faith itself and fought against it viciously. These issues are still argued today, often still with bitter denunciation of those on the other side (or those who might attempt to explain the other side, such as I have in this book).

I will suggest Luther didn't go nearly far enough, and the divisions in the Church today make Luther's time look like unruffled sweet harmony. We *really* have to move past the non-essentials if we are to embody the unity for which Christ prayed.

The risk in even broaching this topic is the fury that arises when religious people fear that their beliefs and practices are being attacked—and calling any one of them "non-essential," even with careful definition of what this means—is often heard as a threat to the faith. Recall Matthew Henry's insight:

> If all the disciples of Christ were of one mind, and kept the unity of the Spirit in the bond of peace, their enemies would be deprived of their chief advantages against them. But Satan's maxim always has been, to divide that he may conquer; and few Christians are sufficiently aware of his designs.

I believe that with care, willingness, and charity for each other, there is a path beyond our divisions, to a common place of safety and godly mutual respect, to Reconciliation.

HOW TO RECONCILE

I want to begin here a series of examples of how Reconciliation can be applied with actual followers of Jesus who differ markedly in their Concepts, Doctrines, Subdoctrines, Worship, Polity, Hermeneutics, dress codes and more. In other words, with Christians who often have little or nothing to say to each other, and even less to do with each other—except perhaps in derision and distancing themselves—lest they be tainted by the other's embodiment of the Faith.

If you begin to live as a Reconciler, an ambassador for the Gospel, and are able to find the unity Jesus prayed for—with others who differ in their Concepts (Doctrines, and so on), visit the Web site[6] for this book, and *please share your story with me.* I will post those that are appropriate online and in future editions of this book, and let this section on Application grow.

---

[5] And more broadly with the Orthodox Church, though it wasn't an issue in this particular dispute.
[6] At WhatWeBelieveAndWhy.com.

Rather than simply proclaim the vital importance of reconciliation, and the differences that the love of Christ can overcome, let me cite a couple of explicit examples of how it can be applied. Note that I am not saying that the differences are overcome by conformity to a single doctrine or view, but rather by respecting other believers as living life in Christ, though differently. It is, if you would, the rabbinic way, where two deep understandings and convictions are *adjacent*, *respected*, with neither eliminating the other.

For instance, consider this classic and often vitriolic debate in the Church:

ARE WOMEN ALLOWED IN MINISTRY?

How do we approach it? One of the challenges in addressing the issue of women in ministry is that we come at it with a view shaped both by our Christian traditions, and by the views and political methods of our culture. These are often so embedded in our ways of thinking that we don't even realize the biases, or how they affect what we perceive or approve.

In some cultures, those who believe that there should be a change in the way things are done would not dare do more than humbly request the appropriate authority to consider the change.

In other cultures, not even this much would be dared; acceptance of the status quo would be expected, regardless of whether you agreed or not. Opposition to it would be swiftly punished.

In still others, rallies would be organized, protests taken to the streets, and the "rights of the disadvantaged" would be proclaimed and struggled for until the change was accomplished.

In the United States and many other countries, the last approach is common, and it obviously affects how we think about gender relations, and in particular in regard to the role of women in ministry.

While some would insist that *the Bible does not permit women as leaders in the Church*, others would counter that *women have the right to be leaders in the Church*. There are many other positions on this issue and I'm not attempting to be comprehensive on the variety of views. I'm merely using these two to illustrate a point about *how we approach issues where we differ*.

I'm also not arguing for one view against the other, just observing that the arguments are not even using the same Concepts, or the same categories of understanding or advocacy. So let's take a few moments to unpack this illustrative disagreement. I'm going to use terminology for ministry leadership that is common to Lutheran, Anglican, Roman Catholic and Eastern Orthodox polity (among others), but uncommon in Baptist, Presbyterian, and most other Protestant usage. Bear with me if you would. The point is not about title here, but role.

Let's consider two of the many varying concepts of women in ministry.

Concept 1: Women Cannot Be Priests

One view would assert that women are *created* in such a way (as childbearers, nurturers and helpers to men) that they are "ontologically" unable to be leaders in their very *being*, in the same way a lily cannot be an oak tree. This view would say that lilies and oak trees are both *valuable* plants, but neither can presume to be the other. Each should be in its *God-given role*. It is an "ontology" issue. This position would be supported by selected verses from Scripture, and by hermeneutical guidelines (concepts) used to interpret those verses.

A second view would say that women are the *equals* of men, intellectually and in every other way, have all of the *rights* of men in this society, and that anyone in authority who would deny them equal opportunity—including in leadership in the Church—should be fought. The rights of women should not be denied, and the Church authorities should be struggled with until they relent, and until the rights are granted. This would be seen as "prophetic" action to force the right thing to be accomplished. *It is a "justice" issue.* This position would be supported by selected verses from Scripture, and by hermeneutical guidelines (concepts) used to interpret those verses.

The debate is over whether the Bible conceives of women "ontologically" as able to be leaders, teachers, pastors, deacons, priests, evangelists, bishops or whatever, and there are advocates who argue from Scripture on both sides of this (and in between!). Those men and women who seriously believe that the Bible does not ontologically conceive of a woman as a pastor or priest, find themselves accused of sin for denying justice. That is, the "rights" supporters say that the advocates of a male-only priesthood or pastorate[7] are against progress for the oppressed, against justice, and therefore *against God*. The "rights" partisans therefore want nothing to do with the all-male priesthood supporters; it would be consorting with the devil, so to speak.

The all-male-priesthood advocates feel God's order of creation is being willfully "stood on its head" by the "justice" advocates, who assert "so-called rights" *against the intentions of the Creator*. They of course want nothing to do with such rebellion; it would be consorting with the devil, so to speak.

Both of these groups are using Concepts they hold dear as the guide to the order of worship, of authority, and of polity, and for their often dismissive view of the others' beliefs.

Among the more-liturgical denominations, one view is that what happens at Communion during worship is a "Eucharistic Sacrifice" with the "Real Presence of Christ." I won't go into detail about the specifics (and they vary depending on the sect), but they see the priest as standing in Christ's place, and making, through

---

[7] "Priesthood" is used here as a term that encompasses both those Christian denominations that call their ordained clergy "priest," as well as those that use "pastor" or other terms. I'm not engaging the issue of title here, just the broader issue of gender and leadership. For some revealing history on the issue of title in Christian leadership, see the entry for *priest* in the Glossary Plus.

the bread and wine, a sacrifice for the remission of sin of Jesus' body and blood (because His Real Presence is there).[8] Further, the priest is seen metaphorically as the bridegroom (Christ); the congregation as the bride of Christ.

There are variations on this theme across denominations and through history, but the basic image is the same: The priest represents Christ and sacrifices Christ in body and blood, in the presence of and for His bride, who He will present to Himself, "without spot or wrinkle."[9]

The themes for this Concept are drawn from Scripture and knitted together quite thoroughly to produce this approach to worship and the theology that makes and defends it. This Concept, so constructed, would naturally find a woman in the role of priest to be impossible. It goes *against the theme*, and against history. If we re-enacted the Exodus, would we cast a woman as Moses? Just so, Jesus wasn't a woman, and more: The bride of Christ (the congregation) is not made clean in order to marry her to a woman. Quite apart from all of the sexual diversity debates of our day, for advocates of this Concept the insertion of a person of the female gender into the role of Jesus Christ is just wrong. They would argue passionately that it has nothing to do with respect for women—they just can't be a man.

Concept 2: Women *Can* Be Priests

Advocates for women in the priesthood would argue from two key points of view (among others): Even if they accepted the Eucharistic Sacrifice concept, they would say that neither a male nor a female priest is *actually* Jesus. It is a *role* the priest plays, and the body shape and gender of the person playing the role is irrelevant. It doesn't make the Sacrifice or the Presence less real. Maybe no one should be allowed to play that role unless they are male, Jewish, olive-skinned and circumcised! And besides, if the priest represents Jesus and therefore must be male, shouldn't then the congregation also be all-male, since His disciples at the Last Supper were all male? And were all of those *guys*, then, the "bride of Christ"?

You see how complicated all of this can get as Concepts begin to conflict!

Parallel debates rage where the churches are less liturgical. Many Baptists, for instance, would also argue that a woman cannot be a pastor because none of the disciples were women, and because the qualifications for pastor (also called an overseer) define it as a man, as in, "Now the overseer must be above reproach, the *husband* of but one wife..."[10]

Other similar passages speak of leaders as men, and refer to how they must manage their *wives* and families. Those who are against women as pastors would say the language is quite clear: Women are even prohibited from teaching men.

---

[8] From the Council of Trent, 1545–1563.
[9] From Ephesians 5:27.
[10] See 1 Timothy 3:1-7, NIV. This is from verse 2.

Paul says, "I do not let women teach men or have authority over them. Let them listen quietly."[11]

On the other side of this issue it would be argued that the language and social customs of the day always expressed leadership in male terminology,[12] but that this is incidental to the important point being made. I've italicized the key qualities of an overseer (pastor) according to this view, in what follows:

> Here is a trustworthy saying: If anyone sets his heart on being an overseer, he desires a noble task. Now the overseer must be *above reproach*, the husband of *but one*[13] wife, *temperate, self-controlled, respectable, hospitable, able to teach, not given to drunkenness, not violent but gentle, not quarrelsome, not a lover of money*. He must *manage* his *own family well* and see that his *children obey* him with *proper respect*. (If anyone does not know how to manage his own family, how can he take care of God's church?) He must *not be a recent convert*, or he may become conceited and fall under the same judgment as the devil. He must also *have a good reputation with outsiders*, so that he will not fall into disgrace and into the devil's trap.[14]

No writer in that day and age would ever say something like, "Now the overseer must be above reproach, the husband of one wife, or the wife of one husband. ... He or she must manage his or her own family well, and see that his or her children obey him or her with proper respect, etc." No one wrote that way! Even the Declaration of Independence, far more recent, says, "We hold these truths to be self-evident, that *all men* are created equal..."

This is jarring to some modern ears, but "all men" didn't mean all *males*. The term "men" was understood to encompass men and women. I'm not suggesting there wasn't gender discrimination in those days—there was—but that isn't what was at work here. It was a grammatical convention that the plural "men" encompassed both genders. This is still true in many languages other than American English.

Advocates for women in leadership would say that the mere use of male terminology in Scripture does not prove that God intended certain roles just for men. The language of the day *often* meant men and women when only male terms were used. It's the way the Greek language works!

But what about Paul saying he doesn't permit women to teach men? Advocates for women pastors would say this passage is either mistranslated[15] (because of a conceptual bias on the part of the translators), or was possibly appropriate for an era when few women were educated, and when they were generally not culturally permitted to have leadership roles—anywhere. Since we

---

[11] 1 Timothy 2:12.

[12] Aristotle even referred to the "king bee" of a beehive because he never imagined such a leader could be female.

[13] i.e., not divorced or a polygamist.

[14] 1 Timothy 3:1-7, NIV.

[15] For more detail see my online article on GeorgeKoch.com, titled *Shall a Woman Keep Silent?*

live in a culture where women *are* educated and permitted to have leadership roles, those old cultural norms are irrelevant.

Reconciliation

I've given a quick overview of the two positions on women in leadership—priesthood, pastorate or teaching—in order to suggest a model for reconciliation.

To be honest, I've given short shrift to each of these arguments. Those who advocate each of these positions have volumes of closely argued Concepts, supported by volumes of scriptural references, countless hypotheses, syllogisms, deductions and inductions, and deep studies of the underlying languages and church traditions. We would be at it for months if we were to try and fully explain or defend each position—and not a step closer to Reconciliation or unity. *It isn't about agreeing on Concepts.*

HOW DO WE GET CLOSER TO RECONCILIATION?

So, how do we get closer to Reconciliation? By these intentional steps:

- Confess and Stop
- Tolerate
- Protect
- Fall In Love

I'll spell out specifically what these mean and give practical examples.

Step 1: Confess and Stop

Remember the woman caught in adultery who was about to be stoned according to the Law of Moses? Jesus intervened and said to the mob that was about to kill her, "Let the one who has never sinned throw the first stone!"[16]

We all see the unloving words and behavior of others on issues of doctrine, polity, interpretation of Scripture—on religious Concepts. Religious people are pretty mean and spiteful out there, from nasty personal attacks, to sarcastic belittlements, to physical violence and even murder—over the centuries and even in our own day. But how about *our own* words and actions—yours and mine? Is any one of us without sin in this area? If so, throw stones.

If not, don't melt away in silence, like this woman's accusers did. *Confess it and be forgiven.* And then be intentional to "go and sin no more" in this way. You know that gossip and personal attack, division and disunity, are not what Scripture commends, not what Jesus prayed for.

So stop doing it.

---

[16] John 8:7b.

Step 2: Tolerate Other Views

Perhaps you've heard of the "Edicts of Toleration." There were many of these issued over the course of the centuries. The first one (related to Christians) in A.D. 311 officially ended the persecution of Christians in the Roman Empire. After the Protestant Reformation in the 16th century, numerous rulers and countries issued similar Edicts to end the persecution of various sects, including Unitarians, Lutherans, Jews and Roman Catholics, and stretching from Rome to Bohemia to England to Hawaii to China. The need was there because the dominant religious group in a given area often persecuted others not of their particular brand of Christian Church, or not of the national religion (as in China, Spain, etc).

Historically, persecution ranged from not being allowed to own property or hold office, to being horribly burned to death atop a pile of dried sticks.

Clashes among Protestants and Roman Catholics still rage today, as well as among native religions, Hindus, Muslims, Christians and Jews, and among rival sects *within* each of those faiths.

Many of these clashes still result in jail or murder for holding the wrong beliefs, or for refusal to convert to the dominant religion, or for "proselytizing" to convert someone from the dominant religion to another one.

Even in countries where Edicts of Toleration were issued, they were often overturned as quickly as a new ruler or government came into power, and persecution resumed.

Such persecution is a direct and profound violation of the commandments to love God, neighbor and even enemy. It cannot be justified by a Christian. It is sin.

We must *at a minimum* tolerate the Christian faith of others who do not agree with us, as well as non-Christian faiths. This is not to say we should be silent or fail to wrestle over issues where we differ, but how we go about this is of paramount importance to God, and so far we have done it horribly.

Tolerate others.

Step 3: Protect the Other, the One With Whom You Disagree

This is a step beyond "tolerance," which itself is usually *grudging* at best, and leaves intact a condescension toward, and fear of, people with views other than your own.

But protect the one with whom you disagree?

This is a new idea for most of us. We tend to imagine our role as both advancing our Concepts on the field of battle, and defending them against the assaults of those with other Concepts. We promote and defend ourselves. You promote and defend yourselves.

Yet this aggressive/defensive behavior further hardens our conceptual fortresses, and darkens the windows to any light that might be given by others. It provides no way or willingness to foster self-criticism, nor seriously to ponder criticism from without. The whole world is inside our own Concept Fortress. Nothing exists outside except danger.

Instead, let's consider this new idea of *protecting each other*. You protect me. I protect you. We protect each other.

Even though we disagree—even on important issues—we *safeguard* each other, *respect* and *pray for* each other. We intentionally *love each other*, which means to *act* for each other's blessing, safety and well-being.[17] We do what the despised Samaritan did for the wounded Jew he despised: He guarded his life, tenderly cared for him, paid for his shelter and time to heal, followed up to make sure he was recovering. Their doctrines were very different; neither saw the other as worshiping God rightly. But the Samaritan fully protected the Jew, and brought him healing and safety.

Does this ring a bell? Meiderlin said,

> We would be in the best shape if we kept in essentials, Unity; in non-essentials, Liberty; and in both *Charity*.

This is more than just "be nice." *Charity* is to "act for each other's blessing and well-being." It is from Scripture. It is the King James Bible rendition of the word now usually translated *love*. It is *agape* in the Greek.

It means to act for someone's blessing, safety and well-being. "Feelings" of love may follow, but this word *agape* is about *caring* for others—*acting, doing.* It is the word Jesus used while telling us to love God, and to love our neighbors, and to love even our enemies, and pray for them. It is what Peter tells us when he says,

> *Most important of all*, continue to show deep love for each other, for love covers a multitude of sins.[18]

It is the action James is describing when he tells us,

> So you see, we are shown to be right with God by *what we do*, not by faith alone.[19]

It is the word Paul uses in saying,

> Love *does no wrong to others*, so love *fulfills* the requirements of God's law.[20]

And also when he says,

> Love is *patient* and *kind*. Love is not jealous or boastful or *proud* or *rude*. It does *not demand its own way*. It is not *irritable*, and it *keeps no record of being wronged.*[21]

---

[17] With no funny business by defining "well-being" to mean "make them to be just like we are."
[18] 1 Peter 4:8.
[19] James 2:24.
[20] Romans 13:10.

Those are our guidelines, our chart, our course, in learning to *protect* each other. But it isn't a new idea at all! It is the parable of the Good Samaritan, which Jesus uses to illustrate *who our neighbor is*: The one despised helps the one he despises!

It is what Jesus told us to do, and what is stressed again and again in Scripture. It is how love is made manifest: You protect me. I protect you. We protect each other. Even though we disagree—even on important issues—we *safeguard* each other, *care for* each other, *respect* and *pray for* each other.

We intentionally *love each other*—which means to *act* for each other's blessing and well-being.

Love and protect each other!

A real-life example of mutual protection: I started this chapter looking at the issue of women in ministry because it affects many Christian organizations, but also because I have worked deeply and seriously *to live and work together* with churches that *differ* on this issue. What follows is a true story.

I cite it as an *example*, but I intend that the *model* be one that is applied *broadly across other denominational differences and distinctives*. We cannot come together in the unity Jesus desires if we continue to divide again and again, and draw ourselves into hardened fortresses of imagined doctrinal perfection, windows closed against any possible wisdom that differs with our "settled" views. I'll address how to handle such differences in the next section—HAVERIM—but for now please consider this example of what we've done with the issue of women in ministry to live out the love which Jesus commanded.

I know churches locally and nationally who are convinced that women cannot be priests,[22] pastors or leaders in the Church. I know others that believe they can. Some of the churches on either side will simply not associate with each other, or worse.

But a significant number have now gathered in an intentional association where they do not simply tolerate each other, but *safeguard* each other, and stay together in unity even when that unity is assaulted from outside by those who consider such protection of the other to be treason to the Concept they hold dear.

In one instance, a small group of Christians who strongly believe only men can be priests was under assault within its denomination—a denomination that had a long tradition of women in leadership. A local congregation with women clergy (in the same denomination), gave this "only men can be priests" group sanctuary for their meetings, loving and respecting them.

Next, a group of churches that only permit men as priests, chose to establish a formal working relationship with this congregation and others that had female priests. Neither forced its views on the other, but the found unity in Christ. The

---

[21] 1 Corinthians 13:4-5.

[22] By the way, it is not just the Roman Catholic Church that uses this title for its pastors. It is also common among Eastern Orthodox, Anglicans and others, including many Protestant denominations. As noted earlier, I use the term generically here to include pastors, overseers and other such ministry leadership roles in the church, not just those with the title of "priest." Also see *priest* in the Glossary Plus.

first group of churches was then taken to task by outsiders for abandoning the established "true tradition" of the faith (the male-only priesthood) and exhorted to leave the association because some congregations had women priests (including the very one that had given sanctuary to a male-only group!)

But the congregations that had only men as priests rose to the defense of the unity and the women clergy, and refused to be driven apart from them! The unity grew stronger!

Several similar incidents have occurred, both big and small, and the action of both sides within the whole group has been consistent: They *love* and *respect* each other, and they *protect each other*, even though they differ on this issue.

To be frank, *this is very unusual behavior for Christians.* We tend (all of us) to be so devoted to our Concepts, our doctrines, subdoctrines, worship practices, polities, hermeneutical methods and traditions, that we rabidly jump to their defense *at the expense* of the people who view things differently.

Stop it. Protect *each other.*

Step 4: Fall In Love

In the example here—of each side actually protecting the other—an extraordinary thing has happened: *We have fallen in love,* and the issue that separated us, though still an area of respectful disagreement, *has lost its charge.* It is no longer a source of irritation, fear, stress or isolation. This last step, falling in love, was not anticipated. The *doing* of love—*protecting each other*—happened out of obedience to the commands of Jesus and Scripture. The "feeling" of falling in love happened in its wake. What a wonderful and surprising gift from the Lord!

This model can and should be applied throughout the Church throughout the world. It is a healing balm that will dress wounds that have gaped and bled for centuries. But it takes daily intention, prayer, repentance, hard work, and love.

Such love covers a multitude of sins.

HAVERIM

First, a little Hebrew and history, and then I'll suggest a means to truly deal with areas where we disagree—that is, with theology and doctrine, with the Concepts we hold dear, and the desire to promote and defend. This "way out" is proposed assuming the four steps of the previous section have been understood and are put into practice. Intentionally. Profoundly.

Perhaps this section here will provide even more justification for mutual protection and the love it requires:

The Hebrew word for love is אהב, *ahav.* If you want to look it up in *Strong's Concordance*, its number is H157.

The following image is from Gesenius' Lexicon.[23] I put the whole section in so you can peruse it and enjoy its depth, but look closely at this: *Ahav* means to *desire* or *to breathe after anything*. This gives a sense of how deeply felt this love is—as close as one's breath: deep desire.

Read the Gesenius entry from top to bottom now. It will be worth your time.

---

[23] A famous and detailed work on the Hebrew language, in German, by Heinrich Friedrich Wilhelm Gesenius, who lived 1786–1842. The English translation below is by Samuel Tregelles (1813–1875).

אָהַב & אָהֵב fut. יֶאֱהַב and יֶאֱהַב‎; 1 pers. אֹהַב Pro. 8:17; and אֹהֵב Hos. 14:5; inf. אֱהֹב Ecc. 3:8 and אַהֲבָה.

(1) TO DESIRE, TO BREATHE AFTER anything. (The signification of breathing after, hence of longing, is proper to the syllables הב, חב, and with the letters softened, אב, או, comp. the roots הָבַל, חָבַב,

حَبَّ to desire, to love; אָוָה and אָבָה to breathe after, to be inclined.) Construed with an accusative, Ps. 40:17; 70:5, seq.; בְּ Ps. 116:1.

(2) *to love* (in which signification it accords with עָגַב ἀγαπάω), construed with an acc. Gen. 37:3, 4; Deu. 4:37; more rarely with לְ Lev. 19:18, 34, and בְּ Ecc. 5:9; 1 Sa. 20:17, אֲהֲבַת נַפְשׁוֹ אֲהֵבוֹ "he loved him as his own soul." Part. אֹהֵב *a friend,* i.e. one who is loving and beloved, intimate; different from רֵעַ a companion, Pro. 18:24; Est. 5:10, 14; Isa. 41:8, זֶרַע אַבְרָהָם אֹהֲבִי "the seed of Abraham my friend."

(3) *to delight* in anything, in doing anything; construed with a gerund of the verb; Hos. 12:8, אָהֵב לַעֲשֹׁק "he delights in oppression," or to oppress; Isa. 56:10; Jer. 14:10.

NIPHAL part. נֶאֱהָב *to be loved, amiable,* 2 Sam. 1:23.

PIEL part. מְאַהֵב.—(1) *a friend,* Zec. 13:6.

(2) *a lover,* especially in a bad sense; one given to licentious intercourse, a debauchee, Eze. 16:33, seq.; 23:5, seq. Always thus used, metaph. of idolaters. [Hence the following words.]

(related entry)

אָהַב a root unused in Hebrew. In Chaldee, in Pael אַהֵב to produce fruit, especially the first and early fruit; Syr. ܝܚܒ to produce flowers. It appears in Arab., as well as in Heb., to have signified *to be verdant, to germinate;* see the derivatives אֵב greenness, אָבִיב ear of corn. I consider the primary sense to have been that of putting forth, protruding, germinating with impetus, shooting forth; Germ. treiben, whence אֵב junger Trieb, young shoots; so that it is kindred to the roots אָהַב, יָאַב, אָבָה, having the sense of desire, eager pursuit of an object; see אָהַב.

FIGURE: GESENIUS' LEXICON ENTRY FOR אהב, *AHAV*

Ahav is just the word used for the relationship between Jonathan and David:

> Now Jonathan again caused David to vow, because he *loved* him; for he *loved* him as he *loved* his own soul.[24]

That is, this kind of friend is "one who is loving and beloved, intimate; different ... from a companion."[25] It is also the word that God uses to describe His relationship with Abraham:

> But you, Israel, are My servant, Jacob whom I have chosen, the descendants of Abraham My *friend*.[26]

Those are the basics of this Hebrew word for love and for an intimate, beloved friend (this intimacy does not imply sexual relations, but a closeness of hearts).

It is also the root of the word חבר, *haver*, which means "friend," pronounced hah-*ver* (ver as in *very*). The plural is חברים, *haverim*, which is pronounced *hah-ver-eem*, with the accent on the last syllable.

Why do we care?

We began to look at this back in Chapter 14, "Covenant—The Law of Moses," in relation to *yeshiva* and the study of the Talmud. The men in *yeshiva* are studying together in pairs: Each is *haver*—beloved friend—to the other, and they search the Scriptures, and the commentaries on the Scriptures in the *Talmud*, and they debate, listen, consider, respond, stretch, reply, in great detail—and with more biblical and Talmudic references and connections than you can imagine! One takes one side. His *haver* takes the other. It is intense. Sparks fly!

It would seem that they try to exhaust the issue, and each other. And then often the *rosh*—the head rabbi of the yeshiva—will tell them to *switch sides!* They have to argue the other side's case!

What is remarkable about this is that for the most part, the specifics of each side of a particular issue (and there may be more than two "sides"), is of long-standing—hundreds if not thousands of years.

No winner!

A highly regarded rabbi has given each opinion recorded in the *Talmud*, and they stand there adjacent to each other, each respected for its wisdom. Each is a careful exegesis of Scripture, Law and Tradition. Their conclusions differ and often diverge or disagree.

These conclusions are studied historically, and studied *for how they apply to today*—they are striving to write the Law on their hearts. This is done with great

---

[24] 1 Samuel 20:17, NKJV.
[25] Like the word "love" in English, it can also be used with any other word to mean to *enjoy* or *delight in* something.
[26] Isaiah 41:8, NKJV.

vigor, and with great care. But what is so notable about it is that for the Jews, aside from a handful of essentials on which there is consensus, *the non-essentials are permitted to have more than one point of view.*

Of course there are individual Jews and groups who violate this and are as mean-spirited as other religious zealots. But the rabbinic model, which is lived out with great intentionality in yeshiva, is one Christians need to embrace and embody.

In yeshiva, the non-essentials are keenly important, so important that no nuance is allowed to be lost. The wisdom of each differing view is considered as an indispensable part of the whole, and each is honored and studied.

I call this *havering*—a wonderful Hebrew word turned into a English verb—and meaning to be able to debate and wrestle with an issue vigorously, but without condescension, harm or defeat to the other. When we *haver* with each other, we let God come in; in fact, we positively invite the presence of the Holy Spirit to inspire our conversation, even our spiritual wrestling, so that we might know the things of God more deeply. This is the spirit (and Spirit) of the yeshiva. (It would help deeply in our discussions with Jewish friends over who the Messiah is!)

But we Christians instead seem to ignore, fight or discard any view or nuance, even on non-essentials, that does not conform precisely to our own, and we end up in thousands of hardened fortresses, unwilling to let in air or light. We excel at sly sarcasm, bitter accusation, name-calling and condescension. The hatred, viciousness and fear-mongering is stunning. And it is sin.

The *haverim* in yeshiva are not permitted any such personal animus, venom or disrespect as they debate. Respect of the other's intention is fundamental.

But the *haverim* in yeshiva believe that it is precisely because they are willing to challenge each other forcefully—to wrestle each issue with vigor, to explore and *preserve* each nuance, to respect the wisdom and intent of each view, that *they make room for the Spirit of God to blow through their understandings.*

The question we Christians need to ask is this:

Aside from the core *essentials* of the faith, is it possible God actually countenances more than one approach to Him, or His love, or His worship, or the love of His creatures for one another, or is there just precisely one Concept that is correct in each case, for all believers?

If the answer is *just precisely one*, then why did Jesus tell *parables*—stories that can be applied in so many ways in so many circumstances? Why are all of both Testaments such a *narrative adventure*, with so many twists and turns, with even the Law (with a few specific exceptions) laid out in broad terms and able to be set aside for good reason (e.g., you can work on the Sabbath if it is to rescue your donkey from a ditch)?

It seems like Jesus would have been better off just giving us the answers. Exactly one for each question. A spreadsheet.

But of course He wasn't a Greek philosopher (and even *they* wouldn't do that). He didn't erect a new Philosophy, or populate a conceptual array with syllogisms, categories, doctrines and subdoctrines, hermeneutical methods and complex structures of authority.

He was a rabbi, a teacher, rooted in the *rabbinic way*, a tradition that *valued vigorous debate* and *allowed differences to persist*—that could see truths side by side, *adjacent*, each a nuance, a piece, of a greater whole, rather than one declared right and one declared wrong. Paul did this too. And Peter. And James.

Jesus challenged others in His tradition—some quite pointedly—but aside from those who were self-righteous and hypocritical, these challenges were typically rabbinic. They would have been expected, normal, *even welcomed!* It's how the breath of God comes in!

So, was Jesus a teacher, or a carpenter?
Did He walk on water, or ride in a boat?
Did He heal Jews or Gentiles?
Did He stay by Himself or mingle with large crowds?
Is He the great high priest, or a suffering servant?
Is He slave or King?

Is He a man or is He God?

Our traditional dialectical, binary approach to our faith would suggest if these were doctrines, then they would be *choices*, and in each case we would get to pick just *one*. The last is the one that should rock us back on our heels. The Christian faith declares that Jesus is *both* fully man and fully God, *not* one or the other.

THE RABBINIC WAY

Beyond the essentials, perhaps we can wrestle with competing Concepts (and their offspring), but *get benefit from all of them*, and their *nuances*, rather than forcing each other to choose or be cast out. Perhaps we can preserve and protect them and each other, rather than insist that one triumphs and the other is defeated.

This is the *rabbinic way* of hearing and applying Scripture, and it is *fundamentally Christian*. Jesus lived it. Paul lived it. But we lost it somewhere in the transporting of the Gospel from Israel to the rest of the Greek-speaking Hellenized world. We adapted a way of doing philosophy that was foreign to the tradition of the faith from Abraham to Paul, but that grew dominant in the Church over the two millennia that followed.

What was begun as a convenient way to explain the Son of God to the Greek philosophers[27] became instead a Greek philosophy[28] in its own right. The faith in God was turned into concepts, the revelation diced up into pieces and put into an

---

[27] Acts 17, Paul's "Mars Hill" speech.
[28] Including, if not beginning with, *Against Celsus* by Origen. See Chapter 22.

organized categorical array, with patterns of syllogisms: major premises, minor premises, conclusions. Inferences. Deduction. Induction.

Concepts!

Worse, we ended up worshiping these Concepts, promoting *them* and defending *them*, instead of worshiping, loving and having a relationship with the One who made us.

The flaw in this is partly in the manufacturing of Concepts at all, but even more so in the insistence that we *choose* one over another, and hurt (physically or verbally) those who do not choose as we do. We discard wisdom when we do this.

HOPE AND THE MEANS TO UNITY

Back to my illustration about women in ministry, as an example of how we should approach most such issues of the faith: I watched once as two scholars each presented papers on women in ministry before a gathering of religious leaders. One defended the *male-only priesthood*, and mustered capable arguments from Scripture, Tradition and History. It was quite an impressive and thorough presentation, done with a persuasive and non-belligerent spirit.

The other stood and presented the case *for women as priests*. It was similarly thorough, and also drew its arguments from Scripture, Tradition and History. It showed remarkable insight into human culture and God's interactions with it over time. It was competent, collegial and persuasive.

Both presenters were prepared. They were respectful of each other as believers. *Wisdom* came from each. *Insights and nuances* were revealed by both. God's light shone *from each* on the topic before them, though they disagreed.

When they were done, some of the gathered leaders present asked, "Are we going to vote now?" They assumed that after debate, proper doctrine and polity for leadership in the church would be decided by majority rule.

The most senior leader, who had called the meeting, said *no*—not only were they not going to vote, they *never would*. They were not going to *choose* one over the other. Adjacent, *both would stand.*

Some accepted this with equanimity and even joy; others were clearly agitated. One side likely had more supporters than the other, and hoped this would be the moment when they could stop the other side, and at last win.

The wisdom of the moderator prevailed, though not without considerable dismay from those who thought this would be their moment of victory.

I recall this incident because it illustrates yet again the flaw in our approach to God. Somehow we have gotten stuck on the notion that in a given instance, only one metaphor, only one description, only one nuance, only one understanding of God is acceptable, and others must be suppressed. *This is a thoroughly bad idea.* We have to stop acting this way, and not only *tolerate* each other's approaches, but *protect* them—safeguard each other's views, not just because it is polite and collegial, but because *it is more complete and true.* More of the Spirit of God is allowed to breathe through us when we do not shut ourselves off from each other.

Essentials Defined

I've been consistent throughout this book in not suggesting that "believing anything" is okay or that every religious idea is equally valid. There are essentials. This will bring some howls from every quarter, but those essentials of the faith are *not* in the Traditions or any of the Concepts so dear to each denomination and local church. Those things may define movements and doctrines, they may help us understand and live the faith, but they do not define a Christian.

Salvation, Sanctification and Glorification are the *essentials* of Life in Christ, of *Covenant*. Re-read the three chapters on Covenant to recall fully what this means. These three are the essence and foundation of all of which our relationship with God consists. They are Life in Christ, where we have union with God. It is where we must have unity with one another. They are our common roots.

Non-Essentials Defined

Most of what we reject each other over are *non-essentials* in the most important sense: They are not *required* for salvation, not *required* for sanctification and not *required* for glorification—these three can proceed with or without them. The non-essentials are not *required* by Covenant, by Life in Christ.

For any element of doctrine, tradition, polity or practice, if salvation is possible without it, if sanctification can proceed without it, if glorification can come without it, it is non-essential.

It may be useful, but if it is not *required*, if it is not an *if-and-only-if* of a Life in Christ, of His Covenant, it is *non-essential*. It may be valuable and important in our doctrine, tradition, polity or practice, but it is non-essential if it is not *required* for life in Him.

This may be hugely disturbing to contemplate. It upends much that our lives have focused upon. But it is key to recognizing the true unity we have with other followers of Jesus Christ. In spite of our huge differences of religious concepts, of doctrine and practice, we are *rooted* together in the essentials, *in life in Him*. We vary widely in the way we explain and manifest the life that flows out from these roots, but that doesn't mean one of us is rooted in Him and the other is not.

This singular revelation should allow us to realize at last the unity for which Jesus prayed.

COMMUNION

Here's a practical, common example to help us understand this and embody unity, through several ways in which something very important—Communion—is explained and manifested in different denominations:

- The presentation of the Last Supper, the Passover Meal, with the priest or pastor recalling Jesus words to His disciples, and the invitation of the blessing of the Spirit unto the bread and wine, that they would be for us "His body and blood." Whether His presence is seen as Real, or Dynamic, or Consubstantial, He is understood to be there. I can value and gain from this Concept, even if it is not my own.
- The metaphor of Christ sacrificing Himself for us in the Eucharist, and doing so before His bride the Church. This is beautiful and heart-rending. That some can accept only a man standing in the role of Christ is comprehensible. I can value and gain from this Concept, even if it is not my own.
- The practice of the Lord's Supper as a memorial, a *remembrance only* of an important moment in the life of Jesus. This is also clear and comprehensible. It doesn't require a male priest, a Eucharistic Sacrifice nor the Real Presence, and still it is wonderful and filled with deep meaning. I can value and gain from this Concept, even if it is not my own.
- The experience of Communion as a coming together, a "love feast" of the Body of Christ, done to remember Jesus' last meal with His followers, and share as He did with His disciples. It is an encouragement—to be one with other believers, grateful to share Him so easily. I can value and gain from this Concept, even if it is not my own.

Each of these—and *several others*—are typical of "Communion" in one branch or another of the Christian faith, yet the followers of each typically reject the others as *invalid* or *untrue* to Scripture or Tradition or both. Denominations and churches tend to insist that *just one be accepted by you for you to be acceptable*. In so doing, the blessings, insights and heart of the others are lost, and our union is broken.

In no case is the form of Communion, the Concept, *required* for salvation. A Christian can live a lifetime without ever once receiving Communion and it has no effect whatsoever on salvation. For *salvation*, it is *non-essential*.

Each of these methods, and others, *can be* a part of a believer's sanctification. Each of them can have a *profound* effect on the individual believer's growth, and his understanding of Jesus' sacrifice. They can have a similarly profound effect on the whole body of believers, as they gather to share the Lord's Supper. But a believer can live an entire lifetime of Spirit-filled sanctification without receiving Communion even once. For *sanctification*, each of these methods and even Communion itself are *non-essential*, not *required*.

The key point here is that Communion, and a host of other practices, methods, doctrines, concepts and structures, though they may be *valuable* and *important* in the life of a Christian, a denomination, or a local church, are nevertheless *non-essential* to salvation, sanctification and glorification, to Life in Christ, to Covenant.

As such, we need to grant liberty in their use, and *charity* in our regard for those who *choose differently* than we do. This is Meiderlin's deep insight, and *it reflects the heart and teaching of Jesus.*

CONCLUSION

Liberty is vital. But *merely* granting each other *liberty* still leaves us self-focused and living in our protected and isolating fortresses. That does not qualify as the unity that Jesus prayed for. That's why *charity* is the necessary final step: *Loving each other.* True unity requires that we see, care for, bless and protect *each other*. It is the example given us when Jesus prayed:

> "Holy Father, you have given me your name; now *protect them* by the power of your name *so that they will be united just as we are.* During my time here, *I protected them* by the power of the name you gave me. *I guarded them* so that not one was lost, except the one headed for destruction, as the Scriptures foretold."[29]

Jesus didn't pray that we all organize, worship, share communion, pray, dress, baptize, sing, teach or understand identically. Jesus says He protected His disciples—who got their Concepts right *and wrong* all the time, and whose faith wavered and failed with stunning regularity. Did He cast them out for this? No, He protected them. In spite of the chaos and differences of their doctrine and behavior, He protected them.

And He prayed that we would be one, united. How can we just *ignore* Him?

Listen to how He describes the unity for which He prays: It is to be as *the unity of Jesus with the Father.* They are *in one another*—an intimacy of love—*ahav!*—that doesn't make them identical, but gives glory, honor, respect, care, thanksgiving *to the other.*

> "I am praying not only for these disciples but also for all who will ever believe in me through their message. I pray that they will all be one, *just as you and I are one*—as you are in me, Father, and I am in you. And may they be in us so that the world will believe you sent me. I have given them the glory you gave me, so they may be one as we are one. I am in them and you are in me. *May they experience such perfect unity* that the world will know that you sent me and that you love them as much as you love me."[30]

We do not experience "such perfect unity" when we hurt, ignore or even just *tolerate* each other. The unity begins with charity, when we love as Jesus loved, when we *bless, care for* and *protect* each other as Jesus did His disciples. When we are *other*-focused instead of self-focused. When we acknowledge His disciples, even when then are not like us. As Matthew Henry said, "*Let us*

---

[29] John 17:11b-12.
[30] John 17:20-23.

consider all who seek the glory of the Redeemer, as our brethren and fellow-travellers, without regarding differences which do not affect our eternal welfare."

We must acknowledge and live out our *common roots in Him*, despite our differences. In the *essentials*, we are one. It is time to act like it.

> *Most important of all*, continue to show deep love for each other, for love covers a multitude of sins.[31]
>
> So you see, we are shown to be right with God by *what we do*, not by faith alone.[32]
>
> Love *does no wrong to others*, so love *fulfills* the requirements of God's law.[33]
>
> Love is *patient* and *kind*. Love is not jealous or boastful or *proud* or *rude*. It does *not demand its own way*. It is not *irritable*, and it *keeps no record of being wronged*.[34]

> Don't think you are better than you really are. Be honest in your evaluation of yourselves, measuring yourselves by the faith God has given us. Just as our bodies have many parts and each part has a special function, so it is with Christ's Body. *We are many parts of one body*, and *we all belong to each other*. ... Don't just pretend to love others. Really love them. Hate what is wrong. Hold tightly to what is good. Love each other with *genuine affection*, and take delight in *honoring* each other. ...
>
> *Bless those* who persecute you. Don't *curse them*; pray that God will bless them. Be happy with those who are happy, and weep with those who weep. *Live in harmony with each other*. Don't be too proud to enjoy the company of ordinary people. *And don't think you know it all!*
>
> Never pay back evil with more evil. Do things in such a way that everyone can see you are honorable. *Do all that you can to live in peace with everyone.*[35]

> This is my commandment: Love each other in the same way I have loved you.[36]

It is His Way. Embody it.

---

[31] 1 Peter 4:8.
[32] James 2:24.
[33] Romans 13:10.
[34] 1 Corinthians 13:4-5.
[35] Romans 12:3b-5, 9-10, 14-18.
[36] John 15:12.

Appendix 1
Glossary Plus of Terms

This is a "Glossary Plus" of terms used in this book. It is intentionally more than just definitions, but rather helps to explain some of the foundations of the book itself, organized alphabetically by word and phrase, rather than by chapter topic. Entries here appear in the book **Index** in boldface.

Bolded words within a definition are cross-references to separate entries.

613 laws, rules, commandments, *mitzvot* (plural of *mitzvah*). Refers to all of the commandments of the Law of Moses found in the **Torah**, or Five Books of Moses (Genesis, Exodus, Leviticus, Numbers, Deuteronomy). Their enumeration is typically attributed to **Maimonides**, though others also numbered them prior to him. There are 365 negatives (e.g., "do not steal") and 248 positives (e.g., "love your neighbor"). The sages also divide them into three categories: those that are logical and make sense (e.g., not committing murder), those that sustain or testify to the faith (e.g., keeping the Sabbath), and those that seem to defy logic and common sense (e.g., Numbers 19:1-22). All are binding nonetheless, though all are subject to interpretation and elucidation by the **Oral Law**. Christians, when they learn of these, often dismiss them as "mere legalism," but that is a serious misunderstanding of their purpose and application.

Abenezra. Abraham ibn Ezra, circa 1089–1167. Also known as Abenezra. Spanish rabbi and brilliant expositor of Scripture.

Abram/Abraham. God changed the name of Abram, "exalted father," to Abraham, "father of nations," in Genesis 17. Husband of **Sarai/Sarah**. See Chapter 13, "Covenant – Abraham."

Acolyte. One who assists the **celebrant** in the performance of the **liturgy**.

Ad hominem. A form of **misdirection**, by attacking the motives or character of an opponent, or appealing to the emotions of the listener, rather than focusing on the opponent's position, argument or logic.

Adiaphora. Translates as "matters of indifference" or "indifferent things." A term from Greek **Stoic** philosophers to refer to things that were morally neutral. In Christian usage, typically refers to things neither required nor forbidden by Scripture.

Adonai. See also **Hashem.** One of the three most common names for God in the Old Testament; the others are **Yahweh** and **Elohim. Adonai** means "lord," and in most Bible translations into English is rendered "Lord" (uppercase *L*, lowercase *ord*). **Yahweh** is an English pronunciation of the Hebrew letters YOD-HEY-VAV-HEY, יהוה, sometimes also pronounced "Yehovah" or "Jehovah." Many Jews do not say this Name aloud, out of respect and in order never to "take it in vain." In prayer, they substitute "Adonai" anywhere "Yahweh" appears in prayers or Scripture, and in daily conversation they substitute "Hashem" ("the Name") rather than, say, "God." Similarly, they write "G-d" rather than write out God's Name. Yahweh is usually rendered "LORD" in English translations (uppercase *L*, small-caps ORD). **Elohim** is another common name for God (and gods) in the Old Testament. Usually rendered "God" in translations. When used as such, it is with a singular verb, though the suffix *-im* is plural. When it refers to other gods, it takes a plural verb.

Agape. Love. From the Greek ἀγάπη, *agápē.* Distinguished from three other common terms for love, *eros*, *philia* and *storge*, the first of which refers to romantic desire and affection, the second to love for family and close friends, and the third to fondness that arises between acquaintances. "Agape" is a relatively uncommon word for "love" in Greek, though the verb form was used to translate the Hebrew word for love, אהב, *ahav*, in the **Septuagint.** The **New Testament** uses it to denote a love that is less of a feeling than an intentional action for someone else's blessing or well-being, including most especially God, neighbor and even enemy. It is the word used almost exclusively for love by Jesus, Paul and others. The King James Bible renders this word as *charity.*

Agnostic. Literally "not knowing." In modern usage, an agnostic is unconvinced whether God exists or not, or believes such existence is unknowable. Apparently coined by T. H. Huxley, who said, "I took thought, and invented what I conceived to be the appropriate title of 'agnostic' … antithetic to the 'gnostic' of Church history, who professed to know so much about the very things of which I was ignorant." From *Science and Christian Tradition*, Forgotten Books, 2010 (originally published 1889), p. 239. See also **Atheist, Deist** and **Theist.**

Ahav. Love. From Hebrew אהב, *ahav.* Also the root of *haver* and *haverim*, denoting intimate friend and friends, as well as study partners in a *yeshiva*.

Alexander the Great. (356–323 B.C.) Greek military ruler who conquered Northern Africa, the Middle East (including Israel and Judea) and the Mediterranean. He was a pupil of **Aristotle.**

Alfred North Whitehead. (1861–1947) English philosopher and mathematician. Co-author of the famous *Principia Mathematica* with Bertrand Russell, who had been one of his students.

All the Law and the Prophets. An expression that refers to all of the parts of the **Old Testament** (see also **Tanakh**) that give instruction: both the *mitzvot*, or commandments, and the exhortations of the prophets, as they spoke for God.

All things depend on one thing. An ancient grammatical form used to highlight something as extremely important. May be meant literally, but may also be meant simply to draw close attention to a point being made. Used by Jesus about the **Law and the Prophets**, by the **Talmud** about the Second Commandment, and by **Rashi** about circumcision, among others.

Allah. "The God." An Arabic word related to the Hebrew **Elohim**, used by Muslims to refer to God, but also by some Arabic-speaking Christians and Mizrahi Jews.

Altar Book. A service book used on the altar table in liturgical churches, such as Roman Catholic, Methodist, Anglican, Lutheran and so on, and containing orders of service for prayer, Communion, baptism, marriage, ordination and the like. Each of these services, in turn, consists of instructions for liturgy, Scripture passages and prayers.

Anabaptists. Re-baptizers. A group of Protestant Christians that arose in Europe in the 16th century, and that insisted baptism be restricted to adult believers who make a profession of faith in Jesus. They did not recognize infant baptism as valid since infants cannot profess faith in Jesus. Thus they re-baptized anyone who had been baptized as an infant but as an adult was willing to profess faith. They had many other distinctives in their manner of life as Christians. Modern-day Baptists descend from this movement, though there have been many divisions and differences in these groups.

Anglican. Churches related to or "in communion" with the Church of England. Originally begun about A.D. 597 by St. Augustine of Canterbury, but separated from the Roman Catholic Church by King Henry VIII in 1534. Today a worldwide church of over 70 million with the majority of its members in Africa and Asia. The third-largest Christian denomination in the world, after the Roman Catholic and Eastern Orthodox Churches.

Anglo-Catholic. A "stream" within the Anglican Church whose worship and theology is closely aligned with that of the Roman Catholic Church, but is not under its authority.

Animus. From a Latin word meaning "intention," or "inclination," but more commonly means having ill-will or a negative attitude toward another person.

Apocrypha. Also called *pseudepigrapha* or "intertestamental" literature. A set of books written after the Old Testament and before the New Testament. Variously regarded as being inspired by God or not, and therefore included or not, in the Bible. The Roman Catholic Church includes them within its Old Testament. Anglicans and others include them but in a separate section and consider them worthy of study, but not "inspired." Many Protestant churches exclude them from their Bibles.

Apollo. The Greek god of healing, light, music, poetry, and prophecy. Son of Zeus and Leto. Guided an arrow shot by Paris into the heel of Achilles, thus killing him. Achilles' mother Thetis had held him by his heel and dipped him in the river Styx to give him immortality, but his heel had not gotten wet, making him vulnerable. See the section on baptism in "More on Magical Thinking," in Chapter 12, *Obedience and Love*.

Apollos. One of the early Christian leaders and teachers. From Acts 18:24-25: "…a Jew named Apollos, an eloquent speaker who knew the Scriptures well, had arrived in Ephesus from Alexandria in Egypt. He had been taught the way of the Lord, and he taught others about Jesus with an enthusiastic spirit and with accuracy." Also mentioned in 1 Corinthians and Titus.

Apostle. Someone who is sent, including Jesus in Luke 10:16. Also refers explicitly to the twelve disciples of Jesus, to the 70 disciples He sent out (Luke 10:1), as well as to Paul and some others, such as Andronicus and Junia (Romans 16:7). Also used more broadly to refer to someone who starts new churches, or leads those who do.

Apostles Creed. Probably the first of the three most accepted statements of theology of the Christian Church, including the **Nicene Creed** and **Athanasian Creed**. It is dated in its earliest form to the second century. As such, it does not address some of the later theologies that developed in the Church, including those asserting the divinity of Christ and the Holy Spirit. In that way, it is less of a theology fabricated into Concepts, and more a weaving together of verses and parts of verses from Scripture.

Apostolic Authority/Succession. The concept that the original apostles had spiritual authority given to them by Jesus, and that this authority can be passed on or conferred to succeeding generations of leaders in the Church, by the laying on of hands for ordination. This is particularly held by those churches that consider themselves in the "unbroken apostolic succession" of bishops from St Peter and the Apostles. Roman Catholic, Eastern Orthodox, Oriental Orthodox, Anglican and some Lutheran churches, among others, hold this view. The sentence in the Nicene Creed, "We believe in one holy and catholic and *apostolic* Church…", refers to this concept. Most non-Anglican Protestants do not hold this view. See also **Apostle**.

Apostolic Succession. See **Apostolic Authority/Succession**.

Aquinas, Thomas. (1225–1274) One of the fathers of the Church. Aquinas predated the Protestant Reformation, and by most any measure was among the most brilliant people who ever lived. His writings are widely respected by both Protestants and Roman Catholics. Even the Eastern Orthodox Church has commended parts of them (in particular they agreed with his thinking on **Transubstantiation** and said so in a letter to the Roman Catholic Church).

Aramaic. The common language of the people of Judea at the time of Jesus, along with Greek. Only the more educated Jews of that day knew Hebrew. Thought to be a dead language until its rediscovery among Kurdish Jews in the 19th and 20th centuries. See *My Father's Paradise* in the Bibliography.

Argument from ignorance. A fallacy in informal logic where something is claimed true because it hasn't been proven false. "Ignorance" in this context means "absence of evidence to the contrary." Conspiracy theories typically use this kind of assertion, and when opponents of their theories ask for *proof* of the conspiracy, they say the *absence of evidence* is proof of how good the conspirators are. They say that since we can't prove there is no conspiracy, it must be real. Similarly, if someone asserts all of the original New Testament documents were without error, or dyed pink, this is an argument from *absence of evidence*. It's true that I can't *disprove* the original New Testament documents were all pink, but that doesn't prove the person who insisted they *are* pink is right. See also **Infallible** and **Inerrancy of Scripture**.

Argumentum ad ignorantiam. See **Argument from ignorance**.

Arianism. A theology attributed to Arius (~A.D. 250–336), which says the Son of God (Jesus Christ) is not equal to the Father, but subordinate to, and created by, the Father. Based on John 14:28, *"I am going to the Father, who is greater than I am."* Arius was deemed a heretic for this doctrine, later cleared, then (after his death) deemed a heretic once again. The issue of the relative status of Father, Son and Holy Spirit was a matter of intense debate. In A.D. 393, Gregory of Nyssa complained that you couldn't go to market or baths without getting into an argument about Trinity. By 493 the debates were over and the equality of the Father, Son and Holy Spirit had been made the settled doctrine of the Church.

Aristotelian. Following the teachings and worldview of **Aristotle**.

Aristotle. (384–322 B.C.) Greek philosopher and student of Plato. Also the teacher of **Alexander the Great**, whose military campaigns Hellenized Africa, the Mediterranean worlds and the Middle East. That is, the Greek worldview became the dominant worldview of the lands Alexander conquered, including Israel and Judah. Aristotle's writings cover many subjects, including physics, metaphysics, poetry, theatre, music, logic, rhetoric, linguistics, politics, government, ethics, biology and zoology. Together with Plato and Socrates (Plato's teacher), Aristotle is one of the most important founding figures in Western philosophy. His writings were the first to create a comprehensive system of Western philosophy, encompassing morality and aesthetics, logic and science, politics and metaphysics.

Ark of the Covenant. A chest made of acacia wood and gold, used to hold the tablets of the Ten Commandments. See Exodus 25.

Ark, for Torah scroll. A cabinet in a synagogue specifically for the storage and safekeeping of the scroll of the Torah. Also called *Aron Kodesh*, from the Hebrew for "holy ark," a reference to the **Ark of the Covenant**.

Asimov, Isaac. (1920–1992) Science-fiction writer, professor of biochemisty, and one of the most prolific authors of all time, having written or edited some 500 books on a huge range of topics, including math, science, and his own guide to the Bible. Humanist. Originator of the **Three Laws of Robotics**.

Athanasian Creed. The last of the three most commonly accepted statements of theology of the Christian Church, including the **Nicene Creed** and **Apostles Creed**. The author and origin of this creed are unknown, except that it is unlikely to have been written by the author whose name it bears, Athanasius. It is probably from the 5th or 6th century A.D., and contains language from Augustine's *On the Trinity* (A.D. 415). A rhythmic, thorough, strong declaration of Trinity, asserting the equal divinity of Father, Son and Holy Spirit, their being of the "same substance" (*homoousios*), and their being separate Persons. It also declares the necessity of holding the "Catholic Faith … whole and undefiled," and says of anyone failing to do so "without doubt he shall perish everlastingly."

Atheist. A-theist, literally "not theist," from Greek *atheos*, literally, "without god," meaning someone who does not believe in God (or gods, or divine beings, or the supernatural). See also **Agnostic**, **Deist** and **Theist**.

Atom. The smallest subunit of an element (such as iron, hydrogen, uranium), consisting of a nucleus with one or more protons (and zero or more neutrons), surrounded by one or more electrons. Neutrons and protons are themselves made up of subunits called quarks. See also **Subatomic particle**.

Augustine of Hippo. (A.D. 354–430) Bishop of Hippo. One of the most influential theologians of the Church, revered by Roman Catholics, the Eastern Orthodox and Protestants (especially Calvinists) alike. Developed the concepts of original sin (after Paul, and Irenaeus) and just war, and wrote extensively on grace, salvation and predestination. His writings attacked many heresies, including Donatism, Arianism, Manichaeanism and Pelagianism. His most famous works include *Confessions*, *The City of God*, *On Christian Doctrine*, *On the Trinity* and *The Retractions*.

Autograph (of Scripture). Refers to the original document the author wrote, whether of Scripture or any other form of writing. In theology, refers specifically to the original manuscript of any book of the Bible. Those who believe in biblical inerrancy assert that such manuscripts are without error. Other versions of this claim would assert inerrancy in matters of faith and morals, but not necessarily grammar, history or science. See also **Inerrancy of Scripture**.

Baptism. An enormous topic that will only be touched on here. At its core, baptism is a symbolic washing, rooted in the Jewish *mikvah* (ritual cleansing bath), and the baptism that John the Baptist (hence his name) offered to repentant Jews. But among Christians, it signifies both the washing away of sins, and entrance into membership in the Church—not a denomination or local church, but the very Body of Christ, the entire fellowship of His followers in all places throughout all time.

It is done with water. Beyond this simple common element, there is enormous range and difference across the denominations as to how it is done. Even this simple element is sometimes missing. Some churches baptize without water by the laying on of hands. Others do not require baptism at all. Of those that baptize with water, some do so by full submersion in water, some with the person clothed and others with them naked (normative until the Middle Ages), some by pouring, sprinkling or partial immersion; some will baptize infants, and some only adults who profess faith in Jesus. Some require certain words be used without fail.

Baptism, Eucharist and Ministry – Faith and Order Paper No. 111 from the World Council of Churches, meeting in Lima, Peru in 1982, attempted to draw together the many denominations and streams of Christendom and find agreement or common ground on Baptism, Eucharist and Ministry. Much agreement was accomplished, though in many ways it remains more theory than practice. At its conclusion, it urged all churches to recognize as valid baptisms done in other denominations, so long as they were done with the intention to baptize, and were Trinitarian in form; it also said baptism can be done only once. This was a positive step, though it does illuminate how seriously we have been distracted by differing Concepts, and our disputes over them, rather than reaching the world Jesus sent us to, to tell about the Gospel.

Baptist Church. Christian churches and denominations that came out of the Anabaptist movement. Anabaptist literally means "re-baptizer" and refers to churches that reject the validity of infant baptism, and require an adult profession of faith in Jesus before baptism can occur. Beyond this common trait, there is wide variety in how various Baptist denominations and independent churches are organized, and in what they believe.

Bar Kochba, Simon. (ca. A.D. 50–135) Jewish leader of a revolt against the Roman Empire in A.D. 132. Established an independent Jewish state, which lasted three years, then was reconquered by the Romans. A contemporary, Rabbi Akiva, had declared him the Messiah and renamed him from "ben Kosiba" to "bar Kochba," meaning "son of a star," from Numbers 24:17, "A star will rise from Jacob; a scepter will emerge from Israel." After the fall of his government, rabbinical writers began referring to him as *Simon bar Kozeba*, which means "Son of Lies."

Bar mitzvah. See also **Bat mitzvah**. The "coming of age" ritual when a Jewish boy reaches 13. The term means "son of commandment" and signifies that the boy is now spiritually responsible for his own actions. His parents were responsible until this time. After *bar mitzvah*, the boy is allowed to participate in ritual, read Torah, and be numbered as one in the making of a *minyan* (ten adult Jews necessary for public prayer).

Barth, Karl. (1886–1968) Swiss theologian widely regarded as one of the most important and capable since Thomas Aquinas, but in the "Reformed" tradition; an interpreter of Calvin's doctrine of election, with a focus on the sovereignty of God. Usually pronounced "bart."

Bat mitzvah. "Daughter of commandment." See **Bar mitzvah**. Basically the same except that it refers to girls.

Begotten, Only. From the Greek *monogenēs*. *Mono-* means "single" or "only"; *-genēs* means "originated" or "born" from. Same root as "Genesis" and "genetics." Much theological ink has been spilled on just what this word means in John 3:16, and whole denominations have sprung up because of differing Concepts about it.

Berit milah. "Covenant of circumcision." From Deuteronomy 10:15-16. מילה ברית, *berit*, the Hebrew word for "covenant," also means "to cut." See also **Bris**.

Bishop. See **Overseer** and **Priest**.

Book of Common Prayer. The title of books used for prayer and other services of the church within the Anglican Communion, and others who follow its practices. The first was authored by Thomas Cranmer in 1549, and subsequent editions and versions of it are used throughout the world.

Book of Mormon. The key religious text of the Church of Jesus Christ of Latter-Day Saints, the Mormons, and the several similar churches that have split from this church. Written by Joseph Smith, Jr. prior to 1830, but attributed by Smith to an angel named Moroni.

Book of the Covenant. The Torah, containing all that the Lord told Moses, and that Moses wrote down for the people. See Exodus 24:3-7.

Born again. In many English translations of the New Testament Greek, an expression Jesus uses in talking to Nicodemus in John 3, meaning that a person must be born into the Kingdom of Heaven to become aware of it and be a part of it. The Greek actually says "born from above."

Born from above. See **Born again.**

Bris/Brit. The Hebrew word for covenant, *berit* ברית, which also means cut, select, winnow or cleanse. The Jewish rite of circumcision is called ***berit milah***, or covenant of circumcision. In the West, and generally among the European Ashkenazi Jews, this is usually pronounced "bris." Among Middle Eastern and other Sephardic Jews, it is pronounced "brit."

Brit. See ***Bris.***

Canon. In religious institutions, a synonym for law or rule. Also the title of an assistant to a bishop or other church authority.

Canon of Scripture. The set of books (histories, prophecies, stories, letters, etc.) declared to be inspired by the Holy Spirit and worthy of inclusion in the Bible. Certain books written between the time of the Old Testament and the New Testament (hence called "intertestamental books"), known as the Apocrypha, are included in the Canon of Scripture for the **Roman Catholic** and **Eastern Orthodox** churches, but typically excluded by most modern **Protestants**. Some, such as the Anglicans, bind them in a separate section in their Bibles and say they are worthy of study but considered non-canonical (not a part of the canon and not inspired by the Holy Spirit in the way that the canonical books are).

Carbon dating. A method of estimating the age of ancient organic materials, such as wood and other plants, based on the amount of carbon-14 they contain.

Cardinal. The highest rank of clergy in the Roman Catholic Church, other than the Pope.

Category error. Placing something into a category to which it does not belong, or that makes no sense. This can be done unintentionally or colloquially, such as calling a tomato a vegetable, or with intent to mislead, such as bottling tap water and calling it "pure mountain stream water." Both kinds of category error have occurred in theology, as they do in many human arguments and discussions, and care is necessary to avoid them.

Catholic. Used in two different senses. Capitalized, it refers to the **Roman Catholic Church** or its members. With a lowercase C, as in "one holy catholic and apostolic Church" (from the Nicene and Apostles Creeds) it means simply "worldwide" or "universal" and does not refer exclusively to the Roman Catholic Church, but to the whole Body of Christ.

Celebrant. In liturgical church such as Roman Catholic, Eastern Orthodox, Anglican and others, a common term for the person who leads a worship service.

Celsus. (A.D. ?–?) Greek philosopher, 2nd century A.D., who wrote *The True Word* as an attack on Christianity. This was rebutted by the early Christian writer Origen in his work *Against Celsus.*

Charity. The English word used in the King James Version of the Bible, and others, as a translation of the Greek word ***agape***. Meiderlin used *Charity* in just this way to mean that we treat others with respect and love, even when we disagree or differ on *either* essentials or non-essentials. See Chapter 1.

Chassidic Judaism. One of the main sects of modern Judaism. The others are **Orthodox, Conservative, Reform,** and **Reconstructionist**. Founded in Eastern Europe, and focused on Talmud study, ecstatic worship and loving kindness. Actively seeks new members from other Jewish sects, as well as from unaffiliated Jews. Founded by Rabbi Israel Baal Shem Tov as a reaction to the legalistic Judaism of the time. The most recent head of one branch of this movement, known as the Lubavitcher Rebbe, was long expected to announce that he was the Messiah, but he never did. He died in 1994.

Chiasmus. A pattern of symmetry in verses, usually where the second half is in reverse order to the first: A-B-C-B-A. From the Greek *khiasmos*, "a crosswise, diagonal arrangement." A common pattern in Scripture where it is found in many forms, often to highlight an important verse, such as the "C" in the pattern above.

Christ. Greek word for **Messiah**, or "anointed one." The word first appears in the **Septuagint**, the Greek translation of the Old Testament. "Anointed" refers to the practice of pouring oil on the head of a prophet, priest or king as a symbol of God's favor or calling. "Jesus Christ" effectively means "Jesus the one anointed by God."

Christian Humanism. An ancient stream of Christianity that believes every person should be regarded as having worth, dignity and individual freedom, because they are made in the image of God. Though today it might be considered a union of Christian and Humanist ideals, both ideals are rooted in the teachings of Jesus as part of an indivisible whole. Familiar exponents of this view include Justin Martyr, Blaise Pascal, Dorothy Sayers, Immanuel Kant, Pope John Paul II, Thomas Merton, Søren Kierkegaard and T. S. Eliot.

Christian Sabbath. The seventh day of the week is given by God in the Fourth Commandment as a day of rest from all work. Religious Jews and some Christians (Seventh-Day Adventists, for example) continue this practice. The vast majority of Christians, however, have changed this practice to an observance of "The Lord's Day" or "Christian Sabbath" on Sunday, the first day of the week, corresponding to the resurrection of Jesus.

Christianity. Refers broadly to all followers of Jesus Christ. This movement was originally called simply "The Way" by early followers of Jesus: "But this I confess to you, that according to the Way which they call a sect, so I worship the God of my fathers" (Acts 24:14). Followers were also referred to as "Christians" in Antioch as early as the first century. See Acts 11:26.

Church Tradition. The combination of doctrines, writings, decisions of councils, polity, worship forms and practices, and other specifics in the evolution and growth of the Church over the course of centuries, which have become established and accepted ways of understanding and living out the faith of the followers of Jesus Christ. Of course, which elements of the Tradition are accepted as normative varies quite widely in the main streams of the Church—**Roman Catholic, Eastern Orthodox** and **Protestant**—as well as in the countless other smaller groups and unaffiliated churches. Tradition is also one of the three key legs of the "three-legged stool," **Scripture**, **Tradition** and **Reason**, which are followed by **Anglicans** and (at least implicitly) by other churches in the **Apostolic Succession**.

Commandment. Refers to both explicit directions ("you must," or "you must not") in the **Ten Commandments** and the full 613 rules, teachings and counsel of the Old Testament, as well as the two Great Commandments of the New Testament (Love God and neighbor), and the Royal Law of Love spoken of in James 2:8.

Communion. See **Eucharist**.

Composite unity. The idea that something regarded as a single entity is actually composed of any number of subunits. A pencil is a composite of graphite, wood, eraser and metal ring. A molecule of water is a composite of two atoms of hydrogen and one of oxygen. An atom is a composite of protons, electrons and neutrons. A family is a composite of parents and children. This idea is used to illustrate the Trinity: Father, Son and Holy Spirit are not three separate gods, but one God composed of three Persons. This is why Christians and others consider it a *mono*theistic religion, not a polytheistic one, such as Hinduism.

Conceptual fortresses. The idea that Concepts about God and the Church can be used to isolate Christian groups from one another, because each group becomes so defensive of its favorite Concepts (whether fundamental or simply incidental) that it builds walls to keep itself separate from others who do not precisely share those Concepts.

Conservative Judaism. One of the main denominations of modern rabbinic Judaism, which typically stands between **Reform Judaism** and **Orthodox Judaism** in its beliefs and practices.

Councils of Bishops. Formal gatherings of bishops of the Church whose purpose is often to resolve disputes over theology, worship practice, or polity in the Church. Their rulings are normatively considered binding over those they oversee, as well as over future generations of the Church.

Covenant. In the Bible, an agreement binding on both (or all) parties that agree to it, but lived out more like a marriage relationship than a business contract or will. It is the plan, structure and means of **Salvation**, **Sanctification** and **Glorification** initiated by God out of love as a means to reconcile everyone to Himself, but constrained by the freewill of those sought by Him to refuse. Three key covenants in Scripture are those through **Abraham**, **Moses** and **Jesus**.

Covenant of Circumcision. The covenant God established with Abraham in Genesis 17.

Covenant That Jesus Declared. This is the covenant in His body and blood, which will be fulfilled by the presence of the Holy Spirit in the heart and minds of believers, so that the Law is written on their hearts and lived out in their daily actions, as foretold in Jeremiah 31:31-34.

Covenant Theology. A Calvinistic method of theology, stressing the covenants of redemption, grace and works, and using these as the organizing principle of Scripture. **Not** what is meant by "Covenant" in this book.

Covenant, Everlasting. A promise made by God to Abraham in Genesis 17.

Creed. A statement of doctrine derived from Scripture and Concepts about Scripture (including choices of verses, imputed meanings and relationships, abstractions and broader philosophical propositions), which affirms or denies various explanations of the nature of God and human relationships to Him. These were created and modified over the course of centuries as various factions within the Church disagreed about specific Concepts, such as the divinity and nature of Christ. The creeds established a perimeter for who was "in" and who was "out" of the group. Those who affirmed a certain creed could be "in," while those who refused to affirm it were "out." The biggest portion of the Christian Church affirms at least two creeds, the **Apostles Creed** and the **Nicene Creed**. Many of them also accept the **Athanasian Creed** and some affirm the Chalcedonian Creed as well. Membership or ordination in various subgroups of the Church often requires assent to one or more of these creeds.

Cynics. A Greek school of philosophy founded originally by Antisthenes, a pupil of **Socrates**. Diogenes was a subsequent leader of this school of thought. Its basic principles were not cynicism as we think of it today, but rather a rejection of wealth, power and fame, in order to live a simple life, free of the bonds of possessions, and treating all humans as equals (everything belongs to everyone), and cultivating virtue. Their intentional lives of poverty and asceticism were adopted by early Christians and still find expression in groups such as monks and nuns sworn to poverty, and Protestant groups such as the Amish, Mennonites and Hutterites. The critics of the Cynics in their time called them "dogs" (the root meaning of "cynic" in Greek) and despised them for their rejection of common cultural values.

Deist. Generally, someone who acknowledges there is a Supreme Being, but believes that though the universe and human being were created by this Supreme Being, it is not involved in the individual lives of human beings. The classic metaphor for this theological view is of a watchmaker who, having created a watch, winds it up and sets it aside to run on its own. Thomas Jefferson and some of the other founders of the United States were Deists. See also **Agnostic**, **Atheist** and **Theist**.

Denomination. Means simply "named." Among Christians this refers to different religious streams or sects, named to distinguish them from each other, such as **Roman Catholic**, **Eastern Orthodox**, **Protestant** (at the highest level of distinguishing), but also including such labels as Byzantine Catholic, Russian Orthodox, Hutterite, Methodist, Baptist, Free-Will Baptist, Universalist, and so on. Normatively designates a group with more than one church. This term is also applied to differing groups within other religions.

Denominationalism. The defense or promotion of one denomination over others, usually insisting on the superiority of one and the inferiority of another, for reasons of theology, worship, polity or tradition. See also **Conceptual fortresses**.

Devarim. Hebrew title in the Torah for Deuteronomy. Means "words" and derives from the first sentence of the book, "These are the words that Moses spoke to all the people of Israel…"

Didaskalia. Greek word meaning "doctrine, teaching, instruction." Compare **Torah**.

Disciple. In the New Testament from the Greek *matheteuo*, meaning someone who learns by use and practice. It implies not a student who merely takes notes and learns intellectually, but is more like someone who is taught carpentry by working with a carpenter. Hence, someone mentored to gain skills, to become like the teacher in knowledge and ability. In a sense someone who is aware of and intentionally chooses **sanctification**, not just to unlearn sinful or hurtful habits, but to gain skill in order to help others.

Disfellowship. To expel someone from a group.

Dispensationalism. The theological idea that God works with mankind in a series of "dispensations," each of which has characteristics of interaction that differ from other dispensations, i.e., Old Testament times, New Testament (Apostolic Age) times and the Church Era. Common to this idea is the assertion that miracles occurred only until the completion of the Apostolic Age (~A.D. 100) and stopped after that. This school of thought has now developed into numerous streams with considerable differences.

Divinity, of Christ. The idea that Jesus was not merely a man, or merely a prophet, but was actually divine, i.e., a member of the Godhead, fully God and fully man.

Docetism. The idea that Christ was fully God but not fully man, and simply "inhabited" a human body but did not experience human feelings or shortcomings, and at His crucifixion did not experience pain, even though the human body He had "borrowed" did experience pain. A heterodox idea, because, like **Modalism**, it implies fraud on the part of God.

Doctrine. Greek *didaskalia*, doctrine, teaching, instruction. A set of agreed-upon theological principles or rules, which are generally considered binding on Christians within the church that holds that Doctrine to be true.

Donatism. A heretical holiness movement in North Africa during the 4th and 5th centuries, it asserted that only those bishops or priests who were sinless could do **Baptism** or **Eucharist**; otherwise either was ineffective and meaningless. Also believed that only those ordained by Donatist bishops were truly ordained. Named after the Berber Christian bishop Donatus Magnus.

Eastern Orthodox Church. Officially called the Orthodox Catholic Church, and sometimes just the Orthodox Church. It traces its roots back to St. Paul and considers itself "the One, Holy, Catholic and Apostolic Church." It is the second-largest Christian denomination in the world only to the Roman Catholic Church; the Anglican Church is third. Currently its primary areas of dominance are Belarus, Bulgaria, Cyprus, Georgia, Greece, Macedonia, Moldova, Montenegro, Romania, Russia, Serbia and the Ukraine, though it is active even in countries where it is not dominant, such as the United States. The Bible it uses includes the Old and New Testaments, plus seven of the intertestamental books (Apocrypha) accepted by the Roman Catholic Church and rejected by most Protestants, plus three additional books not recognized by either the Roman or Protestant Churches. However, these last ten books are considered worthy of reading, but not at the level of holy inspiration of the books of the Testaments. The Orthodox Church split with the Roman Catholic Church in 1054 in a dispute over the coming of the Holy Spirit as represented in the Nicene Creed.

Echad. אחד. The number 1 in Hebrew, as in the *Shema* (sheh-<u>mah</u>), "Hear O Israel, the Lord our God, the Lord is One" (Deuteronomy 6:4), which is the key declaration of monotheism among Jews. *Echad* also appears in many Old Testament passages as a **composite unity**, such as when a man and woman together become "one flesh" (Genesis 2:24).

Edicts of Toleration. The early Church suffered considerable persecution and martyrdom primarily at the hands of the Roman Empire and its local rulers, often directed from the reigning Caesar. Rome had its own pantheon of gods, and the Christians would not worship them, opening them to suspicion of disloyalty (especially since the Caesar was himself considered a god). This changed with the ascent of Constantine as Caesar, whose first Edict of Toleration, issued in A.D. 311, called for Christians to be "tolerated," that is, left alone in their religion. Constantine himself became a Christian, leading to the incorporation of the Christian faith into the very structure of the entire Roman Empire. The letters "IHS" (*in hoc signo*, literally, "in this sign") seen on some crosses refer to the reason for his conversion. Christianity replaced the Roman pantheon of gods as the state religion, and led to rapid expansion of the faith and its eventual domination throughout the Mediterranean, the Middle East, North Africa and Europe. However, as Christianity broke into factions, fights regularly broke out between them, and often the dominant faction in a given country would suppress or persecute the others. This in some cases led to new Edicts of Toleration as rulers tried to quell the conflicts in their countries. These were issued in many locales, from Bohemia to China, over the course of centuries, and covered both other Christian groups and other religions (they were also issued toward Christian groups by leaders of other religions). In many cases these were later withdrawn, and persecution resumed when new leaders rose to power.

Electron. One of the three basic particles that make up an atom (along with proton and neutron), and the means by which electricity flows through wires, lightning, people and everything.

Elohim. אלהימ. One of the names for God in the Old Testament. See **Adonai** for more detail.

Elohim, and Allah. *Allah* is an Arabic word for God and is related to the Hebrew word for God, *eloah* אלוה and *el* אל both singular, and *Elohim* אלהימ (plural). See **Adonai** for more detail on Elohim.

Enlightenment. Also called the French Enlightenment, the Age of Enlightenment and the Age of Reason. An intellectual revolution and cultural movement that celebrated reason as the key means to reform and order society and help the advancement of knowledge. It directly affected the American Revolution (Franklin and Jefferson among others) and led to the overthrow of the French aristocracy and the power of the Roman Catholic Church in France.

Ennui. Bored and listless; unmotivated, weary, dissatisfied.

Epiclesis. "Invocation" or calling down of the Holy Spirit by a priest upon the bread and wine of the **Eucharist**.

Epicurean. Follower of a Greek philosophical school founded by Epicurus before 300 B.C. Although "epicurean" today implies expensive or sophisticated foods or tastes, the actual Epicurean school was quite modest, and advocated a simple life that sought tranquility and freedom from fear. This is defined as pleasure, with freedom from pain as the highest pleasure. This group contested with the followers of **Plato** and the **Stoics**, and eventually died out with the rise of Christianity. It was later given new life and incorporated into Christian practice by Pierre Gassendi (1592–1655), a French priest, philosopher and scientist.

Episcopal. Refers to churches whose upper leadership consists of bishops. From Greek *episkope*, meaning "overseer." See **Overseer**.

Epistle of straw. A term of disrespect used by Martin Luther in reference to the New Testament book of James. **Luther** denied that it was written by an apostle, or James, brother of Jesus, at least in part because he believed it conflicted with Paul on the doctrine of Justification. An example of how a **Concept**, such as **Justification**, can affect **hermeneutics**—how the Bible is read and interpreted. See Chapter 22 on "Religious Concepts."

Eros. The Greek word for romantic love. See *Agape* for further explanation.

Essentials and Non-Essentials. An *essential* is something that is *necessary*, utterly *required* for something to be effective, true or real. You may recall this expression from mathematics: *if and only if*. That defines an essential.

A *non-essential* may be profoundly important, valuable or highly regarded, but it is not *necessary*, not *required*. This is a critical distinction.

Eucharist. From the Greek *eucharistia*, "thanksgiving, gratitude." Used by some churches to refer to the celebration of **The Last Supper**, or **Communion**, which remembers the meal of bread and wine of Jesus and His disciples on the night before He died. See Matthew 26:17-30, Mark 14:12-26, Luke 22 and John 13-17. First Corinthians 11:18-34, probably written before the Gospels, refers to the Last Supper and its meaning.

Eucharistic Sacrifice. The **Roman Catholic Church** and the **Eastern Orthodox Church**, as well as some others, consider the celebration of **Communion**, or **The Last Supper**, to be a literal sacrifice of Christ Himself, present in the bread and wine, to God: Father, Son and Holy Spirit, and a propitiation (payment) for sin. On this point both the Orthodox and Roman churches follow the theology of **Thomas Aquinas** and his concept of **Transubstantiation**, appropriated by him from **Aristotle**.

Faith in Christ. "But now God has shown us a way to be made right with him without keeping the requirements of the law, as was promised in the writings of Moses and the prophets long ago. *We are made right with God by placing our faith in Jesus Christ.* And this is true for everyone who believes, no matter who we are. For everyone has sinned; we all fall short of God's glorious standard" (Romans 3:21-23). The italicized line (v. 22a) highlights the Covenant that begins with Salvation. The Greek actually reads, "righteousness of God through faithfulness of Jesus Christ into all and onto all the believing-*ones*." That is, that the faithfulness OF Jesus places the righteousness of God into and unto those who trust Him. Faith shines both ways in this Covenant: We have faith that He will do what He promises, and He is faithful to do what He promises.

Faith Once Delivered to the Saints. An expression from Jude 1:3, commonly used by advocates of certain Concepts or Doctrines to assert that their exposition of the faith is true to the teachings and faith of the earliest Church. Of course, though this is to be desired, it may or may not be true of any particular Concept.

Faithfulness of Jesus. An expression common in the Greek of the New Testament, but often wrongly translated "faith in Jesus," and similarly with "faith in Christ." BOTH expressions are present; one refers to a believer's trust in Jesus, and the other refers to His reliability, His faithfulness, to God and to us. This mutuality is characteristic of Covenant, which in part is why *both* expressions should be rendered accurately into English, and not compacted into a single "faith in Jesus" in every case.

Fall. The Christian Concept that Adam and Eve, living in innocence in paradise, fell from this state of grace by disobeying God and eating the fruit of the Tree of Knowledge of Good and Evil. The term "The Fall" does not appear in Scripture, but the story (or reference to it) appears in both Testaments. Interpretations of it differ among Protestants, Roman Catholics and Eastern Orthodoxy.

Fisk, Randy. Author of *The Presence, Power and Heart of God*, and *The Amazing Word of God: Seminary-Level Information Anyone Can Understand*. A Vineyard-trained pastor, a teacher at Resurrection Anglican Church, and a close friend of the author for many years.

Five Books of Moses. Refers to Genesis, Exodus, Leviticus, Numbers and Deuteronomy. Also referred to as the **Pentateuch** (Greek for "five books") and Torah. See **Torah** for more detail.

Forgive. In the Bible, this means to pardon, set free, release a just claim, or cut a cord (in the sense that if you owe me something, that ties me to you until it is paid or forgiven).

French Enlightenment. See **Enlightenment**.

Frontlet. A small box tied to the forehead and containing Scripture from the Torah. Based on Deuteronomy 6:8. Also called **Tefillin** or **Phylactery**.

Galilei, Galileo. (1564–1642) Italian astronomer who supported the **heliocentric** (Sun-centered) model of the universe, resulting in his arrest for heresy by the Roman Catholic Church for contradicting the Church's concept of the universe with the Earth as its center.

GeorgeKoch.com. The author's Web site.

Gesenius' Lexicon. A famous and detailed work on the Hebrew language, in German, by Heinrich Friedrich Wilhelm Gesenius (1786–1842). The English translation by Samuel P. Tregelles (1813–1875) is listed in the Bibliography.

Girgashites. A tribe that inhabited Canaan before the Israelites, descended from the fifth son of Canaan (mentioned in Genesis 10:16, 15:21 and Deuteronomy 7:1). Beyond this, little is known.

Glorification. The life *after* this earthly one. It is eternity in God's presence, gained in our **salvation**. Its nature and content is determined in part by the life we live *here* after we are saved, during **sanctification** and by being a **disciple**.

Glorified bodies. See Philippians 3:21 and 1 Corinthians 15:36-55. Although little detail is given in Scripture, these are the transformed and resurrected bodies in which we will live forever.

Gnosis. Greek for "knowledge," but used by the **Gnostics** to assert a special spiritual knowledge available only to an elite few.

Gnosticism. Refers to the idea held by a variety of sects that a special esoteric hidden knowledge of spiritual realities was available to select "initiates" of the sect. Some "Christian" Gnostics believed Jesus came to bring this secret knowledge to earth. The early Christian author Irenaeus called this a heresy in his *On the Detection and Overthrow of Knowledge Falsely So Called*.

Gnostics. See **Gnosticism**.

God. The English word for the Supreme Being and Creator of the universe. Christians normatively believe there is just one God, but that this one God consists of three Persons, Father, Son and Holy Spirit, in eternal relationship with each other, and in whose image humans are made.

"God forbid!" An expression used in the Talmud and by rabbis at the time of Jesus, in arguing about how the Law should be applied or fulfilled. Appears in the New Testament many times when similar discussions are taking place. See Luke 20:16 for an example. This and **"May it never be!"** are used interchangeably as English translations.

God particle. A term used for the **Higgs boson**, an elementary particle smaller than an electron, proton, neutron or quark, which is believed to be the smallest particle, or building block, from which matter is constructed.

God's Word. A term generally used to refer to the Old and New Testaments. Occasionally used to refer to Jesus, from the reference to Him in John 1.

Gödel, Kurt. (1906–1978) Austrian mathematician, logician and philosopher. Author of *"On Formally Undecidable Propositions."* See Chapters 11 and 23.

Godhead. For Christians, a term referring to the essential being of God, and especially to the **Trinity**.

Gospel of Thomas. A book found with the Dead Sea Scrolls near Nag Hammadi, Egypt, in 1945, and not a part of the New Testament. Considered by many scholars as a Gnostic text, though others would say it is ambiguous on that point. The early Church considered it a "false gospel."

Grammatical convention. Refers to a grammatical method to draw attention to a particular word, sentence or idea in a text. In a sense, this is a long-established equivalent of boldface, underlining or highlighting, but accomplished by using techniques in the text itself, rather than modifications of the form of the letters. Chiasmus and repetition are examples of this.

Great Thanksgiving. Another term for Eucharist, Communion or The Last Supper. See **Eucharist** for more detail.

Greek language. The language spoken in Greece, but also the common language of the Mediterranean, North Africa and the Middle East (and all the way to the Himalayas), after the conquests of Alexander the Great. An ancient form of Greek, also known as "*koine*" or *common language* Greek, widely used from 300 B.C. to A.D. 300. The New Testament was written in this language.

Greek Orthodox Church. See **Eastern Orthodox Church**.

Greekified. The idea that Christians have been misdirected from the life and teachings of Jesus, and the God of Israel, into a theology based upon Greek philosophical structure and debate. Though it has Jewish and Christian terminology, much of its worldview is based on Greek philosophy—and this has become so much a part of how Christians do theology, that it is virtually invisible.

HaKodesh. Hebrew for "the holy." See *Ruach HaKodesh*.

Hairesis. See **Heresy**.

Hashem. Hebrew for "the Name." Often used by Jews in place of "God," or any Hebrew word for God, in daily conversation and writing, as a sign of respect, and in order to avoid taking the name of God in vain.

Hassidic Judaism. See **Chassidic Judaism**.

Haver/Haverim. Hebrew for "friend" and "friends" (the *-im* suffix is the plural form). Used generally, but also specifically for a *yeshiva* study partner. Pronounced "hah-*ver*" (as in *very*) and hah-ver-*eem*."

Havering. Inspired conversation. An English verb formed from the Hebrew *haver*, meaning to converse, contest, argue or debate deeply, inspired by the willing invitation of the Holy Spirit, and without personal attack or bitterness. Spiritual wrestling for a deeper understanding of the things of God. Pronounced "hah-*ver*-ing," as in *very*.

Head coverings. Ranging from a kippa or yarmulke to a scarf or veil, they are often used to protect the head from weather or sunlight, but are also used as a sign of religious respect for God, or modesty. In biblical times, a woman's exposed hair was considered salacious, or a sign of a prostitute, so covering it indicated modesty and religious devotion. This tradition survives today in Islam, Orthodox Judaism, and among Amish and other conservative and plain-dressing Christian groups.

"Hear, O Israel." First words of the most important prayer in Judaism. See **Shema**.

Heart. The primary organ of the body for pumping life-giving blood to all of its parts. Also used metaphorically to refer to the emotions, and emotional understanding, as opposed to reason and logical understanding.

Heart-understanding. An understanding that is different than, and often deeper than (but not necessarily at odds with) a reasoned or logical understanding of something. It includes emotions such as empathy, sympathy and love.

Heart and reason, according to Pascal. "The heart has reasons which reason knows not of. We feel it in a thousand things. It is the heart that experiences God, and not the reason. This, then, is faith: God felt by the heart, not by the reason."

Heaven. In both Testaments, from a Hebrew or Greek word for "sky," and intended to mean that God's abode is elevated above the earth and humans—not literally but in terms of authority, power and place.

Hebrew. עברית. Pronounced "eev-reet" in Hebrew. The language of the Old Testament (called Biblical Hebrew) as well as of modern Israel (called Modern Hebrew). Biblical Hebrew is the language used in synagogues in the reading of Torah.

Hebrew Scriptures. Another term for the Old Testament, or *Tanakh*.

Hebrew word for love. See *Ahav*.

Heisenberg, Werner. (1901–1976) German theoretical physicist, Nobel Prize winner, and creator of the **Uncertainty Principle**, which states that there is a limit on the precision with which the momentum and location of a particle can be determined. The greater the precision of one measurement, the less the precision of the other.

Heliocentric. "Sun-centered" model of the relation of Earth, the planets and the stars to the Sun, as opposed to geocentric, which is an Earth-centered model.

Hellenization. Refers to the spread of Greek culture, philosophy and language throughout the Mediterranean, North Africa and Middle East, all the way to the Himalayan Mountains, after their conquest by **Alexander the Great**.

Heresy. From Greek *hairesis*. "Heresy" can be used positively or neutrally to refer to a sect, choice or way of life, or negatively, to refer to an action or belief that causes factions, disunion or division in a group. Although used colloquially to mean "bad doctrine," its actual sense is the division that it causes. Thus, even good doctrine can be heresy if used in a way that causes division. See **Schism** and **Heterodoxy**—related words but *not* synonyms.

Heresy of the Gospel. An expression by an early Christian writer that refers to the *way* of the Gospel. It is not a criticism of the Gospel, but simply the use of the word *haireses* in Greek to mean a way or a path. In fact, Paul uses the word *haireses* this way in Acts 24:14, meaning a sect, choice or preference.

Heretics. People who cause division. See **Heresy**.

Hermeneutics. The interpretation of Scripture. In theory, it is to be objective and careful, but in practice it is greatly affected by religious Concepts—developed through Greek philosophical methods—that influence and often warp the understanding of what is read. See Chapter 22, "Religious Concepts," for more detail. Ironically, the root of the word *hermeneutics* is the Greek god Hermes, the one who brought the messages of the gods to people, and the patron of orators, literature, poets, dreamers and thieves.

Herodotus. (ca. 484–425 B.C.) Greek historian and considered the "Father of History" for his systematic collection historical materials, and his organization of them into narrative.

Heterodoxy. "Error of opinion," from *heteros* ("the other") and *doxa* ("opinion"). The proper term for wrong or bad doctrine or teaching, rather than **heresy**. See also **Schism**.

Higgs boson. An elementary particle smaller than an electron, proton, neutron or quark, which is believed to be the smallest particle, or building block, from which matter is constructed. Nicknamed the **God particle**.

High Church. An expression used by Anglicans and others to refer to a church whose worship services tend to be formal, often with ornate vestments, altar and Communion vessels, with incense and complex liturgical actions (bowing, processing, candle-lighting, bell-ringing).

High Priest. The top religious authority from the formation of the Israelite nation under the destruction of the Second Temple in A.D. 70. Also applied to Jesus in the book of Hebrews.

Hippolytus of Rome. (A.D. 170–235) Theologian, probable disciple of **Irenaeus**. Conflicted with the popes of his era and may have led a schismatic (see **Heresy**) group as rival bishop of the bishop of Rome.

Holy of Holies. The inner sanctuary of the **Tabernacle**, and then the **Temple** in Jerusalem, where the **Ark of the Covenant** was kept, containing the tablets of the **Ten Commandments**. There the **High Priest** could enter only on Yom Kippur, to make atonement for all of Israel.

Holy Spirit. The third Person of the Trinity. Also known as the Holy Ghost in earlier translations of the Bible.

Homoiousios. Of "similar substance," with the emphasis on *similar*. In the early debates about the nature of the Trinity, some argued that each Person of the Trinity was of similar substance, while others contended that they were of the same substance. See also *Homoousios* and **Iota**.

Homoousios. Of "same substance," with the emphasis on *same*. In the early debates about the nature of the Trinity, some argued that each Person of the Trinity was of similar substance, while others contended that they were of the same substance. See also *Homoiousios* and **Iota**.

Human Potential Movement. A movement that arose in the 1960s, based in part on the work of Abraham Maslow and his theory of "self-actualization." Also considered a part of the "New Age" movement, and linked to existentialism and humanism, the key idea being that humans have untapped and extraordinary capacities that can be "unleashed" with proper training and willingness, and that this can in turn transform society at large.

Humanism. A view of human nature that is concerned primarily with human values, needs and concerns. Its two primary branches are Religious Humanism, which integrates religious beliefs and practices with humanist ethical philosophy, and Secular Humanism, which rejects religious and supernatural elements, and focuses on reason, ethics and justice.

Humanist. An adherent of **Humanism**.

Hyper-belief. An assertion of belief "above and beyond" what is given in Scripture, or perhaps even in the oldest and longest-held traditions of the Church, but that is given elevated prominence and even required acceptance by a denomination, theologian or partisan.

Hypocrisy. Not simply the act of preaching one thing and doing another (since one may desire to act in the manner he preaches, but have not yet attained it), but rather *pretending* to be doing (or being) the thing one preaches, while not actually doing or intending to do it.

Hypocritical. To act with hypocrisy.

Hypotheses. Plural of *hypothesis*, an explanation of a phenomenon that has not yet been proven true or accurate, but is held up for examination and testing. Concepts, which are abstractions from the details of events or narratives, are used to develop and then test hypotheses. Unfortunately, in religion, the development of **religious concepts** (see Chapter 22, "Religious Concepts"), leads not to hypotheses, but Doctrines, which are then promoted as if proven, or revealed by God. In fact, that very claim is made, that they have been given by the leading of the Holy Spirit and are therefore **inerrant** or **infallible**.

"I Am that I Am." From Exodus 3:14. Also rendered "I am who I am" and "I am what I am" in other translations. This was in response to Moses asking who he should say had sent him to lead the Israelites out of Egypt. The Hebrew actually says something more like "I will be what I will be," or "I shall become who I am becoming."

"I Will Be What I Will Be." See **"I Am that I Am."**

I, Robot. The name for a collection of nine science-fiction stories by **Isaac Asimov**, written between 1940 and 1950, which deal with the relationships of humans to robots, and the moral dilemmas this poses. Includes the story in which the **"Three Laws of Robotics"** appears (see Chapter 11, "Rule-Following And Transcendent Love"). A movie based on the Three Laws was released in 2004 with the same title.

Ibn Ezra. See **Abenezra**.

Iconoclasm. The destruction of religious symbols, statues, icons and the like, generally in a dispute between sects of the same religion. In Christianity it arose as a literal reading of the commandment to make no images. Also used in relation of the destruction of the artifacts of one religion by another, and of a ruler who has been overthrown. Also used to refer to any rejection of tradition.

Iconoclasts. Individuals who favor or act with iconoclasm, for instance in destroying statues, or challenging a tradition or the "common wisdom."

Icon. From the Greek word for "image." Typically refers to a stylized form of painting, often in gold, representing a biblical scene or a **saint**. See Chapter 8, "Images and Icons."

Idolatry. Used literally to refer to the worship of an idol or a physical object, and figuratively to refer to undue attention, honor or obsession with fame, human beings, wealth, and so on. This is a negative and forbidden act in Judaism and Christianity, but a common one in some other religions.

If and Only If. An expression used to define an **essential**. Borrowed from logic and mathematics.

"In Jesus' name." An expression often thought to mean the use of the literal name "Jesus" was required, as in a prayer, in order to be effective—but this would be a kind of talisman, or magic. The expression actually means "by the authority of Jesus," and has the same sense as the expression "power of attorney," where one individual is granted the right to make decisions and act in another person's name.

Incompleteness theorems. Two related theorems, proven by mathematician **Kurt Gödel** in 1931, that demonstrate that (1) within any logical system (such as arithmetic) there will be some statements that are true but unprovable within the system, and (2) logical systems cannot prove their own consistency. See Chapters 11 and 23 for how this applies to theology and faith.

Inerrancy of Scripture. "Being wholly and verbally God-given, Scripture is without error or fault in all its teaching, no less in what it states about God's acts in creation, about the events of world history, and about its own literary origins under God, than in its witness to God's saving grace in individual lives." That is Summary Statement 4 (of 5) from the 1978 Chicago Statement on Biblical Inerrancy, of the International Council on Biblical Inerrancy, a gathering of over 300 Protestant Evangelicals, including James Boice, Norman L. Geisler, John Gerstner, Jay Grimstead, Carl F. H. Henry, Kenneth Kantzer, Harold Lindsell, John Warwick Montgomery, Roger Nicole, J. I. Packer, Robert Preus, Earl Radmacher, Francis Schaeffer, R. C. Sproul and John Wenham. It is followed by 19 Articles of affirmation and denial, including Article X, "We affirm that inspiration, strictly speaking, applies only to the authographic text of Scripture [See **Autograph, of Scripture**], which in the providence of God can be ascertained from available manuscripts with great accuracy. We further affirm that copies and translations of Scripture are the Word of God to the extent that they faithfully represent the original. We deny that any essential element of the Christian faith is affected by the absence of the autographs [See **Argument from ignorance**]. We further deny that this absence renders the assertion of Biblical inerrancy invalid or irrelevant." See Chapter 21, "Bible Authority," and 22, "Religious Concepts." See also **Infallible** for a similar assertion in relation to the Church.

Infallible. Infallibility means "incapable of error." The Roman Catholic and Eastern Orthodox churches maintain that the Holy Spirit will not allow error in the Church's teachings, within ecumenical councils, and (within Roman Catholicism) for certain declarations of the Pope (such as the Immaculate Conception of Mary and the Assumption of Mary), and the teachings of the "ordinary and universal Magisterium."

Without going into detail, it should be noted that this infallibility is asserted for 21 councils (historical meetings over many centuries, mostly of bishops, which made doctrinal statements) by the Roman Catholic Church, for 7 by the Eastern Orthodox Church, for none by many Protestants, and for the "Christological statements" of the first seven by some Protestants. (A reader will search in vain for a Christological statement in the seventh council. It's in a footnote.)

I believe the teachings of the Church and the councils can be taken with great gravity without imposing upon them either the idol or the onus of infallibility.

Ironically, those Protestants who reject the concept of *infallibility* in the teachings of the Church are often the same who affirm it in the **Inerrancy of**

Scripture. Both concepts represent claims that—because of the leading of the Holy Spirit—certain writings (whether Scripture or Church teachings) are without error.

See Chapter 21, "Bible Authority," and 22, "Religious Concepts."

Intercession. Intervening on behalf of another, especially in prayer.

Intertestamental. The period between the time of the writing of the Old and New Testaments, about 400 years, during which the books of the **Apocrypha** were written.

Iota. Greek letter roughly equilvalent to the Engish letter I. The difference between the words (in Greek) of *homoiousios*, "similar substance," and *homoousios*, "same substance," in the debate about the nature of the three Persons of the Trinity. The wags of that day thus said there was only "one iota" of difference between them. "Iota" was also used by Jesus in Matthew 5:18, "For truly, I say to you, until heaven and earth pass away, not an iota, not a dot, will pass from the Law until all is accomplished."

Irenaeus. (A.D. ? – 202) Early Christian bishop and apologist of the second century, and author of *Against Heresies*, an attack on **Gnosticism**. Irenaeus contended that Christian unity was to be found only in accepting the doctrinal authority of councils of bishops in union with the bishop of Rome.

Isaacs, Ronald. See **Rabbi Ronald Isaacs**.

Jefferson, Thomas. Third President of the United States and one of the chief authors of the Declaration of Independence. Also the author of a Bible in which he chose all of the verses he found helpful in making moral and ethical decisions. This is called *The Life and Morals of Jesus of Nazareth*. Jefferson was a **Deist**.

Jehovah. A pronunciation for the Hebrew letters יהוה (YHWH), whose earliest use is debated, but arose anywhere between the second and 12th century as a means to pronounce the proper name of the God of Israel. This is not a Hebrew pronunciation.

Jehovah's Witnesses. A nontrinitarian sect that arose in the 1870s, founded by Charles Russell, who use their own translation of the Bible, known as the New World Translation. They anticipate the certain and soon destruction of the present world-systems and the coming of God's Kingdom on Earth. They are well-known for their door-to-door evangelism and for distribution of *The Watchtower* magazine.

Jesus. Also known as Jesus of Nazareth, Jesus Christ, or Christ. Regarded by Christians as the Son of God and second Person of the Trinity. See also **Yehoshua/Yeshua**.

Jew. From the word *Judah*. A member of the Jewish people, which originated in the Ancient Near East; the Jews trace their ancestry to Abraham, Isaac and Jacob in the second millennium B.C. (2000–1000 B.C.). Judaism is the traditional religion, and converts to **Judaism** are regarded as equal to those born into it. The two primary modern branches of Judaism are the Ashkenazi (primarily European; the term literally means "German") and Sephardic (primarily from Spain and Portugal, though the term is now used to include Jews from Africa, Asia and other parts of the Middle East). These communities were formed after the Diaspora (scattering) when the Jews were driven out of their traditional land in Israel (more than once before the time of Jesus, and after A.D. 70 and 132, after conflicts with the Romans).

Jewish. See **Jew**.

Jewish Bible. Also called the Hebrew Bible or *Tanakh*. Refers typically to the books of the **Old Testament**, though they are in a different sequence in a Jewish Bible.

Jewish Law. Refers generally to the Ten Commandments and the additional 603 rules (of various sorts) throughout the **Torah**, or Five Books of Moses (Genesis through Deuteronomy). These are also called the **Law of Moses** or the Mosaic Law, and the rules themselves are called *mitzvot* (plural; singular is *mitzvah*). See also **613** and Chapter 14, "The Law of Moses."

Jewish Oral Law tradition. A tradition, now embodied in the Talmud, that says that at the same time as the Law was given at Sinai, a parallel oral tradition to aid in interpreting and applying the Law was given.

Jewish Publication Society. Oldest nondenominational and nonprofit publisher of Jewish works in English. Founded in 1888. The JPS Tanakh, or Hebrew Bible, is the authoritative translation among Jews.

Joshua. Biblical leader after Moses who led the Israelites into the Promised Land. Fundamentally the same name as Jesus. See also **Yehoshua/Yeshua**.

Judah. Fourth son of Jacob, who was renamed Israel after wrestling with God. Refers also to a kingdom and later a Roman province. Root of the word *Jew*.

Judaizers. Early Christians who insisted that converts to Christianity must first convert to Judaism and follow all of its Laws and customs.

Justification. A term closely related but not identical to **salvation**. It is that the righteousness of Jesus is credited to us. In spite of our sin, because of Jesus, we are declared innocent, acquitted of our sin before God.

Kierkegaard, Søren. (1813–1855) A Danish theologian and critic of the intellectual debates of his time over the Christian faith. Focused on the difference between theoretical "proofs" of Christianity, and a life lived in *relationship* to Jesus Christ.

Kosher. From a Hebrew word that means "clean" or "fit" for use as food, following the dietary laws set forth in Leviticus and Deuteronomy, as well as the **Oral Law**, used to interpret them.

Last Supper. See **Eucharist**.

Law of Moses. Refers broadly to the **Torah** (or **Pentateuch**), the first five books of the Bible. Also refers to the **613** *mitzvot*, or rules, contained in those books.

Law. A broad term with numerous related definitions, ranging from secular law in a country, state or city, to scriptural law (see **Law of Moses**, to the **Royal Law**, "Love your neighbor as yourself"), to scientific law, which follows the pattern *observation leads to concept leads to hypothesis leads to theory leads to law*, if certain criteria are met at each stage.

Liturgics. The study of the doing of worship, particularly the actions of clergy, assistants and the congregation, in a worship service. This includes clothing, decorations, ritual actions, sequence, content (words, music, prayers, etc.), in any kind of worship service, including those churches that might call themselves "non-liturgical."

Liturgy. From Greek, literally, "the work of the people." *Liturgy* does not mean "ritualistic," nor does it imply robes, priests, processions or candles (though it can include them). Rather, liturgy is the overall concept covering all of the *actions of the people*—lay and clergy both—that *constitute a worship service*.

Lord's Supper. See Eucharist.

Love feast. An expression from Jude 1:12 (NKJV), "These are spots in your love feasts, while they feast with you without fear, serving only themselves." May refer to **Eucharist**, or to meals the early followers of Jesus shared together.

Lubavitcher Rebbe. The title of the head of a sect of Chassidic Jews, the most famous of which in modern times being Menachem Mendel Schneerson (1902–1994). *Rebbe* is the title only of the head of the movement. Within the movement are many rabbis and their followers.

Luther, Martin. (1483–1546) The founder of the **Protestant Reformation**. A German Roman Catholic priest and professor of theology who confronted the selling of "indulgences" by the Church in order to raise money. These indulgences were sold with the promise that dead ancestors could have their way to heaven assured by the Church. Luther's *Ninety-Five Theses* challenged this and other practices of the Church that were unscriptural or in error. In this he challenged the authority of the Pope, and asserted instead that the only source of divinely revealed knowledge is the Bible. His concept for this was "*Sola Scriptura*," or "Scripture Alone." He married Katharina von Bora, thus setting an example of clerical marriage still followed by Protestants to this day. In his declining years he became increasingly anti-Semitic, advocating violence against Jews and confiscation of their property.

Lutheran. Member of a Lutheran church, or a follower of the ideas of Luther. Lutheran churches come in many denominations, ranging from quite conservative to quite liberal.

Maimonides. (1135–1204) Moses ben-Maimon, or Rambam. Prolific medieval Jewish philosopher and Torah scholar. A rabbi, physician and philosopher in Morocco and Egypt. Author of the *Mishneh Torah*, a massive codification of Talmudic Law. Nicknamed "the great eagle" for his stature in the Oral Law tradition. Maimonides wrote *The Guide for the Perplexed* and greatly advanced Greek Concepts and philosophy within Jewish thought (seeing allegory where others saw miracles and the supernatural)—not unlike Thomas **Aquinas** did for Christian theology.

Mars Hill Speech. A speech given by Paul to Greek philosophers at the Areopagus in Athens, recorded in Acts 17.

Martyr. A Greek word meaning "witness," in the sense of one who testifies about something (as in a court trial). Because early Christians would testify about their faith in Christ even on threat of death, and were subsequently murdered, the term came to refer more specifically to those who were killed for their faith.

"May it never be!" An expression used in the Talmud and by rabbis at the time of Jesus, in arguing about how the Law should be applied or fulfilled. Appears in the New Testament many times when similar discussions are taking place. See Romans 7:7 for an example. This and "**God forbid!**" are used interchangeably as translations into English.

Meiderlin, Peter. (1582–1651) Lutheran educator and theologian, also known by the pseudonym Rupertus Meldenius, under which he published *Paraenesis votiva per Pace Ecclesia ad Theologos Augustana Confessionis auctore Ruperto Meldenio Theologo* ("A reminder for peace at the Church of the Augsburg Confession of theologians"). This is the source of his quote, *"Verbo dicam: Si nos servaremus IN necesariis Unitatem, IN non-necessariis Libertatem, in utrisque Charitatem, optimo certe loco essent res nostrae."* ("Word I will say: if we preserve unity in essentials, liberty in non-essentials, and charity in both, our affairs will be in the best condition at all events.") See Chapter 1, "What We Believe and Why." Later in the same book Meiderlin also says, *"Vincat veritas, vivat charitas, maneat libertas per Jesum Christum qui est veritas ipsa, charitas ipsa, libertas ipsa."* ("Let truth prevail, live in charity, abide in freedom through Jesus Christ who is truth itself, love itself, freedom itself.")

Melchizedek. Also known as Malki Tzedek, which means "king of righteousness." Sometimes identified as a son of Noah (Shem). Mentioned in Genesis 14:18-20, Psalm 110 and the book of Hebrews.

Messiah. See **Christ**.

Metaphor. A word, phrase, figure or speech, object or concept that is representative or symbolic of something else. Examples: "All the world's a stage." "Dad was a rock." *"You know how I carried you on eagles' wings and brought you to myself"* (Exodus 19:4b).

Middle East. A somewhat imprecise term for the area of Western Asia and Northern Africa, generally including the modern countries of Egypt, Syria, Israel, Lebanon, Jordan, Iraq, Saudi Arabia, Kuwait, Bahrain and Qatar. Judaism, Christianity and Islam all have their origins here.

Middle Platonic. A stage in the development of Plato's philosophy (by others) starting near 100 B.C. and continuing into the 3rd century A.D., with the development of Neoplatonism. Both Middle Platonic and Neoplatonic schools held the concept of a "demiurge," which was the uncreated second god, wholly benevolent, through whom the world was made.

Midrash. A Hebrew word meaning "story," but typically used by Jews to describe a method of hermeneutics and exegesis to understand and apply the Old Testament. It operates at four different levels, from the simple or literal through "hints," "seeking," and "secret." The focus of *midrash* is either "*Halakha*" (law) or "*Aggadah*" (mostly teaching and homily).

Minor Prophets. Refers to the prophets Hosea, Joel, Amos, Obadiah, Jonah, Micah, Nahum, Habakkuk, Zephaniah, Haggai, Zechariah, Malachi and the biblical books attributed to them.

Misdirection. A technique used by thieves, magicians, politicians, religious partisans and others to direct the attention of someone away from the actual topic at hand in order to accomplish something, usually nefarious, without it being seen.

Mishneh Torah. Hebrew expression meaning "repetition of the Torah," authored by **Maimonides** between 1170 and 1180. It is a treatise on Jewish religious law (*Halakha*), and is enormous in the breadth of the study. Though innovative—and therefore hotly opposed—in its time, it is today regarded as one of the key approaches and resources in the understanding and application of the **Oral Law**.

Mitzvah. Hebrew for "commandment" (plural *mitzvot*), and referring to the **613 rules** present in the Torah. Can also refer to a "good deed" or moral act performed in carrying out one's religious duty. See also *Bar mitzvah*.

Modalism. Also known as Sabellianism after its conception by Sabellius, a third-century priest and theologian, who imagined that God acted in three modes, or wore three masks, as Father, Son and Holy Spirit, but was not three separate Persons. This is a nontrinitarian theology, but one that does consider Jesus Christ to be fully God.

Modernism. A movement of the late-19th and 20th centuries that denied the existence of a Creator God (at least one with any personal engagement with humans), as well as the self-satisfaction of the Enlightenment, and embraced instead the abstract, unconventional and ambiguous morality of the modern age.

Monotheist. One who believes in only one God. Trinitarians consider themselves monotheists (three Persons in one God), but most Jews and Muslims do not consider **Trinitarians** monotheists.

Montanism. Early Christian sect founded by the priest Montanus in the late 2nd century A.D. Very charismatic and popular, with an emphasis on personal holiness. A strong attention to prophetic teachings (the "New Prophecy"), said to be from the Holy Spirit, eventually led to it retroactively being regarded as a heresy. Even so, in many areas the Church continued to accept the movement as orthodox. Montanus had two women, Prisca and Maximilla, who claimed that the Holy Spirit spoke through them.

Moshiach. Hebrew pronunciation of **Messiah**.

Moses. Considered the author of the **Torah**, the first five books of the Bible, and therefore of the **Law of Moses**. Though born a Jew, was raised by Pharaoh, and later led the Israelites out of Egypt and into the Promised Land.

Moses ben-Maimon. (a.k.a. Rambam.) See **Maimonides**.

Mother Teresa. (1910–1997) Albanian Roman Catholic nun who started the Missionaries of Charity in 1950, to serve the dying on the streets of Calcutta, India. Her work drew others also so inclined, and became a worldwide movement.

Murmuring. As used in the Bible, particularly by Jesus, refers to complaining or gossiping about others, generally in a belittling or condescending way, and not contributing to the solving of whatever was complained about.

Music of the Spheres. An expression referring to imagined concentric invisible crystal spheres in which were embedded the planets, Sun and stars, all circling around the Earth. The idea can be traced to the Greek philosopher Pythagoras (ca. 570–495 B.C.) and his students and was a "geocentric" concept about how the universe was organized. Later overthrown by Copernicus and Galileo. See Chapter 3, "Sanctification."

Muslims. Also known as Moslems (meaning "those who submit to God"). Followers of Islam, a religion founded by Mohammed around A.D. 610. Muslims regard the Qur'an (or Koran) as their holy book, written by Mohammed, whom they consider a prophet. Muslims are monotheistic and consider themselves descendants of Abraham. They believe that prior to Mohammed and the Qur'an, God gave the Torah to Moses, Psalms to David, and the Gospel to Jesus. They consider Jesus a great prophet, but deny His divinity.

Nachmanides. (1194–1270) Also known as **Ramban**. Rabbi Moshe ben Nachman, also known as Bonastruc de Porta. A rabbi, physician, kabbalist and philosopher. Ramban opposed the ideas of **Maimonides (Rambam)** in part because of their advancing of Greek concepts and philosophy. He tried to act as a reconciler of those who opposed and those who favored Maimonides; both sides rejected his efforts and proposed solution.

Neoplatonism. See **Middle Platonic**.

Nestorianism. A 5th-century movement that considered Jesus both human and divine, but considered the relation between these two to be loose: The Son of God lived in Jesus Christ, but was not identical with Him.

Neural net. Human brains are made up of neurons, small cells that can be excited electrically, and that communicate with each other through the synapses by the exchange of neurotransmitter chemicals such as serotonin. A neural net is a computer system—hardware and software—designed to replicate or mimic the actions of neurons, and therefore an attempt to create computers that "think" like humans do. All of this is categorized generally as "artificial intelligence," or "AI."

Neutron. One of the three key particles of an atom, and found normally in the nucleus of the atom, along with protons and other neutrons. Electrons orbit around the nucleus of an atom.

Nevi'im. Hebrew word for "prophets," used to describe those books in the Hebrew Bible that are between the *Torah* (teachings) and the *Ketuvim* (writings).

New Age. A term used generally to describe any of several spiritual movements that began in earnest in the mid-20th century, and including Eastern religions (primarily from India), yoga, Zen, enlightenment, astrology, meditation and so on.

New Commandment. From John 13:34-35, "So now I am giving you a new commandment: Love each other. Just as I have loved you, you should love each other. Your love for one another will prove to the world that you are my disciples."

New Covenant. An expression used by Jesus during the Last Supper, and recorded in Matthew 26, Mark 14 and Luke 22. Also referenced In 1 Corinthians 11 and 2 Corinthians 3, as well as in Hebrews 8, which quotes its original use in Jeremiah 31:31. In both the Hebrew and the Greek, the word translated "new" does not mean more recent in time, but *fresh*, or *renewed*.

New Testament. The title given to the books produced by the followers of Jesus, beginning with Matthew and extending through Revelation; most, if not all, were written during the first century after the Crucifixion. This is also the expression used in the King James Version; other translations render it "new covenant." See **New Covenant**, and Chapter 15, "Covenant – Jesus."

New World Translation. The translation used by the Jehovah's Witnesses church, and questionable for some of its intentional choices in rendering both Hebrew and Greek into English.

Nicene Creed. The second of the three most-accepted statements of theology of the Christian Church, including the **Apostles Creed** and **Athanasian Creed**. Originating in the early fourth century, this was a statement of doctrine to oppose the teachings of **Arius**, who declared Jesus was divine, but created by God the Father. The Nicene Creed declares, instead, that Jesus Christ is "very God of very God, begotten, *not made*, being of one substance with the Father." This creed underwent some change and development in the years following, and one element of it, inserted in the late sixth century, led to the division of the Church, with the Orthodox Church separating from the Roman Catholic Church in A.D. 1054.

Nicodemus. A renowned Pharisee and teacher of the Law who encountered Jesus three times in Scripture: first in John 3:1-21 (See Chapter 2, "Salvation"), and later at Jesus' arrest (John 7:45-51) and after His Crucifixion (John 19:39-42).

Noah. In Genesis 6-9, the man who built the Ark to save his family and two of each kind of animal, having been told by God of His intention to destroy mankind for its wickedness.

Noahide Laws. Also known as Noachide Laws or Code. Some religious Jews consider certain commands of God to be binding on all people, while some are binding only on Jews as a part of their covenant with God. Any non-Jew who abides by these Noahide Laws is considered a "righteous Gentile" and is assured a place in the world to come. These laws (usually numbered as seven) include the prohibitions of idolatry, murder, theft, sexual immortality, blasphemy and eating flesh from an animal that is still alive. The seventh establishes courts of law.

Non-Christians. Used generally to refer to those who do not affirm faith in Jesus, but also used pejoratively of Christians of one group against Christians of another group that do not subscribe to all of their doctrines.

Non-Essentials. See **Essentials and Non-Essentials**.

Non-Jews. Generally used to refer to those who are either not born into a Jewish family, or who have not converted to Judaism. The biblical Hebrew word for this is *goyim*, simply meaning "nation." It is used in the Bible to refer both to the Israelites and other nations, but over time began to be used typically to refer to people other than Jews. In modern Jewish usage sometimes a pejorative reference to Gentiles.

Nonbelievers. Another term for non-Christians.

Nuance. A subtle or slight difference in understanding or interpretation. From a French root meaning "to shade" or "shade of color." Also related etymologically to *cloud* and *fog*.

Obedience/obedient/obey. All of these convey the sense, in English as well as in Greek and Hebrew, of listening attentively, and then complying with what was ordered, especially by one in authority over you. In Hebrew, often also the same word as in the command "Hear O Israel, the Lord our God, the Lord is one." The word "hear" in this sentence is *shema*, and it means to hear attentively and respond by obeying. See also *Shema*.

Observer/observed phenomenon. The concept that the observer often affects the phenomena under observation, whether intentionally or unintentionally, and thereby *changes* the event itself, *or interprets the event* in such a way as to render the description biased, incomplete, or wrong.

Omnipotent. Meaning all-powerful, almighty, able to do anything at will, and used in reference only to God.

Omnipresent. Present at all times and places. Used in reference only to God.

Omniscient. All-knowing. Used in reference only to God.

Ontologically. See **Ontology**.

Ontology. The "science" or philosophical study of being, existence and reality. More specifically, refers to that part of **metaphysics** that considers what kinds of things can and do exist, and how they can be categorized and subdivided by similarities and differences. This approach to reality is thought to have begun with the 5th-century B.C. Greek philosopher Parmenides of Elea, founder of the Eleatic school of philosophy.

Oral Law. In Rabbinic Judaism (descended from the **Pharisees**, a holiness movement), the idea that at the giving of the written Law to Moses at Sinai, there was simultaneously given an oral law, which was the method to understand, interpret and apply the written law in specific cases at specific times. The written Law is found in the **Torah** (literally "instruction" or "teaching," and found in the first five books of the Bible) and the **Tanakh** (all of the **Old Testament**, including the Torah). The Oral Law is recorded in the **Talmud** (the "learning") and the *Midrashim* (the "interpretations"). Thus Jewish Law in total, called *Halakha* (meaning "the path"), is the authoritative reading of the Torah based on the Talmud and Midrashim. The Torah does not stand alone and is not read literally, but is applied situationally based upon careful interpretation and study of Oral Law.

Oral Tradition. See **Oral Law**.

Orans position. *Orans* is Latin for "praying," and is usually used to refer to the position of hands raised and held to the side, palms forward. See Chapter 10, "Prayer – Object, Posture, Purpose and More," for an illustration.

Ordination. The act of conferring holy orders, or a ministry position, on an individual pastor, priest, deacon, etc. often done with the laying on of hands.

Origen. (A.D. 184–253) Early Church father, highly regarded for his scholarship and expertise in many areas of theology. Later scorned for his views on the **Trinity**, the pre-existence of the soul, and the possibility that God would ultimately reconcile everything and everyone to Himself, even Satan. To be fair to Origen, many of the decisions of the Church on **Doctrine** related to these issues came much later in its life, and Origen wrote while many of these **Concepts** were still undecided and in common debate.

Orthodox. From Greek *ortho-*, "right, true, straight" (as in a right angle, which is orthogonal), and *doxa*, "opinion, praise." In normal use this means "having the right doctrine or opinion," that is, one that is congruent with the teaching of the Church. Who determines this is a matter of some dispute, particularly on **non-essentials**. See **Infallible** for further discussion.

Orthodox Church. See **Eastern Orthodox Church**.

Orthodox Jewish. One of the main sects of modern Judaism. The others are **Chassidic, Reform** and **Reconstructionist**. Orthodox Jews affirm and live according to traditional interpretations and application of the **Torah** and **Oral Law**. Sometimes also called "observant" Jews, though this adjective can also be applied to others. There are many movements of Orthodox Judaism, and not all congregations nor rabbis fall under just one overarching group. There are two main Orthodox groupings, Modern and Haredi, but there is wide variety even within these.

Orthodoxy. Refers usually to either the **Eastern Orthodox Church**, or to correct doctrine. See **Orthodox** and **Infallible**.

Overseer. 1 Timothy 3:1 says, "This is a faithful saying: If a man desires the position of a bishop, he desires a good work." The word translated "bishop" is *episkopes* in Greek, meaning overseer or supervisor (that is, someone who oversees the work of others). In the **New Testament**, the teachings on the roles of **Presbyter** and overseer do not clearly distinguish the two, but *episkope* quickly came to refer to those who (usually while remaining pastors themselves) oversaw the work of younger and less-mature pastors. Thus emerged the hierarchy of bishops over pastors, with both mentoring and directive authority. See **Priest** for a more detailed discussion.

Pagans. In Christian usage, anyone who is not either a Jew or a Christian. Typically refers to someone who worships local gods, or no god at all.

Papyrus. A kind of early paper made from the papyrus plant.

Partisan. Someone who has taken one side in a dispute or disagreement, and advocates or fights passionately, sometimes violently, for that position.

Partisan spirit. Having the tendency to fight rather than seek compromise or reconciliation.

Pascal, Blaise. (1623–1662) Brilliant French mathematician, physicist and philosopher. Invented the calculator, and wrote on geometry, probability theory, economics and social science. Author of "Pascal's Wager," to wit: Even if God cannot be proved by rational means, a rational person should choose to live as if He did, because he thereby has everything to gain, and nothing to lose. If there is a God, he gains heaven. If there isn't, nothing is lost. Pascal also had a profound spiritual experience that he recorded on a piece of paper and sewed into his coat, where it was found only after his death. It read, "From about half-past ten in the evening until about half-past twelve … FIRE … God of Abraham, the God of Isaac, the God of Jacob, and not of the philosophers and savants. Certitude. Certitude. Feeling. Joy. Peace."

Passover. Also called *Pesach*. Refers to the "Passover" of the Spirit of the Lord, when the firstborn of all families in Egypt were killed, except those of the Israelites who placed the blood of a lamb on their doorposts. The Jewish celebration of Passover commemorates this event, and it is the event celebrated by Jesus with His disciples as the **Last Supper**, on the night before He was crucified. Christians thus also remember Passover, and their salvation by the "blood of the Lamb" every time they celebrate the Last Supper, also known as **Eucharist** or **Communion**.

Pastor. See **Priest** for a detailed explanation.

Paul (ca. A.D. 5-67). Also known as Paul of Tarsus, the Apostle Paul, and Saul (before his conversion). A highly religious and zealous Pharisee who persecuted Christians prior to an encounter with Jesus (after the Ascension) on the road to Damascus. The author of a major portion of the New Testament, and responsible for the growth of Christian communities throughout the Mediterranean.

Pentateuch. See **Torah**.

Pentecost/*Shavuot*. A celebration of the coming of the Holy Spirit 50 days after the Last Supper. See Acts 2. This exact same holiday is celebrated in Judaism as *Shavuot*, the commemoration of the giving of the Law at Mount Sinai, and is counted as seven weeks from the second day of the celebration of **Passover**. The Jews present in Jerusalem who witnessed the coming of the Holy Spirit on Jesus' followers had come there for the festival of Shavuot.

Pentecostal. A term applied in the last century or so to Christians who seek and have an experience of the Holy Spirit. Named after the coming of the Spirit in Acts 2 (see **Pentecost**), and subsequently common in the early Church. Some theologians asserted the supernatural works of the Holy Spirit had ended with the death of the last Apostle, around A.D. 100, and thus opposed the Pentecostals and claimed their present-day experiences must be demonic. But the rise and faithfulness of this stream of Christianity proved so powerful, and so effective in spreading the Gospel, that this criticism is now confined to a relatively small number of Dispensationalists and other theologians and groups.

Pharisees. A Jewish religious sect that arose after the Maccabean Revolt (Hanukah celebrates this revolt). The Pharisees stressed personal holiness, both the Torah and the Oral Law, and believed in the resurrection of the dead. Their primary opponents at the time of Jesus were the Sadducees, made up of a wealthier class of people, and descended from Solomon's high priest, Zadok. The Apostle **Paul** was a Pharisee.

Philia. One of four Greek words for love. See ***Agape***.

Photon. Elementary particle of light that exhibits properties of both a particle and a wave. It is the means by which things are seen or detected. A beam of light is basically a group of photons traveling together. We see objects when these particles bounce off of them and then into our eyes, where they (the photons) interact with our retinas, which sends a signal to our brains.

Phylactery. See **Frontlet**.

Piety. Piety is considered one of the seven gifts of the Holy Spirit. It is reverence, love and humility before God.

Placebo effect. The idea that a person may feel better or even be healed of a disease if they believe they are taking something that can cure it, even if what they are taking has no ability to do so.

Plain dress. A mode of dressing that stresses modesty of behavior and avoids showy materials and designs. Common to Mennonite, Amish and similar conservative religious groups.

Plato. (ca. 424–347 B.C.) Greek philosopher, student of Socrates, teacher of **Aristotle**. One of the greatest and most prolific minds of all time. See **Aristotle** for more detail.

Platonic. An adjective meaning that a Concept can be traced to Plato or his followers. (Occasionally used to describe a non-sexual friendship.)

Platonic ideal. Simply put, the concept that behind each tangible thing, including people, dogs, love, tables, color and more, there is a universal Form, in a sense the "perfect" model of the thing, of which the actual thing—like a cocker spaniel named Toby—is a mere shadow, a mimic, of the real substance, the true perfect universal Form of a dog. This "ideal" is unseen by humans, but is considered more real than the thing that humans perceive.

Pleroma. Means "fullness" in Greek. Used by Paul in Colossians 2:8-9, "Don't let anyone capture you with empty philosophies and high-sounding nonsense that come from human thinking and from the spiritual powers of this world, rather than from Christ. For *in Christ* lives all the *fullness* of God in a human body." Here Paul in effect is rejecting the use of the term by the Gnostics, who believed that spiritual beings or powers emanated from the pleroma, the "heavenly light above our world."

Pneumatos Hagiou. Greek for, literally, "breath holy," normally translated as *Holy Spirit.*

Polemic. From the Greek *polemikos*, meaning "warlike, belligerent." Can be used neutrally to simply refer to someone who writes against the beliefs of another, but typically polemical writings have implications or outright accusations about the character or ability of the person whose ideas are opposed.

Polity. Refers to the organizational structure of an institution or government, or the rules and practices that support it.

Polygamy. Literally means many marriages, regardless of the gender of the parties involved, but often used colloquially to refer to one man with several wives—which more correctly is called polygyny. One woman with multiple husbands is called polyandry.

Pope. From the Greek *papas*, "father." Originally used by bishops in Rome, Asia Minor and Egypt, but restricted to the Bishop of Rome after 1073.

Presbyter. Elder or pastor. See **Priest** for a detailed explanation.

Priest. To understand the various terms that are used, often inaccurately, to refer to spiritual leaders in the Church, we need especially to look at three terms: **pastor, presbyter** and **priest.** In normal English usage, they are roughly equivalent: They refer to a person called and trained to care for and to lead others in a church. **Pastor** (as in Ephesians 4:11) is from the Greek *poimen*, literally, "shepherd." **Presbyter** is from the Greek *presbuteros*, meaning "elder"—as in someone mature and experienced in the faith, and called upon to lead in the church. This is the word Paul used, for example, in Titus 1:5 (KJV), "ordain *elders* in every city" (and is the root of *Presbyterian*). The two concepts are basically the same in most Christian churches (some others distinguish them).

But it gets interesting with the word **priest** in English, because it actually has two *different* root meanings: The first root refers to those who were descendants of

Aaron and served in the Temple. This is *cohen* (in Hebrew) and *hiereus* (in Greek) meaning "offerer of sacrifices," and describing what Old Testament priests did. The second root is *presbuteros*, which, in its long etymology, contracted over time, losing some of its letters, until it *coincidentally* became *prest*, or *priest*.

So our English word *priest* can refer either to the root *cohen / hiereus*, "one who sacrifices," or *presbuteros*, an elder in the faith, a pastor.

Here's where it gets confusing (and important to understand!): *Cohen* is the Old Testament word for the one who comes to the altar of God and makes sacrifices, but its Greek equivalent, *hiereus*, is NEVER used in the New Testament to describe a pastor or elder in the Church. Instead, it is used only to describe ALL BELIEVERS, as in 1 Peter 2:5, "And you are living stones that God is building into his spiritual temple. What's more, you are his holy *priests*. Through the mediation of Jesus Christ, you offer spiritual sacrifices that please God."

Hiereus is also used to describe Jesus, when combined with the adjective for "high," as in Hebrews 4:14-16, "So then, since we have a great High *Priest* who has entered heaven, Jesus the Son of God, let us hold firmly to what we believe. This High *Priest* of ours understands our weaknesses, for he faced all of the same testings we do, yet he did not sin. So let us come boldly to the throne of our gracious God. There we will receive his mercy, and we will find grace to help us when we need it most."

So the idea that the priest in a Roman Catholic or other church is sacrificing at the altar comes from the church's religious Concept, a metaphor, that the priest is "standing in the place" of Christ and re-enacting His sacrifice. The difficulty with this concept is twofold: It confuses us because all believers are called priests by Scripture, yet in the church these same believers are called the *laity*, and the *pastor* is often called the priest; and also because the appropriate title for the pastor, *presbuteros*, has etymologically come down to us as *priest*. It is further confused by the practice of the Roman Catholic and other churches of conceiving of their pastors as modern-day *cohens*, still at the altar as in the days of the Old Testament. Incidentally, a Latin word also shows up in these discussions: *sacerdotal*, meaning duties restricted to or pertaining to a *sacerdos*, a priest who offers sacrifices. Not surprisingly, this confusion of terms has led not only to huge misunderstandings, but countless religious battles. See also **Overseer**.

Priesthood of all believers. From 1 Peter 2:5. See **Priest**.

Principalities and Powers. An expression used variously in the New Testament, positively, negatively and neutrally, to refer to earthly or spiritual authorities.

Principles Through Which Torah Is Expounded. Means both a set of hermeneutical rules (such as from Rabbi Ishmael) to guide the interpretation of Torah, or a general approach to Torah interpretation which guides application in specific circumstances.

Prisca. One of the leaders of **Montanism**. There are others with this name, both in Scripture and tradition, but in this book, refers only to the Montanist.

Progressive Tradition. Also called progressive Christianity. Refers to a movement that often questions tradition, is open to human diversity (often in ways rejected by more-traditional Christians), and has a strong focus on social justice, especially for the poor, oppressed groups, and the environment. Jesus' command to "love one another" leads to a strong emphasis on the "social gospel," and the solving of the world's ills.

Prophecy. In Scripture, a term that means both "foretelling" events that will or may come, depending upon a response to God's direction; and, a "forth-telling" of truth—that is, speaking out, regardless of opposition, of a truth that needs to be heard. Thus prophecy can be about the future, or about needed truth-telling.

Prophetic action. An action intended to produce a perceived needed change in the Church, society, or someone's behavior. Jeremiah demonstrated prophetic action when he put a yoke on his shoulders (Jer. 27-28). Modern Christians demonstrate prophetic action when they protest or support the actions or needs of others. Sometimes this is dramatic so as to "make a point." Other times it is simply illustrative of living out the love Jesus commanded of us.

Prophets. Refers to both a set of books in the **Old Testament**: the "Major Prophets," Joshua, Judges, Samuel, Kings, Isaiah, Jeremiah and Ezekiel, plus the 12 "Minor Prophets," Hosea, Joel, Amos, Obadiah, Jonah, Micah, Nahum, Habakkuk, Zephaniah, Haggai, Zechariah and Malachi. Also refers to individuals who were given the spirit or ability to prophesy. There we many in addition to those named in this list of books. See also **Tanakh**.

Propositions, Undecidable. See **Gödel, Kurt** and Chapters 11 and 23.

Proselytizing. Attempting to convince another of the truth of your religious beliefs, with the intention of conversion.

Protestant Reformation. A split (schism) in Western Christianity following the publication of Martin Luther's *Ninety-Five Theses on the Power and Efficacy of Indulgences*. Luther wrote and nailed it to the door of the Castle Church, in Wittenberg on Oct. 31, 1517. Luther *protested* (hence the name) the church's selling of "indulgences" that supposedly would get one's ancestors out of purgatory and into heaven. Others, including John Calvin and Ulrich Zwingli, followed, and virtually all Protestant churches flowed from these events, including the establishment of many denominations of Protestants, as they disagreed and split from each other.

Protestant. A member of a church descended from the **Protestant Reformation**. This includes Lutherans, Presbyterians, Reformed, Puritans, Methodists, Anglicans, Baptists, Assemblies of God and many more.

Protestantism. The movement that developed from the **Protestant Reformation**.

Pythagoras. (ca. 570–495 B.C.) Greek philosopher and mathematician. Founded a religious/philosophical movement called Pythgoreanism. He (or his students) conceived of the "harmony of the spheres," the idea that the Earth was at the center of a series of concentric spheres, in which the other planets, the Sun and the stars were embedded, and therefore moved around the Earth. The Pythagoreans studied music, and musical intervals, and believed the "spheres" in which the planets were embedded must produce a sound, since they were of different sizes, and arranged together at specific harmonic intervals from Earth. This "geocentric" model was adapted by the Church and led to Galileo's arrest and the accusation of heresy against him. See Chapter 3, "Sanctification," for more detail. The term "**music of the spheres**" comes from this idea.

Pythagorean. See **Pythagoras**.

Quantum theory. A part of physics that studies and describes the "wave/particle duality" of matter and energy. That is, that particles such as electrons and photons exhibit properties of both particles and waves. Quantum mechanics allows for the defining of the effect of the observer on measurements of the thing observed, but also demonstrates that there are limits of precision due to the effect of the observer. See also **Werner Heisenberg** and **Uncertainty Principle**.

Quark. An elementary, subatomic particle, from which protons and neutrons are composed. See also **God particle**.

Rabbi Moshe ben Nachman. Also known as **Ramban**. See **Nachmanides**.

Rabbi Ronald Isaacs. Author of *Mitzvot: A Sourcebook for the 613 Commandments*, an excellent introduction to Jewish thought and belief on the Law of Moses. See Chapter 14, "Covenant – The Law of Moses."

Rabbi. Also *rebbe* (though this term is usually used to refer to the head a a Chassidic sect). A Hebrew word meaning "teacher."

Rabbinic way/model. The method of debate and relationship which permits fervent disagreement but disallows personal attack. Rather, those who discuss, agree, disagree or explore together are intentionally friends, **haverim**, and care for each other, protect each other, and regard ongoing, loving relationship as more important than concepts or things.

Rambam. See **Maimonides**.

Ramban. See **Nachmanides**.

Ramchal. Moshe Chaim Luzzatto (1707–1746). Italian rabbi, who said, "Whoever sets God always before him and is exclusively concerned with doing God's pleasure and observing God's commandments will be called God's lover. The love of God is, therefore, not a separate commandment but an underlying principle of all of God's commandments." See Chapter 14, "Covenant – The Law of Moses." Quoted in *Mitzvot: A Sourcebook for the 613 Commandments*, by Rabbi Ronald Isaacs.

Randy Fisk. See **Fisk, Randy**.

Rapture. A term used to refer to the event described in 1 Thessalonians 4:17, "…we who are still alive and remain on the earth will be caught up in the clouds to meet the Lord in the air." The term "rapture" doesn't appear in Scripture, but has been used in connection with certain relatively recent Concepts from 18th- and 19th-century theologians.

Rashi, Shlomo Yitzhaki. (1040–1105) The most famous, highly regarded and most-referenced of all rabbinic commentators on both the **Talmud** and the **Tanakh**. Famous for the clarity and conciseness of his comments.

Real Presence of Christ in the Eucharist. The Concept that Jesus is actually fully present, in person, in the bread and wine of Communion. This idea stems from the **Last Supper** (see Matthew 26) when Jesus said of the bread, "this is my body," and of the wine, "this is my blood." The early Church accepted this as true, but did not try to explain how it was true. **Thomas Aquinas** and others tried to create Concepts that explained *how*.

Reason. The ability of the human mind to think through things, create logical categories, make assumptions and draw conclusions.

Rebaptizing. See **Anabaptists**.

Rebbe. A rabbi, though this term is usually used to refer to the head of a Chassidic sect. A Hebrew word meaning "teacher."

Rebbe of Kotzk. R. Menachem Mendel (1787–1859). Chassidic rabbi in Kotzk, Austria. Said the prohibition against idolatry extends to making an idol out of the Commandments.

Redeemer. From the concept of paying a ransom to get something back that was sold or lost. The concept of the redeemer is used in Ruth 4:14 to refer to a redeemer for a family, and in many places in the Book of Isaiah to refer to God, as in Isaiah 59:20, "The Redeemer will come to Jerusalem *to buy back* those in Israel who have turned from their sins." This title is not used directly in the New Testament, though Paul uses *redemption* to refer to what Jesus did.

Redeemer of Israel. A reference to God in the book of Isaiah.

Reform Jewish. See also **Orthodox Jewish** for more detail. The Reform movement in Judaism tends to be liberal in its theology and interpretation of the Law of Moses, adapting it to the modern culture, and working to "heal the world" by its advocacy of social reform and justice.

Reformation. See also **Protestant Reformation**. A process that changes the "form" of the Church, in particular to correct widespread error or abuse. Those who initiate or promote reform in the Church often do so against great opposition from those currently in positions of power or influence. This is not to imply that the reformers are right and those who oppose them are wrong. It can go either way, or (more commonly) error and truth are on both sides in a dispute.

Reformed Tradition. Another term for Calvinism, and followers of Calvin and other theologians in his tradition. Stresses the Five Points of Calvinism (TULIP): Total depravity, Unconditional election, Limited atonement, Irresistible grace, and Perseverance of the saints, as well as predestination, **Covenant Theology**, and the sovereignty of God.

Reincarnation. The Hindu and Buddhist idea (plus some Jewish and Christian mysticism) that human beings return in a series of lives on Earth, striving for greater holiness or enlightenment in each subsequent life, until finally reaching liberation from the cycle of death and rebirth. Mentioned here only because some "conspiracy theorists" claim the Bible once taught about reincarnation, but that the idea was removed by Justinian and Theodora. See Chapter 21, "Bible Authority."

Relics of saints. Typically either body parts (usually bones, or pieces of bones) or possessions of famous saints, which are venerated by some Christians. These relics are often kept in a "reliquary," and put on display in a church. Sometimes they are believed to have miraculous powers because of the holiness of the saint.

Religious Concepts. See Chapter 22. The foundational idea that the narrative of Scripture was mined to extract themes, ideas, parallels, grammatical structures and textual forms, and these were then abstracted into categories, and philosophical Concepts were fabricated. These complex Religious Concepts then led to the creation of Doctrines, Rituals, Canons, Worship, Practices, Polities, Creeds (conceptual statements of faith) and Hermeneutics (ways of reading and interpreting Scripture).

Religious idolatry. Making an idol of any religious concept, tradition, practice or form of worship.

Renaissance. A cultural phenomenon from the 14th to 17th century that involved a revival of Greek philosophical ideas, and a flowering of science, mathematics, literature, art, politics and religion.

Revisionism. The process of rewriting history or the telling of events, usually in order to support one's point of view or hinder another's.

Right Doctrine. The idea that some **Religious Concepts** more accurately describe God or God's will than others. See also **Orthodox**.

Ritual. A physical action done in a certain and consistent way, usually as part of a liturgy or religious act.

Robot. From a Czech word meaning "slave," and popularized by Isaac Asimov in his science-fiction and scientific writings. Used to refer to a computer-based machine that does complex work, and may mimic human actions.

Roman Catholic Church. A denomination whose name means, essentially, "the universal church headquartered in Rome." The world's largest Christian church, headed by the Pope, and administered by layers of authority from Cardinals down to Priests, in a pattern based on the Roman Empire's administrative structure.

Rosh Yeshiva. Head **rabbi** of a **yeshiva**. Sometimes called *roshi*.

Rousseau, Jean-Jacques. (1712–1778) A Swiss philosopher.

Royal Law. "Love your neighbor as yourself," from James 2:8.

Ruach HaKodesh. רוח הקודש. The word "spirit" in Hebrew is *ruach*, and it means "breath" as well as "spirit." This same word is used both to describe what God breathes into Adam's lungs to give him life, and the Holy Spirit (*Ruach HaKodesh*, literally *spirit the holy*, or *breath the holy*) in the **Old Testament**.

Sabbath. The seventh day of the week, according to Jewish reckoning, as commanded by God in the Fourth Commandment, to be a day of rest: "Remember the Sabbath day, to keep it holy. Six days you shall labor and do all your work, but the seventh day is the Sabbath of the LORD your God. In it you shall do no work: you, nor your son, nor your daughter, nor your male servant, nor your female servant, nor your cattle, nor your stranger who is within your gates. For in six days the LORD made the heavens and the earth, the sea, and all that is in them, and rested the seventh day. Therefore the LORD blessed the Sabbath day and hallowed it." The only one of the Ten Commandments that Christians broadly seem to consider no longer binding.

Sabellianism. A heresy and heterodoxy attributed to Sabellius, a third-century priest. See **Modalism**.

Sacrament. A sacred rite of the Church denoting a specific spiritual event or reality. Defined by some as "an outward and visible sign of an inward and spiritual reality." Some churches have no sacraments, others two (Baptism and Eucharist), while still other have seven (Baptism, Eucharist, Confirmation, Penance, Orders, Matrimony, and Extreme Unction).

Sacrifice. The idea of offering something—food, animals or humans—to God, in order to gain favor, or as an act of thanksgiving, penitence or worship.

Sadducees. A Jewish religious movement from the time of Solomon until about A.D. 70. Believed to be descendants of Zadok (or Tzadok), the priest who served under King Solomon.

Saint. A term often used to refer to a Christian of great distinction, or a martyr, and in some churches given a special day of honor. In the New Testament, "saint" is from the Greek *hagiois*, meaning "holy ones," and is used generally for all believers, not just those worthy of special honor.

Salvation. In the New Testament, from the Greek *soteria*, meaning to be rescued, or delivered away from danger. In the Old Testament the word typically is *yeshua* (also the Hebrew name for Jesus!) and means deliverance, safety, help, victory, welfare and even prosperity, or *teshua*, meaning deliverance by God but through humans. See **Yehoshua/Yeshua.** For Christians, salvation means being rescued or saved from a life poisoned by sin, thus being born into eternity and a life and relationship with God. This comes simply by recognizing that we sin, that we hurt others, ourselves, and the world around us; and accepting the forgiveness that God offers through Jesus. That is salvation.

Salvation and Sanctification, Distinction Between. See Chapters 2 and 3. See also **Salvation** and **Sanctification**.

Samaritan. Followers of Samaritanism, a religion closely related to Judaism, and descendants of Abraham, who studied the Samaritan Torah. Their name is from a root that means "keepers of the Law." At the time of Jesus, generally disrespected *by* the Jews, and themselves disrespectful *of* the Jews. Jesus' story of the "Good Samaritan" used this mutual disrespect to illustrate what true love really was.

Sanctification. Allowing ourselves to be changed in our thought-life, in our behavior, in the way we live in the world—in essence, to become more and more conformed to the image of Christ. Said differently, to learn to live and love like Jesus did—that is sanctification. See Chapter 3, "Sanctification."

Sanctuary. From the Latin *sanctus*, "holy." Normatively refers to a building or place set apart, "consecrated," for worship. Can also mean a place where a fugitive can be hidden and protected from pursuers.

Sarah/Sarai. The name of Abraham's wife. She was known as Sarai, a name whose meaning is not known; in Genesis 17:5, her name was changed by God to Sarah, meaning "princess," just after God changed the name of Abram, "exalted father," to Abraham, "father of nations." See Chapter 13, "Covenant – Abraham."

Satan. A Hebrew word, *satahn*, meaning adversary, or enemy. In the book of Job and elsewhere, a being who moves on Earth causing strife, but also stands in heaven and argues with God. Also used as a word simply to mean an adversary, as when an angel of the Lord blocked the path of Balaam in Numbers 22:22. In the New Testament Greek, *satanas*, the prince of evil spirits and the enemy of God and man.

Satan's Counterfeit. A pejorative expression used by some Christians who believe only in full immersion for baptism, in relation to baptism done with sprinkling or pouring of water.

Schism. Split or torn apart. Generally refers to a division in the church, with people choosing sides or starting new denominations in reaction to some perceived error. See **Heresy** and **Heterodoxy** for differences and similarities.

Schleiermacher, Friedrich Daniel Ernst. (1768–1834) German theologian and philosopher. Sometimes called the "father of modern liberal theology." Rejected many traditional teachings of the Church, and loved Plato and Aristotle.

Scribal error. An error in copying. Even with extraordinary care, those who copy documents sometimes make errors, from mistaking one character for another, to skipping a whole sentence or verse. I have a modern Bible with each section of verses of Psalm 119 marked with a Hebrew letter. The entire Hebrew alphabet is used in this Psalm as an acrostic, from *alef* to *tav*. The third-to-last letter in the Hebrew alphabet is *resh* (ר), and it begins verse 153. But in my Bible, verse 153 begins with *dalet* (ד). That's close (they look similar), but it is not the right Hebrew letter. Whoever set the type mixed up the two similar letters. That is a "scribal error." These errors can often be found by careful comparison of documents that are supposed to be identical, though if the original document is not available, which of several differing documents is correct is always open to question. See Chapter 21, "Bible Authority," for a discussion. Though these kinds of error are possible, their occurrence is rare at best, and none of those discovered in the copies that we have has made any substantive difference in the content.

Scribal tradition. Refers to the extraordinary skill and care of the "scribes" who hand-copy the Tanakh (Old Testament), to make certain no **scribal errors** are made. The scribes' expertise is so exceptional that they can look at a tiny piece of paper with a single verse on it from anywhere in the Tanakh, and tell you immediately where it is from, and if any characters are missing or wrong.

Scripture Alone. Also known as ***Sola Scriptura***, from the Latin for this expression. An expression arising out of the Protestant Reformation and attributed to Martin Luther, that the final authority of the faith rests not in the Church, or Reason, or Tradition, but in the Scripture itself, alone, and any other authority by the Church must be subsidiary to that which is plain (or able to be readily deduced) from Scripture. Chapter I, Section VII of the Westminster Confession puts it this way: "All things in Scripture are not alike plain in themselves, nor alike clear unto all: yet those things which are necessary to be known, believed, and observed for salvation are so clearly propounded, and opened in some place of Scripture or other, that not only the learned, but the unlearned, in a due use of the ordinary means, may attain unto a sufficient understanding of them." Some denominations take Scripture Alone beyond this, and say, effectively, that only Scripture can be used to understand and interpret Scripture. Other denominations (e.g., the Roman Catholic, Eastern Orthodox and some others) claim equal authority of Scripture, Tradition and Bishops (or Reason).

Scripture, Tradition and Reason. Also known as the "three-legged stool" of Anglicanism, it describes 3 sources of authority in the Church: the Bible; the understanding of the Bible and the established Doctrine of the Church coming through the "fathers" of the Church and its Councils; and the use of thoughtful insight, guided by the Holy Spirit. Anglican priest and theologian Richard Hooker (1554–1600) is often cited as the source of this approach.

Second Temple. The first Jewish temple was built by Solomon in Jerusalem about 1000 B.C. It was destroyed by the Babylonians in 586 B.C., and the Jewish people were exiled to Babylon (in modern-day Iraq). After their return from exile, a second temple was built there and completed around 516 B.C., renovated by King Herod around 19 B.C., and stood until destroyed by the Romans in A.D. 70.

Second Temple Period. The period from about 530 B.C. until A.D. 70, during which the Jewish people faced three significant crises: the destruction of Solomon's Temple in 586 B.C. and their exile to Babylon (rebuilt; see **Second Temple**); the **Hellenization** of all of Israel and Judea by and following its conquering by Alexander the Great, and the Maccabean Revolt of 167 B.C. (which is remembered in the celebration of Hanukkah); and then the Roman occupation (which also led to the destruction of the **Second Temple**).

Semantic misdirection. The technique of drawing an opponent's or listener's attention away from an important issue (or flaw) by sarcasm, shouting, *ad hominem* attack, revision, redefinition, or other verbal or dramatic means.

Septuagint. Translation of the Torah, and eventually all of the Tanakh, or Old Testament, into Greek. Held in high regard, with some early writers (e.g., Philo and Josephus) believing the translators to have been divinely inspired.

Shabbat. Hebrew word (also *Shabbos*) meaning "rest," for the day of rest ordered by God in the 4th Commandment. Begins approximately at sunset on Friday evening, and ends shortly after sunset on Saturday evening.

Shema. שְׁמַע. Hebrew for "hear!" and used as a short label for (sheh-<u>mah</u>), "Hear O Israel, the Lord our God, the Lord is One" (Deuteronomy 6:4). In Judaism, considered the key statement of the faith; the full *Shema* consists of Deuteronomy 6:4-9 and 11:13-21 and Numbers 15:37-41, though often just the first two verses are used. The following is from the NKJV.

Deuteronomy 6:4-9. "Hear, O Israel: The LORD our God, the LORD is one! You shall love the LORD your God with all your heart, with all your soul, and with all your strength. And these words which I command you today shall be in your heart. You shall teach them diligently to your children, and shall talk of them when you sit in your house, when you walk by the way, when you lie down, and when you rise up. You shall bind them as a sign on your hand, and they shall be as frontlets between your eyes. You shall write them on the doorposts of your house and on your gates."

Deuteronomy 11:13-21. "And it shall be that if you earnestly obey My commandments which I command you today, to love the LORD your God and serve Him with all your heart and with all your soul, then I will give you the rain for your land in its season, the early rain and the latter rain, that you may gather in your grain, your new wine, and your oil. And I will send grass in your fields for your livestock, that you may eat and be filled. Take heed to yourselves, lest your heart be deceived, and you turn aside and serve other gods and worship them, lest the LORD's anger be aroused against you, and He shut up the heavens so that there be no rain, and the land yield no produce, and you perish quickly from the good land which the LORD is giving you. Therefore you shall lay up these words of mine in your heart and in your soul, and bind them as a sign on your hand, and they shall be as frontlets between your eyes. You shall teach them to your children, speaking of them when you sit in your house, when you walk by the way, when you lie down, and when you rise up. And you shall write them on the doorposts of your house and on your gates, that your days and the days of your children may be multiplied in the land of which the LORD swore to your fathers to give them, like the days of the heavens above the earth."

Numbers 15:37-41. Again the LORD spoke to Moses, saying, "Speak to the children of Israel: Tell them to make tassels on the corners of their garments throughout their generations, and to put a blue thread in the tassels of the corners. And you shall have the tassel, that you may look upon it and remember all the commandments of the LORD and do them, and that you may not follow the harlotry to which your own heart and your own eyes are inclined, and that you may remember and do all My commandments, and be holy for your God. I am the LORD your God, who brought you out of the land of Egypt, to be your God: I am the LORD your God." See also *Echad* and **Obedience/Obedient/Obey**.

Skeptics. Originally a member of a Greek philosophical school founded by Pyrrho (ca. 360–270 B.C.), which doubted that it was possible to truly "know" anything (with some parallels to both **Heisenberg** and **Gödel**). Much later took on the meaning of someone with a critical and doubting point of view. Still much later (20th century), someone who disbelieves in the supernatural and either sets out to prove it mistaken, or assumes it is mistaken and speaks condescendingly toward those who believe in it.

Social Action. Also called the Social Gospel. Although there is a whole school of thought called "Social Action," related to how individuals and society (or others) interact, in the Church the term typically refers to those who believe the primary purpose of the Church is to change existing social structures, governments, laws and institutions, in order to bring justice and equity to all people—particularly the poor, marginalized and disadvantaged. Although in the West this is primarily seen as a politically and theologically "liberal" movement, in other parts of the world, such as Africa and the Middle East, it is considered simply a natural and integral part of the Gospel.

Social Contract. A Concept that came out of the Enlightenment (and traceable back to the Greeks) that the appropriate relationship among individuals, and with their government(s), is best understood as a "contract" where the individuals have intrinsic rights and collateral responsibilities toward each other. Thomas Hobbes, John Locke and Jean-Jacques Rousseau were the philosophers who brought this Concept to the modern era. Its development continues.

Social Gospel. See **Social Action**.

Socrates. (ca. 469–399 B.C.) Greek philosopher and the "father" of all Western philosophy since his time. If Socrates wrote anything, none of it survived or is known. What we do know of him comes through the writings of his students, primarily Plato and Xenophon. Socrates is famous for his method of dialogue, in which probing questions are asked in order to both understand what someone else is asserting, but also to gain deeper insight into the issue being considered. His influence on all modern thought, including ethics, politics, religion, knowledge and life itself, is virtually unmatched. Socrates taught Plato, who taught Aristotle, who taught Alexander the Great. See **Aristotle** for more detail.

Sola Scriptura. See **Scripture Alone**.

Solar system. Refers to the Sun and the planets, asteroids and other objects that revolve around it.

Solomon. (ca. 1000–922 B.C.) Son of King David. Builder of the First Temple in Jerusalem.

Søren Kierkegaard. See **Kierkegaard, Søren**.

Soul-rest. One of several Concepts among Christian theologians about what happens at death. Some believe a person who dies goes immediately to the "afterlife." Others believe that all who die "sleep" (soul-rest) until the Second Coming of Christ, at which point they all are awakened—some to glory, some to destruction. There are other views.

Speaking in tongues. A phenomenon among Christians of speaking, praying, singing or prophesying in a seemingly unknown language. Also called glossolalia; a related phenomenon is xenoglossy, speaking in a normal human language that the speaker doesn't know. Apparently common in the early Church (1 Corinthians 12-14). Now common in some denominations and nearly absent in others.

Speechless idols. A term Paul uses in 1 Corinthians 12 to distinguish idols made by man, such as those carved from wood or stone, and God. Paul's point is that idols made by man cannot speak because they are not gods at all, whereas Christians worship a real God who can and does speak.

Spirit of God. See **Holy Spirit**.

St. Augustine. See **Augustine of Hippo**.

Stigmata. A phenomenon whereby some Christians spontaneously exhibit wounds similar to those described as having been suffered by Jesus Christ at His Crucifixion, such as pierced and bleeding hand, feet, side and head.

Stoics. A Greek philosophical school founded by Zeno (3rd century B.C.). The Stoics believed a person's character and philosophical view of life was demonstrated by behavior, not simply words. They also believed that one's will should be in harmony with nature, and that when it was, this was virtue.

Storge. One of four Greek words for love. See *Agape*.

Styx. In Greek mythology, the river that separated the Earth from the Underworld, or place of the dead. It was believed that the water of the river Styx gave immortality, and Achilles' mother dipped him in the river, holding him by his heel. See **Apollo**.

Subatomic particle. Typically, a particle smaller than an atom. This includes electrons, which orbit around the nucleus, protons and neutrons, which make up the nucleus, and a host of other particles.

Substance and Accident. These are terms from **Aristotle**, to express the Concept that what is seen by the senses, the "accident," is not the same as the reality, the "substance." The term **"transubstantiation"** was meant to describe a change that bread and wine underwent during the **Eucharist**, in which they literally became the body and blood of Jesus Christ. However, this change took place not in the accident, which people see, but in the *substance* that was invisible beneath or behind the *accident*. **Thomas Aquinas** borrowed this Concept from Aristotle and applied it to the bread and wine used during **Communion**.

Summa Theologica. The massive summary of theology written by **Thomas Aquinas**.

Summary of Theology. See *Summa Theologica*.

Syllogism. Although the term has other meanings, typically it refers to a logical structure consisting of a major premise, a minor premise and a conclusion.

Synagogue. A very general term used by Jews to denote a place of assembly, usually with a large room for prayer, and smaller rooms for study or fellowship.

Syncretism. The blending together of various beliefs, usually religious. In a positive sense, this means they share a common underlying truth. In a pejorative sense (more common), this means they have been blended to accomplish a false inclusiveness that does not do justice to the beliefs that were blended.

Systematic theology. An intentionally comprehensive, orderly and rational approach to explaining or defending the beliefs of the Christian faith.

Talmud. A record of rabbinic commentaries on Jewish Law, as well as comments on the commentaries, all applied as a means to understand the Law, and apply it to religious and every day life.

Tanakh. An acronym for the books of the Old Testament, formed from the first letter of the names of the three main sections: the *Torah* (teaching), the *Nevi'im* (prophets) and the *Ketuvim* (writings). *TNK*, those letters, are thus used and pronounced "ta-nakh."

Tautology. In logic, a formula or statement that is true in all circumstances, always valid. Pointlessly obvious. Can also be used negatively to refer to something that proposes to be proved true, but actually assumes the truth it pretends to prove, or needlessly repeats an assertion, seeming to prove the assertion by repetition.

Tefillin. See **Frontlet**.

Ten Commandments. Also called the Decalogue. Ten instructions given to Moses by God for the Israelites. See Chapter 14, "Covenant – The Law of Moses."

Tertullian. (ca. A.D. 160–220) Early Christian writer and apologist, from whom we get the Trinitarian concept of "three Persons, one Substance," although he was later spurned as unorthodox by the Church when he became a **Montanist**.

Textual criticism. A technique intended to recover, as well as possible, the original text based on a multitude of copies. The technique is quite ancient (it was in use thousands of years ago) and consists of looking at how the copies we have *differ* from one another. See Chapter 21, "Bible Authority."

Theism. From the Greek word *theos*, "god." A belief that a God, or gods, exist. Also refers to how God relates to the universe and human beings.

Theist. One who believes in at least one God.

Theopneustos. Greek for "God-breathed," but implying something that is inspired by the Holy Spirit.

Thetis. Mother of **Achilles**.

Thomas Aquinas. See **Aquinas, Thomas**.

Thomas Jefferson. See **Jefferson, Thomas**.

Thought-forms. A habitual or learned way of thinking that affects or biases perception, and hence leads to loss of objectivity and understanding.

Three Laws of Robotics. Created by **Isaac Asimov** for a series of sci-fi stories written between 1940 and 1950, and compiled in a book (and later a movie) called *I, Robot*. The laws are: (1) A robot may not injure a human being or, through inaction, allow a human being to come to harm. (2) A robot must obey orders given to it by human beings, except where such orders would conflict with the First Law. (3) A robot must protect its own existence as long as such protection does not conflict with the First or Second Law. See Chapter 11, "Rule-Following and Transcendent Love."

Tongues. See **Speaking in tongues**.

Torah. Hebrew for "instruction." Compare to *Didaskalia*. Also known as the five Books of Moses (Genesis, Exodus, Leviticus, Numbers, Deuteronomy), and the Pentateuch. The fundamental text of Judaism; held in high regard by Christians and Muslims as well.

Transubstantiation. A term meant to describe a change that bread and wine underwent during the **Eucharist**, in which they literally became the body and blood of Jesus Christ. See **Substance and Accident**. This Concept is held by the Roman Catholic and the Orthodox Church, but is rejected by many Protestants, some of whom substitute similar Concepts, such as Consubstantiation or Dynamic Presence, both of which imply that Jesus Christ is present during Communion, but not through any transformation of the actual bread and wine.

Triadic Emanation. A Concept from what is called "Middle Platonism" about the divine realm emanating three gods (look into Numenius of Apamea and the Platonic *Second Letter* for more detail, though they are beyond the scope of this present book). This Concept informed **Celsus** in his writing of *On First Principles*, where he developed his ideas about the **Trinity**.

Trinity. Normative Christian doctrine asserts that God exists as three divine Persons, each fully God, who are distinct, but live in constant eternal unity and equality, and are of the same substance. See Chapter 20, "Trinity."

Unbroken Apostolic Succession. See **Apostolic Authority/Succession**.

Uncertainty Principle. Developed by Werner Heisenberg. States that there is a limit on the precision with which the momentum and location of a particle can be determined. The greater the precision of one measurement, the lesser the precision of the other.

Universalism. In a Christian context, the belief that all humans will be saved by Jesus Christ and be reconciled to God. (A less-common meaning is that all humans may be saved, but not all will choose to be.)

Veneration of the Saints. The concept that those Christians in history that showed special holiness or dedication, or gave their lives for the faith (**martyrs**), are worthy of special attention, praise and study: This is *veneration*. It is distinct from *worship*, which is reserved for God alone.

Virgin Mary. Mary, the mother of Jesus, was engaged to Joseph, but was still a virgin, when she conceived Jesus by the power of the Holy Spirit. See Luke 1:26-36. In some Christian circles Mary is deeply venerated, and some believe she remained a virgin for the rest of her life. The term "Immaculate Conception" actually refers to the conception of Mary in her mother's womb, not Mary's conception of Jesus. Many believe Mary lived without sin.

Voltaire. (1694–1778) Pen name of François-Marie Arouet, French philosopher of the Enlightenment, and advocate of social reform, separation of church and state, and freedom of religion.

(The) Way. "The Way" was the term used to designate the early followers of Jesus. See Acts 9:2 and 22:4, among others. See **Heresy**.

"What shall we then say?" An expression used in the Talmud and by rabbis at the time of Jesus, in arguing about how the Law should be applied or fulfilled. Appears in the New Testament when similar discussions are taking place.

Yahweh. An English pronunciation of the Hebrew letters YOD-HEY-VAV-HEY, יהוה, sometimes also pronounced *Jehovah* or *Yehovah*. See **Adonai** for more detail.

Yehovah. See **Adonai**.

Yeshiva. Hebrew for "sitting." A school that focuses primarily on the study of the **Talmud** and the **Torah**. This is done with daily lectures, and by working in pairs to discuss or debate a particular passage or rabbinic opinion. The head of a yeshiva is called *rosh* or *roshi* yeshiva. The members of the study pairs are called *haverim*, Hebrew for "friends," or *chavrutas*, Aramaic for "friends."

Yehoshua/Yeshua. Hebrew: יהושע Yehoshua, or ישוע Yeshua (shortened version of the same name). The name **Jesus** and **Joshua** in Hebrew.

Yom Kippur. Also called the Day of Atonement, the holiest day of the year for Jews, calling upon them for deep repentance and atonement.

Appendix 2
Bibliography
& Recommended Reading

This bibliography contains most of the books that were used in the preparation of *What We Believe and Why*. Their presence here does not mean I agree with their premises or everything they assert (often quite the opposite!), but they all were uniquely valuable in understanding and describing the issues addressed in my text. Those that I found particularly worthy of study are in **boldface**, and good resources for anyone wishing to delve more deeply into these themes.

Absent are the many volumes of theology usually a part of a course of seminary study, not because they are unhelpful—some are quite valuable and important—but because they can be found in any good list of books on theology. Most of those listed here are more unique and less known.

ARTICLES AND ESSAYS

"Early Christianity Was…Jewish?!" Rev. Dr. Les Fairfield. *Seed & Harvest* 34.3 (Summer, 2011): pp. 6-7. Trinity School for Ministry, Ambridge, PA. Discusses the Jewish background of Christian teachings and prayers. Excellent.

"The Origin and Terminology of the Athanasian Creed." Robert Krueger. Western Pastoral Conference of the Dakota-Montana District. Zeeland, ND. October 5-6, 1976. www.wlsessays.net/files/KruegerOrigin.pdf.

"Why We Need Hell." Frederica Mathewes-Green. March 23, 2006. www.frederica.com/writings/why-we-need-hell.html.

50-Day Spiritual Adventure series. Dr. David Mains. Mainstay Church Resources, West Chicago, IL.

50 Jewish Messiahs: The Untold Life Stories of 50 Jewish Messiahs Since Jesus and How They Changed the Jewish, Christian and Muslim Worlds. Jerry Rabow. Jerusalem: Gefen Publishing House, 2002. Examines the significant Jewish "Messiahs" since the time of Jesus. These were often little-known characters who inspired messianic fervor, including the Messiah who killed the Pope; the "Second "Moses"; the Messiah who demanded his head be cut off in order to prove his immortality; and the Messiah who defied the Roman Empire.

52 Lies Heard in Church Every Sunday ... and Why the Truth Is So Much Better. Steve McVey. Eugene, OR: Harvest House Publishers, 2011. Shows how pastors and churches can distort biblical truths. Offers an examination of these misconceptions.

A Life God Rewards: Why Everything You Do Today Matters Forever. Bruce Wilkinson. Colorado Springs: Multnomah Books, 2002. A scriptural study of heavenly reward.

Against Celsus. Origen. Whitefish, MT: Kessinger Publishing, 2004. English translation of *Contra Celsum* (*Against Celsus*), Origen's defense of the Christian faith mounted against criticism from the Greek philosopher Celsus.

Against Heresies. Irenaeus. Whitefish, MT: Kessinger Publishing, 2004. English translation of *Adversus Haereses* (*Against Heresies*). Ancient, classic defense of the faith.

Anti-Judaism and the Gospels. Ed. William R. Farmer. Harrisburg, PA: Trinity Press International, 1999. Poses these questions to the readers: "When and under what circumstances did the Gospel texts begin to serve anti-Jewish ends? Can it be said, accurately and fairly, that the evangelists were anti-Jewish?"

Apologeticus. Tertullian. Tertullian: Apology and De Spectaculis. Minucius Felix: Octavius (Loeb Classical Library No. 250) (English and Latin Edition). Cambridge, MA: Loeb Classical Library, 1931.

Are the New Testament Documents Reliable? F. F. Bruce. Mansfield Centre, CT: Martino Publishing, 2011. Excellent review of the issues and evidence of the reliability of the New Testament.

As the Rabbis Taught: Studies in the Aggados of the Talmud (in *Tractate Megillah*). Ed. Chanoch Gebhard. Trans. Dovid Landesman. Northvale, NJ: Jason Aronson, Inc., 1996. A compilation of the teachings on the Talmud. Incorporates teachings from the Babylonian and Jerusalem Talmuds.

Backgrounds of Early Christianity. Everett Ferguson. Grand Rapids, MI: William B. Eerdsman Publishing Company, 1993. An analytical and systematic introduction to the Roman, Greek and Jewish political, social, literary and religious backgrounds that are necessary for a historical understanding of the New Testament and the early Church.

The Beauty of Spiritual Language: Unveiling the Mystery of Speaking in Tongues. Jack Hayford. Nashville: Thomas Nelson, 1996.

The Bible and Archaeology. Sir Frederic Kenyon. New York: Harper & Row, 1940.

The Canon of Scripture. F. F. Bruce. Downers Grove, IL: IVP Academic, 1988. The choice of the canon of Scripture has been an issue of debate for nearly 1900 years. A solid review of the issues.

The Case for Jesus the Messiah: Incredible Prophecies That Prove God Exists. John Ankerberg, Dr. John Weldon and Dr. Walter C. Kaiser, Jr. Chattanooga, TN: The John Ankerberg Evangelistic Association, 1989. The authors examine evidence in the Bible that reveals the reality and nature of God.

Celsus on the True Doctrine: A Discourse Against the Christians. Celsus. Trans. R. Joseph Hoffman. New York: Oxford University Press, 1987. Translation of *Alethès Lógos* (*True Doctrine*), the Greek philosopher's dismissal of the philosophical basis of Christianity.

Christianity and Rabbinic Judaism: A Parallel History of Their Origins and Early Development. Ed. Hershel Shanks. Washington, D.C.: Biblical Archaeological Society, 1992. Covers six centuries of the parallel histories of Jews and Christians.

***Christianity in Talmud and Midrash*. R. Travers Herford. London: Williams & Norgate, 1903.** This book gives an account of the similarities that exist in Rabbinic teaching and Christianity.

Churches That Make a Difference: Reaching Your Community With Good News and Good Works. Ronald J. Sider, Philip Olson, and Heidi Rolland Unruh. Grand Rapids: Baker Books, 2002.

A Commentary on the Jewish Roots of Galatians. Hilary Le Corner, Joseph Shulam. Swindon, Wiltshire, England: The British and Foreign Bible Society, 2005. Challenges the assumption that the theological argument of Galatians is characteristically Pauline in both method and content.

Commentary on the Jewish Roots of Romans. Joseph Shulam, Hilary LeCorner. Baltimore: Ledener Books, 1997. Supports the idea that the Book of Romans is a classic Jewish text.

Critical Documents of Jewish History: A Sourcebook. Ronald H. Isaacs, Kerry M. Olitzky, eds. Northvale, NJ: Jason Aronson Inc., 1995. Documents the history of their development of the four primary Jewish movements in North America.

Death and Resurrection of the Beloved Son: The Transformation of a Child Sacrifice in Judaism and Christianity. Jon D. Levenson. New Haven: Yale University Press, 1993. Explores child sacrifice in Judaism and Christianity emphasizing the biblical texts on Isaac, Ishmael, Jacob, Joseph and Jesus.

Dialogue Concerning the Two Chief World Systems: Ptolemaic and Copernican. Galileo Galilei. Ed. Stephen Jay Gould. Trans. Stillman Drake. New York: Modern Library, 2001. One of the most important scientific papers ever written, proving that the Earth revolves around the Sun, showing the truth of the Copernican system over the Earth-centered Ptolemaic.

The Disputation at Barcelona. Nachmanides (Ramban). New York: Shilo Publishing House, 1983.

Doctrine and Practice in the Early Church. Stuart G. Hall. Grand Rapids: Wm. B. Eerdman's Publishing Company, 1991. An account of the major doctrines and practices of the early Church.

Doctrine of the Trinity: Christianity's Self-Inflicted Wound. Anthony Buzzard, Charles F. Hunting. New York: International Scholars Publications, 1998. Looks at the relationship of Jesus to the One God of Israel. The author asserts that within the bounds of the canon of Scripture Jesus is confessed as Messiah, Son of God, but not as God Himself.

Eerdman's Concise Bible Handbook. David and Pat Alexander, eds. Minneapolis: Lian Publishing, 1980. Handbook designed to guide readers through the Bible in book-by-book order.

Encyclopedia Judaica. Jerusalem: Keter Publishing House Jerusalem, Ltd., Israel, 1971-1972. An enormous 17-volume work on the history of the Jewish people and Judaism.

Epistle 185. St. Augustine of Hippo. *Nicene and Post-Nicene Fathers, First Series, Vol. 1*. Ed. Philip Schaff. Trans. J. R. King. Buffalo, NY: Christian Literature Publishing Co., 1887. www.newadvent.org/fathers/1102185.htm

Epitoma Rei Militaris. Flavius Vegetius Renatus. *Vegetius: Epitome of Military Science*. Trans. N. P. Milner. Liverpool: University Press, 1996.

Ethics of the Talmud: Pirke Aboth Text, Complete Translation and Commentaries. R. Travers Herford. New York: Schocken Books, 1962. This book is a collection of words of wisdom from the early writers of post-biblical Judaism. The *Pirke Aboth* gives an introduction to Jewish piety, saintliness, love for God and man, and devotion to learning.

Ethics of the Talmud: Sayings of the Fathers. R. Travers Herford. New York: Schocken Books, 1962. A collection of the ethical words of wisdom of the "fathers" of post-biblical Judaism. This book is a mirror of the spiritual life of Rabbinic Judaism, and a record of the teachings of the 65 sages quoted within it.

Every Man's Talmud: The Major Teachings of the Rabbinic Sages. Abraham Cohen. New York: Schocken Books, 1995. A classic introduction to the teachings of the Talmud. A summary of the wisdom of the rabbinic sages on the dominant themes of Judaism: the doctrine of God; God and the universe; the soul and its destiny; prophecy and revelation; physical life; and more.

First Apology. Justin Martyr. *St. Justin Martyr: The First and Second Apologies (Ancient Christian Writers)*. Ed./trans. Leslie William Barnard. Mahwah, NJ: Paulist Press, 1996.

The Five Books of Moses: Genesis, Exodus, Leviticus, Numbers, and Deuteronomy. Everett Fox. New York: Schocken Books, 1997. Fox's translation helps his readers hear the echoes, allusions, alliterations and wordplays of the Hebrew original.

Flatland: A Romance of Many Dimensions. Edwin Abbot, Mineola, NY: Dover Publications, 1992.

Forgotten Trinity: Recovering the Heart of Christian Belief. James R. White. Minneapolis: Bethany House Publishers, 1998. Asserts that the heart of the Christian belief has lost its foundation; examines ways to recover the ancient Christian tradition.

Gesenius' Hebrew and Chaldee Lexicon to the Old Testament Scriptures. Heinrich Friedrich Wilhelm Gesenius. Trans. Samuel P. Tregelles. New York: John Wiley & Sons, 1877.

God in Search of Man: A Philosophy of Judaism. Abraham Joshua Heschel. New York: Farrar, Straus and Giroux Publishers, 1955. Extraordinary scholarship and compassion demonstrates that God reaches out to man.

Gödel, Escher, Bach: An Eternal Golden Braid. **Douglas Hofstadter. New York: Vintage, 1989.** Pulitzer Prize-winning insight into patterns and the thinking of Kurt Gödel, M. C. Escher and Johann Sebastian Bach.

The Hebrew Yeshua vs. the Greek Jesus: New Light on the Seat of Moses From Shem-Tov's Hebrew Matthew. Nehemia Gordon. Mansfield, TX: Hilkiah Press, 2006. Explores the ancient Hebrew text of the Gospel of Matthew and how it differs from the contemporary Greek text of Matthew from which the Western world translations derive.

Hebrews Through a Hebrew's Eyes: Hope in the Midst of a Hopeless World. Dr. Stuart Sacks. Baltimore: Ledener Books, 1995. Insights into the Book of Hebrews that only a Jewish-rooted believer in Yeshua (Jesus) can give.

Hillel and Jesus: Comparisons of Two Major Religious Leaders. James Charlesworth, Loren L. Johns, eds. Minneapolis: Fortress Press, 1997. Compares the lives and teachings of the two major religious leaders in the Jewish and Christian traditions.

The Historical Jesus Through Catholic and Jewish Eyes. Bryan LeBeau, Leonard Greenspoon, Dennis Hamm, eds. Harrisburg, PA: Trinity Press International, 2000. Asks the question: "What can the historical Jesus research contribute to the life of faith?"

A History of Messianic Speculation in Israel: From the First Through the Seventeenth Centuries. Abba Hillel Silver. NY: The Macmillan Company, 1959.

The History of the Jewish People in the Age of Jesus Christ, 175 B.C.–A.D. 135, Volume III. Emil Schürer. Edinburgh: T & T Clark, Ltd., 1987. Jewish history, institutions, and literature from 175 B.C. to A.D. 135.

The Hole in Our Gospel: What Does God Expect of Us? The Answer That Changed My Life and Might Just Change the World. Richard Stearns. Nashville: Thomas Nelson, 2009. True story of a corporate CEO who set aside worldly success and discovered the Gospel of Jesus Christ.

How Does Jewish Law Work?: A Rabbi Analyzes 95 Contemporary Halachic Questions. J. Simcha Cohen. Northvale, NJ: Jason Aronson, Inc., 1993. Summary of how Jewish Law molds character and sets the guidelines for Jewish life.

How Firm a Foundation: A Gift of Jewish Wisdom for Christians and Jews. Rabbi Yechiel Eckstein. Brewster, MA: Paraclete Press, 1997. Answers questions about the Jewish life: beliefs and practices, festivals and holy days and the Jewish life cycle, including rites of passage, worship practices and dietary laws.

I Asked For Wonder: A Spiritual Anthology. Abraham Joshua Heschel. New York: Crossroad, 1987. A wonderful account of and insight into a life with God.

I, Robot. Isaac Asimov. New York: Fawcett Crest, 1969.

If Not Now, When? Joseph Telushkin Hillel. New York: Schocken Books, 2010. Discusses the most famous teaching of Hillel, one of the greatest rabbis just before and at the beginning of the time of Jesus.

In the Shadow of the Temple: Jewish Influences on Early Christianity. Oskar Skarsaune. Downers Grove, IL: IVP Academic, 2002. The history of the early Church with an emphasis on the Jewish influence through the pre-Constantinian period.

The Influence of Judaism Upon Jews in the Period From Hillel to Mendelssohn. R. Travers Herford. Whitefish, MT: Kessinger Publishing, 2009. Explores the differences and similarities of Jews and non-Jews in this long period from Hillel to Mendelssohn. Incorporates religious and secular influences upon the Judaism practiced during this period.

The Interlinear Bible: Hebrew-Greek-English (English, Hebrew and Greek Edition). Ed. Jay P. Green. Peabody, MA: Hendrickson Publishers, 2005.

Jesus: A Biblical Defense of His Deity. Josh McDowell, Bart Larson. San Bernadino, CA: Here's Life Publishers, 1983. Asserts many people in history have claimed they came from God. The authors claim there is one who can prove he came from God.

Jesus and the Judaism of His Time. Irving M. Zeitlin. Cambridge: Polity Press, 1988. Explores how Jesus saw Himself within His time and religious tradition, as well as the varieties of Judaism present: Pharisees, Sadducees, Essenes, Zealots and Sicarii.

Jesus and the World of Judaism. Geza Vermes. Philadelphia: Fortress Press, 1983. This book carries on from Vermes' books *Jesus the Jew* and *The Dead Sea Scrolls* and sheds light on different issues from that period.

Jesus in the Talmud. Peter Schafer. Princeton and Oxford: Princeton University Press, 2007. Explores how the rabbis of late antiquity understood and utilized the New Testament Jesus narrative to conclude that Judaism was superior to Christianity.

Jesus Was Not a Trinitarian: A Call to Return to the Creed of Jesus. Anthony Buzzard. Morrow, GA: Restoration Fellowship, 2007. Looks at Jesus' Jewish Creed, and His recitation of the Shema, which proclaims God to be the one single Lord. Buzzard asserts that defining God and God's Son biblically remains part of the unfinished work of the Reformation.

Jesus Within Judaism: New Light From Exciting Archaeological Discoveries. James H. Charlesworth. New York: Doubleday Publishers, 1988. Looks at Jesus and the time period in which He lived.

Jewish Believers in Jesus: The Early Centuries. Oskar Skarsaune, Reidar Hvalvik, eds. Peabody, MA: Henrickson Publishers, 2007. A detailed account of Jews who believed in Jesus during the first few centuries of Christianity.

Jewish Christianity Reconsidered: Rethinking Ancient Groups and Texts. Ed. Matt Jackson-McCabe. Minneapolis: Fortress Press, 2007. An introduction to the origin of Jewish Christianity and Christian Judaism.

***Jewish Messiahs: From the Galilee to Crown Heights*. Harris Lenowitz. Oxford: Oxford University Press, 1998.** Explores the history of Jewish messianic movements. Looks in detail at all the Jewish messiahs, and gives a biographical account of each.

Jewish Roots: A Foundation of Biblical Theology. Daniel Juster. Pacific Palisades, California: Davar Publishers, 1986. Messianic Judaism is a movement among Jewish and non-Jewish followers of Jesus of Nazareth. Messianic Jews recognize and identify with their Jewishness and also proclaim Jesus as Messiah.

***The Jewish Trinity*. Yoel Natan. Chula Vista, CA: Aventine Press, 2003.** Declares that Moses and other Bible writers wrote strikingly and often, both about the Trinity and the deity of the Messiah.

***The Jewish Trinity Sourcebook: Trinitarian Readings From the Old Testament (B&W Text)*.** Yoel Natan. Raleigh: Lulu Press, 2003. Trinitarian evidences and proofs from the Old Testament.

The Jewish World in the Time of Jesus. Charles Guignebert. New York: University Books, 1959. A detailed account of the history of the time in which Jesus lived from a Jewish perspective.

Judaism and Christian Beginnings. Samuel Sandmel. New York: Oxford University Press, 1978. Traces the history, institutions and ideas of Judaism from 200 B.C. to A.D. 175. Drawing on many sources ranging from the Apocrypha and Pseudepigrapha, it documents the growth of Synagogue Judaism and its influence on the early Christian Church.

Judaism in the Beginning of Christianity. Jacob Neusner. Philadelphia: Fortress Press, 1984. Answers questions about the world of Judaism in which Christianity was born. Gives an overview of the religion and the history of Israel. Analyzes the Judaic legacy as it endured among those who did not convert to Christianity.

Judaism in the New Testament: Practices and Beliefs. Bruce Chiltan, Jacob Neusner. London: Routledge Publishers, 1995. Explains how the books of the early Church came about.

Judaism: Practice and Belief, 63 BCE–66 CE. E. P. Sanders. Philadelphia: Trinity Press International, 1992. A comprehensive view of Judaism as a functioning religion over this period.

Karaite Rabbis: Aaron Ben Elijah, Abraham Firkovich, Anan Ben David, Elijah Bashyazi, Daniel Al-Kumisi, Jacob Qirqisani, Yefet Ben Ali. Books LLC. Memphis: General Books, 2010. A biographical account of these Karaite Rabbis.

The Life and Teachings of Hillel. Yitzhak Buxbaum. Northvale, NJ: Jason Aronson, Inc., 1994. The author carefully separates the teachings of Hillel from Shammai, his contemporary.

The Life and Times of Jesus the Messiah. Alfred Edersheim, Ph.D. McLean, VA: MacDonald Publishing, 2009. Since Jesus was a Jew, asserts importance of the surroundings of location, society, popular life, and intellectual and religious development during Jesus' time on Earth.

Lost Heritage: The Heroic Story of Radical Christianity. Dr. Kim Tan. Godalming, Surrey, England: Highland Books, 1996. Asserts that the zeal of the New Testament believers, and their practices, has been lost.

Lost In Translation: Rediscovering the Hebrew Roots of Our Faith. John Klein, Adam Spears, Michael Christopher. Bristol, TN: Selah Publishing Group, 2007. Using ancient Hebrew language and culture, clarifies many of the Bible's so-called "mysteries" and helps the reader uncover foundational truths that have been "lost in translation."

The Malbim Haggadah (Translated, Adapted & Annotated). Jonathan Taub, Yisroel Shaw. Spring Valley, NY: Feldheim Publishers, 1993.

Man Is Not Alone: A Philosophy of Religion. Abraham Joshua Heschel. New York: Farrar, Straus and Giroux Publishers, 1951. Heschel examines the ingredients of piety: how man senses God's presence, explores it, accepts it, and builds life upon it.

Matthew Henry's Commentary on the Whole Bible: Complete and Unabridged. Matthew Henry. Nashville: Thomas Nelson, 2008.

Meet the Rabbis: Rabbinic Thought and the Teachings of Jesus. **Brad H. Young. Peabody, MA: Hendrickson Publishers, 2007.** Shows that despite the common values and Scriptures shared by Judaism and Christianity, many Christians have little knowledge of the great Jewish rabbis who wrote from the time of Jesus and the writing of the New Testament in the first century to the completion of the Talmud in the seventh century.

Memory and Manuscript: Oral Tradition and Written Transmission in Rabbinic Judaism and Early Christianity. Birger Gerhardsson. Grand Rapids: William B. Eerdmans Publishing Co., 1961. Contains two of Gerhardsson's works on the transmission of tradition in Rabbinic Judaism and early Christianity. Examines the way in which Jewish rabbis during the first Christian centuries preserved and passed on their sacred tradition. In addition, shows how early Christianity is better understood in light of how that tradition developed in Rabbinic Judaism.

Messiah: Developments in Earliest Judaism and Christianity. Ed. James H. Charlesworth. Minneapolis: Augsburg Fortress, 1992. An international group of scholars addresses central issues regarding messianic beliefs in Judaism and Christianity from their origins to the close of the New Testament, as well as the editing of the Mishnah.

Messiah Texts: Jewish Legends of Three Thousand Years. Raphael Patai. Detroit: Wayne State University Press, 1979. Tracks the progress of the messianic legend from its biblical beginnings to contemporary expressions.

Messianic Exegesis: Christological Interpretation of the Old Testament in Early Christianity. Donald Juel. Philadelphia: Fortress Press, 1973. An exegesis of how early Christians understood Jesus, the Messiah and how they interpreted Old Testament passages that referred to Messiah.

Messianic Judaism: A Modern Movement With an Ancient Past. David H. Stern. Clarksville, MD: Ledener Books, 1988.

Mitzvot: A Sourcebook for the 613 Commandments. **Ronald H. Isaacs. Northvale, NJ: Jason Aronson, Inc, 1996.** The conduct of the Jews has been governed by the religious commandments, or *mitzvot*. These commandments have been interpreted many times from biblical times to the present day. The author explores the ways of classifying and reasons to obey them.

Mystery of Bar Kokhba: An Historical and Theological Investigation of the Last King of the Jews. Leibel Reznick. Northvale, NJ: Jason Aronson, Inc., 1996. A detailed account of the life of Bar Kokhba, who attempted to end Roman domination over the land and people of Israel.

Nine O'Clock in the Morning. Dennis Bennett. Alachua, FL: Bridge-Logos Publishers, 1970. The story of Bennett's discovery of "praying in tongues" and the effect it had on his ministry and life.

On First Principles. Origen. *Origen on First Principles: Being Koetschau's Text of the De Principiis Translated Into English, Together With an Introduction and Notes by G. W. Butterworth.* Trans. G. W. Butterworth. Introduction by Henri De Lubac. Gloucester, MA: Peter Smith Publisher, Inc., 1973.

On Formally Undecidable Propositions of Principia Mathematica and Related Systems. Kurt Gödel. Trans. B. Meltzer. Edinburgh: Oliver & Boyd, Ltd., 1962. The groundbreaking paper, written in 1930 (later published in English), that demonstrates that in any formal system of logic, including even elementary arithmetic, there are propositions that cannot be proved within the system where they are proposed.

On the Absence and Unknowability of God: Heidegger and the Areopagite. Christos Yannaras. New York: T & T Clark International, 2005.

Pharisaism: Its Aim and Its Method. R. Travers Herford. London: Williams & Norgate, 1912. Reprinted from the public domain by Nabu Public Domain Reprints. Excellent exposition of the teachings and practices of the Pharisees.

The Pharisees. R. Travers Herford. Boston: Beacon Press, 1924, 1952. An extraordinary history and examination of the teachings and observances of the Pharisees, correcting much of the misreading and misunderstanding of this sect over the ages.

The Presence, Power and Heart of God. Randy Fisk. Second Ref Press, 2011.

Process and Reality. Alfred North Whitehead. New York: Free Press, 1978.

The Puzzle of the 613 Commandments and Why Bother. Philip J. Caplan. **London: Jason Aronson, Inc., 1996.** The significance of the 613 Commandments and why they are still being studied today.

The Real Kosher Jesus. Michael L. Brown. **Front Line, Lake Mary, Florida, 2012.** Easily one of the best introductions to why Jesus is truly the Jewish Messiah, despite centuries of opposition to this idea. Brown quotes Bible, history, Talmud and Jewish scholars in making his case, and he does it expertly.

Questions of Life. Nicky Gumbel. Colorado Springs: David C. Cook, 1996. A wonderful presentation of the basics of the Christian faith.

Rabbi Akiba and His Contemporaries. Judah Nadich. Northvale, NJ: Jason Aronson, Inc., 1998. A collection of legends and anecdotes about the great rabbis of the Talmudic period. Includes their moral and ethical teachings as well as their understanding of historical information, biblical stories and biographical info.

The Religious World of Jesus: An Introduction to Second Temple Palestinian Judaism. Frederick J. Murphy. Nashville: Abingdon Press, 1991. An introduction to the Second Temple era, 520 B.C.E.–70 C.E.

Resurrection: The Power of God for Christians and Jews. Kevin J. Madigan, Jon D. Levenson. New Haven and London: Yale University Press, 2008. The origins of the belief in resurrection. Why some early Christians and Jews opposed the teaching, and why others felt belief in resurrection was essential to faith.

Sage From Galilee: Rediscovering Jesus' Genius. David Flusser, R. Steven Notley. Introduction by James H. Charlesworth. Grand Rapids: Wm. B. Eerdmans, 1968. Looks at historical sources about first-century life, especially through archaeology and the Dead Sea Scrolls.

The Sequence of Events in the Old Testament. Eliezer Shulman. Israel: Investment Co. of Bank Hapoalim: Ministry of Defense Publishing House, 1987. Sets biblical dates chronologically. Excellent.

Should Christians Be Torah Observant? The Answer Will Astound You! Carmen Welker. Bellingham, WA: Netzari Press, 2007. Asserts that every believer should ask the question: "Am I really worshiping God according to what the Bible says?"

Simple Words: Thinking About What Really Matters in Life. Adin Steinsaltz. New York: Simon & Schuster Paperbacks, 1999. Examines some of the meanings of the words: friends, family, love, God, death and faith.

Strong's Exhaustive Concordance of the Bible With Greek and Hebrew Dictionary. James Strong. Ventura, CA: Regal Publishers, 1990.

Talmud: The Steinsaltz Edition. Rabbi Adin Steinsaltz. New York: Random House, 1995.

Teachings of Maimonides. Jacob S. Minkin. Northvale, NJ: Jason Aronson, Inc., 1987. An introduction to the writings of Maimonides.

The Message: The Bible in Contemporary Language. Eugene H. Peterson. Colorado Springs: NavPress, 2005. The Bible in very contemporary English.

They Loved the Torah: What Yeshua's First Followers Really Thought About the Law. David Friedman, Ph.D. Clarksville, MD: Lederer Books, 2001. Asserts that Paul did not teach against the Law.

They Never Told Me This in Church! Greg S. Deuble. Atlanta: Restoration Fellowship, 2010. Suggests that much of what the historical Jesus and His Apostles taught has been overrun by an influx of post-biblical tradition.

TrueFaced. Bill Thrall, Bruce McNicol, John S. Lynch. Colorado Springs: NavPress, 2004. An insightful look at what God really desires from His followers.

Until the Mashiach: Rabbi Nachman's Biography – An Annotated Chronology. Rabbi Aryeh Kaplan. Jerusalem: Breslov Research Institute, 1985. Rabbi Nachman lived during the time of Ukraine's Industrial Revolution. Gives the chronology of his life and of significant events in the history of the Jews.

Uses of the Old Testament in the New. Walter C. Kaiser, Jr. Chicago: Moody Press, 1985. Argues that New Testament authors used Old Testament Scriptures properly and with due regard of the intent of their authors.

Ways That Never Parted: Jews and Christians in Late Antiquity and the Early Middle Ages. Adam H. Becker, Annette Yoshiko Reed, eds. Minneapolis: Fortress Press, 2007. The essays in this collection assert that Jews and Christians did not entirely part ways in the early Middle Ages.

What the Rabbis Know About the Messiah: A Study of Genealogy and Prophecy. Rachmiel Frydland. Columbus, OH: Messianic Publishing Company, 1991. The common 21st-century Jewish view of the Messiah is not the traditional Jewish view of the Messiah. Messiah as servant is overlooked by the current view of Messiah as king who will establish peace on Earth.

What the World Owes to the Pharisees. R. Travers Herford. London: George Allen & Unwin, Ltd., 1919. Shows the Pharisees were the founders of Talmudic Judaism, and looks at their influence on contemporary Judaism and Christianity.

Yeshua: A Guide to the Real Jesus and the Original Church. Dr. Ron Moseley. Clarksville, MD: Messianic Jewish Publishers, 1996. Describes the lifestyle of Jesus as being characteristic of Jews during that day. To fully understand the New Testament, it should be read from this perspective.

Yeshua the Messiah. David Chernoff. Havertown, PA: MMI Publishing Co., 1993. In 1967, the city of Jerusalem was reunited under Jewish rule. This event fulfilled a Biblical prophecy. Since that year, the world has been witnessing the growth of the Messianic Movement.

Appendix 3
Relevant Humor

A small collection of very funny jokes that illustrate many of the points made in *What We Believe and Why*. Other than the last one, I do not know the source or author of these, which I found many years ago. I'd be happy to give credit where it is due if anyone knows to whom they should be attributed.

THE CAT SAT ON THE MAT

How would various Christian denominations and theologians deal with the phrase "THE CAT SAT ON THE MAT" if it appeared in the Bible?

The liberal theologians would point out that such a passage did not of course mean that the cat literally sat on the mat. Also, "cat" and "mat" had different meanings in those days from today, and anyway, the text should be interpreted according to the customs and practices of the period.

This would lead to an immediate backlash from the Evangelicals. They would make it an essential condition of faith that a real, physical, living cat, being a domestic cat of the *felix domesticus* species, and having a whiskered head and furry body, four legs and a tail, did physically place its whole body on a floor covering, designed for that purpose, and which is on the floor but not of the floor. The expression "on the floor but not of the floor" would be explained in a leaflet.

Meanwhile, the Roman Catholics would have developed the Feast of the Sedentation of the Blessed Cat. This would teach that the cat was white and majestically reclined on a mat of gold thread before its assumption to the Great Cat Basket of Heaven. This is commemorated by the singing of the *Magnificent Cat*, lighting three candles, and ringing a bell five times.

This would cause a schism with the Orthodox Church, which believes that tradition requires Holy Cats Day (as it is colloquially known) to be marked by the lighting of six candles and ringing the bell four times. This would partly be resolved by the Cuckoo Land Declaration recognizing the validity of each.

Eventually the Anglican House of Bishops would issue a statement on the Doctrine of Feline Sedentation. It would explain that, traditionally, the text describes a domestic feline quadruped superadjacent to an unattached covering of a fundamental surface. For determining salvific and eschatological significations, they follow the heuristic analytical principles adopted in dealing with the Canine Fenestration Question ("How much is that doggie in the window?") and the Affirmative Musaceous Paradox ("Yes, we have no bananas"). And so on, for another 210 pages.

The General Synod of the Church of England would then commend this report, without officially endorsing it, as a helpful resource material for clergy as they explain to the man in the pew the difficult doctrine of the cat sitting on a mat.

Finally, in a backlash against this "extensive and boring religious spirit," a modern "emergent church regular guy," in sandals and shorts, boldly proclaims the yoking of emergent theology with quantum mechanics: He recalls the "Schrödinger's cat" thought experiment—a cat is in a box with poison, and it will kill the cat, but according to the "Copenhagen interpretation," the cat will enter a state of "quantum superposition," and be simultaneously alive and dead—yet if an observer opens the box, the cat will either be dead or still alive, not both.

Applying this to "a cat in a box with a mat," the emergent theologian concludes that the cat *both is and is not* on the mat, but if the box is opened, it will be *either* on the mat, or not.

Hence, he concludes, "quantum entanglement," proves again that God sees the cat as both dead and alive, and on the mat and not. How this applies to daily life for human beings is not exactly clear, but the emergent theologian is pretty sure it is really important.

– Author unknown

HERMENEUTICS IN EVERYDAY LIFE

Herme'neutics. [f. hermeneutic *a*.: see -ics. Also in form *hermeneutic*. Cf. L. *hermeneutica*, F. *l'herméneutique*.] The art or science of interpretation, esp. of Scripture. Commonly distinguished from *exegesis* or practical exposition. (*Oxford English Dictionary*)

Suppose you're traveling to work and you see a stop sign. What do you do? That depends on how you hermeneutically understand the stop sign.

1. A postmodernist deconstructs the sign (knocks it over with his car), ending forever the tyranny of the north-south traffic over the east-west traffic.

2. Similarly, a Marxist refuses to stop because he sees the stop sign as an instrument of class conflict. He concludes that the bourgeois use the north-south road and obstruct the progress of the workers in the east-west road.

3. A serious and educated Catholic rolls through the intersection because he believes he cannot understand the stop sign apart from its interpretive community and tradition. Observing that the interpretive community doesn't take it too seriously, he doesn't feel obligated to take it too seriously either.

4. An average Catholic (or Orthodox or Coptic or Anglican or Methodist or Presbyterian or whatever) doesn't bother to read the sign, but he'll stop if the car in front of him does.

5. A Fundamentalist, taking the text very literally, stops at the stop sign and waits for it to tell him to go.

6. A seminary-educated evangelical preacher might look up "STOP" in his lexicons of English and discover that it can mean: (1) something that prevents motion, such as a plug for a drain, or a block of wood that prevents a door from closing; (2) a location where a train or bus lets off passengers. The main point of his sermon the following Sunday on this text is: When you see a stop sign, it is a place where traffic is naturally clogged, so it is a good place to let off passengers from your car.

7. An Orthodox Jew does one of two things: (1) Take another route to work that doesn't have a stop sign so that he doesn't run the risk of disobeying the Law; or (2) Stop at the sign, say, "Blessed art thou, O Lord our God, king of the universe, who hast given us thy commandment to stop," wait 3 seconds according to his watch, and then proceed. Incidentally, the Talmud has the following comments on this passage: Rabbi Meir says: He who does not stop shall not live long. R. Hillel says: Cursed is he who does not count to three before proceeding. R. Simon ben Yudah says: Why three? Because the Holy One, blessed be He, gave us the Law, the Prophets, and the Writings. R. ben Issac says: Because of the three patriarchs. R. Yehuda says: Why bless the Lord at a stop sign? Because it says, "Be still and know that I am God."

8. A scholar from the Jesus Seminar concludes that the passage "STOP" undoubtedly was never uttered by Jesus Himself because, being the progressive Jew that He was, He would never have wanted to stifle peoples' progress. Therefore, STOP must be a textual insertion belonging entirely to stage III of the Gospel tradition, when the church was first confronted by traffic in its parking lot.

9. A New Testament scholar notices that there is no stop sign on Mark Street but there is one on Matthew and Luke Streets, and concludes that the ones on Luke and Matthew Streets are both copied from a sign on a street no one has ever seen called "Q" Street. There is an excellent 300-page doctoral dissertation on the origin of these stop signs and the differences between stop signs on Matthew and Luke Street in the scholar's commentary on the passage. There is an unfortunate omission in the dissertation, however: It doesn't explain the meaning of the text!

10. An OT scholar points out that there are a number of stylistic differences between the first and second half of the passage "STOP." For example, "ST" contains no enclosed areas and 5 line endings, whereas "OP" contains two enclosed areas and only one line termination. He concludes that the author for the second part is different from the author of the first part and probably lived hundreds of years later. Later scholars determine that the second half is itself actually written by two separate authors because of similar stylistic differences between the "O" and the "P."

11. Another prominent OT scholar notes in his commentary that the stop sign would fit better into the context three streets back. (Unfortunately, he neglected to explain why in his commentary.) Clearly it was moved to its present location by a later redactor. He thus exegetes the intersection as though the sign were not there.

12. Because of the difficulties in interpretation, another OT scholar amends the text, changing the *T* to *H*. "SHOP" is much easier to understand in context than "STOP" because of the multiplicity of stores in the area. The textual corruption probably occurred because "SHOP" is so similar to "STOP" on the sign several streets back, that it is a natural mistake for a scribe to make. Thus the sign should be interpreted to announce the existence of a shopping area. If this is true, it could indicate that both meanings are valid, thus making the thrust of the message "STOP (AND) SHOP."

13. A "prophetic" preacher notices that the square root of the sum of the numeric representations of the letters S-T-O-P (sigma-tau-omicron-pi in the Greek alphabet), multiplied by 40 (the number of testing), and divided by four (the number of the world—north, south, east and west), equals 666. Therefore, he concludes that stop signs are the dreaded "mark of the beast," a harbinger of divine judgment upon the world, and must be avoided at all costs.

– Author unknown

Die, Heretic Scum!

Comedian Emo Phillips tells a terrific joke about heresy that has been voted the funniest religious joke of all time. Since I don't have permission to reprint it, I suggest you search for it on the Internet. Emo's name and "heretic," ought to locate it.

Index

Entries in this Index that have a page number in **boldface** are definitions included in the **Glossary Plus**; if Capitalized As Titles they refer to sections or chapters in this book. *Entries in italics* are titles of books or essays. Hebrew language entries follow the letter **Z**.

E

Gassendi, Peter (1592-1655), a French priest, philosopher and scientist · 284
gender · 13, 17, 217, 218, 222, 251, 252, 253, 254, 302
gender discrimination · 254
gender relations · 251
genealogies · 225, 240
Gentile · 46, 82, 110, 111, 112, 115, 126, 129, 134, 135, 145, 146, 171, 172, 198, 211, 264
gentle · 254
gentleness · 46, 56, 155
geocentric · 288
geometric forms · 209
GeorgeKoch.com · 254, **285**
Gesenius' Lexicon · 260, **285**
Gesenius' Lexicon, illustrated · 262
Gethsemane · 148
getting even · 236
Gideon · 137
gifts of the Spirit · 69
Girgashites · 107, **285**
glorification · 4, 21, 22, 29, 30, 31, 35, 37, 136, 266, **286**
glorification, defined · 29
glorification, part of Covenant · 280
glorified bodies · 30, **286**
Gnosis · 165, **286**
Gnosticism · 157, 165, **286**, 292
Gnostics · 165, **286**
God · 1, 2, 3, 4, 5, 8, 9, 10, 11, 12, 13, 14, 15, 16, 17, 19, 20, 21, 22, 23, 24, 25, 26, 27, 29, 30, 31, 33, 34, 35, 37, 38, 39, 40, 41, 43, 44, 45, 46, 49, 50, 51, 52, 53, 54, 55, 56, 57, 61, 64, 66, 67, 68, 69, 70, 71, 72, 73, 75, 76, 77, 78, 79, 80, 81, 82, 83, 85, 86, 87, 88, 89, 90, 91, 92, 93, 94, 95, 96, 97, 98, 100, 101, 103, 104, 105, 106, 107, 108, 109, 110, 111, 112, 113, 114, 115, 116, 117, 118, 119, 120, 121, 122, 123, 124, 126, 127, 128, 129, 131, 132, 133, 134, 135, 136, 137, 138, 139, 141, 142, 143, 144, 145, 146, 147, 148, 149, 150, 153, 156, 157, 158, 159, 161, 162, 163, 164, 166, 167, 168, 169, 170, 171, 172, 173, 175, 177, 178, 179, 180, 181, 182, 183, 184, 185, 186, 187, 188, 189, 190, 191, 193, 198, 199, 200, 201, 202, 203, 205, 206, 207, 208, 211, 216, 217, 218, 219, 222, 223, 225, 226, 228, 229, 230, 231, 232, 233, 236, 237, 238, 239, 240, 241, 242, 243, 244, 245, 246, 247, 249, 252, 254, 256, 257, 262, 263, 264, 265, 266, 269, **286**, 301
God forbid! · 127, **286**
God particle · 179, **286**
God talk, theology · 3
God, covenant with · 132
God, love for · 122

God, love of · 66, 93, 94, 122, 135, 188, 206, 223, 241, 246, 305
God's counsel · 208
God's faithfulness, reliability · 106
God's lover · 93, 122, 305
God's nature · 181
God's Word · 200, **286**
Gödel, Kurt · 79, 91, 92, 93, 144, 227, 228, 229, 236, **286**, 291, 322, 327
Godhead · 75, 136, 148, 156, 157, 165, 180, 181, 185, 186, 187, 190, **286**
gold, refining · 26
good deeds · 32, 33, 232, 233
good reputation with outsiders · 254
Good Samaritan · 308
good-luck charm · 87
Gospel message of reconciliation · 226
Gospel of Thomas · 165, 166, 200, **286**
gossip · 155, 255
goyim, Hebrew word for non-Jews · 298
grammatical convention · 254, **286**
granite monument · 106
grape juice, in communion · 221
great eagle, Maimonides · 294
Great Thanksgiving · 222, **286**
Greece, ancient · 209
Greek Concepts, in Jewish thought · 294
Greek language · 254, 287
Greek Orthodox Church · **287**
Greek philosopher, Jesus not · 263
Greek philosophical methodology · 231
Greek philosophical methods and culture · 210, 211
Greek philosophical schools, listed · 170
Greek philosophical teaching and culture · 211
Greek philosophy · 23, 170, 171, 211, 212, 216, 238, 264
Greekified · 172, **287**
Greeks, philosophical approach · 170
Greek-speaking hellenized world · 264
Gregory of Nyssa · 275
guidance · 80
gullibility · 141

H

hairesis, Greek for heresy · 153, 154, **287**, 288
HaKodesh, Hebrew for the holy · **287**
Halakha (law) · 295
Hanukah · 301
hard heart · 236
hardened fortresses · 258, 263
harmless · 69
harmless High Priest · 133
harmony · 20, 22, 23, 24, 47, 106, 108, 168, 240, 250

CPSIA information can be obtained at www.ICGtesting.com
Printed in the USA
LVOW111430300912

300867LV00003B/3/P

9 780977 722631